Rule of Law

'I don't understand what you want from me.'

'The truth. Your government will not tell us the truth.'

'About what?'

'You will be approached. Asked to prosecute a case.'

'What case?'

'The only case that means anything. Montford. You will use your evidence and . . . you will win.'

'And what will happen . . . if—'

'You refuse? Nothing. Nothing at all.' Yuri smiled, his face again riddled with lines like deep cuts. 'I want to make it perfectly clear to you that your life is not at stake, Mr Becket. But . . .'

'But what?'

'But every time your daughter looks in the mirror and sees the acid burns on her face, she will curse you. And you will have achieved . . . what? Prevented the truth coming out? Prevented justice from being done?'

Also by Dexter Dias

False Witness
Error of Judgement

About the author

Dexter Dias is a barrister specialising in criminal defence and practises from a set of chambers specifically created to represent people disadvantaged by poverty and discrimination. He had already written on a variety of legal and political issues, but the real stimulus for writing fiction came when he met Ruth Rendell while he was defending a murder in 1993. *Rule of Law* is his third novel.

RULE OF LAW

Dexter Dias

CORONET BOOKS
Hodder and Stoughton

First published in Great Britain in 1997
by Hodder and Stoughton
A division of Hodder Headline PLC

First published in paperback in 1997
by Hodder and Stoughton
A Coronet Paperback

10 9 8 7 6 5 4 3 2 1

British Library Cataloguing in Publication Data
Dias, Dexter
Rule of Law
1.English fiction – 20th century
I.Title
823.9X14[F]

ISBN 0 340 66715 X

Typeset by Palimpsest Book Production Limited,
Polmont, Stirlingshire
Printed and bound in Great Britain by
Clays Ltd, St Ives plc

Hodder and Stoughton
A division of Hodder Headline PLC
338 Euston Road
London NW1 3BH

For my father
sine qua non

And for Katie

This book is also dedicated to Katie, without whom both the process and the purpose of writing would be for me immeasurably diminished. Perhaps you will allow me these few lines (and the only lines in this book not to quiver under your red pen) hurriedly scribbled while you are downstairs asleep, to record the many, many happy hours we have spent together discussing, debating and agonising over Dan's pain and Jo's courage and Chrissy's hope and Sophie's love. This book owes so much to your unswerving faith in the simple tale it tells, through its various drafts and revisions, both at home and on holiday. I know these lines can never be adequate recompense for the numerous hours I have locked myself away from you. But in a special way, the time I have spent in the company of these characters (whom we have both come to know so well) has never seemed to me like time spent entirely apart from you. Thank you.

The Rule of Law. All men are equal before the law, and the fundamental rights of the citizen, the freedom of speech, the freedom of association, the freedom of the person, are exempt from arbitrary powers, privileges and prerogatives.

Dicey, *Law of the Constitution*

PART I

JANUARY

Chapter 1

As Dan Becket sat in the witness stand, the names were hurled at him as though he were to blame for it all. Auschwitz, Bergen-Belsen, Buchenwald, Dachau; Chelmno, Treblinka, Sobibor, Birkenau. And within those infamous names, other names, ordinary names, six million more, so many that no one could ever know them.

High to Dan's left, the brilliant light of a cloudless January day in Manhattan poured into the well of the court. It coated his face, half blinding him like an interrogator's spotlight, whilst the hard wooden benches of the public gallery were thrown into shadow. In between these pools of light and darkness stood an old man, Aaron Stein. It was Stein who had asked the question that had changed the whole tone of the proceedings.

Stein supported himself with both gnarled hands on the top of a cane walking-stick. He had cataracts in his pale eyes which made it difficult for Dan to discern whether he was staring him out or not. Dan looked closely into the milky whiteness of Stein's irises when suddenly the old man repeated the question.

'Do I understand you to say, Mr Becket, that for the *first* time since the Second World War, the British courts intend to prosecute war crimes?'

'Yes,' Dan replied.

'And you have written a legal paper arguing that these prosecutions should be ... *stopped*?'

Dan paused. How should he answer? This was a distortion of the meaning of his lecture, but he could not say that. Here he was, a British barrister amongst American attorneys, on foreign soil and thousands of miles from home. What could he tell them about crime? After all, every year there were more murders in this one city alone than there were in the whole of his home country. But this symposium wasn't about ordinary murders. It was part of the United Nations Conference on War Crimes, following allegations of 'ethnic cleansing' in Bosnia. Dan tried to keep his voice even, controlling the urge to shout: For Christ's *sake*, why do you have to make it so personal? This is just one lecture on one part of the problem, isn't it? It's just a research paper, it's not real life.

Instead he said, 'I'm very grateful for your question.' He used the gambit he had used many times in court. 'But I fear you have misconstrued the thrust of what I was saying.'

Suddenly the *sotto voce* whisperings amongst the audience of one hundred and fifty lawyers ceased. Dan immediately recognised the moment, the awful hanging silence; for he had experienced it many times in trials he had conducted at the Old Bailey. This was a flashpoint. A confrontation. The issue would be decided one way or another by the next exchanges. Slowly, the dark blur of the public gallery resolved itself as, one by one, the faces came into focus: frozen features, as if captured in oils like the confused, angry and hateful faces of the condemned in Michelangelo's *Last Judgment*. All the benches were full, Dan noticed, except the last one on the right-hand side, upon which a man sat alone.

'My argument . . .' Dan said, pausing as he noticed how strangely the lone man stared at him, with a cold intensity that conveyed no emotion, with eyes that didn't appear to blink. 'My argument is simply that stale prosecutions should be stopped. Justice cannot be done by bringing people to trial after fifty years. It demeans the integrity of the whole judicial process.'

'*People?*' Stein rocked back on his heels and pointed the end of his walking-stick across the well of the courtroom towards Dan in an accusatory manner. 'You talk about *people*? These are war criminals.'

'Accused war criminals,' Dan replied, adjusting his position in the witness stand uneasily.

He had always thought it odd that American witnesses were allowed the luxury of sitting down, even when they were under the most intense scrutiny. How much easier than standing up as they were obliged to do in the British courts, he had assumed.

Now, as he was being attacked in an American courtroom fifteen floors above the downtown Manhattan sidewalks, he knew how wrong his assumption was. Sitting within the narrow confines of the wooden box, he felt rather like a caged animal, or worse still, like someone sitting in *the* chair waiting for the current to be switched on.

'So what do we do with your *alleged* war criminals, Mr Becket?' Stein continued. 'Forget their crimes?'

'Certainly not.'

'Forgive them?'

'No.'

'So we don't prosecute them, we don't forget them and we don't forgive them.' Aaron Stein hesitated and then said, 'I'm afraid I'm just a simple old Jewish lawyer, Mr Becket, but what do you suggest we do? *Nothing?*'

This was the question Dan dreaded. In the three months it had taken him to research his paper for the London Bar Conference – on what was technically called Abuse of Process – this was the question to which he had constantly returned. Like so many other aspects of his life, he could say with certainty, even at times with confidence, what he should *not* do. After all, the majority of the Commandments were Thou shall *not*. That was the easy part. But advocating a positive plan of action, in his experience that was where the demons lay, in life, in law, in this case.

Dan Becket could see no useful purpose in trawling through the wreckage of war-torn Europe fifty years previously – to do what exactly? To prosecute a small group of octogenarians who had led perfectly normal lives for half a century? There was no point. That was the theoretical answer. It was logical. But in his experience, logic did not always lead to the right answer, just as the law did not inevitably lead to justice. Nor love to happiness. So the thought that these men, these mass murderers, people who had participated in killing on an industrial scale, should live out the rest of their lives in *peace*, that stuck in Dan's throat.

There was more. Dan knew, although he rarely admitted it, that the reason for this confusion of thought, this tumult of emotion that tore him one way and then another, stemmed from one person. His father.

Suddenly, for the first time since he had been trapped in the witness box, the sunlight disappeared from the side of Dan's face.

The sun had moved behind one of the skyscrapers next to the court complex, setting the other building impossibly alight by lighting up its glass structure. It was another of the myriad minor miracles Dan had witnessed on his first trip to New York.

Stein was prepared to wait no longer.

'There was *a boy*,' he said. 'No, I tell a lie, he was little more than *a baby*, born in the camp, lived in the camp, if you can call it life – what with those . . . experiments Klaus Keller performed on him.' The agony of this recollection compelled Stein to pause before he could continue. 'In April 1945, the British soldiers came. Sitting on their tanks – I see them now, they seemed as big as . . . gods. They gave us food, threw out chocolates. And we ate. And because we hadn't eaten like that for months, years, we were sick. But this boy had never really eaten anything before. I still remember his face as he put the chocolate into his mouth. He looked at me, with those innocent eyes that had never seen outside the camp, and he chewed slowly. The look that came over his face as the chocolate melted. He must have felt . . . he was in heaven. He asked the soldiers for another. Then another. And soon something stopped . . . inside him. Like his heart seized up with – *joy*.' Again, Stein paused. 'Then he died. He's the one I think of most.'

Aaron Stein's voice trailed off. Dan felt a pang deep inside, the irrepressible tug that he felt whenever anyone spoke of the camps.

'You see?' Stein said to all the lawyers and at the same time to none of them. 'Can't even remember the boy's name now. But I won't forget what *happened*. Any of it. Even after fifty years, I can tell you what they did to us. The camp was the only world that boy ever knew. That was the worst of it. That was the new world, *die neue Welt*, they wanted to create for all of us Russian Jews.' His breath was becoming shorter. More pained. 'And you, *sir*, a *barrister*, a man of the law, come all the way from England, to tell me that these men, these *accused* war criminals, should not be prosecuted?' He coughed painfully. Then again. 'They should not be . . . should not . . .'

Suddenly the old man's body appeared to wither and he collapsed on to the hard floor in a fit of retching. Other lawyers swiftly gathered around him, undoing his tie and loosening his suit jacket, then his waistcoat.

It was a hideous moment for the sun to break through again, suffusing the court with a warm glow as Aaron Stein, Holocaust survivor, struggled for breath. Dan rushed towards the wooden benches and the knot of lawyers around the prostrate man. One of them, Lisa Hartman, the young attorney who had invited Dan to New York, looked around rapidly and mouthed to him, 'He's *fine*.'

Still Dan advanced to help, if he could. Seeing how the horror could return in an instant, though fifty years of happiness, success and achievement in Aaron Stein's life stood between those camps and this courtroom. The other lawyers melted away and soon Dan stood above the crumpled man.

He noticed that Stein's face glistened with sweat, a transparent film which had suddenly broken out as if an ancient fever, originating deep inside him, was consuming his body. Lisa held Stein's right hand and the old man's fingers gripped hers, tightly squeezing the blood away from her delicate palm.

'I'm sorry,' Dan said.

Stein tried to effect a smile but burst into another cruel fit of coughing. Then the old man held out his left hand towards Dan, holding it up vertically from the floor, with the fingers widespread, trembling. Dan saw numbers carved into his wrist. His camp number. His allotted place in the Final Solution. And Dan wondered about his own father, whom he had never seen. A father who also lived in New York, whose wrist would bear similar numbers.

At the very back of the room, Dan again noticed the man sitting alone. Unlike everyone else in the courtroom, this man had not moved, as if he were riveted to his seat and Aaron Stein's collapse had not happened. Still the man stared, not, Dan felt, at the chaotic scene, but simply, unwaveringly, at Dan.

Chapter 2

In London, a woman screamed loud and long before she managed to move her head away from the man moving between her legs. She gripped the side of the bed so tightly, as another shock of pain convulsed her body, that the nail of her left index finger snapped halfway, revealing the soft, semi-bloody flesh beneath.

Sophie Chase held her sister's other cramped hand, and in doing so felt the pain shooting into herself. She saw the doctor working away furiously as the glint of the metal instrument in his hand ignited the room. But Sophie could not have felt prouder.

Another scream: of pain, of joy. Yes, Sophie thought, this is the very best moment of my life. She looked at her sister's drenched auburn hair, now black with sweat, and smiled to herself. Here in the white-cream-grey hospital-coloured delivery room were the two sisters; the confirmed, militant, *fanatical* career girls who swore a secret pact that they would never have babies, who vowed to cut their separate paths into this world of men, remaining single, loyal and devoted to the calls of their respective professions. Sophie the barrister, Helen the doctor. Sophie's big sis, the doctor, giving birth to the next generation of career women. For they had checked. The foetus was female, no offending dangly bits, no testosterone, and soon it would be here. Sophie wanted to cry.

Another convulsion tore through Helen's body, making her spine arch. But through the pain, she looked up with the big almond-shaped eyes that were Sophie's abiding memory of her own childhood.

'Love you,' she said through gritted teeth.

Sophie was about to reply when the midwife insisted, 'Pant, try to pant.'

'I'm trying,' Helen said, squeezing Sophie's hand tighter.

'Try harder.'

'*Fuck*,' Helen shouted.

Sophie burst out laughing. The prim and proper army doctor, Captain Helen Chase, uttering expletives with a platoon of strangers hovering around her groin.

'Come on,' Sophie said, squeezing her hand in time, 'do it with me: fuck, fuck, fuck, *fuck*.'

Helen responded.

'Good,' the doctor beamed from the other end. 'Keep going.'

'I love you,' Helen gasped.

'Pant.'

'*Fuck*.'

'Yes, fuck.'

The doctor looked up. 'I can see the head.'

He adjusted the mirror and Sophie could see the crown of the head emerging slowly. Suddenly she saw the nose.

Oh *God*, she thought. It was the most miraculous thing she had ever seen. For years, throughout their teens, she and Helen had fought and argued and all along Helen was secretly capable of creating something as astonishing as that *nose*. How was that possible? In that precise instant Sophie resolved that one day, she would create a replica, with two equally perfect nostrils, only it would be as good – no, better – because Sophie would find the ideal man who would be there at the birth, unlike the male humanoid who had donated half the ingredients to Helen.

Helen had said she didn't care, was even relieved, as the disgusting man was a soldier, married to the British Army and incapable of marriage to anything female. He was a Gulf War vet, someone who had seen active service in Desert Storm, who put Queen and Country before ... well, everything. Sophie knew that Helen's baby had already changed her own life, and consequently she could no longer fight nature and her bloody biology. She wiped the sweat away from Helen's brow with her free left hand and kissed her sister as gently as her excitement would allow.

It was then that the doctor whispered something. At first it was incomprehensible. Then again, 'There's ... some maternal distress,' he hissed to the midwife.

'*What* did he say?' Helen cried.

Sophie spoke with a calmness that surprised her. 'It's all right.' But something inside her began to tear.

'The baby has stopped descending,' the doctor said.

'What *did* he say?' Helen tried to raise her head but Sophie immediately stroked her forehead, covering the eyes.

'The mother has stopped pushing,' the midwife shouted.

'Forceps delivery,' the doctor replied. 'With episiotomy.'

Sophie could see how the pressure of the moment distorted the doctor's eyes. Before she knew it, there was a scalpel in his right hand, small and sharp and lethal. Sophie shuddered at the thought of this instrument, this weapon, in the hands of her criminal clients.

She lowered her head and rested it on the sweat-soiled pillow – was it just compassion for her sister? Or her own fear? The recollection returned to her in a flash: this was why she objected to childbirth, it was the blood and the butchery that she despised.

'Push,' she said.

'I *can't.*'

'You've *got* to, Helen. Your baby needs you, Jenny needs you.'

It now sickened Sophie that the two of them had agonised over a name and had rejected many before they had named the foetus Jenny. She was crushed that giving it a name was her idea, though Helen had protested that it was tempting fate, or at the very least enticing it a little. But Sophie had a strong sense of destiny, which she called her *Que Sera* philosophy, the old wives' wisdom which said: What will be, will bloody well be. *Why* had she visited this stupidity upon her sister?

'Prepare yourself,' the doctor said.

'I w-want drugs,' Helen screamed.

'I can't give you any more drugs,' he replied.

Helen looked wildly at Sophie. And Sophie was terrified, for she could see the knife held precisely between the man's thumb and fingers, with the sharp edge about to cut her sister's vagina.

Helen screamed. Her nails cut into the flesh of Sophie's wrist, drawing blood.

'It's coming,' the midwife said.

'Jenny's coming,' Sophie whispered in Helen's ear, despite her sister's inhuman groans. 'Oh, my darling, little Jen is coming. You are *so* brave, and I love you so much.'

Helen was now gasping for breath.

'Here it is,' the doctor said as, with the aid of forceps, Jenny entered the world.

Sophie held Helen's head up, supporting the crook of her neck with her left hand.

'Chest clear,' the doctor said.

'Stomach next,' replied the midwife.

Sophie glimpsed a smile on the nurse's face, but it rapidly turned to shock. To horror.

'Breathe, breathe, *breathe*,' the doctor shouted.

Helen began panting, but it was crystal clear to Sophie that the man was no longer talking to her sister.

'*Breathe*,' commanded the doctor.

Helen sank back with relief. The baby was out. But there was no sound. Sophie saw the look of horror on the midwife's face now reflected on the doctor's.

'I want my baby,' Helen moaned.

'Mrs . . . Miss Chase,' he replied.

'I want *my* baby,' she cried.

There was then a pause. Sophie could see silent activity at the end of the room. But it was when the small knot of arms and legs, bloodied and quite still, was gently lifted and placed on to Helen's chest that Sophie was truly deafened by her sister's scream.

Chapter 3

Lisa Hartman had waited with the collapsed Aaron Stein until the paramedics arrived. Once Stein was placed on a stretcher, the group of besuited lawyers began to melt away slowly.

Dan sat on a wooden bench at the back of the courtroom. As he observed the scenes of controlled chaos, the oxygen masks, the precise routine of the medics, the gawping lawyers with expressions of sincere concern they would pay handsomely for to use in front of a jury, he felt dismally responsible.

In the course of his legal practice in England he had inflicted all kinds of carnage upon opposing witnesses: sudden faints, cataclysmic fits, confessions of guilt, even that true legal rarity – unexpected compulsions to tell the truth. There was one case, in which he was leading Sophie Chase, when the witness ran straight out of the box and vomited profusely in the general direction of his solicitor's leather briefcase. What would Sophie be doing now in London? he wondered. It would be the early hours of the morning on the other side of the Atlantic and he briefly imagined Sophie curled up in bed. Her blond bob spread out on the pillow, sleeping peacefully. And in this particular imagining, he had the power to see through her duvet, and his mind's eye scanned her naked body beneath: five foot eight of toned, tanned, female, feminine barrister. Of course, if her sister had actually given birth by now, and it was due any day, Sophie would be up all night with the screaming and wailing of the newborn child. He half smiled at these recollections of the bitter-sweet joys of parenthood, recalling the first moments of the life of his own daughter, Christine.

'*Hey*, Counsellor,' Lisa whispered. She had come up to his shoulder unnoticed, but now that he had been stirred from his

daydreaming, he again became aware of her delicious, clean
smell.

'I'd better take you back to the hotel,' she said.

'What a success,' he replied.

'Dan—'

'I bet you're just *thrilled* you invited me over. You want to see
me on a bad day,' he said, forcing a smile.

She lightly rested her hand on his shoulder. Strands of her
chestnut hair curled around her chin and framed the youthful
face. She had large brown eyes that watered frequently, and a
mouth that was just slightly crooked when she smiled.

'Look, Aaron Stein is an old man. Last month he even collapsed
in court. You're not to blame. It was the Holocaust, not you.'

Dan nodded for a moment, absorbing her words. Then he said,
'Do you think they'll ask me back?'

'Do you joke around like this in court?'

'Always.'

They left the courtroom and turned left down a bleak corridor
until they came to the lifts. They descended in silence and it was
only when they reached the steps outside the huge brass doors
of the Criminal Court Building that they spoke.

'Let's get a cab,' she said.

'Can't we walk?'

'Yeah, we can walk all right. But we're fifty blocks from your
hotel. That's not a walk, that's a safari . . .'

She broke off and let out the most piercing wolf whistle
Dan could remember hearing, running with her left arm raised
towards the kerb. A yellow taxi yanked to the right, causing a
cacophony of hoots from other vehicles as it pulled up in front
of the court.

'Your carriage awaits,' she called to Dan, opening the door.

When he got in, Lisa leant forward on the shiny back seat
and spoke to the cabbie through the small hole in the thick
glass panel.

'We need Central Park South,' she said.

The man looked around, his face wincing with bemusement.
He had gaunt features and could have been little older than
Lisa. Clearly he had not shaved for a couple of days, and the
prickly growth merged with his close-cropped hair, giving Dan
the impression that he was wearing a spiky balaclava.

'Central Park South,' Lisa repeated, brushing the hair away from her face in irritation.

Still the man stared.

'Central Park?' she said. 'Ever heard of it? Fifty-ninth Street?'

The man's face lit up and the grimace broke into a smile, exposing more clearly his tobacco-stained teeth. 'Ah, Fifty-ninth Street.'

'Yes,' Lisa said, flopping back against the seat next to Dan.

The taxi jolted to the left, incurring further wrath from the downtown traffic – horns, flashing lights, cars right up to the bumper. A police car drove past and the passenger wound down his window.

'What the hell you playing at?' a thick-set officer shouted.

The cabbie smiled back uneasily. But eventually they became part of the crawl up the island of Manhattan, racing against the lights, block by arduous block.

Lisa moved close to Dan's ear. 'Russian,' she whispered, 'right off the boat. Our taxi drivers don't have to pass the . . . what is it London cabbies have?'

'The Knowledge,' he replied. 'Not to mention the odd hundred thousand opinions.'

'Yeah, well, these guys have any knowledge, they fail them.'

The taxi was stuck in an avenue going north. On either side Dan could see a canyon of vertical stone and steel façades, rising dizzyingly from the sidewalk, drawing the eye miles up the island, past the undulations of the prehistoric bedrock, to a dim horizon, a little like an indistinct patch of light at the end of an incomplete tunnel.

'Russian?' he said.

Lisa pointed to the man's identity tag. There was a small colour picture of the cabbie even more unshaven, looking as miserable as if someone had asked him the quickest way to Harlem. His name was Savchenko. The ID, Dan noticed, was above a sticker on the back of the driver's seat setting out the passenger's charter. The charter stressed that Dan, as a paying customer, had the right to a taxi driver with at least a passing acquaintance with the city he navigated on a daily basis.

'New York is flooded with Russians,' Lisa whispered. 'I blame the end of the Cold War.'

'Surely,' Dan said, 'you should blame capitalism for winning it.'

'Do you remember?' she asked, smiling. 'That delegation of Russian lawyers? Bad suits or what?' When Dan stared blankly at her, she added, 'You know, at the London Bar Conference. They came to hear you speak.'

'God, I was so nervous the whole thing's just a blur.'

'You were great.'

'As good as today?' he asked ironically. It had been four months earlier, at the annual symposium of the British Bar, that the two of them had first met.

'You spoke with such passion,' she said. 'God, most of the other speakers were just so boring. And to be honest, when I read the title of yours . . . abuse of whatever—'

'Process.'

'Yeah, I just thought here we go again, another Mogadon meeting.'

'Thanks.'

'No, you brought it so alive. All that war crimes stuff. It was so—'

'Anyone would have done the same,' he said, feeling distinctly embarrassed. 'The London Bar was full of rumours about war crimes prosecutions.'

'I can't believe that you guys are going to prosecute a bunch of Nazis after fifty years.'

'That's the plan.'

Lisa paused and pursed her lips before she asked, 'And you don't approve?'

'I'm . . . I'm not sure.'

This appeared to infuriate her. 'Hey, Dan. This is one of those kinds of issues. You know, either you're part of the solution or you're part of the problem. Not sure?' She paused. 'What is that?'

A silence descended upon them and Dan knew that despite the provocative way in which they had been spoken, there was more than a grain of truth in her words. It was only when they neared the hotel that Lisa spoke again. 'I finally talked to him.'

'Who?'

'Jesus, you asked *me*. That guy, my client from Brighton Beach.'

'He knows my father?'

Lisa hesitated. 'Look, he just said he'd meet with you.'

'And is he,' Dan asked with increasing embarrassment, 'well
. . . Jewish, too?'

She stared at him sternly and he was unsure if she was
serious. 'His name's Ira Gottlieb, Dan. So he's *bound* to be a
Buddhist monk.'

'Ah,' he said, 'you're joking.'

'Jesus, are you Brits wound tight? Look,' she said, laughing,
'the Jewish Mafia is pretty small in New York. Everyone knows
everyone, or knows someone who knows.'

'I get the picture.'

'See you tomorrow, Counsellor.'

Chapter 4

The hotel lobby was a neo-classical extravaganza: weighty colonnades supporting nothing but the exorbitant room tariff, statues of eagles in stone and marble. Dan went to the polished wooden reception desk and asked for the little strip of magnetised plastic that was his key. The boy on reception, Dmitri, had started just after Dan arrived the previous week and had always been cheerful and helpful.

'Did I get any messages?' Dan asked.

'Sorry, your daughter didn't call.'

Dan had been waiting all week for Chrissy to contact him. She was staying with Dan's in-laws in Devon and whenever he rang her, she was either out or asleep.

'Maybe tomorrow,' Dmitri said.

'Maybe.'

'Is she pretty?'

'Beautiful.'

'Kinda like her mother, I bet?'

Dan did not reply. To him, Chris was growing to look more like her mother every day. Sometimes it was a pleasure, but more often it was a punishment, reminding Dan cruelly of Vivienne's death.

'So a beauty, eh?' Dmitri asked.

'I'm biased.'

'Bet you kill any boy that go near her?'

At this, Dan felt a pang of anxiety. Chris was thirteen and he had never once talked to her about sex. He assumed that Vivienne had dealt with all that. What was more, Chris was always reading those women's magazines and seemed to know an unhealthy amount about summer sex and penis envy for a thirteen-year-old girl.

But Vivienne had disappeared from their lives so suddenly he had never actually asked her about it. That was one of the things he resented most. Sometimes he would secretly beg the God he no longer believed in for just one hour with his wife, when he would ask all the things he never got around to asking while she was alive, an hour during which he would gladly tell her all the things he never got around to saying. In the course of the previous week, he had seen couples in the hotel, and others on the flight from Heathrow to JFK, who were about the same age as he and Vivienne were last year, and all these people did was to sit sitting glumly next to each other, silent. Dan wanted to go up and shake them and shout: God, say it all now, tell her, tell him, how you really feel, how much you love each other.

He couldn't even remember the last time he had told Vivienne he loved her before she died. Dan began to walk to the lifts when Dmitri called him back.

'Mr Becket,' he said, 'you got a call.'

Dan was directed to the banks of phones in the marbled lobby next to the lifts. Around him, people were speaking in a variety of languages: a Japanese businessman, a woman speaking French very loudly, a tanned youth speaking heavily accented Spanish, probably South American.

'Chris?' Dan gasped into the receiver.

'Dan?'

'Who is this?'

'Sophie.' Silence down the phone line until she continued. 'Well, don't sound *so* delighted to speak to your former pupil.'

Several years previously, Sophie Chase had undertaken her legal apprenticeship, her pupillage, with Dan.

'Soph, I'm sorry. It's just that I was expecting a call from . . . why are teenage daughters so unreliable?'

'Being teenaged has nothing to do with it.' Sophie laughed uneasily, and yet Dan was certain he sensed an underlying sadness. 'So how is the Big Apple?' she asked.

'Big, I suppose.'

'And when are you home?'

'Couple of days.'

'And back at the Bar?'

'Come on, Soph.'

'Look, Dan, I don't know what happened. I don't *care* what happened, but you're too good a barrister to have hung up your wig and gown.'

Since the night Vivienne had died the previous April, Dan had not donned his gown. It was not something he had planned; he had at first just returned the cases scheduled to be heard in the month after Viv's death. But one month had become two, then three, and he had begun to turn away new cases, staying at home with his daughter, until the inactivity had become too much and he had flung himself into his research paper on Abuse of Process.

'I'm sorry about Vivienne,' Sophie continued. 'But there's got to come a time when you stop feeling sorry for yourself.'

'It's Chris I worry about.'

'Look, some children are tough.' Suddenly, there was a cold edge to her voice. 'Children,' she said. '*Bloody* children.'

'Was there some reason you called, Soph?' There was no reply – only a faint whispering down the phone. 'Soph, speak up,' he said, but it made no difference. 'Soph, I said . . .' He put his hand over his other ear to cut out the background noise and it was then that he heard her.

'Oh God, Dan,' she wept quietly. 'Oh my God, Dan.'

'What's the—' He realised before he finished the question. He knew there was only one thing it could be. 'What time is it over there, Soph?'

'Early hours.'

'Are you still in the hospital?'

She did not reply, but he could hear the sobbing.

'Oh, Dan, it's so unfair.'

'Poor Helen.'

'Why couldn't it happen to me?' she cried, anger sharpening her words.

'Come on, Soph, don't say—'

'Say what? I never really wanted children, but Helen always talked about them after she joined the army. I used to catch her watching mothers with their babies riding in trolleys at Safeway or kids learning to swim at the pool, and I'd tease her, but it was what she really wanted, Dan. It was what she really . . . how could it have happened?'

He had no answer.

'You know, in court,' he said, 'you always say that I can't shut up, that I have an answer for everything? Well, Soph, I'm afraid I just don't know what to say.'

'Then don't say anything. But do something. Come home.'

They each waited in silence for the other to speak but for a short while neither did so. Dan for his part raced through a dozen neutral things he could say, rejecting them all as insensitive or trite or intrusive. He hesitated to the extent that it was Sophie who spoke next.

She sniffed heavily down the phone, and then he heard her exhaling, trying to revert to her professional voice. 'I've got the Montford brief,' she said eventually.

It was a *cause célèbre* in England. Former government minister Simon Montford, accused of murder. A murder from 1945.

'*You've* got the Montford brief?' Dan asked.

'Don't sound so flabbergasted.'

'It's only the show trial of the year.'

'I've only got the magistrates' committal, actually. I think you'd be interested in the war crimes allegation. I mean, you're the one against old prosecutions and all that?'

'In principle.'

'Principle? Jesus, Dan. Don't forget you're a lawyer, what the hell have principles—'

'Soph, if I change my mind, you'll be the first to know.'

'God, I'd forgotten how infuriating you could be.'

'Thanks.'

'But I miss you, anyway.' There was the hint of a more reflective tone in her voice. 'Dan, I think you should take the case.'

'Why?'

'It'd be good for you – for me, too . . . am I allowed to say that? – you know, getting back into the saddle. Of course, don't pull your weight and I'd rip your throat out in court, but we'd have a bit of fun in the process.'

'If anyone's going to tear out my throat, I'd want it to be you.'

'You know, I still don't understand.'

'What?'

'Why the worst things always seem to happen to the nicest people.'

Again he had no answer and there was an uneasy silence on the line.

'See you soon, Soph. I'm truly sorry.'

'So am I.'

When he put the phone down, he reflected that he hadn't cried after Viv's death. Not once. He told himself that he was being strong for his daughter. But he wasn't. He was being male and macho and stupid. He hadn't cried openly. But inwardly, he hadn't stopped.

Later that evening, Dan was at the window in his room looking over Central Park, at the bare skeletons of the trees, at the sheer cliffs of concrete apartment blocks on the east side of the park, at the buildings on the west side sparkling with lights. He thought again about the meeting the next day. Did Lisa's client really know his father? If he did, what sort of man would he turn out to be? He had waited so many years to find out. In truth, it had been Viv's death that had concentrated his mind. In a crude trade-off Dan did not really understand, he hoped to gain a father now that he had lost a wife. At least, that was the plan.

The telephone rang.

'Hello?' he said, flicking on the speakerphone.

'Dad?'

'Chrissy. Is that you, Chris?' He hurriedly picked up the receiver.

'How many other daughters have you got?' She paused, but before he could reply said, 'Why haven't you rung me, Dad?'

'I've tried.'

'I mean, today.'

'I've been . . . busy, Chris.'

'You're always busy.'

It was the old complaint, Vivienne's complaint, now taken up by Chris. He didn't answer back. It was true. 'How's your nan?'

'She's always making stuff. Cakes, jumpers.'

'Are you helping her with the housework?'

'*Yes*, Dad.'

It was something else he had noticed only after Viv died. Along with puberty came an adolescent inability to pick up a Hoover or any other contraption that would improve the hygiene of the house. 'You must help them, Chris. They're old people.'

'So are you.'

'How's your grandpa?'

'Always making me practise piano. Dad, they haven't even got a computer.'

'You can sail your Internet when you get—'

'It's surf, Dad. Surf. And if I don't soon, my cyber friends will think—'

Then he realised. 'Chris, what time is it over there?'

She was suddenly silent, and when she spoke again it was in her Daddy's-little-girl voice. 'I couldn't sleep, so I sort of sneaked down.'

'Well, sort of sneak up again.'

'I . . . miss you, Daddy.'

'I miss you, too,' he said instinctively. She always outmanoeuvred him. She could always diffuse his anger.

'When are you coming home?' she asked.

'Soon.'

'But your soon and my soon are not the same.'

'Couple of days more.'

'You haven't sent me a postcard.'

'Hasn't it arrived yet?' Dan guiltily glanced at the desk at the bottom of the bed where he could see a couple of cards in the letter tray beneath the smoky mirror. He resolved to write one immediately. 'I love you, Chris.'

'I *know*.'

Did she sound bored or embarrassed?

'Do you love me?' he asked tentatively.

'Dad!'

'Wrap up warmly.'

'Dad, I'm not eight years old.'

'No, you're thirteen. By the way, you're not wearing your short skirts and clumpy shoes, are you? They arrest young girls for things like that in Devon.'

'Ring me.'

'See you soon.'

'Not if I see you first.'

When Dan put the receiver down, his whole body tingled from the contact with his daughter. He loved her awkwardness, her obsession with her shoes and computers. He loved it when she called him Dad. But he noticed again that she had not actually said that she loved him. And his good humour was tempered because he knew that she had not said it once since the night Vivienne had died.

Chapter 5

The next morning the winter weather in London could not have been further removed from that in New York.

Sophie Chase's taxi was brought to a virtual halt on the Mile End Road as the rain made visibility poor and driving to the east of London treacherous. But Sophie did not worry unduly about the delay as she had left her chambers in the cloistered legal world of the Temple in good time for court.

Sophie had spent her first day as a baby barrister perched on the end of Dan's desk, and doing her pupillage with him had been one of the happiest years of her life. That was five years ago and she was no longer fresh out of Bar school. Now she was pushing thirty, had some positive experience of life, some negative equity, a lot more debt in the bank, vast sums of outstanding fees from cases she would never be paid for conducting, and the first traces of lines around her eyes. But more than all of that, she was still alone. She had a sister who would need her greatly in the coming months, but essentially Sophie was alone.

The rain was easing off and the cab started to accelerate out of London towards the East London Magistrates Court on the Tilbury Road. Normally, Sophie got to court by Tube or in her Citroën 2CV. But this case was different. Simon Montford was a private client and would foot the bill for the taxi.

As the cab approached the red-brick court building, built in the last ten years to deal with one of the nation's most reliable growth industries, crime, Sophie told herself that she should have forgotten about Dan years ago. Of course, he was married then, happily married to Vivienne, and Sophie was no home-breaker.

The taxi driver half leant over his shoulder, and intruded upon her mental ramblings. 'Can't take you right there, love. See the crowds? Don't know what all the fuss is for.'

But Sophie knew.

'Can I have a receipt, please?' she asked, opening the door and swinging her bag and law books out of the cab.

'What do you suppose is going on in there?' the cabbie asked.

'Murder,' she replied.

All of what was once known as Fleet Street was there. And Sophie had no doubt: this was a great story. The former government minister for industry, special portfolio chemicals and petroleum, a stalwart of the party, murdering a concentration camp inmate in Germany in 1945. Well, allegedly. Keep it in perspective – she was defending him after all.

But two things puzzled Sophie. Why had it taken all these years for charges to be brought? And what was the motive?

When the hacks spotted Sophie's sharply cut court suit and the brief she carried, tied with legal pink ribbon, they rushed towards her.

'You representing Montford?'

'What's the story?'

'Does he deny the charges?'

'Is Montford going to appear?'

'Fancy a drink tonight?'

It was a scene you would imagine in Los Angeles and not in East London. She walked in a dignified silence as, ahead of her, a cameraman scuttled backwards, training his lens on her face. Dictaphones were shoved under her nose; she could faintly smell the alcohol on the breath of one unshaven reporter, while the scrum crowded around her begging for a quote.

Sophie pushed her way to the front and turned and stopped. In a flash, the journalists were silent, waiting for her words.

'No comment,' she said, spinning on her heels sharply and running up the courthouse steps. She knew she must look dreadful; after all, she had stayed up all night with Helen after she had rung Dan. She hadn't given up, even if she was trying to console the inconsolable.

Suddenly, she noticed a distinguished-looking man behind the metal detector inside the front doors, watching carefully and smiling at her. It had to be Montford. Once she had collected her brief and her handbag and the private security guard was satisfied that she was not smuggling Semtex into the building, she looked again at the man.

'Mr Montford?'

'I see you've run the gauntlet,' he replied, smiling.

'How did you get past that lot?'

'Back way.'

'The *magistrates'* entrance?'

'My office arranged it. One of the perks, I suppose, of once wielding some power. Now, can I buy you a cup of what they tell me is tea, although I'm sure it should be referred to the Office of Fair Trading.'

She nodded.

As she walked up the stone staircase behind him, she realised that he wasn't what she had expected at all. Not as tall as he appeared on television, and older. Or was it the result of the years that had passed? Montford had really disappeared from public view after his sudden retirement from politics in 1991.

His tone was less strident than she had remembered from the dispatch box, his eyes were softer, he was very avuncular. As they reached the first-floor landing, Montford turned around.

'Can I say something, Miss . . .'

'Chase.'

'You're not quite what I expected.'

'Really?' She had heard it so many times before from her criminal clients: We were expecting someone older, you know, a man. 'What did you expect?' she continued, a hint of hostility in her voice. 'Someone . . . older?'

'Plainer. You know, my wife will be absolutely furious seeing on the national news that such a beautiful young lady is representing me.'

'Only for the committal hearing,' Sophie replied. 'Julian Waugh will, of course, represent you at trial.'

'If there is a trial. Now where is that tea dispenser?'

As they walked to the end of the corridor, Montford's penultimate comment sent a shiver of anxiety through Sophie's body. Montford had instructed Julian Waugh, QC, to conduct his defence. Waugh, Sophie's head of chambers, was reputedly the best, certainly the most expensive, barrister in the country. Rumour had it that now he would not even take the ribbon off a private brief for less than £250,000. And given the notoriety of the case, and the celebrity status of the defendant, Sophie could only guess at how much Montford would have to fork out in legal costs.

Montford put a fifty-pence piece into the machine and a steamy sludge-coloured liquid was sprayed out, some of it even managing to find its way into the plastic cup. He handed her the tea.

'To be honest,' she said, 'I was a little surprised that I was chosen as junior on the case.'

Montford put another coin into the machine, which promptly swallowed it without spluttering out any tea.

'Britain today,' she said.

'Actually, it's made in Taiwan.' He pointed to the trademark at the bottom of the machine.

'Please, you have it,' Sophie said, handing the cup to him.

'Certainly not. I insist.'

'Thanks.'

She took a sip, which seared off the top layer of skin on her lips, then she nodded towards a conference room.

'To answer your question . . .' he said.

'What question?'

'Why you've been chosen as junior. Julian Waugh felt it would be good PR if we had a young lady on the team.' He paused. 'Women are supposedly so much less capable of evil than men.'

It was a decidedly odd comment and she was unsure what to make of it. She tried to joke. 'You want to see some of the women I went to Bar school with.'

Montford remained deadly serious. 'I believe in calling a spade a spade, Miss Chase. Let us, for argument's sake, accept that a murder has been committed. The only question is: was it me?'

'Can they *prove* it was you.'

'The same thing?'

'Not always.'

'So sometimes the guilty go unpunished?' he said.

'Sometimes.'

'And is that something you are *happy* to be a part of, Miss Chase?'

Sophie remembered the first speech that she had heard Dan Becket make at the Old Bailey, five years previously. He was prosecuting a terrible case of parental sex abuse; the allegations of the violations could not have been worse, but Dan was almost outrageously fair.

She repeated what Dan had said then. 'It's better that ten guilty men go free than one innocent man is wrongly convicted, Mr Montford.'

'Doesn't it depend upon *which* guilty men go free?' he smiled.

It was not a comment Sophie had ever heard before and she was not quite sure how to answer it. But when she looked into his soft eyes, she was certain that he had no intention of saying anything else until she replied.

'I suppose that's the price we pay,' she said.

'There always seems to be a price. I found that out in politics. It just depends who pays it. Now, what are the chances of you getting my case thrown out at this stage?'

Chapter 6

When Julian Waugh had asked Sophie into his room in chambers and had given her the brief, he had insisted that she conduct the magistrates court hearing on her own. This was part of the deal. He had said that it was because tactically Montford didn't have a chance of getting the case thrown out in this lower court if a highly paid, polished QC appeared on his behalf. Magistrates were more used to having solicitors and baby barristers appearing in front of them. They invariably equated the appearance of a legal big-hitter with the defendant's guilt. Waugh also added that if Sophie could get the case discharged, it would make her career. It was, however, only when she first read the prosecution evidence that she realised Waugh's real motivation: the case was almost certain to be sent to the Old Bailey for trial. The charge was too serious and there was just too much evidence. Waugh hated losing and was very rarely defeated. Sophie would be the sacrificial lamb in the magistrates court.

After Douglas Wallace, head partner from solicitors, Wallace Howard, had arrived at court, Sophie left Montford and went in search of the prosecutor. It was part of the routine on a typical court morning: hunt down the opposition, appease them, goad them, spike their guns or negotiate. It was all part of legal warfare.

As she passed the usual assembly of the dispossessed, dispirited and drunken in the foyer of the magistrates court, she reflected on her position. The stakes could not have been higher, the rewards could not have been richer, and her chances could not have been slimmer. At the end of the dirty carpeted corridor, protected from the people they claimed to serve by a security lock, was the office of the Crown Prosecution Service. It was a modern room, but grubby for all that, with battered metal filing cabinets along three walls. On the fourth, there was a window giving a view of the industrial sites along the lower Thames. Ensconced at the desk in the middle of the office, as if it were his personal fiefdom, was her prosecutor of the day, Robert Lancing.

The case being a high-profile show trial, the CPS had brought in a barrister at an early stage. But Lancing was no ordinary barrister. He was one of the élite, on the special list of prosecutors who conducted the most serious and difficult cases at the Old Bailey. He was a Treasury Counsel. It was the same élite that Dan had resigned from at the time of his wife's death. Sophie remembered that Lancing had been elevated in Dan's place, one's loss being the other's gain.

'How are you doing, old thing?' Lancing said as she came in.

'Fine,' she replied.

Minions and clerks shot around Lancing, photocopying documents, filing his papers, providing him with coffee in a china cup – a rare distinction in a court building.

'What's all this nonsense I hear, Soph, that you're *trying* to get the case booted out?'

'I'm not trying.'

'Good.'

'I'm going to succeed.'

'That's my girl. Always a scrapper.'

'I'm not your girl, Rob. Not any more.'

It had all been a horrendous mistake. The previous year, she had somehow ended up in bed with Lancing after a legal summer ball, and the affair had fizzled on until the beginning of the next legal term in the autumn. There was no denying that Lancing was outstandingly attractive in a clean-cut, public school, nanny-reared sort of way. But she was really just filling in, comforting herself; he was a sort of bar of chocolate on two legs and by October she had had her fill.

'Why don't you just accept that we have a case?' Lancing said. 'Then we can all have an early bath – I might even be tempted to buy you lunch. There's this delicious little seafood restaurant—'

'It's not even ten o'clock.'

'Look, if you fight the case down here, things might get a bit messy.'

'How?'

'Can't say.'

'You're bluffing.'

'Try me.' He stood up and approached her, sweeping back his dark immaculate hair, whispering, 'Why don't we give it another shot, Soph?'

'Hopeless.'

'Why?'

'Don't you know? It's been biologically proved. Love between two barristers doesn't work. Some polytechnic did a survey.'

'You're still hung up on *him*, aren't you?'

She still didn't understand why she had ever mentioned her feelings for Dan to Robert Lancing in the *de rigueur* splitting-up argument. She thought it kinder to say there was another man than just claiming: We're incompatible, Rob, we have different dreams, you're a lousy lay.

'Is Becket going to represent Montford as well, then?' Lancing asked.

'I don't know. He doesn't know. It hasn't really been discussed.'

'You don't have a chance. Even with Waugh and Becket.'

'That's what they said to David.'

'David?'

'As in Goliath. The Bible. Religion. God.'

'Oh, you have the forces of goodness on your side?' Lancing said. 'That's not what my witnesses say.'

She paused, inspecting his patrician features. Good cheekbones, thin lips, only a soupçon of arrogance, which was unusual from someone from one of the great public schools. He was being deliberately provocative, having hinted at further evidence, undisclosed evidence. But time was too short to rise to his bait.

'See you in court, Rob.'

As she walked back to the conference room in which she had left Simon Montford, she asked herself the question again. Why do I always end up with the most inappropriate men at the most inappropriate times in the most inappropriate positions? Why were all the best men married or gay or your father or dead? There must be, Sophie thought, some kind of basic law of natural selection operating here. The best men were like the decent stuff at the Harrods sale, a ritual at which she always arrived too late.

Consequently, she always had to choose from the chipped vases and ghastly tartan jumpers.

As she opened the door to the conference room, she decided that her affection for Dan Becket was a bit of cliché really, like having a schoolgirl crush on the English teacher. The need for a father figure? The sort of thing Freud would invent a perversion about.

'I've spoken to the opposition,' she told Montford, as he sat in the square, dark room.

'Any surprises?'

'They think they're going to win. Is that a great surprise? Come on, the court is ready for us.'

Fifteen minutes later, Robert Lancing addressed the court in his precise tones.

Sophie sat at the front of the modern, stripped-wood courtroom, with Lancing along the advocates' bench to her left. In front of her, raised from the well of the court, was the bench, containing three lay magistrates, all women. They each made notes as the prosecutor stood in front of them, oblivious to the royal crest above and behind them: *Dieu et mon droit*. Montford sat at the very back in the dock with an air of genuine interest, as if he too were finding out about the crime for the first time. Sophie's eyes met Montford's: either he was innocent, she thought, or he was an extremely talented deceiver. Of course, in this regard he had a head start – he was both a politician and a man.

Lancing looked briefly at Sophie before he launched himself into the crux of the case.

'Madam, this case concerns war crimes. Or rather, one crime committed in the heat of warfare, in April 1945. At that time the German Army was in retreat, being chased across the Rhine by the Allies. This defendant, Simon Sinclair Montford, was then a major in the British Army. He commanded one of the tank units spearheading the Allied advance. However . . .'

Here Lancing stopped to allow the reporters to catch up. Sophie knew that it was important for the next words to be broadcast around the world. Yet she couldn't help but be sickened by the sight of Lancing preening himself. She took it personally. How on earth could she have ever been naked in bed with such a creature?

Lancing took a sip of water and then said, 'On the east bank of the Rhine, somewhere between the more famous – or infamous – camps of Bergen-Belsen and Buchenwald, lay Neuwelt.'

Sophie noticed a few journalists looking at each other, checking each others' spelling. Some had never heard of Neuwelt before. But she knew that before the case ended, Neuwelt would be as notorious in Britain as any other camp.

'Even before the British Army had been in control of Neuwelt for twenty-four hours,' Lancing continued, 'a Holocaust survivor, a Russian soldier, had been executed.' Again he paused. This was the very heart of the allegation. 'The prosecution's case is that this camp survivor, Ivan Basarov, was executed on the orders of Major Simon Montford.'

There was consternation around the court. People muttering, savouring the accusation, Sophie thought. Lancing now drew to a complete halt until the court was silenced.

'Madam, the evidence will really speak for itself. We propose to call, *inter alia*, soldiers who served alongside Mr Montford in Germany. There will be eye-witnesses testifying as to the surrounding circumstances of the case. I do not propose to outline the facts any further, but will begin by calling the evidence.'

This was the moment when the prosecution began to reveal its hand. Sophie opened her blue counsel's notebook and waited.

Lancing coughed. 'I would ask that the court goes into closed session.'

Sophie shot to her feet. 'I must object. We have been given no notice of this highly unusual step.'

He bent his head towards her. 'I told you it would get messy if you persisted in fighting the case down here.'

'What's going on?'

'It's called a secret, Soph.'

The chairwoman of the bench leant forward to the court clerk for legal advice. Being lay justices, they were reliant upon the legally trained court clerk for technical advice on the law. The clerk stood up and said, 'Madam, I advise that the court is cleared while the prosecution address you in private.'

In a flurry of activity, the dock was opened, Montford was escorted out, and an usher stood at Sophie's side asking her to leave. Lancing smiled annoyingly, smirking as Sophie was expelled from the courtroom before the case had even begun.

Outside court, Montford approached her, red-faced and confused. 'What on earth is going on?' He watched as the usher shut the door on the two of them, hanging a 'Private Hearing' sign on the outside.

'I don't know,' Sophie replied.

'But didn't you speak to the prosecution before the case started?'

'Yes, but—'

'Isn't it your job to find out what evidence they have?'

'In theory. But in practice, often—'

'Forgive me, Miss Chase. But isn't it a fundamental principle in this country that we have open justice?'

'Yes.'

'So why is the court in *closed* session? In *my* case?'

Sophie's mind raced through the permutations. Lancing had tried to warn her in his bumbling way. There could be only one plausible explanation.

'I served this country in government,' Montford continued, 'I fought for it in World War II – and this is how I am treated? I was decorated, I was mentioned in dispatches.'

The court usher rushed towards them, clipboard in hand. 'Mr Lancing has told the court that he could well be addressing them into the afternoon.'

'The *afternoon*?' Sophie was incredulous.

'In the circumstances,' the usher continued, 'the Bench has released you and your client until tomorrow.'

Sophie and Montford watched in silence as the usher hurried back to court, her tatty gown trailing behind her.

'I smell a rat,' Sophie finally said.

'A what?'

'A rat.'

'What kind of rat?'

'An undercover one.'

'How do you mean?' he asked.

'They have some sensitive evidence. Something about you. Perhaps something they've just found out about. Something that they don't want us to know.'

'So today has been a complete waste of time? I have been hanging around here for . . . over an hour now, Miss Chase. Don't you think I've got better things to do?'

Sophie was secretly relieved that the day's proceedings had finished so rapidly. Her mind flashed again to Helen's hospital room, and she allowed herself to see the prostrate figure of her elder sister, lying between the crisp white sheets, motionless. When Sophie had left, Helen's face had turned towards the high windows that gave on to the City reach of the Thames. She was cried out – or was she just controlling herself? Helen had always been stronger than Sophie, but now Soph wanted to try and take some of the pain on to herself, if only she knew how.

Montford stood with his back to the court door. 'My time is very precious, Miss Chase.'

Sophie wondered if there had been even a flickering of life as the child had emerged from the womb, or was it stillborn? Did it live – even for a few precious seconds? She didn't know, but she knew that she didn't want to reply to Montford.

Chapter 7

The Moscovitz Deli was situated downtown, opposite the court complex, and was more than a mere Manhattan restaurant: it was a place of pilgrimage.

Dan arrived there at one o'clock the next day and dutifully waited in a queue of the faithful on the pavement outside. However, within a minute Lisa tapped on the glass window from the inside, and to the irritation of several people ahead of him, Dan walked into the deli.

'I've been waiting ten minutes,' she said, ushering him to the back of the room. 'You English. Always joining the back of lines.'

'We call them queues – and it's polite.'

'So is being on time.'

'Am I late?' he asked.

'He hasn't arrived yet.'

The other tables were a blur as she took him by the hand and negotiated her way around two waitresses with platters full of carved, congealed cold flesh. The room was very basic. Twenty long varnished tables. Neon lights flashing the names of famous Broadway shows on the walls, and circumnavigating it all, like pocket battleships, sturdy waitresses with pink pinnies and white hats.

When he sat down, he pointed to their trays and asked, 'What is that?'

'The beef sandwich.'

'How many cows did they sacrifice for one of those?'

'You don't eat it all. People like to feel they're getting value for money,' she laughed. 'Better let me handle things,' she added, smiling at the waitress who arrived at their table.

As Dan picked up the wipe-clean plastic menu, a metal tray of gherkins and other more indistinct pickled things was placed on the table. The waitress had a name-tag that said Iris.

'Something to drink?' she snapped, managing to fake a grin at the same time.

'I'll get a coffee,' Lisa said. She held up her menu and whispered behind it, 'What would you like?'

'Can't he speak English?' Iris demanded.

'He is English.'

'Tea, then. Milk not lemon?'

Dan nodded, feeling extremely foolish. As Iris moved off, he tried to absorb the menu. There was almost a page for each type of sandwich.

'How many ways can you make a beef sandwich?' he asked.

'Try the pastrami. It's the best in Manhattan. And the cheese-cake. It's the best in the universe.'

He looked at Lisa carefully. She still exuded the strange, exotic air that had intrigued him at the Bar Conference in London the previous September. He had thought that it must have been a combination of the American accent, the fact that she called herself an attorney, her energetic way of talking, her youthfulness. But even in the middle of Manhattan, she had a rare aura around her that made him want to know more.

Dan saw Iris approaching with the drinks. The tea was dropped down, splashing on to his trousers. 'Are you folks ready to order?'

'Can we just have two minutes?' he asked.

'Honey, you can have two days, but the menu ain't going to change.'

Dan looked at Lisa. What should he say to that?

'He'll have the pastrami on rye, side order of onion rings, and I'll have the special.'

'*Thank* you.'

It was only when the waitress walked towards the kitchen, shouting out Lisa's order like a grotesque echo, that Dan began again to breathe.

'What's the special?' he asked.

'No idea. But it always shuts 'em up.'

They both sipped their drinks. Her jet-black coffee was too hot, and as Lisa half closed her eyes to blow over it, Dan used the opportunity to sneak another look at her face. Her skin was perfect, no blemishes or lines to disrupt the beauty of the healthy sheen. Her hair was longer than he remembered from four months earlier, and with the extra length, the gentle wave in its dark lustre was more obvious. But it was the eyes that fascinated him. They were a rich brown, almost teak, like his daughter's. But there was a special quality to Lisa's eyes, a fleeting sadness, all the more noticeable because it was so rarely there, something that hinted at a buried vulnerability, a hidden side he had not yet discovered.

Lisa suddenly put down her coffee and stood up, extending her right hand to someone behind Dan. Dan heard the voice before he saw the face.

'Lisa . . . honey!'

When Dan looked round, he saw a man well into his seventies. He was completely bald but had a well-trimmed grey moustache – a dapper dresser, fastidious and neat. His eyes had the sparkle of a ladies' man.

'Dan,' Lisa said, 'this is Ira Gottlieb. Ira, this is—'

'The guy you told me about?'

Lisa smiled as Ira sat down with them. Dan offered his hand across the table.

'Mr Gottlieb, pleased to—'

'Call me Ira for Chrissake. Only the judge and the IRS call me Mister.'

The waitress returned with the order. In a flash, she had placed plates stacked with food all over the table.

'What'll it be?' she asked Ira.

He looked at her, smiled back widely. 'Tell me I'm wrong. But you're wearing Obsession by Calvin Klein, ain't you?'

'No.'

'Well, you should . . . uh . . .' He examined her name-tag. 'Iris. Gee, that's a pretty name.'

She still froze him with her look. 'Do you wish to order . . . sir.'

'I ain't hungry,' Ira replied. 'Yet.'

Iris stormed off, muttering to herself.

'Younger women,' Ira whispered, his eyes twinkling.

Dan and Lisa burst out laughing as the old man grabbed Dan's fork and started digging into the food.

'Lisa told you about me?' he asked with his mouth full.

'Sort of,' Dan replied.

'Christ, you *never* ordered the special?'

'What's wrong with the special?' Lisa asked.

'Sucks. You should come down to Brighton Beach. Get some real Russian food.'

All three now began to demolish the food, with Ira leading the way, almost as if it were a race.

Lisa said, 'I'm representing Ira on—'

'I'm *allowing* Lisa to represent me on a claim for wrongful dismissal.'

'If it hadn't been for Ira,' Lisa said, 'I might never have been interested in your speech at the Bar Conference, Dan. Ira worked at the Holocaust Archives.'

'I don't understand.'

'Till the bastards sacked me. Jesus, all I wanted—'

'Which one's the special?' Dan asked.

Ira pushed a plate towards him. 'Enjoy.'

Lisa tried again: 'Ira wanted to put on an exhibition.'

'My life's work. My Sistine fucking chapel.'

'The special sucks,' Dan agreed. 'So what do you do?'

Ira suddenly put down his fork and didn't speak again until his mouth was empty. The change of face, the hesitation, created tension around the table.

'Fifty years ago,' Ira said quietly, 'the Nazis hunted me.' Again he paused. 'Now, I hunt them. What the hell is wrong with that?' He looked at Lisa as if there must be a simple answer to his question.

'It's not as simple as that, Ira.'

'The hell it isn't.'

'Hey, I'm on your side. Remember?'

'Yeah, yeah. I'm sorry, honey.'

Slowly, they all began to eat again, for a while in silence. Iris came by and freshened their cups without asking, huffing as Ira winked playfully at her.

Lisa began, 'Ira's theory—'

'It ain't no theory.'

'Ira's researches,' she corrected herself, 'prove that the Allies smuggled Nazi scientists to safety after the war.'

'The museum wouldn't put it on.'

'But don't we already know that the Allies recruited some Nazis?' Dan asked.

'Sure,' Ira replied. 'Rocket experts, anti-Soviet intelligence officers. But these chemists were different. These bastards devised the Final Solution.'

Dan, who had been unsure what to make of the meeting, couldn't contain his curiosity any longer. 'So why'd the museum object? Don't people want to remember?'

Ira frowned. 'Some things they want to remember. Some things they want to forget. We were the good guys, they were the bad guys. No one's interested in anything else.'

'Ira thinks,' Lisa said, 'that he can prove that the British and Americans have used Nazi scientists.'

'For what?' Dan asked.

'For every-goddamn-thing,' Ira replied.

Dan was confused. 'What have the British got to do with it?'

Ira laughed out loud, causing a couple on the next table to look over. 'Now don't go all holy on me, Dan. The British invented concentration camps.'

'Nonsense.'

'It's true. In the Boer War. Have you finished with the onion rings?'

Dan shoved the tray towards him. He was beginning to be annoyed by the old man.

'The English,' Ira continued, 'banished all Jews in 1216.'

'We fought the Nazis,' Dan protested.

'You fought *some* of them.'

'Bullshit.'

'How do you know?' Ira shouted. 'You know where Klaus Keller is, then?'

'Hey, hey, hey.' Lisa raised her voice and spread her hands, trying to calm the men down.

Dan sat back in his chair and crossed his arms defensively. Ira mirrored him. Lisa looked from one to the other and then decided to speak herself.

'Ira, Dan wants to know about Josef Rosen.'

'Why?' Ira was inspecting his shoes.

'I just do,' Dan replied.

'He owe you some money?'

'No.'

'That makes a change.'

Lisa gently took Ira's arm and tried to draw him closer to the table. 'Please, Ira.'

'I need your help,' Dan said.

'Why do you want to know Jo?'

'I'm . . .' Dan hesitated. But he decided that the old man deserved to know the truth. 'I'm his son.'

'Jo hasn't got a son.'

'No,' Dan replied. 'He doesn't *want* a son. It's not the same thing.' He paused and allowed his eyes to meet the old man's. 'I'm truly sorry if I offended—'

'Forget it, kid. It's just . . . look, I was at Auschwitz, OK? Kind of makes you sensitive.' He stared into the mid-distance as he spoke, his voice now slightly broken, no longer confident and vibrant but soft and pained. 'I spent fifty years hunting them down. Fifty years. How old are you?'

'About thirty-nine,' Dan replied. In fact, he had just turned forty.

'Well, there you go. And now? No one wants to listen. I'm just a crazy old Jew. I find out about Klaus Keller, and no one wants to know. You got a pen?'

Dan reached into his jacket and produced a Biro. The old man took one of the paper napkins out of its metal container and began to write. As he did so, Lisa spoke in a hushed voice.

'Klaus Keller was a leading Nazi chemist. Disappeared in 1945.'

Ira handed the pen back to Dan and stood up.

'You're Jo's boy, huh?'

Dan stood too. He didn't know what to say. Ira smiled and held out his hand. Dan shook it.

'Pleased to meet you, Jo's boy.' He handed Dan the napkin with a number on it. 'Ring that.'

'I've tried to ring, no one answers.'

'It's his private line. He knows I gave it to you, I'm a dead man.'

The three of them walked slowly out of the deli; Dan folded the napkin neatly and put it in his pocket. But at the door, the waitress blocked Ira's path.

'So where you taking me tonight, lover-boy?' she demanded.

Ira's face blanched and he looked quite ill. 'I'm sorry . . . I'm – uh – busy tonight,' he said.

*   *   *

Although the clouds swept along the length of Manhattan, depositing a fine drizzle between the Hudson and the East River, Dan decided to walk back to the hotel. He took a cab part of the way and then walked the last dozen blocks uptown, still in awe of the street drama of the city: the sax players on the corners, stalls selling freshly roasted nuts, steam coming from the ducts in the roads, legless Vietnam veterans on church steps. By the time he reached his hotel opposite the park, he had penned a letter to Chris in his head. He bought a postcard in the lobby, and scribbled the lines, telling her again that he loved her, that he would be home soon, that he wanted things to be different between them – better, more open.

What he was trying to say, but didn't dare commit to paper, was that he didn't want to miss her adolescence like he had missed her childhood.

Dan went slowly to the reception desk. Once more the young Dmitri was on duty in his dark waistcoat and neatly pressed shirt.

'I'd like to send this to England, please. Where can I get a stamp?'

'No problem, Mr Becket. Just give it me and we can frank it here.'

'Thanks,' Dan said, handing over the card. 'Any messages?'

Dmitri smiled and shook his head.

When Dan arrived at his room minutes later, it took three attempts to slide the plastic key through the lock correctly. It must have been this which prevented him from seeing the envelope jammed under his door.

He was confused. Dmitri had intimated that there were no messages, but here was an envelope: plain white and self-sealing. He walked the length of the room, right up to the sheet-glass windows that gave on to the panorama of Central Park. He tossed his jacket on to a chair and undid his tie before he opened the envelope. But there was no letter inside.

Dan turned the envelope upside down and, when he did so, a folded piece of green paper fluttered down.

It was a torn dollar bill.

On the front of the note, coming out of the mouth of George Washington, were the words *Bring this with you*.

It was only when he turned the note over that he saw, next to the etching of the pyramid that formed part of the US Treasury seal, *Cleopatra's Needle, 11 a.m.*

Unsure what to make of it all, he instinctively went to the room safe, in a dark wood cupboard by the bed. He crouched down and entered the personalised code number. He couldn't forget it – he had punched in Viv's birthday. The machinery ground ominously and the door suddenly sprung open. Inside was a mess of traveller's cheques, airline tickets and other documents. There was a stash of dollars he had intended to keep for an emergency, and amongst these worn green notes, a sliver of white paper. Nothing had been taken; whoever had left the envelope had probably not even been in the room.

He stood up and took from his jacket pocket the napkin upon which old Ira had written his father's private number. It began with the Brooklyn code, Brighton Beach specifically, and he knew this was where the man whom his mother had loved and hated for forty years still lived. These numbers, too, were some sort of formula or code back into the past, and he felt an urge to dispose of the paper. But he couldn't do it: things had changed since Viv had died.

He pressed '9' for an outside line and then dialled. The phone clicked twice before the connection was made, and then it began to ring. Dan held his breath, aware his palm was sweating – what was he going to say? Remember me? I am your son. Or rather: you don't remember me, you left us before I was born. You broke my mother's heart – I don't know you, but actually, I hate you.

The phone kept ringing. No one answered.

Chapter 8

The next day, parties convened in London for the second day of the committal hearing in the Montford case.

Sophie had to run the gauntlet of ravenous journalists once again, their numbers swelled by the breaking news of a 'secret' application by the prosecution. It was a potent combination: politics, crime and secrets of state. Banner headlines and front-page columns were guaranteed to boost circulations. But the scrum and chaos outside court only added to Sophie's sense of unease and, despite her controlled outward appearance, she kept thinking to herself that she was in over her head.

Montford had not arrived by the time Sophie entered the court building, so she headed straight for the CPS room. However, the foyer of the court was filled with people of Middle Eastern appearance, young men with tanned skin and moustaches, women with fair skin and headscarves, standing around, gesticulating to each other, speaking a language Sophie had never heard. She made her way with some difficulty through the group, and towards the corridor that contained the court offices. If she caught Robert Lancing off guard, she calculated, perhaps she might be able to coax some of the sensitive information out of him. He was hardly very bright; in fact he was more of an intellectual midget, the type of professional man whose common sense frequently absconded when a young woman appeared on the horizon.

Lancing was again sitting in a swivel chair in the middle of the hectic office, his feet on the desk in front of him, revealing patent leather shoes and the hideous red socks he considered a fashion statement. It was a statement Sophie had always loosely translated as: I am a prat in red socks.

Had she really gone out with him? Her heart, she consoled

herself, was a fickle little muscle. But she was no different to most people – except Dan Becket. He seemed to have a different brand of machinery ticking away in there. So many women at the Bar had thrown themselves at him, and he had never, legend had it, succumbed. That was probably why she had never let him know how she felt. Perhaps it wasn't from a sense of decency or respect, but from a fear of failure.

Sophie shut the office door behind her.

'Ah, Miss Chase,' Lancing began. 'Why, you look even more beautiful this morning than—'

'Cut the bull, Robert. Now what's going on?'

He smirked at her and flicked provocatively through a detailed report. 'It's a committal, Soph. It's to send your murdering minister to the Bailey for trial.'

'You know perfectly well that you have a duty to disclose all evidence to the defence.'

'Subject to Public Interest Immunity.'

Sophie was well aware that if any evidence might prejudice the public interest, or national security, then the Crown could seek the court's leave to keep it secret, under the doctrine of Public Interest Immunity – P.I.I.

'So are you saying your evidence is P.I.I.?' she asked.

'I'm not saying we have any evidence.'

These were the usual bizarre games that lawyers played when the issue of P.I.I. arose. It was a battle of mental gymnastics, where the defence tried to embarrass or trap the Crown into a revealing admission.

'All right,' Sophie said. 'On the assumption you have some further evidence.'

'On the assumption, which is not admitted, that we have further evidence, which is not accepted, we cannot confirm or deny that it comes under the protection of P.I.I.' Lancing smirked again. 'I hope that helps.'

'Prat.'

'Come on, Soph. If you were just a *bit* nicer to me, I might just blurt out a state secret or two in a moment of unbridled passion.'

'In your wildest dreams.'

'Oh, but my dreams are wild.'

'No, they're a little on the *wet* side, as I remember. But I don't recall anything particularly wild, Robert.'

A young member of the admin staff in the office, a girl barely out of school, sniggered at the photocopier by the window and Lancing spun his head around.

'This is a private conversation,' he snapped at her. Turning back to Sophie, he said in a cold voice, 'I am formally instructed to keep you up to date on a "need to know" basis.'

'I suppose that's a start.' She waited, hopeful of something she could take back to Montford, any scrap of information to demonstrate she was not completely hopeless.

Lancing was silent.

'So?' she asked finally.

'So there's nothing you *need* to know. We will seek and obtain an adjournment for another day.'

Sophie decided to play her final card. She moved much closer to him, dropped her voice and knew that she was about to hate herself. 'Look, Rob. This case is a real break for me. If I keep getting the runaround I'm going to get sacked. I *need* to know what this is about. Just give me a clue. For old times' sake.'

He examined her face evenly, swivelling from side to side in the chair. 'You always did go for the jugular, didn't you, Sophie? I suppose that's your special talent.'

'Rob—'

'Why don't you ask your client?'

'Montford?'

'Ask him where the skeletons are buried. Ask him what he did after the war.'

'After the war?'

'I've already said too much. I trust you will not oppose the application for an adjournment?'

'No. Rob . . . thanks.'

'See you in court.'

Sophie felt again that she was out of her depth. As she left the office, she could not help wondering again if her leader, Julian Waugh, QC, was using her as a sacrificial lamb. When she reached the foyer of the building, Montford fought his way through the crowd of Middle Eastern people and approached her with the senior partner of the instructing solicitors. Both examined her expectantly. She would just have to bluff it out.

Once they were safely locked in a square conference room, with

a strip light and a rickety desk, the men waited for Sophie to sit
down. Then she told them the news.

'I am afraid we might have another wasted day,' she said as
cheerfully as possible.

Her false optimism was not contagious.

'Do you know what's happening in my case, Miss Chase?'
Montford asked.

'I think they are asking for another day's adjournment.'

'On what basis?'

'They won't say.' She tried to decide whether she should
mention the end of the conversation with Lancing.

'They won't say?' the solicitor, Douglas Wallace, said. 'This is
most unsatisfactory. I don't wish to sound rude, Miss Chase, but
didn't I instruct you to—'

'They hinted at Mr Montford's time after the war.'

'After?'

'*Yes.*' She had had enough. It wasn't her fault that the prosecution were being awkward about disclosing the evidence: why
should she be blamed? Sophie noted that Montford had said
nothing. She stared at him, but his head dropped slightly, and
she saw him slowly opening and closing his right hand.

The solicitor continued. 'I suggest that we move immediately
to have these entire proceedings struck out as an abuse of the
process of—'

'Do be *quiet*, Douglas,' Montford said softly.

'Look, Simon, I've been your solicitor for over twenty years
and—'

'Just shut up, will you?' Montford looked up at Sophie. 'Will
they have to disclose what they know about the war? I mean, at
some stage?'

'Probably,' Sophie replied. 'We can try to flush them out before
trial by listing the case for a disclosure application in front of the
trial judge at the Old Bailey.'

'So you think it will go that far. To trial?'

'I think they have something important,' she replied.

'Well, please be good enough to find out what you can. But
try not to push them too far – not yet.'

'Why not?'

'I learnt in the army that there are many battles to be fought
before the war is won. Let's keep our powder dry for now.'

'Can you tell me what's going on?' Sophie asked.

Montford's eyes flashed once as they looked at her, past her, focusing on some truth she could not even begin to understand.

'I saw a couple of members of the Board of Deputies outside,' he said.

She was still confused. 'The Board of—'

'The British Board of *Jewish* Deputies, Miss Chase. I suppose it was only a matter of time until people like that turned up.'

Montford half smiled. 'The great and the good of our esteemed Jewish community are here to do a bit of old-fashioned gloating. They seem to forget that I commanded the British Army detail that liberated Neuwelt concentration camp in 1945.'

'So, why are they after you?'

'You might remember the furore about the War Crimes Bill a few years ago. Just because I spoke out against it, I was accused of anti-Semitism and all sorts of . . .'

There was a sudden screaming in the foyer outside. A thick-set woman, her face half covered in a scarf, was crying out inconsolably. Sophie rushed past the two men, though they were closer to the door. The large group of people milled around the woman, their faces a mixture of fury and confusion. A young man, possibly still in his teens, approached Sophie.

'You a lawyer?'

'What's the problem?'

'Her son. He in the next court. They refuse him legal money.'

'Legal aid?' she asked.

'They say the offence do not allow legal aid. But the defendant, my cousin, he a political refugee. If he is convicted, then they send him back and he die.'

'Where does he come from?'

'Kurdistan.'

'Which part?'

'Iraq.'

Sophie put her hand on the crying mother's shoulder. At the same time, Montford's solicitor joined them.

'Is there a problem?' he asked.

'They don't have a brief,' Sophie said.

'You be our lawyer,' the youth asked her. 'Yes?'

'No,' the solicitor intervened.

'I'm afraid that you can't instruct me directly,' she added. 'I'm

a barrister and you must go to a solicitor first. It's the rules.'
She turned to the senior partner. 'I believe you're a solicitor,
Douglas.'

'Are you serious?'

'Look, nothing is going to happen on the Montford case until
tomorrow.'

The youth interrupted and gestured towards the astonished
Douglas Wallace. 'We instruct you to instruct her.'

'We only take private clients and require that they open a client
account and deposit a substantial cash sum against potential
legal costs.'

'How much have you got?' Sophie asked the boy.

'One pound.'

'Got another five pence?'

He rummaged in his pockets. 'Yes.'

'Splendid. A one-guinea brief – one pound, one shilling, just like
the old days,' she beamed. 'Now go into court and tell the usher
that your cousin's barrister is going to be delayed a moment,
she's having the Montford murder adjourned. And then I'll be
all yours.'

The youth dashed off with a huge grin on his face.

'Shouldn't we ask Mr Montford first?' the solicitor asked.

'He won't mind,' she said. 'He's a real gentleman.'

Chapter 9

In the next court, an overworked Crown Prosecutor had a pile of grey files on the bench at the front of the court. Each file was kept closed with a large rubber band, and the stressed woman prosecutor was fielding enquiries from half a dozen defence lawyers at the same time.

Other cases in the list ahead of Sophie's were dealt with by the stipendiary magistrate, a former barrister with his first toe on the judicial ladder. He dealt with the unrepresented clients first, obviously relishing the fact that in so doing he kept the lawyers in court waiting.

Sophie watched as case after case was disposed of in summary fashion. First a prostitute, caught for the twentieth time soliciting; then a tramp 'D & D', drunk and disorderly; a shoplifter who was not keeping up with payments of her fines; a motorist, claiming that he no longer had ownership of the car that had been affixed with a parking ticket.

Sophie used the time to speak to the CPS lawyer. They sat next to each other, two professional women dressed in widows' weeds, nondescript black suits, and talked in whispers.

'I represent the Kurd,' Sophie began.

'Thought there was no legal aid.' She checked her files. 'No, there isn't. It's the case of Bicak you're talking about?'

'He's a private client.'

The woman looked at Sophie incredulously. 'What's he paying you with? A string of beads?'

'It's *pro bono*. Can you tell me what the allegation is?'

'Abbas Bicak was arrested for disorderly conduct in the Tilbury Road.'

'What's the story?'

'There was an Iraqi trade delegation visiting an industrial site in the Docklands area. Your man and the others were protesting violently.'

'Others?'

'None have been arrested. They all scarpered. But for some reason your man cannot run.'

'Any of the Iraqis injured?'

'No, but—'

'Isn't this a classic case for a bind-over?' Sophie whispered.

The woman shrugged. 'I agree, but there are orders from on high. It's public policy.'

'What policy?'

'We can't have foreigners fighting out their battles on our soil.'

'But it's all right for us to fight ours on *theirs*?'

The clerk of the court, sitting in a seat in front of Sophie, hissed at her to be quiet.

'Sorry,' the prosecutor said. 'This has to go to trial. There's a date in April.'

'April? Why not sooner?'

'The Iraqi witnesses are abroad. They're returning then. Your punter could always plead guilty, you know. He'd only get a fine.'

Sophie didn't reply. As she walked to the back of the court, another prostitute had been fined for soliciting and was calculating how many tricks she would have to turn to pay off her backlog of £200. She asked for three days – the magistrate allowed her seven.

Sophie asked the jailer, a policeman who stood at the back of the court with the list, to let her into the holding cell behind the rear door.

'Are you sure, love?' he asked, eyeing her up and down. 'Pretty thing like you. We got a couple of murderers behind there. Why don't you stay in here with us?'

'On balance, I think I'd prefer the company of the murderers,' she snapped.

The jailer muttered some expletives under his breath, including the words 'bloody feminist', and knocked on the door. Another, younger jailer inside opened it.

Sophie immediately saw a sick-looking man sitting at the rear of the cell alone. He was a swarthy man of about thirty, lean, with a moustache and a shock of curly dark hair.

'My name is Sophie Chase,' she told him. 'Mr Bicak, your family asked me to represent you.' He didn't look at her until she raised her voice and spoke again. 'They say you were protesting against the Iraqi trade delegation at Tilbury docks.'

'They buy chemicals to bomb my country,' he said indignantly.

'It's alleged that your conduct was disorderly. Do you deny that?'

'I threaten to kill them.'

Sophie looked at the man's face, which was covered in burn marks, like an ancient map. 'It might be that you should plead guilty. You don't seem to have a defence.'

'I defend my country.'

'From what?'

'Genocide.'

The man slowly unbuttoned his shirt. Underneath, his chest was covered in peeling skin and scabs as if something were eating it from inside.

Another of the prisoners in the holding cell, a young black man, looked on, horrified. '*Shit*, man. Put that shit away.'

'In 1987,' the Kurd said, 'my village, near Halabja, is bombed by Saddam's planes. I was on the hillside and I look down, but there is no explosion, no fire, and I think, maybe Saddam just scare us.

'Later, I come down, slowly, and the sheep, they all begin to die. I run to village and everyone on ground, children with foam in mouths, old women eyes open, all dead but no wounds.'

'What happened?' Sophie asked, although she already suspected.

'Chemical attack.' He pointed to the scabs on his chest. 'Cancer. My heart soon dies, too. Arteries. They say I have memory loss, but I remember everything. Every woman, every dead child. I remember them all.'

Sophie was silent while the man did up his shirt. Suddenly her worries about the Montford case appeared frivolous, mere vanity.

'The case can't come to trial until April,' she told him.

'They deport me before then.'

'To where?'

'Back home. The secret police find me, and kill me. I seek political asylum, but they say I cause trouble. True. I do cause trouble. World must know how my people are being killed.'

'Look, I'll try to seek a stay of the deportation,' she said, but he didn't seem to hear.

The door to the court opened and the jailer called the Kurd's case. Sophie stepped quietly to the front row of the court, next to the CPS lawyer.

'Pleading guilty?' she asked.

'Fighting,' Sophie said.

'What on earth is your defence?'

'Genocide. The prevention thereof.'

It was a swift, formal arraignment. Sophie had conducted many in the past, and normally they were unremarkable. But this case was different. Here was a man with a vivid sense of his own demise, admitting to a crime for a greater good, speaking of horrors so far beyond her direct experience that she trembled at his words.

Her client pleaded not guilty to the charge and the matter was listed for a half-day trial in April. As he was led back to the cells, still in custody on the immigration matter, the Kurd smiled at Sophie for the first time. It was this gesture which made her feel wretched walking out of the doors of the court a free person. Images of the children foaming at the mouth filled her head, and she sat in the foyer of the building trying to regain her poise. But then a picture of Helen's baby being neatly wrapped in a sheet and taken away took their place.

Chapter 10

Dan had slept badly, disturbed by the envelope slipped under the door. So on that rain-swept morning in Manhattan, it was with a heavy head and bags under his eyes that he walked with a ninety-nine-cent umbrella through Central Park well before 11 o'clock. He had given himself an extra fifteen minutes and circled wide around Cleopatra's Needle. The Egyptian monument was near to the Belvedere Lake in the heart of Central Park, and he walked as casually as his nerves and the wet conditions allowed, placing himself on the far shore of the lake. The stone needle lay across a sheet of flat water, pitted by raindrops.

From this position, he watched the damp scene, the rain drumming on his umbrella, the water beginning to work its way into the soles of his shoes.

10.59.

He watched a small woman with a walking-stick and a headscarf dawdling towards the West Side. Then a young girl in a Lycra bodysuit jogged around the lake with four dogs on long leads running miserably behind her. But there was no one at the needle.

11.03.

Slowly, he began to edge his way towards the other side of the lake. He was sure that he looked suspicious, he certainly felt suspicious, and the young girl gave him a wide berth as her second circuit of the water crossed his path. The trailing dog sniffed at his foot, but it was too wet and the slack on its lead soon ran out, forcing it to scamper off with the others.

It was 11.11 when he arrived at the foot of Cleopatra's Needle.

Yet no one was there. He decided that he would give it four minutes and then he would walk back to the hotel and order a cup of Earl Grey tea and milk, and to hell with New York.

As he waited, he looked at the engravings on the stone. Some idiot had sprayed it with paint, the sign of a Swastika, some further anti-Semitic abuse. As he stood and waited, Dan felt uneasy, short of breath. The atmosphere and the events of the last few days were unnerving. A mingling of the present and the past, for he knew that somewhere in the city, among the ten million New Yorkers, was his father, Josef Rosen.

After a further short wait, Dan heard approaching steps.

'You've brought your English weather to New York,' a man said quietly, barely above the noise of the raindrops falling through the branches of the trees.

Dan looked at him, his long coat down to the ankles, the collar turned up. This man was in his mid-fifties but very fit, with clear, intelligent eyes; however, the skin on his face was badly marked as if from a terrible childhood disease. And Dan suspected that he had seen him before: he appeared to be the man from the back row of the court-room.

'Who are you?' Dan asked.

'It doesn't matter.'

Dan stared hard at the man and then, when there was no reply, he began to leave.

'Come on, Mr Becket—'

'Who?'

The man paused and examined Dan's face slowly. 'Yuri.'

'Bullshit.'

'I've wanted to contact you for some time.'

'Why?'

'I practise law – but not like you. I'm more interested in what you might call . . . justice.'

'Justice?'

'For those who have evaded it . . . criminals the courts have not reached.'

'Like who?'

'War criminals,' Yuri said, looking at the Swastika on the stone.

Dan stared into the man's dark eyes, trying to get a handle on what he was dealing with. 'What do you want from me?'

The man paused and then said plainly, 'Help.'

The word was spoken with such a lack of emphasis, in such an understated fashion, that despite himself Dan found that his curiosity had been roused. 'What kind of help?'

'There's a war criminal currently in Britain. We need help securing his conviction.'

'I don't practise law any more.'

'No, you don't *want* to practise law because you cannot find a case you believe in. But this case ... this case you might believe in.'

'Why?' Dan asked.

'Twenty million Russians died in the war. This case is about one of them. A conviction in this case would make you proud.' The man hesitated, looked down, and said more softly, 'Would make your daughter proud of you.'

A chill raced through Dan's body. 'Who are you?' he shouted, storming up to the man, grabbing his coat.

'My name is Yuri. I am a lawyer.' He broke free of Dan's grip. 'I practised law in St Petersburg when it was called Leningrad. I defended citizens' rights in Moscow when no one else would. But Russia today, Mr Becket, is just another European state with European unemployment and inflation and ... lawyers. All kinds of lawyers. Some greedy. Some, like you, who want to do the right thing.'

'I don't understand what you want from me.'

'The truth. Your government will not tell us the truth.'

'About what?'

'You will be approached. Asked to prosecute a case.'

'What case?'

'The only case that means anything. Montford. You will use our evidence and ... you will win.'

'And what will happen ... if—'

'You refuse? Nothing. Nothing at all.' Yuri smiled, his face again riddled with lines like deep cuts. 'I want to make it perfectly clear to you that your life is not at stake, Mr Becket. But ...'

'But what?'

'But every time your daughter looks in the mirror and sees the acid burns on her face, she will curse you. And you will have achieved ... what? Prevented the truth coming out? Prevented justice from being done?'

'Simon Montford was a government *minister*.'

'Of course, that puts him above suspicion,' the man laughed. 'We want you to show surprise when you are approached by the British authorities. For you will be approached. But you must hesitate before you accept. And then you will work ... with me.'

The man walked away, his footsteps drowned out by the sound of the rain in the trees, the dream-like quality of the encounter enhanced by the fact that his dark coat soon blended into the wet trunks of the leafless trees in the park. Dan was alone.

11.17.

The world a different place.

A wind got up, blowing from the Hudson River, forcing Dan's umbrella inside out, tearing the lining away from the metal spokes. He wandered aimlessly around the lake. Dumping the tangle of wire and plastic into the first bin he came across, he did not feel the rain lashing against his face as he tried to work out what to do. His shoes were by now sodden, and he thrust his hands deep into his pockets as he walked.

There must be a logical explanation to all of it. Keep calm, he told himself. You've coped with terrible things in the past. Then from somewhere a doubt arose. Had he in fact coped with Viv's death? Burying your head in the sand wasn't exactly coping. So what was the alternative now? Contact the police. Yes, and say what? So they could do *what*?

Dan felt the crash of a body against his.

He looked up. He had bumped into a balding man whose newspaper had fallen into the puddles on the ground near an exit on to Fifth Avenue.

'I'm sorry,' Dan said, bending down, trying to fish the sodden sheets out of the water.

'My fault,' the man replied in an English accent.

Dan looked up. The man was portly, with a tight mouth. He stared resolutely past Dan and into the puddle. And it was only when Dan followed the path of the man's eyes that he saw what the man was looking at.

The other half of the torn dollar note.

'I'm sorry I'm a bit late,' he said.

Chapter 11

He must have been about fifty years old and wore a raincoat that was tightly tied around his large waist. His face was ruddy and he had not shaved properly, missing the odd hair underneath his chin. He carried a large golfing umbrella, under which two small eyes peered out and darted incessantly over Dan's body. The traffic roared from the other side of the fence that separated Central Park from Fifth Avenue, and a large refuse truck blasted its horn at an unseen obstruction, causing the man to shout at Dan above the din.

'I'm so glad you agreed to meet me, Mr Becket.'

'I've agreed to nothing,' Dan said. 'What do you want from me?'

'Five minutes of your time, that's all. After that, it's up to you.'

'I can just walk away?'

'You're right, of course, to be suspicious. But I had to contact you and . . . well, as you've probably guessed, I couldn't phone.'

'Why not?'

'Off the record.'

Dan shook his head, the rain spinning off his hair, and rubbed his eyes.

'I'm afraid that you may be a bit of a marked man, Mr Becket.'

'A bit?'

'True,' the man said. 'I suppose one is either marked or not. Look, we can stand here discussing hit-squads in the rain or we can get a coffee and bagel. How does that sound?'

'You know who I am, but—'

'Didn't I say? Peter Grail. Met.'

'CID?'

'Special squad.'

'Homicide?'

'Worse.'

'*Worse?*'

'Mass murder. War crimes.'

Grail offered Dan the shelter of his golfing umbrella and together they began to walk along Fifth Avenue, stepping over the puddles, but unable to avoid the spray from a passing yellow cab. Grail turned his collar up against the January rain, while Dan looked down at the glistening sidewalk and held his coat lapels together. Neither of them spoke.

It took no longer than ten minutes to reach the five-storey stone building situated on the corner of Fifth and a cross-street in the lower Seventies. Dan had asked at reception for the precise address of the Holocaust Museum from which Ira Gottlieb had been dismissed, and he wanted to see it for himself. It had heavy rustication on the outside, and a pair of workmen were busily engaged in repairing the stonework. There was no written sign indicating what the building was, but carved above the door, barely visible among the accumulated Manhattan grime, Dan spied a Star of David.

Inside the entrance, the furnishings of the reception area were plush and modern, more like a state-of-the-art airport terminal. As they walked, Dan looked at the black-and-white photographs on the walls. Emaciated men, their ribs jutting out painfully from their stomachs, were standing behind barbed wire. There were pairs of small children, identical, holding each other in oversized clothes. An old woman, with a skeletal face, staring at the camera, wearing a Star of David on her arm.

'They must do a pretty brisk trade,' Grail said. 'More Holocaust survivors over here than anywhere else in the world except possibly Israel.'

The cafeteria was empty. There were a dozen tables that were immaculately clean, and a tray of fresh bagels on the counter of the servery. Grail lifted and then rang an ornamental brass bell, causing an old woman with a squint and wafer-thin hair to stick her head around the kitchen door. Grail whispered 'Coffee,' and she nodded.

Dan sat down at the table that Grail had indicated. He looked at the overweight man in front of him, now sweating with the effort of the walk, and asked, 'What brings a British policeman to New York?'

'Can I answer that with a question, Mr Becket?'

'I'd prefer it if—'

'When was the last war crimes prosecution in England?'

'Nuremberg?'

'That was in Germany, of course. But you're in the right general area.' Grail shook his umbrella out, covering the newly Hoovered carpet with droplets. 'In fact, it was in 1948. The German Generals case. And Winston Churchill himself contributed to their defence fund. You see, we English – I include you, of course – have always had an ambivalent attitude to war crimes.'

'How do you mean?'

'Well, it just doesn't seem very English to win the war *and* rub their leaders' noses in it. It's just not cricket or whatever. Of course, all that's changed now. You of course know about the Montford case, Mr Becket? The committal proceedings are going on in London.'

Dan looked on silently. He didn't answer, tried not to express any emotion, though he remembered what Yuri had said in the park. The woman from the kitchen arrived at the table and placed a tray with two steaming cups of coffee in front of them. The bagels had been sliced in half and Dan could see slivers of pink, almost transparent salmon topped with cream cheese.

'Could I have some cream for my coffee?' Grail asked her.

She nodded and returned to the counter.

Grail took a bite of his bagel and began to speak with his mouth full. 'The whole shooting-match has changed with the War Crimes Act 1991. I remember when I heard about it on the news. I thought, talk about chasing ghosts. We can't catch criminals who nick things under our noses. How on earth are we going to catch Nazis who murdered unknown people fifty years ago?'

He took another mouthful of bagel. 'So there I was sitting in my living room when a call comes from my Chief Super. They need someone on this new war crimes squad who is good with paperwork.' He wiped some cream cheese from the corner of his mouth with a shiny paper serviette. 'That's my speciality. Fraud squad for twenty years. Forgery. Fakes. Counterfeiting. And I'm told, Pete, it's a cushy number, sit on your bottom until you retire to the Costa del Crime.'

Dan looked on, unsure as to whether he should respond.

Suddenly Grail stopped eating. 'If I knew the trouble all this would cause, I'd have taken early retirement. It was on the table, government cutbacks and all that. Crime rate goes up, get rid of your senior officers. Blinding policy.' He took another bite. 'You're the lawyer. I'm just a career policeman. You'll know the ambit of the War Crimes Act better than me.'

'It allows for the prosecution of war criminals from the Second World War?' Dan suggested, unsure of the precise drafting of the statute.

Grail put down the bagel for the first time. There was a more assured tone in his voice. 'Section One provides for the prosecution of perpetrators of war crimes in German Occupied Territories between 1939 and 1945. Well, perpetrators who after 1991 were ordinarily resident in the United Kingdom.' He looked at Dan impassively. 'Are you going to finish your bagel?'

Dan waved his hand.

Grail continued, 'Of course, the act was aimed at ex-Nazis and collaborators who had sneaked into the UK after the war. A Home Office report indicated that three foreign nationals should be prosecuted forthwith and seventy-five others should be investigated further.'

'By your squad?'

'I had no problem with *that*. I mean, if we had Nazis in Northolt, let's put them away. But that's not what they're using the statute for. The first prosecution, Mr Becket, won't be of a German or a Lithuanian, or a Croat. It will be of one of us, Simon Montford.' He paused. 'And I want you to prosecute the case.'

Grail took a single bite of Dan's bagel and then stood up. The cafeteria was still empty and he threw a ten-dollar bill on to the table.

Dan affected to be shocked, and in one sense he was. But the cause of the surprise was not the revelation that Dan was to prosecute – Yuri had already told him that. Rather, Dan was astonished that the Russian had access to such accurate information. It raised the more sinister question, what else did Yuri know? There was, of course, the equally disturbing corollary:

was there anything Yuri could *not* find out? About the war crimes case, about Dan, about his family.

'There's one thing that doesn't make sense,' Dan said.

'Only one thing?'

'If the Montford committal's going on now, why aren't you in London?'

Grail paused and smiled. The false kind of smile a detective gives a suspect to soften him up. 'Because, Mr Becket, I'm still looking for witnesses.'

The exhibition rooms of the museum were dark, with spotlights picking out particular items, and the only natural light filtered in eerily from narrow Gothic windows high above the floor. The museum was arranged in a chronological fashion, tracing the history of the Jewish people back to Old Testament times, showing how the Diaspora spread through Europe right up until the Holocaust began.

Dan felt uneasy. These were things, this was blood, he had never acknowledged. He looked on at the images of persecution and did feel sympathy on a gut level, an abhorrence of bigotry and prejudice. But he did not feel part of it. These were not his people in the camps. Why should he be more concerned than anyone else? A Jewish father did not a Jewish son make: especially not this father, especially not this son.

Grail eventually stopped at a room that was labelled 'The Final Solution'. Dan followed him past sepia-coloured railway maps pinned to the wall, showing the routes to Auschwitz and Treblinka, the location of Buchenwald and Belsen, the names of camps he had never heard of such as Masdorf and Neuwelt.

Looking at a plan of a gas chamber, Grail read the quote above it. 'Whoever fights with poison gas will be fought with poison gas. Whoever departs from the rules of *humane* warfare can only expect that we shall do the same.' He looked at Dan. 'Who said that?'

'Churchill?'

'Hitler. But I take your point. You know Adolf was obsessed with gas warfare. Ever since he was temporarily blinded at the Battle of Ypres in 1918. A poison gas attack, launched by the good old Brits. Perhaps that's why he was so keen on *Die Endlösing*.'

Dan looked at him blankly.

'The Final Solution. Devised by Eichmann, developed by Klaus Keller.'

'Keller?'

'The Mozart of Murder. Hitler's pet chemist. A scientific genius. He was developing a new generation of gases when he disappeared in 1945.'

'Why me to prosecute the Montford case?'

'Word has it that you're the expert on Abuse of Process, or whatever the term is. Robert Lancing's fine for now, but didn't you give a paper on it at the Bar Conference last year? And that's why you're in New York, isn't it?'

'So?'

'So the defence lawyers for the war criminal—'

'The alleged war criminal.'

'They are bound to argue that the case is too old and should be thrown out as an abuse of process.' Grail looked seriously at Dan. 'Am I wrong about that?'

'No, but anyone could argue against that legal submission.'

'But not everyone has a reputation as a tough, independent brief. Not everyone was an expert prosecutor. On the Treasury Counsel list.'

'I resigned.'

'I resigned from the porn squad in the seventies. But I'm still a copper. You're still a barrister, Mr Becket.'

'Why can't you get one of the current Treasury Counsel?'

'We want you.'

'I find that hard to believe. People will be queuing up for this brief. This will be the biggest case of the year.'

'Of the decade,' Grail said. Then he paused and appeared totally captivated by the criss-cross railway lines on the ageing map. 'It will be titanic. It will cause waves. It could sink a whole part of the Establishment.'

'Sounds like the sort of case that could make a reputation.'

'Or ruin a life.' Grail turned away from the map. 'What I need is a barrister who has nothing to lose within the profession, within the Establishment. And all my spies – loosely speaking, of course – tell me that is you.'

Dan had said to himself that after his last case, after the resignation, after Viv's death, he would never prosecute again. He no longer wanted to be part of it, he could no longer stomach it: the power; the ability to affect people's lives, to save or destroy them, to have that choice and that responsibility.

'I no longer prosecute,' Dan said.

'Out of principle?'

'Sort of.'

'It's a strange sort of principle, Mr Becket, that will allow some of the biggest mass murderers in history to escape justice.' Grail paused. 'Or is it something else? Something to do with the Iraqi bombing case?'

Dan realised that Grail inevitably would have investigated this.

'I've done my homework, Mr Becket. Terrorist organisation, Sons of Kurdistan, bombed the Iraqi trade mission. Trial at the Bailey last year. Both Kurds convicted on a majority verdict. You resigned from the case and withdrew from the Treasury Counsel list.'

And, Dan silently added, my wife died that night.

'I need someone who is honest,' Grail said. 'Someone who has the guts to do the right thing.'

'That's not me.'

'I think it is.'

'So what is Montford supposed to have done?'

'I can't tell you unless you agree to take the case.'

'That's ridiculous.' Dan looked at the man's ruddy face, trying to find a sign that he was bluffing. But there was none.

'There is a secret annexe to the War Crimes Act,' Grail said, his voice deadpan. 'It contains names of suspects whose identity cannot be revealed on grounds of national security.'

'Nonsense. How is national security threatened by crimes that were committed fifty years ago?'

'Good question.'

'So what's the answer?'

'Can't tell you. But if you take the case, you will be bound by the Official Secrets Act until the trial, maybe longer.'

'Maybe for life?'

'Maybe.'

'So why on earth should I take the brief?'

'Because it is the right thing to do.'

It was with a shudder that Dan recalled the conversation in the park with Yuri. Should he just tell Grail? I have been approached and threatened, I need your help. But how did Yuri know that Grail would contact him? There must be a leak in the police ranks. And if there was, Yuri would find out about Dan seeking the police's help. What would then happen to Chris thousands of miles away?

'I want to stress,' Grail continued, 'that you have an entirely free choice in this matter. I'm a man of my word, Mr Becket, and I told you the moment we met that you can walk away from this right now and that will be the end of it.'

'That offer holds true?'

'Certainly.'

Dan paused to weigh his options, but in the dark room with images of concentration camp survivors appearing to crawl out of the walls like holograms, he found it impossible to think.

'I'll need to know more,' he said.

'I suppose we both will.' Grail smiled, his face creasing, and Dan was offended by the stark contrast between his ruddy cheeks and the hollow faces staring out from behind the barbed wire of the concentration camps in the photographs. 'But the clock is ticking, Mr Becket. Every day the trail gets a little colder, or witnesses die or evidence is buried.'

Chapter 12

By 6 o'clock that evening, the rain had left the city, and Manhattan was cool but not cold. The pavements were covered in a sheer film of surface water that reflected the early evening lights, giving the avenues the appearance of congested waterways, bordered to the east and the west by ever-changing gold-splattered carpets.

Lisa Hartman arrived at Dan's hotel at 6.15 and telephoned him from the lobby. He came down immediately, having shaved and dowsed his cheeks lightly with his favourite aftershave, one to which Vivienne had introduced him. Lisa sat in the lobby, lost in a massive leather chair that surrounded her like a huge hand. Around her, businessmen chattered in small conspiratorial groups and overdressed bell-boys hung about waiting for tips.

'How's my favourite English attorney?' she said, getting up. 'Look, the Plaza is just a couple of blocks over. Why don't we go to the Oak Room there?'

'Have we time?'

'Sure. The play doesn't start till eight.'

'You got the tickets?' Dan asked, smiling.

'Not the ones you wanted. But these,' she said, holding up a yellow and a red ticket. 'I think you'll like them even more.'

He smiled and ushered her towards the revolving door, momentarily placing his palm in the small of her back. He felt how delicate and narrow it was, but immediately took his hand away.

They walked towards the East Side, along the border of the park. The road was lined with horse carriages and fast-talking Ukrainians and Russians touting for trade, offering a romantic ride through Central Park. Dan would have loved to have taken one, except that the horses stood so miserably between the harnesses, and Lisa would probably have thought that it was a terrible cliché.

The Oak Room was a dark bar that gave on to the park. It was filled with sombre wood and men in dark suits, sitting with their preppy sons and immaculately turned-out wives.

Lisa sat down. 'It's where Manhattan fathers are supposed to bring their sons for their first drink. Of course, I was exposed to alcohol much earlier. I was around eight when I realised my mother was not drinking water with her cornflakes at breakfast but something that smelt like paint.'

'Vodka?'

'Amongst other things.'

A waiter came to their table.

'Two vodka tonics,' Lisa said.

Dan looked through the windows and could see a couple, perhaps the age that Viv and he were the previous year, getting into one of the carriages, then he heard the clip-clop as the horse began to trot into the park. The man in the carriage put his arm around the woman and she smiled, resting her head on his shoulder, brushing her hair away from her face. They seemed so content. Silent. At ease. He struggled to find a moment like that between him and Vivienne. Failed.

The waiter came and placed the slim glasses containing the vodka before them. He poured the tonic into each glass, half filling them, and left the bill on the table.

'What were you saying?' Lisa asked. 'You mumbled something.'

'Oh, nothing.'

'*Hey*, I thought you were going to be straight with me, Counsellor.'

He reflected that he had told only one other person what had happened in his last case, the Kurdish bombing trial that Grail had mentioned. And that person was Viv. He was certain that he could not tell anyone in England, not even Sophie, for all her concern. But Lisa was different. Lisa appeared to be like him. Alone.

It was only after they had finished their drinks and ordered another round that Dan began to talk more frankly. The bar was filling up and an even murmur built up around them, insulating them from the neighbouring tables.

'You know, I actually went to the Bar to try to do some good, to make a difference. I thought, all right, Dan Becket, you've got a sharp mind and a quick tongue – or should that be the other way around? – put your money where your mouth is. I wanted to make the world a safer place, if only a little. Get the bad guys off the street. Prosecute. Do justice.'

'So what went wrong?' she asked, sipping her drink discreetly.

'I never cut corners, always was straight with the defence, and although I was the only kid of a single mother – an Irish Catholic, working-class, an outsider – somehow I began to rise quickly up the prosecuting ladder. In 1994, I was finally made a Treasury Counsel.'

'What's that? Like a District Attorney?'

'Treasury Counsel are the first-choice prosecutors at the Old Bailey. Get all the best cases. Or rather, all the worst. Terrorist cases, child abuse, gangland assassinations, serial rapists, wives battered to death, pensioners robbed and tortured.'

'Jesus, Dan.'

'Then last year, I got what was supposed to be my big break. The Iraqi bombing case.'

'I remember – the one that made the international news?'

'The Sons of Kurdistan car-bombed the Iraqi Trade Mission in West London. Only they killed ten ordinary Londoners, including a member of the minor aristocracy.'

Lisa put down her glass. 'That's it. Wasn't it some Lady or other who was always doing charity?'

'You can imagine the public outcry. Blue blood had been spilt. They needed their pound of flesh.'

Lisa looked confused. 'But the reports that I read said that the Kurds confessed.'

'Of course they did. If you put enough pressure on people they will say anything. They were beaten up. I remember their arrest photographs; they were totally black and blue. The trouble was that the details of their confessions did not fit all the forensic evidence that would emerge over the following months.'

'Didn't the defence raise all that in court?'

'Who was going to listen? And then during the defence case, the barrister who was leading me in the prosecution, Julian Waugh, QC, called me into a secret debriefing.'

'Who by?'

'I can't say.' Dan stared out of the window and right through the black winter tree-trunks in Central Park. That appalling day at the Old Bailey suddenly seemed a lifetime away. 'It was the Security Service – MI5.'

'You're kidding.'

'They had arrested another active service unit of the Sons of Kurdistan, another cell who claimed in their interrogations that they were responsible for the Iraqi bombing.'

'But that never came out?'

'We . . . buried it.'

For a moment, both of them were silent. Dan sipped his drink even though he felt sick in the pit of his stomach at what had happened.

'Julian Waugh said that it was standard procedure for terrorist organisations. If they all admitted responsibility, then no one could be sure who was really guilty, and no one would be convicted. It's a ploy, we were advised, that the IRA had used several times.'

'How did you bury it?'

'I didn't. I refused to be part of it. I withdrew from the case and resigned from the Treasury Counsel list.'

'They were convicted?'

'On a majority. I actually sneaked into the public gallery in jeans and a jumper and saw the verdict. When they were convicted – remember, they were just young boys – they refused to be taken down, they clung on to the dock. Christ, the guards had to smash their fingers to get them to let go.'

'But it wasn't your fault? You had done the right thing?'

'Had I? I was bound by the Official Secrets Act. I couldn't say anything.'

'And what happened to the Kurds?'

'The second cell was deported. Secretly to Iraq. In exchange for two British businessmen who had been arrested for spying at an arms show in Baghdad just before Desert Storm.'

'And the first lot?'

'Still languishing in prison in Britain. Probably innocent and still in prison. I know and I can say nothing. The government knows and it will do nothing. Great British justice.'

'And you haven't appeared in court since?'

Dan shook his head.

'I'm sorry,' she said.

She smiled at him as another round of drinks arrived. He stopped the waiter from diluting his vodka, and drank down half the measure. She lightly put her hand on his. He smiled back at her, but he hadn't told her the second part of the story, the part that had resulted in his wife's death.

'We'd better go,' she said.

'Is it on Broadway?'

'Off.'

Chapter 13

The play was in a little alternative theatre off Broadway. Outside the building were scattered groups of young white males, some carrying placards, all shouting a refrain Dan did not hear properly.

'What's all the fuss?' he asked.

'Haven't you seen what's on the signs?' Lisa replied.

There was a cordon of policemen standing around, bored, hands resting on their nightsticks. They ignored the protesters milling behind them and chatted among themselves. Dan momentarily left Lisa in the foyer and moved closer to the police line. There he could read the placards.

Lies ... Jewish Propaganda ... It did NOT happen

When he reached Lisa, her forehead was lined with concern. She led him to the queue at the ticket booth. 'The play's director has been in the news. He claims white supremacists are planning another Holocaust. Last month in Texas? The Klan tried to feed crystals of hydrogen cyanide into the air-conditioning system of the synagogue.'

'Hydrogen—'

'*Giftgas*. Zyklon B. What the Nazis used at Auschwitz. The Holocaust may be over, Dan, but hatred of the Jews isn't. Don't suppose it ever will be.' She looked into his eyes, her hair falling over one shoulder as she looked up at him. 'Are you all right?'

'Yes.'

But he was not. It wasn't just the demonstration he had witnessed, it was the more fundamental question as to why it had hurt.

*   *   *

Inside the theatre, there were no programmes available, nor any
drinks or ice-creams. It seemed as if everyone had arrived at the
same time, and the queue took for ever. The audience consisted
of a strange mixture of young and very old, with the middle
generations conspicuous by their absence. After the usher had
torn the corner off their tickets, Dan and Lisa were finally taken
along with the crush into the warehouse-like auditorium. It was
then that Dan looked at the yellow ticket and saw the name of
the play.

'What does it actually mean?' he asked.

'*Shoah?* It means a great or terrible wind. A holocaust.'

'Yiddish?'

'Hebrew.'

And Dan figured that if part of him was rightly to be called
Jewish, it was a part that could not speak its own language, a
part that would have to remain silent. He noticed that Lisa's ticket
was red. 'Why the different colours?'

'You'll see. But they don't do it every night.'

'Do what?'

A large youth with dyed peroxide hair in a tight black uniform
put his hand on Dan's shoulder. '*Ticket?*' he shouted.

'I don't have the ticket, she's—'

'Everyone *must* have a ticket or they will be sent out of the
theatre.'

Lisa hurriedly gave Dan the yellow one.

The youth smirked. 'You,' he shouted to Dan. 'Over there.' He
turned more politely to Lisa. 'Madam, tonight red tickets will be
in the luxury of the circle.'

Dan looked at Lisa. 'What on earth is going on?'

'Part of the play. See you at the end. It's only one act.'

As Lisa departed upstairs, all the people with yellow tickets
were sent to the pit at the front of the theatre. There were no
seats and the floor was covered in sawdust. One or two people
had cleared a small patch of the floor and sat down. But as more
and more yellow tickets were crowded into the confined space at
the front, everyone had to stand, shoulder to shoulder. Pinned to
the walls of the lower house were maps, the same type of railway
maps as he had seen in the museum.

Dan needed to go to the lavatory and he tried to work his way through the increasingly angry crowd. Tempers had begun to fray, and people were beginning to argue with each other. But when he reached the exit, the way was blocked by another large uniformed youth with fair hair.

'I need to go to the bathroom,' Dan said.

'No one leaves.'

'Look, I really—'

'No one *leaves*. There is a bucket at the back of the room.'

Dan could hear gales of laughter from the circle above, people with prime seats looking down, pointing, enjoying the discomfort of the yellow ticket-holders.

Finally, the play began. It traced the story of a family separated by the *Shoah*, how their paths crossed over the years, with the principal character, the daughter, eventually finding her Jewish mother after thirty years.

In the pit, the heat was unbearable, scorching air being pumped into the confined space, while above, in the circle, Dan could hear the gentle whirr of fans.

At a lull in the action, the exit door was opened, and two metal buckets with a ladle were given to the standing crowd. When Dan looked into the water, there was something dead, a snail perhaps, floating in it. At that stage, a woman in the crowd collapsed. Dan was not sure if it was a hoax or a genuine reaction to the heat, but the play continued obliviously as she was taken away. The actors themselves moved in a shifting halo of light on the stage, and the lighting was such that for extended periods they appeared as little more than shadows, marionettes against a wall.

At the end, when the curtain came down, there was silence in the theatre and total darkness. Then Dan heard people, just one or two in the dozens around him, crying softly. He left the theatre and met Lisa under the awning on the pavement outside. It was now pouring with rain and the protesters had left.

'I hope you understand. But it's important to me. It's part of who I am.' She took his hand gently in hers. 'I wanted to share it with you.' She smiled her faintly uneven smile. 'I see the rain has washed the trash off the streets. I shouldn't say trash. I'm a liberal. God, what a cliché. New York, Jewish, left-wing liberal, fighting for their right to racially abuse me.'

'Do you want to go and get a drink?' he asked.

'I already had one.'

'What?'

'All of us upstairs got a free glass of champagne.' She laughed nervously.

'Can you bear another?'

'Funny you should ask that, Counsellor,' she said, taking his arm. 'There's this little place I know where—'

Dan stopped and looked at her seriously. 'Lisa, one thing.'

'What?'

He stared at her.

'What, Dan?'

'Next time.'

'Yes.'

'You get the yellow ticket.'

They both laughed and walked under her umbrella along Broadway. The neon lights were mirrored brilliantly in the puddles, the city pulsed into the night, even in the rain, even in winter. They walked quickly, without talking, close to one another. Other people flashed past Dan's eyes but they were unreal, because now he saw them with the faces from the Holocaust Museum, all different, but all with the same pallor, emaciation and intensity.

Smoking Billy's bar was not particularly smoke-filled and the proprietor was not called Billy but Miguel Fernandez. Located off East 42nd Street, it was, Lisa assured Dan, the smart place for a post-theatre drink. The lighting was subdued, the service fashionably discreet, and somewhere on the other side of the cavernous room, filled as it seemed to be with a hazy bluish light, a piano played the great tunes of Cole Porter and Gershwin. Only in New York, Dan thought, could this be.

It was, however, Lisa who took the lead, speaking about her family as if they were obliquely linked to the one in the play.

'You see,' she said, having ordered two vodka tonics, 'you don't need to be Columbo to realise my accent's not pure New York.'

'I was trying to place it,' Dan said.

'Do your worst, Counsellor,' she dared him, smiling.

Dan pursed his lips and nodded his head, surveying her closely, as if he were intent on diagnosing a rare ailment. 'New Jersey,' he exclaimed.

She picked up a small paper table-mat and threw it at him.

'I give up,' he said, holding his hands in front of his face in a gesture of surrender.

'My father was a diplomat – God, I hated it. Did the European circuit.'

'London?'

'Never,' she said.

'Shame.'

She paused, thinking. 'I don't know. You see, I grew – I mean really grew – to hate every place we were posted to. Europe was like this huge boarding school for me. Officially, I went to a god-awful international school in Switzerland, but it was full of the diplomatic brat pack. And then Dad went to Austria ...'

Her words trailed off and Dan got the impression that she was addressing a wider audience, though she spoke more softly. It was as if the more quietly she spoke the more Dan concentrated upon her, and this process caused a veil to be drawn around the rest of the bar.

'I just couldn't believe it,' she said. 'This guy who is respected and admired in his country only turns out to be a signed-up member of the SS.'

'Kurt Waldheim?' Dan asked.

Lisa continued without answering. 'And what really made me sick was that all these people in Austria were saying: So what?' She laughed, still struck after all the years by the incredulity of the situation. 'So what? Hey, that changed things. Right there. You know how kids pester their parents about going to Disneyland or wherever?'

'Eurodisney's the last place Chris would want to go.'

'Yeah, well, she's your daughter, so ... anyway, every holiday I insisted we visited every single place I could find. I've seen ... visited ... experienced all of them.'

Dan did not want to interrupt when he realised Lisa was building up to something.

'I even looked up the lesser concentration camps in books,' she said. 'Sometimes Dad would go nuts because there would be nothing left. A field. An empty site. And I never quite knew what was worse.'

'How do you mean?'

'When I went to Auschwitz, there were these Polish soldiers hanging around. The whole thing was like this museum with films about the Great Patriotic War and how brilliant the Russian Army was. I just couldn't believe it. I had just been to see the huts, the wall where people were shot, plans of the gas chambers ... and these two soldiers came up and asked me to sell my denim jacket. For Christ's sake. Dad said you've got to understand that things were tough, Poland was still under martial law, but what the fuck excuse is that?' she shouted.

It was the first time Dan had heard her swear in the months he had known her. A thick film of sweat had broken out on her upper lip with the vehemence of her words, and he allowed her a moment to compose herself. She rested her head in her right hand, her arm propped on the table. With her fingers, she discreetly brushed away the beads of sweat almost as if she didn't want him to see her do it.

She smiled fleetingly and shook her head. 'Dad and I had the mother of arguments about that. I don't really know why. It wasn't his fault. I mean, only his father was Jewish and ... well, my mother, she was Jewish all the way down the line, but she never came with us. Not once. Just lay in a health farm in the Alps with two slices of cucumber over her eyes. How do you figure that?'

'It's odd,' Dan replied. 'Our parents are where we come from, yet they're the people we want to know about least. I mean, do we ever really stop to think about ... I don't know, who were their first loves? What they still want from their lives. That sort of thing.'

The waiter brought the drinks and the conversation was killed until he left.

'I can't believe you never even *met* your father,' she whispered.

'He left England before I was born. Never came back. I was brought up by my mother.'

'You must have a very strong bond with her.'

'She passed on a few years ago.'

'I'm sorry.'

'It was cancer, but mercifully quick. It was as if she called it a day before the pain really set in.'

'Did she never talk about him?'

'Never. Unless I asked. She always said that she would never lie to me about it, but she could never tell me the whole truth either.'

Lisa sat back, and ran her fingers through her hair, bringing out the gentle waves. The melody of a refrain from *An American in Paris* filled the bar.

'Originally,' Dan said, 'he was from Russia. He came over to England after the war as a refugee with the Red Cross. Stayed until 1955.'

'Why did he leave?'

'Mum never said properly.'

'It sounds intriguing.'

'Not from my end.' Dan looked around the room, two dozen tables with couples holding hands, smiling at each other in the moody half-light, enjoying themselves. 'I've denied it all my life, the Jewish thing, lived the lie, and then it just becomes worse and worse until it actually makes you sick thinking about it. But I just want to look him in the eye and say: You ruined my mother's life. It's all your fault. My life's been a mess and it's all your fault.' Dan paused; the intensity of the emotions had creased his forehead and hunched his shoulders. 'Well, that's the theory,' he smiled.

He suddenly felt incredibly tired. He tried to fight back a yawn but failed.

'I guess I have this devastating effect on most men,' Lisa said.

'I'm sorry.'

'I'll take a cab with you uptown and then take it home.'

They hailed a taxi immediately outside the bar and didn't speak again until they neared the park and hotel.

'How come he came to England?' Lisa asked.

'He was a refugee.'

'I mean, if he was Russian.'

'At the end of the war, he was in a concentration camp in West Germany. It was in the British zone of occupation.'

Dan asked the taxi to pull up a block before the entrance to the hotel.

'What's the matter?' Lisa asked.

'Just need some fresh air.'

'Don't go near the park.'

'I'm just going to get a coffee.'

He instinctively reached over and kissed her on the lips, embarrassed when he realised what he had done.

Chapter 14

Sophie could see the first hint of dawn from Helen's hospital window. Far to the east of London, the opaque darkness of the city was melting from the rim upwards, signalling the end of another night of intermittently snatched sleep at her sister's side.

She picked up the telephone the BUPA scheme had finally provided for Helen's private room and, taking the extension lead into the draughty corridor, dialled for an outside line. As she waited for the international number to click through, she gazed out over the hospital courtyards. The yellow squares from various windows suddenly flashed on or off, while far below, nurses in heavy coats returned for the early shift.

The phone was answered at the other end and the receptionist recited the name of Dan's Manhattan hotel.

'This is Dmitri speaking. How may I help you?'

'I would like Daniel Becket's room, please.'

'Putting you through.'

The phone rang a few times at the other end. The line clicked and the receptionist spoke again. 'I'm afraid Mr Becket is not answering.'

'He must be asleep,' she volunteered hopefully.

'Haven't seen him come in yet. And his key is still here. Would you like to leave a message?'

'No. No message, thank you.'

It must have been past midnight in New York, she calculated. She found it hard to believe Dan was still out on the town.

At 10.30 Sophie collected her wig and gown from her room in chambers and, having already put on her winged collar and

bands, rushed over the zebra crossing that divided the Temple
from the Royal Courts of Justice.

She made her way through the metal detectors just inside the
Gothic archway of the court building. As she headed for the
courtroom where her application would be heard, she wondered:
what if Dan had a *date*? She half smiled to herself. Too bad. It
wasn't her business.

That morning, she was due to appear for the first time
in the High Court. She had made an emergency application
for leave to review the decision to remove her Kurdish client
Abbas Bicak from the UK. It was not something she had
ever done before, but the image of her client's scarred and
cancerous body had not deserted her. She was determined to
make a difference.

In the great central hallway of the Royal Court, where the
staff played badminton at night when justice was off duty, she
passed the daily cause list, the names of all the cases to be
heard in the fifty-plus courtrooms. It was a long hall with a
hard mosaic floor and a high, airy ceiling surrounded by walls
of dull grey stone. Concealed steep stairways fanned to the left
and right, leading up to the courtrooms.

For a junior criminal barrister, this was foreign country. They
certainly did things differently here, she thought. A couple
of barristers passed by, going into court with computers.
Computers in court. To a criminal hack, a computer was this
mysterious thing her pro burglar would nick and flog cheaply
at Shepherd's Bush market. It had no place in court except as
Exhibit A for the prosecution.

As she climbed the steep stone stairs and rushed along
the corridor, she heard solicitors instructing their counsel
about collateral proceedings in Hong Kong, there was talk
of sequestration and interim injunctions, and not so much as
a mention of bloodstains or gunshot residue. Keep calm, she
kept telling herself. It's just another court. How alien could it
be? It was only when she reached the door of the court itself
that she panicked.

Her client. Where would he be? She wasn't even sure that he
would be produced from custody. And if he was, where were
the cells in the building? She had seen no signs.

A cold sweat broke out on her forehead. She felt the

dampness down the back of her shirt as if someone had
turned on a cold-water tap somewhere behind her neck. To
make matters worse, her solicitor should have been here by
now, but the reluctant Douglas Wallace had not shown up.
She was alone.

'Are you in the immigration matter?' It was the usher. A
small woman obviously wearing a wig of wiry red hair that
was absolutely immobile as she walked towards Sophie in the
dark first-floor corridor. 'Case of Bicak?'

'I'm in the deportation matter,' she replied.

'You're late.'

'But it was listed for—'

'Don't apologise to me. It's His Lordship you should be
worried about.'

Another pang of doubt and anxiety shot through her. She
had to try to take control. 'What's he like? The judge.'

'In a bad mood.'

'No, I mean normally.'

'In a bad mood.' The usher came right up to Sophie's ear and
whispered. 'Can't abide latecomers.'

Sophie did not know whether to laugh or cry. She had
spent ages researching the case and had prepared almost one
hour of submissions. But it would all be useless without an
open-minded judge.

The usher took down Sophie's name and filled in the
attendance slips for the court record. 'Right, into the lion's
den with you.'

'Wish me luck.'

'You won't need luck. A suit of armour, perhaps.'

She held the door open and Sophie pulled on her wig and
gown as she went in.

The court was full of dark wood, with vaulted ceilings and
huge bookcases of dusty law books to the side. There were
several narrow rows for the lawyers – QCs in front, then
junior counsel like Sophie, then the solicitors; not that Douglas
Wallace would dirty his hands with this guinea brief. The
bench to the front was raised well above counsel's row, and
there were three high-backed leather chairs – but only one
judge. Mr Justice Stephen Staines.

He was dealing with the end of another emergency application which he had taken from the next court to fill in the time while he awaited Sophie. It finally ended, and the barrister who had been refused the court's leave left sweaty and shell-shocked. But before Sophie had even stood up in the second row, the judge shouted at her.

'Where have you been?'

'I'm sorry, Your Honour, but I was told the court sat at—'

'Do not you know the correct form of address in this court?'

This was the High Court, not the Crown Court. 'I do apologise to Your *Lordship.*'

'You are seeking leave of this Honourable Court to judicially review the decision by the Secretary of State, acting in his lawful capacity on behalf of Her Majesty's Home Office, to remove your client from the jurisdiction? A man who was allowed into this country solely because of the largesse of this nation, and who, I understand, has now committed a criminal offence? And you *allege* that the Secretary of State is acting . . . unlawfully?'

It sounded dreadful. For a moment Sophie felt that she should be immediately sent by black cab – no, minicab – to the Traitor's Gate by Tower Bridge.

'Is that your position, Miss . . .'

'*Ms* Chase.'

'I'm afraid the appellation Ms is not one recognised by this court, *Miss* Chase.'

Sophie had had enough. She did the only thing her instincts told her to do. She fought back. 'Can I ask why not? I've just seen barristers take computers into court.'

'So?'

'Microchips are fine, but the term Ms is not? How does it expedite the course of justice to know whether a woman barrister is married or not?'

In the public gallery behind her, she heard a laugh from a court groupie, someone who would sit the whole day, the whole month, in one court after another.

The judge put his robed elbows on the bench and glowered at her. 'You are seeking leave . . . from *me* . . . to have a full hearing so that you can contest the decision to remove? Your client has had his application for political asylum refused, has he not?'

Sophie paused and realised the mistake she had made. There was no jury here. Scrapping with a judge in the criminal courts was an occupational hazard. Judges did not finally decide the outcome of trials, twelve ordinary members of the public did that. But here there was no jury. She had just alienated the one person who could help prevent her Kurdish client from being sent back to Iraq.

She had to swallow her pride – at least for now – and show more respect. 'My Lord,' she began. 'This is an extremely serious case.'

'Miss Chase, if I had a pound for every time counsel in front of me had said precisely that over the years, I would not be sitting on the High Court Bench in the Strand, but on a beach in the Bahamas.'

Sophie forced herself to titter at this attempt at wit. Humour him a little, Soph, she told herself. Get him on your side. She hated herself sometimes. And if I had a pound for every time I had to humour a misogynistic old git at the Bar, she thought, I would not be in front of you, *My Lord*, but on a beach somewhere even more exotic than the Bahamas. But she couldn't for the moment think of anywhere more exotic, and the only other place she'd like to be was New York.

'Is the Treasury represented?' the judge asked.

'It appears not,' Sophie said, failing to find any opponent.

'Very well. It's *ex parte* on notice. If they can't be bothered to turn up,' the judge said, 'that just leaves you and me.'

She opened her blue counsel's notebook and began to recite the first of the many scribbled and cross-referenced pages she had so carefully compiled.

The judge swung back in his chair. His eyes were raised to the Gothic vaults in the ceiling and, dressed as he was in his robes of office, his appearance was suddenly disconcertingly medieval. 'Miss Chase, what is your best point?'

'Well, I shall come to that in due—'

'Come to it now, why don't you?'

She should have prepared herself properly for this. High Court judges were notorious for running the best-laid submissions ragged by their interventions.

'What is your submission *really* about?'

Sophie took a sip of warm water from the cracked glass in front of her. 'Life or death.'

'Pardon?'

She thought of Dan, of his direct style, how he had always encouraged her to tell it how it was. But he had the experience, the gravitas, the balls – physical and metaphorical – to get away with it. It was easier for men at the Bar, which meant, she knew only too well, that it was harder for women. Harder, but not impossible. It was a question of how hard she was prepared to fight.

'I'm not going to beat around the bush, M'Lord, because I know that this court is running on a tight schedule. But so is my client.'

The judge was again looking at her, as if waiting to pounce on a mistake.

'Let me confess,' she said. 'This is the first time that I have appeared in an immigration matter such as this.'

'You are one of our criminal cousins?'

'Yes, M'Lord. And to tell the truth, we pride ourselves that we deal with the most serious cases. But even a life sentence rarely means life these days.' She paused again, the judge leaning a little further forward. Draw him in, Soph. Draw him in. 'For my client, a deportation order will mean one thing: a death sentence. From which there will be no appeal.'

'Do you have any evidence of this?'

She handed up the photographs of her client's deformities which the Kurdish family had delivered first thing that morning to her chambers.

'It's more usual to argue the merits on a full hearing,' the judge said. 'If this is a simple appeal against a refusal of political asylum, then I don't need to see—'

'My client is a Kurd. The Iraqi regime has a simple policy for its Kurds. Genocide.'

She could see the judge pale visibly as he flicked through the prints and she was determined to hit him hard with her client's suffering. Now was the time to press home her advantage. 'Some time before Desert Storm, my client's village was bombed by Iraqi planes. I have here United Nations reports that confirm that nerve agents were used.'

'Nerve agents?' the judge asked.

'Chemical and biological warfare. Poison gases. The UN concluded that the massacre was so merciless because a lethal combination of gases was employed. What is called a chemical cocktail. It was thought to contain, amongst others, the gas Tarin A. Such gases are silent and colourless and deadly. About twenty times more lethal than the cyanide the Nazis used on the Jews in the Holocaust.'

'Your client survived?'

'You'll see at the flagged passage in his affidavit. He arrived in the village after the attack, but his entire body is poisoned. He is decaying from inside. It's somewhat ironic. The gases will kill you immediately and leave virtually no trace – unless you know what you are looking for. But if you live, they will consume your body slowly. He is in excruciating pain. Death is certain either way: it's just a question of how long the victim suffers before the end.'

'But hasn't your client committed a criminal offence?'

'An *alleged* offence. And the supposed victims are Iraqis. The allegation is not so serious that it would exclude him from the benefit of the Geneva Convention on Refugees.'

'I see.'

'My Lord, all I am respectfully seeking is leave to have a full hearing to contest this deportation. If Your Lordship agrees to grant that, you are not overruling the Secretary of State. We will merely have the opportunity to review the decision to refuse asylum.' Sophie paused. 'But . . .'

'But what?'

'But if you refuse leave, my client is going back to Iraq. It's as simple as that.'

She sat down and could see the judge glancing again through the photographs. He wrote something down in his bound notebook before giving his judgment. Mr Justice Staines turned the snaps face down as he spoke, so that he no longer had to endure the close-ups of her client. Then he began. 'This court cannot today rule on the rights and wrongs of the Iraqi regime.'

Why *not*? Sophie thought, her heart sinking. That was her best point.

'But the court does take on board the assistance that counsel has given as to the United Nations analysis of chemical weapons and the potential jeopardy the applicant, one Abbas Bicak, may be subject to should he be removed. This may very well be a life-or-death decision. It must be argued on a full hearing. I grant you leave, *Ms* Chase.'

He smiled at her and then left the bench.

Sophie grabbed her papers and dashed out of court, along the dark corridors echoing with her gait, down the stairs, and out into the natural light of the Strand. She could not remember being so satisfied with any of the criminal verdicts that she had won. Fifty pages of notes and legal research, and she had only used a couple of sentences. She had got to the point. She had told it how it was. Dan would be proud of her.

She crossed the road, thrilled with the result, but as she was about to enter the Temple, her way was blocked by Robert Lancing.

'Thought you were doing the secret bidding of the state down in the mags,' she said.

'Bit later, Soph. After lunch, actually. I've just been to your chambers,' he added. 'They told me you were in the High Court. You've not gone all intellectual on me, have you?'

'You know how it is. Just trying to do justice, Robert.'

'Well, we're trying to do the same to Simon Montford.'

'*Look*, Rob, now we're on neutral territory and all that, why all the secrecy?'

'Ever heard of the Official Secrets Act, Soph?'

'Yes, it's a pile of crap.'

He involuntarily burst out laughing. Then he looked around rapidly and moved closer. 'Look, because it's you, I'll give you a clue. I've already sentenced myself to a stretch in the Tower by talking to you.'

'But if Montford was a decorated officer in the British Army, what have war crimes to do with—'

'I've said *enough*, Soph.'

She paused and then asked, 'Are you ready to go ahead tomorrow at the committal?'

'Oh yes,' he smirked.

'Now you've got me worried. Whenever you smile that means bad news, and when you smirk, that's even worse.'

'We have new evidence against Montford.'

Sophie's excitement vanished. She looked at her brief in the Kurdish case, and then back at Lancing. 'So who is it, then? This great witness.'

'Can't say.'

'Won't say.'

'No, Soph. I simply can't say. Except ... he's an informer.'

Chapter 15

Lisa had arranged to meet Dan for an early lunch at the Russian Tea Room. However, it being only a short walk from the hotel to West 57th Street, Dan arrived a few minutes early. He decided to wait outside until Lisa arrived. Finally, he saw her.

'I'm taking you out tonight,' she said, taking his hand momentarily as she reached him.

'Where?'

'Secret. But I reckon you'll like it.' Her eyes shone mischievously. 'How are you doing with your father?'

'I've tried to phone the deli from the hotel but there was no reply.'

'Then we'll try again.'

When they stood in the crisp air out on the street, Lisa gave him her mobile phone. He took out Ira's napkin and retried the number. The traffic lights that were suspended above the road junction near them changed to green and a stream of traffic roared past. Two cars hooted each other as they raced for the next lights.

'No one there?' she asked.

He shook his head.

She shrugged. 'I'm not particularly hungry. How about a walk in the park? It's lovely by the lake this time of the year.'

Dan was about to agree when suddenly there was a click at the other end. He was caught cold and wasn't sure what to say. He'd rehearsed dozens of ways to introduce himself, to broach difficult subjects, to just talk, but now he was speechless.

'Hello?' the heavily accented voice at the other end said. Then again, more irritably, '*Hello?*'

'Hello,' Dan finally said. 'May I speak to Jo, please?'

'Who wants him?'

'Is that you, Jo?'

'Who wants to know?'

'Dan.'

'Who?'

'Dan. Daniel Becket.'

There was a pause at the other end. Just long enough for a mental connection to be made, sufficient time to formulate a plan of action. 'Where'd you get this number?'

'Somewhere,' Dan said. There was another pause. For his part, Dan tried to visualise his father at the other end, but this caused him great difficulty as the images of the man that he had created in his youth had faded with the years. The father of his imagination was now a shadowy figure, no longer possessing the shock of dark hair and strong features Dan had fondly imagined as a boy.

'What do you want?' Jo asked abruptly.

'To talk.'

'So talk.'

'No, face to face.'

'So come to America.'

'I am in America.'

'The line, it's—'

'I'm on a mobile. West Fifty-seventh Street. Can I come and see you?'

'Can't stop you. Deli's open eight to eight. It's a free country.'

'Do you want me to see you?'

'You want to see me?'

Dan looked at Lisa and she gazed on expectantly. 'Yes, Jo. I want to see you.'

There was another hesitation. Some indecipherable mumblings down the phone until finally the old man spoke. 'I'm in Brighton Beach.'

When Dan's taxi crossed the Brooklyn Bridge, it left Manhattan and entered the borough of Brooklyn. As he gazed out of the window, he understood how Gulliver had felt when he arrived in Lilliput for the first time. For leaving Brooklyn Heights behind and driving south, the contrast with Manhattan could not have been greater. Suddenly there were no high-rise monstrosities. Here life was actually lived on the street.

Throughout the journey the cabbie chattered away in his unique brand of broken English. It was a concoction of ethnic Georgian and the colourful diction of Brooklyn. He was a man in his thirties, unshaven, with the hollow cheeks of a sportsman. In fact he boasted – while a two-inch roll-up hung from the corner of his mouth – that he once played football for Dinamo Tiblisi until the walls came down and he was bought by Aston Villa. Then he was injured and joined the rest of his family in Brighton Beach. He told Dan that the neighbourhood was now known as 'Little Odessa' owing to the waves of East European immigrants. Since the collapse of the Soviet Union, there had been an influx of Russians and other ethnic groups. He said that the Russian Mafia was strong in the area.

The cab ride went quickly and Dan was pleased with the conversation; he was grateful for the diversion from what he knew lay ahead.

The deli was simply called Jo's and was off Brighton Beach Avenue. Once he had paid the cabbie, Dan paused. Suddenly he was there, at his father's doorstep. He had learnt to control his nerves in court, and over the years he had trained himself to perform. But now he wanted to be himself. He didn't want a performance. Counting silently to three, he walked up to the grime-covered glass door. He knocked twice. There was a CLOSED sign hanging inside.

At first, there was no reply. He knocked again, harder, and felt the door move slightly. It was open. Taking a deep breath, he pushed it open and went in.

The room was basic – laminated tables screwed into the floor, a serving counter at the front with a broken glass display that was practically empty. The air smelt of stale food. Dan could hear the faint sound of hushed voices coming from a back room, but he could not find a way in. He left the shop quickly and went round the back, past the lock-up that was open and had contained no car, and it was there that he saw the back room full of dark-suited men.

This was it.

Panic. He did not even know what Jo looked like. His mother had once shown him a sepia photo of him from after the war, while his father was studying in London. He would have been about twenty-five, about the age that Lisa was now, and had the same shock of dark curly hair that Dan had had when he was in college.

He knocked on the back door and an elderly man looked out.

'Hi,' Dan said. 'Is Jo in?'

'The deli's shut,' Ira Gottlieb replied. 'Can't you read the sign?'

'Jo just popped out,' another voice called.

'Jo said his nephew was coming. Come in, take a load off,' said yet another.

So Jo was living a lie, too, not admitting that he had a son. It gave Dan no comfort, but it was not unexpected.

There were perhaps a dozen people in the room, in a mood of what Dan perceived to be false jocularity. He sat down.

'Have we met before?' he asked Ira, playing along.

'Not unless you was in Minsk in 1936 and your name is Sonya.'

The others laughed again, but it was short-lived.

Ira held out his hand. 'My name is Ira Gottlieb. Pleased to meet you, Jo's nephew.' He came close to Dan and whispered, 'Take it easy, kid. He won't bite you.'

Just then another voice interrupted, from the door behind Dan.

He turned around and looked at the speaker, who was holding a crate of vodka. He knew instantly that it was Jo.

'Will you guys excuse us,' Jo said, 'I need to speak to my nephew.'

Dan was led back out to the front of the building and in through the glass entrance of the deli. He followed Jo, who must once have been Dan's height, but was beginning to bend forward with the weight of years. He was still well muscled, but the skin was beginning to hang off what was once an athlete's frame. There were liver spots on his hands. Sprays of wispy, grey hair protruded from the bottom of his New York Yankees baseball cap, especially at the back. Again Dan thought of the many faces of his father he had conjured up through the years: sometimes he was the archetypal villain with a callous stare and a deep voice; other times, when Dan was lonely, the man had an almost saintly shroud, a gentle backlighting from which the young Dan drew comfort. But he had *never* imagined his father as an old man with a baseball cap.

Dan sat down as the door was shut behind him. He pushed himself away from the table edge on a wooden chair that screeched eerily on the hard floor. The back right chair leg got caught on a broken yellowing tile. Again there was the smell of over-ripe food.

'This belongs to you?' he asked Jo.

'Yes.'

'It's nice.'

'It stinks.'

Jo sat down opposite him, took off the cap and rubbed his eyes. Dan noticed the still-long eyelashes, darker than the greying hair on his head.

'Why are you in New York?' he asked Dan.

'Lecturing.'

'Why are you here?'

'In Brooklyn?'

'Here, in this deli.'

Dan paused to consider his reply. There were so many answers, and yet there were none. 'I'm just here, Jo. It's about time.'

'Your mother wrote me.' This was something Dan did not know, and he was stunned. 'Before she . . .'

'Passed away?'

'Died,' Jo said. 'She told me to make sure that I looked after you and that I kept away from you.'

Dan was confused. 'Well, which?'

'Both. They're the same thing.'

'I don't understand.'

'You're not meant to.' Jo looked up. Hanging from the ceiling were dirty fans, rusting into position like the propellers of a sunken wreck. 'She never told you *anything* about me?'

'Not much.' Dan was unsure if it was a trick question, but he was determined to be as open as he could. 'I see you haven't told anyone that I'm your son?'

''Course, you go around and tell everyone that you got a Jewish father who lives in New York?' When Dan did not reply, Jo continued, 'So why you here?'

'I just felt it was time to stop lying. To myself. About who I was.'

'And who are you?'

'Your son.'

'Does your daughter know about me?'

'No.'

Jo hummed to himself. 'Just as well. How about your wife?'

'I lost her.'

'When?'

'Last year.'

'That's tough. Deaths always come in threes.'

It was not the conversation that Dan had planned. He had wanted to shout wildly at his father, to blame him. He wanted cast-iron explanations, the truth, so that he could be secure in the hatred his head told him he should feel towards the old man. But it was not working out so easily. He closed his eyes for a moment and tried to decide where to go next. The wind blew off the nearby ocean, rattling the glass panes of the shop front. 'Can I see you again, Jo?'

'If you want.'

'But if I do want, if we do, there's something I've got to get out of the way first.'

Jo looked into his eyes.

'Why was it you and my mother fell out?'

'There were many reasons.'

'Name some.'

'There are too many.'

'Name one.'

Jo was silent.

'You could have, I don't know, you could have kept in touch. You could have written or something,' Dan insisted.

'I couldn't.'

Dan felt that he had him cornered and, despite himself, his advocate's instincts told him to pursue him and rub his face in it. 'Why not?'

'Because your mother *forbade* me.'

They looked away from each other and were silent for a minute. Dan glanced at the empty tables, the dirty mirrors on the walls with Russian writing painted on them, the menus in a language and script that he did not understand. The fading winter light seeped in through the shop front, lighting one side of his father's face, highlighting his striking profile.

It was Jo who spoke next. 'I did try to write you. Many times at first, after I arrived in the USA. But my letters were always sent back to me "Return to Sender". She never even opened them.' There was a plaintive tone in his voice as he was compelled to recollect the pain he must have felt forty years previously. 'Then on one of my letters, she had written in small capitals on the back of the envelope "LEAVE US ALONE". I never wrote her again.'

Dan was unsure how far he should delve into this secret history. Suddenly the cherished image of his mother had changed, not necessarily diminished, but changed, for good.

'But why did you leave England?'

'She never told you?'

'Never.'

'You don't know why we fell out?'

He paused, and Dan suddenly felt the need to touch this man. He knew it would help him, to feel the vital spark in the body that had given him life. Despite the ageing frame, this was the man his mother had once loved. Dan wanted to like him – he needed to do so.

But Jo continued, 'We disagreed.'

'All married couples disagree—'

'We disagreed about having you.' Jo stood up, and tried to straighten his shoulders. He played nervously with the cap in his left hand. 'In 1955, she got pregnant. She wanted to have the child. I wanted her to have an abortion. Now you know. See? The truth don't always help.'

Ira Gottlieb staggered in the front door, bleary-eyed, a half-finished bottle of vodka in his hand. 'Jo, you coming or what?

'Later,' he replied.

Jo led Dan up on to the boardwalk above the beach. Along the elevated walkway elderly men stood in groups of two or three, all of them with caps, some in long dark coats, others in waist-length leather jackets, cut like the jacket of a demob suit. They talked in whispers, looking out to sea, occasionally turning to greet Jo with a word or two of Russian, or following the progress of the odd jogger, especially if the runner happened to be female. It was a fine afternoon with the clouds breaking up in the west, allowing intermittent bursts of sunshine to be reflected brilliantly in the pools of rain scattered around the wooden planks. Dan estimated that the sun was setting over Staten Island and New Jersey, but all he really had was a two-dimensional image of these places from a map of New York.

'So . . .' he began, quickly running out of steam.

Jo turned around sharply. 'So what?'

'Just . . . so.'

'Uh huh.'

'Well,' Dan replied, but thought better of adding anything further.

After they had been walking a few more moments, he asked, 'So how long have you known Ira?'

Jo had to stop to regain his breath, inhaling and exhaling in shallow puffs, momentarily holding on to Dan's coat for balance. 'Ira?' he wheezed.

Dan nodded.

'For-goddamn-ever,' Jo replied, breaking into a fit of coughing.

But Dan did not want his father to be vulnerable. Throughout his adolescence, and if he was entirely truthful some time beyond that, his absentee father had been the prime focus of his anger. When he had been scolded at school as lacking discipline, the boy explained the failing to himself as being entirely due to the absence of a father. Occasionally, other boys would comment on the fact that Dan never appeared to have new shoes, that his uniform was shabby and didn't fit. He never reported these chides to his mother, but deep down thought: It's his fault. If I had a father, we would have enough money. He took weekend jobs as soon as he could, yet there never seemed to be enough. But the greatest portion of his hostility was created on perhaps two dozen evenings, no more than that. It was on these evenings that his mother would retire early. Although she would turn up the radio in her room, by the time he went to bed he could hear her. Sobbing gently. While some people blamed the existence of evil in the world for their misfortunes, and others blamed fate or the sinfulness of man, Dan blamed his father. But this palliative could never have worked had he seen what he now saw in Brighton Beach: not a monster, or a criminal, but a proud man, bent with the weight of years, holding his sleeve and coughing.

'We can go in if you like,' he said.

'You drink vodka?' the old man replied, wiping his mouth on the back of his coat sleeve.

'Not really.'

'We go back to the deli, we drink vodka.'

They continued walking. A breeze cut through the air, laced with the tang of sea salt, sharpening the dirty white tops to the waves.

'How long have you lived here?' Dan asked.

Jo did not reply directly. He turned his face away from the sea and surveyed the blocks of buildings inland. 'Neighbourhood's changing,' he said.

'For better or worse?'

'It ain't for the better.' He shook his head. 'A different breed of Russian's coming over now. Right here, in Ronald Reagan's back yard. He'd turn in his grave.'

'Reagan isn't dead.'

Jo looked up, apparently not registering that fact. 'You know, some of them can't even speak English. Live in Brooklyn years and still speak Russian.'

Dan heard the comment and then saw that it contained an opening, a small window through which he might reach the past. 'I've often wondered,' he said, knowing that it was a little clumsy, 'how you learnt English.'

The old man indicated with his head, a flick of the peak of the baseball cap, that they should return. Dan buried his hands deep into the pockets of his long coat and, as he walked, his shoulders now and then brushed those of his father.

'Jo, I said—'

'Your mother taught me.'

The revelation didn't startle Dan, but it did catch him unprepared. Over the years, his mother had given various explanations as to how the two of them had met, but never this one. What made Dan feel somewhat naïve was the glaring obviousness of the explanation: Jo was a Russian refugee in London, his mother was an English teacher. He did not understand why she had not told him this simple truth, but guessed that since she had wanted to keep his father a total mystery to him, there was a crude logic in blurring the facts of their first encounter. But now he faced a dilemma: on the one hand he wished to know more, but on the other he had already been stung by the few truths Jo had thrown back at him about the origins of his parents' dispute, about the letters.

'I was the worst student in the whole goddamn class.' Jo smiled. 'But she taught us all to speak with an Irish accent.' He stopped momentarily and tilted his head back as he spoke, a gesture Dan faintly recognised as belonging to his mother when she was angry with him. Jo continued, now in an overblown Irish accent. 'Josef, you are the very worst pupil, so you are.'

Dan laughed, for he could see his mother now, standing at the door to his bedroom in their small flat in the poorer part of Maida Vale and saying: Daniel Becket, you are the very worst son a mother could have, so you are.

'She wasn't really interested in English,' Dan said. 'It was languages she loved.'

'I taught her some Russian,' Jo added.

'God, I never knew.'

'Not much. "Where is the bridge, thank you," was all she could say.'

They both laughed, Jo with his mischievous, almost schoolboyish giggle, and Dan relaxing with relief.

'So how long did you live together?' Dan asked, smiling.

But suddenly the mirth had disappeared from Jo's face as quickly as it had arisen. He pulled his coat tightly around himself, putting up the collar so that it reached the back of his cap, though some wisps of hair still stuck out. Within a moment Dan, too, felt the harshness of the wind cutting off the sea and he cursed himself for having pushed things too far. But if, as was blatantly apparent, there were limits to what he could ask of his father, he could not be sure of them.

'Let's get in,' Jo said.

They walked in silence back to the rear of the deli, and whether by design or accident now no longer brushed against each other. Jo fumbled with a large bunch of keys in the cold before he found the correct one to open the door to his personal flat. A steep, carpetless flight of steps led up to a sitting room that exuded so much heat that by the time Dan could see inside it, he was already sweating profusely. He was immediately struck by a wild profusion of green. From the walls, from shelves and window ledges and tables sprouted plants of all descriptions. Some shot out tendrils which had climbed the walls apparently unaided, circling windows, climbing above and below the black-and-white photographs of Russia on the wall. Others were thick with leaves and spilled out of their pots and prodded chairs and tables nearby; still others, clearly some kind of cacti, sported a multitude of thorns, from long, nail-like spikes to furry balls of prickles; one of these cacti was even in bloom. It was all so unexpected to Dan. From the drab back streets of Brighton Beach on a January day, he was suddenly plunged into this subtropical haven.

'So I like plants,' Jo said, immediately fetching a green watering can from beneath the window and moving to the open-plan kitchen to fill it up.

Dan carefully placed his overcoat on the ramshackle sofa, one leg of which consisted of a sawn-off stump supported by yellowing papers.

'Don't tell me,' he said, 'you prefer plants to people.'

The old man turned off the tap sharply and looked over as if to say: What planet are you on? Dan immediately regretted the comment but decided to attempt an explanation.

'I only mean, you know, plants can't hurt you.' His father continued to stare at him, and although Dan felt he was slowly sinking into mud, he tried to claw his way out. 'You know, they're natural. Safe. Well, apart from Venus fly-traps, I suppose. They're—'

'I like growing things,' Jo said, finally putting Dan out of his misery.

'It's a nice apartment,' Dan ventured, hesitantly. 'I can say it's nice, can't I?'

'Saying it's nice don't make it nice.'

'And being grumpy doesn't make this any easier for me, Jo.'

It was more than he had intended to say, but the words had formed themselves and burst out of their own accord. Dan was pleased, as well as confused, when he saw his father grin.

'Your mother said I was grumpy. Could never stay up in the evenings. From the camps, I guess. Used to getting up at dawn.'

'And you couldn't get out of the habit?'

'Tried. Failed. After a while grew to like the mornings. Best time of the day.' He began watering the nearest plant, the cactus with the flower. 'You want something? To eat? Drink?'

'Tea would be nice.'

'Are you ever an Englishman?'

'OK, some vodka then.'

Jo half looked around with a wicked grin. 'Truth is, I could murder some tea.'

Dan ran his hand through his hair. 'Jesus Christ, Jo, is everything between us going to be a battle?'

But before he could reply, there was a sharp rap on the apartment door.

'Yeah,' Jo said, but he said it in such a way that Dan couldn't be sure whether this was an answer to the door or to Dan's earlier question.

'It's me,' the voice outside called.

'Who's me?' Jo snapped in mock anger.

'A litre of vodka.'

'Why didn't you say?' Jo said, moving across the length of the rectangular room to open the door.

Ira entered the flat only a few inches behind the bottle of vodka. 'We missed you,' he said to Jo. His bald head was already sweating from the heat of the room.

'What? You can't get smashed without me now?'

'Sure. But we needed someone to poke fun at.' Ira laughed loudly at his jibe, holding the bottle of spirits out towards Dan as if it were an invitation to join in the bantering.

'Ira,' Jo said seriously, 'don't give up the day job.'

'Huh,' he replied. 'It gave me up, all right.'

'I thought you was going to sue?'

'Suing's one thing. Being reinstated? That's another ball game.' Ira wiped his hand quickly across his mouth and moustache as if there were suddenly a bad taste in his mouth.

Dan, who was beginning to feel left out, sat forward and said, 'Actually, I went to that place. The Holocaust Museum.'

Although there was no instant reply from the two elderly men, the contrast in expression upon their faces spoke volumes. While Ira smiled widely because someone had taken an interest in his affairs, Jo's face creased up and set hard, his jaw jutting slightly forward in annoyance.

'Ira's crazy,' he finally said.

'Oh. I'm crazy, huh?' Ira replied. 'Well, you're crazy, you mad Muscovite.'

'Yeah, well, I don't go round chasing dead Nazis.'

Ira put, or rather dropped, the bottle on to the table nearest him. 'Well, you show me where every Nazi is buried. Or you know what? I'm going to be hunting them.'

Jo stared at him, but more gently now, and spoke as if this were a conversation the two of them had had a thousand times before. He enunciated his words carefully, in a reassuring manner, rather as a parent would soothe a child awoken by a recurring nightmare. 'Ira,' he said, 'Mengele is dead, and Boorman is dead, and . . .' He paused, then said more quietly still, 'Klaus Keller is dead.'

The final name resonated in Dan's head. Klaus Keller. He trawled through his memory. Where had he heard it before? Then it came to him: Ira had discussed Keller in the deli with Lisa. As these thoughts turned through his mind, Ira walked slowly to the sofa and sat next to him. Jo came closer too, first lowering the watering can on to the ground two feet in front of them, then squatting uneasily, using the top of the can as a balancing point. For his part, Ira's eyes had glazed over, almost as if he saw many things now, only some of which were actually in the room.

'Are they all dead, Jo?' he asked.

'They're all dead, Ira.'

Dan felt embarrassed and out of place, sensing that he was intruding in some private ceremony, a private grief.

'You know,' Ira said, slowly following with his eyes insubstantial images, unseen to the others, 'they say Mengele used to stand on the railway ramps at Auschwitz, all dressed up, when he made his selections. But Keller? He was never like that. You never saw him at Neuwelt – until it was too late. They said he was always in his lab. Experimenting. Gases. Chemicals. I once sneaked a look in the window. It was a beautiful sunny day. You remember sunny days in the camps, Jo?'

'I remember.'

'The sun poured through that window and the room: I thought it was a cellar full of diamonds and stars. Shining. Everywhere.'

'Must have been the lab equipment,' Jo said.

'Everything was polished and clean and sparkling. How could he have done . . . those things there?'

Jo moved forward and took Ira's hand; he gently held it to his face, as if Ira were suddenly blinded by the brilliance of the lights he saw in his mind. 'I don't know how it happened, Ira. It just happened.'

Ira burst into sobs, his body convulsing from his midriff, though no tears fell. Dan shot a glance at Jo and raised his eyebrows, asking if there was anything he could do. Jo shook his head and there was a hint of a smile, thanking Dan for the gesture.

'I . . . I'm afraid, Jo,' Ira said.

'They can't hurt us no more,' he replied.

'What if for fifty years I've been chasing shadows? Ghosts?' He sobbed again. 'I wasted my life.'

'Now, Ira Gottlieb,' Jo said, pretending to scold him, 'you didn't lie down. They had an army. But you were a soldier. On your own. Jesus, what the hell did I ever do?' Jo paused and laughed. 'I made coleslaw. So, hey, it ain't you who's wasted your life.'

Dan noticed that, as Jo spoke to him, Ira's eyelids became progressively heavier, now and then closing.

'I'm tired, Jo.'

'We're both tired, buddy.'

Jo then gestured to Dan to help him lift Ira by the other shoulder, and the two of them slowly took him towards a half-open door leading off the living room. Once past this, Dan saw Jo's bedroom. A simple room with a single bed. The curtains were already drawn, but in contrast to the living area, there were no plants in the room. They lowered Ira gently on to the bed, face down. Ira instinctively rolled to his side and reached out with his right hand to make himself comfortable. Jo sat on the side of the bed and ran his hand over Ira's brow, trying somehow to smooth out the wrinkles. And it was then that Dan saw it, on the bedside table, under a simple terracotta vase with three fresh white roses: a photo. He looked at Jo, surprised, but his father merely got to his feet and walked back to the lounge. Dan picked up the photo frame and examined the image: Jo and Dan's mother, in black and white, almost lost in the crowds around Piccadilly Circus. They both looked totally in love.

When he followed his father into the lounge, the old man gestured that he should not shut the bedroom door. Jo sat on the very edge of the sofa, from where he could keep watch over Ira.

'First time I asked her for a date,' he said, 'she refused. Said something about not . . . what was the word? Yeah . . . consorting, not consorting with her students.'

Dan sat on the sofa next to him.

'Second time I asked her,' he continued, 'she agreed, but only if one of her friends could come to the pictures too. Jesus. You should have seen the size of that one. They could have played the whole movie on her backside.'

'What was the film?' Dan asked.

'Oh, I forget. Some musical.'

'She liked musicals.'

'Hated this one,' Jo said. 'Complained all the way home. When we got rid of her friend, I walked her home to Maida Vale.' He rubbed his cheek, remembering. 'Tried to kiss her.' He paused and then groaned. 'Oh boy. Could she slap hard. Wow.'

'You know, she never hit me,' Dan said.

'No? Well, you was lucky. Oh boy, *baam*. Right on the kisser. I think my lip bled a little on the inside but I didn't tell her.' He stopped then, lowering his voice, said, 'Never told her. Second date, I didn't go near her. Now I *wanted* the incredible hulk along to protect me in case your beloved mother got it in her mind to remind this red-blooded Russian how to treat a Catholic girl.'

'Did you go to the cinema again?'

'The movies? No. A meal. Small Italian place. Her friend couldn't come. Washing her hair – hair under her armpits, I guess – so we was alone.' He grinned to himself. 'So help me, I didn't go near her. Barely looked at her during the meal. Paid the bill as quick as possible and walked her home. I stand on her doorstep as polite as I can and say goodbye. She looks at me and says I must learn to treat her like a lady. She says: Josef, you are a foolish man, so you are. She raised her hand and I was about to duck – Jesus, I could already feel the blow, *baam* – but she grabbed me by the back of the neck, pulled me forward and . . . if I'm lying, I hope I never see the blue skies of Ireland again, Jesus H. Christ . . . she kissed me.'

Dan couldn't help but be transported, too, by his father's infectious joy at these memories.

'Of course,' Jo said, 'by then it was too late.'

'Too late?'

'I was head over heels in love.'

He got up and went to the sink, picking up the watering can

along the way. He turned on the taps, harder than was necessary, and water splashed out from some dirty plates in the cracked porcelain basin.

'Come to England,' Dan whispered.

Without looking around, Jo shook his head.

'Please, Jo. I want you to spend some time with me and my daughter.'

Jo walked slowly over to the flowering cactus and was about to pour when he realised that it had already been watered. 'You know, these things, you can leave them for months and they don't need you. But get a flower? Then you got to watch them like a hawk.'

'Please, Jo. Come.'

'I wish,' Jo said, not looking at his son, 'I wish they didn't get no flowers.'

Chapter 16

Sophie calculated that it must be some time in the late afternoon or early evening in Manhattan. Dan was likely to be out, but she had been working late in her chambers in the Temple, researching the latest legal authorities on the use of informers. She was tired and lonely. It was approaching midnight. Her room looked out on an ancient cobbled courtyard, in which a single lantern shone eerily through the descending fog. The room itself was mock period with large oak desks, thick blue carpet and a disgusting oil painting of a judge. No one could remember who it was.

Flicking open her black mini-Filofax, she punched the telephone number with her fountain pen. The familiar international dialling tones gave way to the same heavily accented American-East European voice.

He gave the name of the hotel and then said, 'This is Dmitri, how may I help you?'

'I'd like to speak to Mr Becket, please.'

'Mr Becket? Let me see . . .'

'Or leave a message. He's probably out at this time—'

'Let me put you through.'

Sophie felt her breathing quicken. The phone clicked as the connection was made, and then she could hear further, more muted ringing. She was about to hang up when it was answered.

'Hello, Dan Becket speaking.'

'Dan, it's me.'

A pause. 'Sophie?'

'Sorry to disturb you, but—'

'No. It's great to hear your voice, Soph.'

'I tried to phone you last night.'

'I was out.'

'Of course you were out, or I would have spoken to you, Dan.'

'Good point. I was just out by myself, having a bite to eat.'

'So late?' she asked. 'So late, you must have been hungry.'

'You see,' he continued, 'Lisa – Lisa Hartman, you know the . . . she dropped me off and then I went to . . .'

So he was calling her Lisa now?

'When are you heading home?' she asked dejectedly.

'Tomorrow. Don't sound so miserable about it.'

How should she broach the subject? She had never asked a man for a date before, and certainly not down an international phone line. But it wasn't a date, she just wanted to see him.

'It would be great to see you, Soph,' he said first.

'*Really?*'

'Of course. And I know that Chrissy would love to see you and talk about all those girl things.'

He wants me as an elder sister for his daughter. That was it. Still, it's a start.

'Ring me the instant you get home,' she said.

'How is the case going?' he asked.

'Pardon?'

'Montford. You know, war crime. As in a politician accused?'

She had forgotten her excuse for calling. 'Oh, that case? Just doing a bit of research in chambers. They've got some new evidence. A grass.'

'Any idea who?'

'Not yet. Can't wait to tear his head off, though.'

She could hear him laughing down the phone. Had she made a joke? She hadn't meant to. Was he laughing at her?

'I'd better let you go, Soph. I'll speak to you soon.'

She put the receiver down, happy, confused, frustrated and jealous. She picked up the Montford brief, a bundle of papers eighteen inches thick, neatly tied with pink ribbon. Then she placed Volume 1 of Archbold, the Bible of criminal law, in her black leather briefcase. The content of her brief conversation with Dan played again and again in her head as she strolled through the deserted courtyards of the Temple, suddenly emerging from the cloistered calm into the fading bustle of a central London night.

Chapter 17

Having met Lisa in the lobby of his hotel a couple of hours after Sophie's phone call, Dan accompanied her down Fifth Avenue. By this time, a light snow had begun to fall. The dozens of lights that were intended to illuminate tall buildings managed only to light up little pockets of air many feet above, through which the spinning flakes fell silently.

As Lisa crossed 54th Street, he noticed again what an effort she had made. Her make-up was perfect, setting off those searching eyes, that delicate mouth. Her hair shimmered in gentle waves behind her, glistening with odd snowflakes before they melted and died.

'Hope you like dancing,' she said, linking arms with him, pulling him tighter.

'Dancing? You mean disco dancing?'

'Proper dancing, dummy. Proper music, proper tunes, man and woman together.'

'I love it,' he said.

Lisa tugged him to the right and they entered a narrow parade of expensive boutique-like shops set back from the street with neat gardens running through the middle.

'The Channel Gardens,' she told him.

'Why are they called that?'

'Who cares?'

At the end of the parade there was an ice rink that had been built below the surface of the street. A couple of skaters with their scarves flying out behind them like tails glided around the perimeter, in perfect harmony, their movements fluid, effortlessly beautiful. Behind Dan cars hooted, people bustled past and no one else, he thought, seemed to notice.

A chalky tower rose in front, the RCA Building, and Lisa led
Dan into the Rockefeller Center beneath. Once inside the echoing
art deco lobby, they took a lift that shot rapidly upwards, and
before Dan quite knew what was happening he was in a corridor
sixty-five floors above Manhattan. There were stunning views of
the city lights.

'Where are we?' he asked.

'The Rainbow Room.'

They were led into a salon with dimmed lights and a revolving
wooden dance-floor, a room in which a band in tuxedos played
softly, while waiters brought huge salvers of seafood to the
semicircle of discreet tables. Men sported bow ties, women wore
ball-gowns or cocktail dresses, and on all sides massive windows
revealed the rooftops of New York and the descending snow.

'My God, Lisa. Isn't this expensive?'

'Only if you eat.'

'So we aren't eating?'

'No, Dan, we're the floor show. Of course we're eating.
My treat. How does lobster thermidor and a chilled Puligny-
Montrachet grab you?'

She had reserved a table directly in front of a window, and
Dan could see the lights of Fifth Avenue and the Empire State
Building painted with a kaleidoscope of neon light.

'Shall I ask for the menus?' he said.

'No need. I've arranged everything.'

The wine waiter arrived with an ice bucket and opened the
Burgundy. He poured a little, a precise amount, into Lisa's glass.
There was something sensuous about the way she swirled the
pale green liquid around, a certain poise that Dan found hugely
enticing – the way she took a sip in her mouth, rolled it over
her tongue, swallowed imperceptibly, smiled and nodded her
approval.

When the waiter left them, Dan said, 'You're a bit of an
expert.'

'It's just a question of how you're brought up, I guess. We
never ate except in the best restaurants. All I really wanted was
a simple meal at home.'

Dan took a sip of the wine, noticing that his glass was already
slightly frosted on the outside.

'How was your meeting with your father?' she asked.

'Fraught.'

'But you've broken the ice.'

'Trick is not to fall in the hole. There are so many things I hadn't properly considered. You see, if I'm partly Jewish, what does that make my daughter?'

'It makes her your daughter. Nothing has changed. At least, nothing important. Don't start worrying until she discovers boys.'

Dan was aghast. 'Boys?'

'You got them in England too, I guess.' She paused when he did not reply. 'Has Chrissy got a boyfriend?'

'I don't know. How do you tell?'

'You'll get strange, inarticulate youths phoning for her and she'll wash her hair a lot.'

She poured another glass of wine for each of them as the music started up with a new song, one from Cole Porter. It was an unwritten law that boys and all things embarrassing were Viv's province; Dan had never even spoken to Chris about sex. Things would have to change: he would have to sit down with her when he got home. No, he would first have to buy some books, read them, and then sit down with her.

'Drink it down in one,' Lisa insisted.

'All of it?'

'All of it.'

The wine slid down smoothly and he felt a warm glow in his stomach.

'Dance?' she asked.

But before he could reply, she grabbed his hand and led him past tables at which couples were absorbed in their food. When they arrived on the dance-floor, an elderly, distinguished couple, the man in a white tuxedo, the woman in a flowing ruby gown, were moving elegantly over the revolving surface.

'I can't do it like that,' he whispered.

'Just follow me.'

'Shouldn't the man lead?'

'Not always.'

During the first dance he was self-conscious, during the second he relaxed a little more, but by the third, a cha-cha-cha, he was thirsty. They rushed back to their table and downed another glass of wine. Soon the food came, the lobster the size of a Cadillac. He ate voraciously, losing himself in the magical ambience, in Lisa's company, so much so that no sooner had they finished than he took her hand, actually wanting to dance. By now they were on to the second bottle of Burgundy and the slow rotation of the dance-floor seemed to compensate for the alcohol-induced spinning of his head.

By the time a really smoochy slow dance had been introduced, Dan was totally besotted.

They stood together, almost motionless, lost in a crowd of dancing couples, as the floor turned slowly. The huge windows came into view in turn, disclosing the best of the Manhattan skyline, then the Hudson River, then the tops of skyscrapers further downtown, while the snow continued to fall.

He could feel the gentle contours of Lisa's body against his, her fragrance not diminished by the blush of sweat from the dancing, but enhanced by it, in the way the bouquet of a fine wine comes out when it is allowed to breathe. He knew at that moment that he wanted her.

'Can I say something?' he whispered.

'You don't need to, Dan.'

'So how do we deal with this?'

She put her head on his shoulder. 'I don't want to hurt you, Dan.'

'What do you mean?'

'I'm trouble.'

'I find that hard to believe.'

'Do you think if you're told you're a bad person enough, you actually become a bad person?'

'Lisa, just kiss me.'

'I can't.'

'You don't want to?'

'There's nothing I want to do more.'

'Then do it.'

She stopped dancing. 'Dan, this is not a good time for me.'

'Why not?'

'I'm seeing someone else.'

'What?'

'Well, sort of seeing him. It's on and off, has been for the last four months or so.'

'What does that mean?'

'It means I shouldn't kiss you, Dan.'

But he didn't care. He took both sides of her face in his hands and put his lips to hers, just once, gently, then withdrew. But she came after him, and her tongue melted into his.

'Let's go home,' she said eventually.

When he nodded, Lisa smiled. Then she blinked slowly, and when she opened her eyes again Dan felt as though he were looking at her for the first time.

Chapter 18

Lisa's apartment was on the Upper East Side. Owing to his persistent questioning, she was compelled to admit, albeit with embarrassment, that it was reputedly the richest neighbourhood in the world. The buildings were elegant, the hotels grandiose; it was a world of designer shops and cultural institutions.

Her block was, however, a brownstone somewhat more run-down than the others around it, but there was a balcony outside her apartment, affording stunning views of Central Park.

Thirty minutes after they had arrived, he sat on a thick white rug in the lounge in front of the fire. The room was comfortingly warm and, sipping on a Courvoisier, Dan was half asleep. From behind his closed eyelids he heard the soft footfalls of her bare feet moving away and then back towards him.

'Great fire,' he said, as she sat next to him.

'It's fake.'

'I wouldn't have guessed.'

'It's like everything else here.'

'Here? New York?'

'New York. The apartment. Me.'

She moved in front of him, so that he saw her back. Then she shook her hair, letting it fall forward over her face so that he could see none of her delicate features save for the back of her smooth neck.

He picked up his glass and drank down the remains of his brandy in one gulp, waiting for the alcohol to bite in the back of his throat. She tossed her hair back from her face and he saw her flushed cheeks. Without any make-up, she looked infinitely more appealing than at any time he could remember.

'I kind of think a lot about your daughter,' she said.

'Chris?'

'Well, since you've been in New York. I keep thinking, yes, it was a tragedy that her mother was taken from her so cruelly, but at least she had someone who loved her all those years. And now, she still has someone who will look after her no matter what.'

'True.'

'I never had either of those things. I guess that's why I've always gone for older men. Jesus, it's so pathetically Freudian. I should be in some journal or something.'

He looked at her profile as she stared straight into the fire. When she turned he saw the tears beginning to roll down her cheeks. She sniffed and used the back of her hand to wipe them away. And then she took his face in her hands as he had done in the Rainbow Room and kissed him. He could taste the brandy on her lips and how warm her mouth was when her tongue met his. She took his hand and directed it on to her body. He could feel her firm breasts, the hard tips of her nipples, and the skin that was so smooth he barely dared touch it.

They rolled back on the floor, and soon he was on top of her, tearing away the clothes, their legs tangling, moving over each other until her thighs parted slightly and he was between them.

They made love again, this time in Lisa's bedroom.

It was the sort of room, full of junk that his daughter would have been too embarrassed to have owned. Lisa had created for herself a comforting private world, one that attempted to compensate for an arrested childhood that had been starved of affection. After they rolled apart, the only thing in Dan's mind was sleep, but Lisa shot out of bed full of energy, in the way only women can after sex. She capered around the room naked.

'You realise, don't you, that I'm bound to fall hopelessly for you,' she said.

'Can't we just take it one step at a time, Lisa?'

'It depends on who takes the step – and who gets trodden upon.'

'I don't want to hurt you.'

'So don't. But, you know, in the colonies it is common courtesy, if nothing else, when someone tells you they're nuts about you, for you to reply—'

'I'm sorry, but it's all happened so quickly. You see, I haven't been with a woman since . . .'

'Your wife?'

'A part of me says I'm being disloyal to her. And she died so suddenly that we never discussed any of this.'

Lisa came to the foot of the bed and slipped her feet under the covers. 'You still love her, don't you?'

'Yes.'

'So you can never be with anyone else as long as you live?'

'That's not what I said.'

'Well, imagine that you had died. What would you have wanted for her? Would you have wanted her to be alone?'

'No, that would be selfish—'

'Was she far more selfish than you?'

'Certainly not.'

'Well, then. What makes you think that she would not have wanted you to find somebody? Not anybody. Not any time. But somebody who could love you, who could love Chrissy, who could understand your love for Vivienne, who could even love you all the more because of it.'

Dan was silent.

'Well, Dan. Why can't that somebody – one day, whenever it comes – be me?'

'But you said you were involved with someone else.'

'I said I was sort of involved. It's more off than on. I want to end it. He can't accept it. But I'll deal with it. I'll sort it out. For you. Do you want me to do that?'

'You must do what you want.'

'*Objection*. Witness non-responsive.'

She climbed back gingerly under the sheets. He could feel the warmth of his body running into hers as she wrapped herself around him, holding him close with her thighs and arms, skin on skin.

'You'd better know about me and Viv,' he said. 'I mean, if this is going to continue—'

'Don't. Not if it's too painful.'

'You see, the truth is . . .' He hesitated and took a deep breath before continuing. 'I was so incensed by the corruption in the Kurd case that I resigned there and then. I didn't even try to speak to Viv about it. And thinking back now, I could have

phoned her from the Old Bailey or something. It wouldn't have
been difficult. But as usual, I thought this is a question of
right and wrong. I can see clearly what to do and I'm going
to do it.'

'What did she say?'

'I don't know – I think I expected her to admire my fortitude
or something, at least to respect my decision.'

'But you never consulted her?'

'Viv had worked her guts out to put me through Bar school,
to keep us afloat during the early days of my legal practice when
I had more debts than clients. She came from an affluent family.
Could have been a very good pianist. But she volunteered to do
a whole load of menial jobs, sometimes two or three at once, so
that I could survive as a barrister.'

'Didn't her family help?'

'They objected to me as a husband for their precious daughter.
Working-class, Catholic, half Irish. They didn't even know about
the Jewish side. Viv refused to go to them for anything. And in
truth she never wanted anything for herself. She just thought
about Chris. A decent school, a house in a nice area of London.
Was that too much to ask? And then there I was, after all the
years of struggle, throwing away a quarter-million-per-year meal
ticket. So we rowed. I said some terrible things.'

'Such as?'

'I said that if it was the money she was after, she should
never have married me. That she would be better off with
her parents, that kind of rubbish. We argued for about two
hours, drinking all the time; there was some music on a repeat
loop, Beethoven, the Moonlight Sonata. Can you imagine? We
shouted so loud, and Chris was upstairs in bed . . . when finally
Viv stormed out.'

'Where?'

'She grabbed the car keys, even though she had had far too
much gin, and . . .' His voice trailed off and he had a fleeting
image of the car wreck, the tangle of crushed metal, and inside
it, somewhere, his wife. 'I never saw her again. Alive.'

'Oh, Dan, I'm so sorry.'

'I suppose that's why I've tried to make it up with my father.
A crude trade-off. I've removed one person from my life. If I
can bring back another, then . . .'

'Are you going to see your father again?'
'I'm leaving for England tomorrow.'
'Oh, God. You got to go back right now?'
'I want to see my daughter.'

Chapter 19

The media again gathered in large numbers outside the doors of the East London Magistrates Court at 10 o'clock the next morning. As her black cab pulled up, Sophie wondered whether they had had a tip-off; perhaps there had been a leak about the informant.

She noticed a cameraman in a leather jacket from a cable TV station filming her as she walked less elegantly than she wished up the stairs to the court building, staggering under the weight of the brief and her law books. Then there was a notorious tabloid hack, the definitive cheque-book journalist, unshaven and scruffy, who followed her annoyingly up the steps, not offering to help with her load.

He whispered as he held open the door to the courts, 'I could do with the *names* of any witnesses.'

Sophie stared at him with as much withering contempt as she could muster. It was this man who had been found in contempt of court when he had paid for the exclusive stories of key witnesses in a serial murder trial.

Montford was already in the conference room on the first floor. When she saw him, she wondered for a moment how she should break the news to him, or whether the solicitor had done so already. That's what she hoped. But as she opened the glass door, she again thought of Dan. She knew what he would do. Confront it head on. Deal with it.

So the moment she put her bags down in the room, she began. 'Mr Montford, I'm afraid I have to tell you—'

'They have an informer,' he said, completely deadpan.

'The solicitor told you?'

The senior partner, Douglas Wallace, was also in the room,

standing by a plastic chair. He looked embarrassed. 'Actually, Miss Chase, I was waiting for you, for counsel to—'

'So how do you know?' Sophie asked.

'I just do,' Montford said. 'Let's not get distracted with side issues. The real question is whether we can do anything about it.'

Sophie closely examined Montford's face. He had retained a remarkable amount of his good looks for a man in his seventies, but now his forehead was permanently creased. It was something that she had not noticed before.

'I suppose we could object,' she said. 'We could argue that it is too late to produce this evidence, that we need time to investigate it.'

'What would the court do?'

'Adjourn. Perhaps for a couple of months. Give us a chance to prepare.'

He hesitated. 'Can't we get the evidence excluded? Ruled out of court?'

'Perhaps at the Bailey. Not a prayer now.'

'I see,' Montford said, crossing his arms and putting his left hand to his lips.

'Do you know who the informer is?' she asked.

'Not for sure. But I have an idea.'

'And if your idea is correct?'

'Then he won't testify.'

'Why not?'

'He would have too much to lose.'

Robert Lancing was already in court when Sophie entered ahead of Montford and the solicitor. The case papers were arranged in perfect, precise piles in front of him, and he leant towards the row behind him where a pretty young CPS representative sat. Sophie could just see his red socks.

He looked up when he saw her, smiled but kept talking to the rep. As Sophie sat down on the right-hand side of the front row, he slid a couple of sheets of white paper her way.

It was the informer's statement.

The name and personal details had been blanked out.

She got up and moved two paces closer to Lancing. 'What sort of a stunt is this, Robert?'

'A cheap, underhand, totally unfair stunt. I love it.'

'Tell me his name. That at least.'

'But surely your innocent client knows.'

'I don't care what he knows or doesn't know. I want the prosecution to comply with its duty of full disclosure.'

'Soph, if I disclosed everything we had on Montford, you would get the declaration of war on Germany, the Yalta Agreement and the greatest hits of Vera Lynn. You wouldn't want me to burden you with that lot.'

'Why don't you let me be the judge of that ... or the court. It's up to you.'

'Fighting words. Well, Soldier-boy certainly has instructed the right barrister.'

'The name, Rob.'

'Didn't I say?' He smiled falsely. 'Just call him Jerry.'

She noticed that the usher was busy at the back of the court, taping old newspapers over the glass panels in the doors. By the time the magistrates entered, the court had gone into private session.

Sophie walked quickly to the waist-high dock, having glanced at the pages of the statement but not having had time to absorb it fully.

'Tell me about him,' she ordered.

'There's nothing that you need to know.'

'I'm going to ask for an adjournment.'

'No,' Montford insisted. 'Let's just see how far it goes.'

'What?'

'Just do what I say, Miss Chase.'

Sophie again tried to read the statement as she returned to the front of the court. But her mind was racing with images, thoughts, suspicions. This was dangerous country. It would probably decide the case at the Old Bailey. She wished she could speak to Dan.

Lancing stood up to address the bench. 'Madam,' he said, speaking to the chairwoman, 'we have next an important witness. I should add for the sake of the court record that certain ... steps have been taken to protect the identity of this man.'

Sophie heard another door open, this one nearer the prosecution position in court, a side door that she had not even noticed before. And from it walked a youngish man, perhaps mid-twenties, blond hair, long and swept back, fine classical features, a trim body. He walked cautiously to the witness box.

He took the Bible in his right hand and said, 'I swear by Almighty God that the evidence I shall give shall be the truth, the whole truth and nothing but the truth.'

When he had placed the Bible carefully down on the stand beside him, he looked briefly at Montford. Sophie glanced quickly at her client, but he was impassive, his lips tightly pursed, his face all concentration.

To her left, she heard Lancing clear his throat. 'The police know your real name.'

'Yes.'

'We are going to call you Jeremy or Jerry.'

'So I understand.'

Lancing paused and looked at Sophie. 'Do you, Jerry, know the defendant?'

The man said nothing.

'Do you know Simon Montford?'

The witness clasped his hands together, the fingers intertwining as if he were praying. 'Yes, I know Mr Montford.'

Sophie was staring hard at the witness's face. What was he feeling? Satisfaction? Embarrassment? Guilt? He stared at Montford. Montford stared at him. Something passed between them. Then she felt someone at her shoulder. It was the usher.

'Your client wants a word with you.'

Sophie got up and hurried to the back of the court. When she arrived at the dock, she asked, 'Do you recognise him?'

'Just listen.'

'Is he telling the truth?'

'Listen, Miss Chase.'

She looked at Montford, at the deep lines in his forehead.

'I want these proceedings to be terminated – *right* now. Can we do that?'

'Yes, but—'

'You're here to do what I say.'

'I'm also here to advise you.'

'Tell the court, Miss Chase.'

'But why?'

'I'll fight the case, but not here. Not now. Not like this.'

*   *   *

Subsequently, everything happened extremely quickly. Not five minutes later, the witness had been taken back into the side room, the witness orders had been called out, the alibi warning had been given, and Montford was told to stand up.

The chairwoman of the bench addressed him directly, over Sophie's head. 'Simon Montford, I have to tell you that you are committed to stand trial at the Central Criminal Court, the Old Bailey, on one charge. In that on the said date in April 1945 you murdered Ivan Basarov, contrary to the War Crimes Act 1991 and common law.'

Chapter 20

Dan was surprised that he could fit all his luggage into the taxi. The back seats were crammed with his suitcases and two bags of assorted souvenirs he had bought for Chris on Fifth Avenue.

Owing to the snow, the traffic was heavier than he had anticipated, and when the cab pulled up off Brighton Beach Avenue he had little time left until he was due to check in. He asked the taxi driver to keep the engine ticking over while he jumped out and headed for the deli. He had tried to ring Jo from the hotel but the phone kept ringing.

In the distance, he could hear the ebb and flow of the waves beyond the boardwalk. But as he reached the door to the deli, the characteristic tang of the ocean salt in the air had been replaced by a more acrid smell.

He put his hands to the dirty glass, cupping them around his eyes, and tried to peer inside, seeing nothing, no lights nor any signs of life.

It was only when he walked slowly along the alley to the side of the shop, pacing softly in the snow, that he heard the humming sound. At first he thought that the muffled buzzing belonged to an air-conditioner, but it was the wrong season for that.

When he passed the small lock-up behind the deli and he saw that the grimy windows were clouded up, and smoke was coming from gaps in the garage door, he feared the worst.

He wrenched hard at the metal door handle, but it was already open. The garage door rose off the ground, spewing toxic clouds at him, making him cough and choke, burning his eyes, leaving a bitter taste in his mouth.

He pulled his coat lapels over his nostrils and tried to control his breathing. Narrowing his eyes into slits, he could just discern the shape of a car, and a hosepipe leading from the exhaust to the driver's seat. He reached the driver's window and to his horror saw the crumpled figure of an old man.

What had Jo said about deaths in the family coming along in threes? Guilt stabbed at Dan's heart. Why had he been so harsh on Jo about his mother?

He could barely keep his eyes open now, the carbon monoxide stinging them badly, but he had to persevere. He pulled the door open and the body slumped out of the car. The discoloured arms fell around Dan's feet.

He knelt down, trying to cradle the head, and instantly heard another noise from the other side of the garage.

The breaking of glass, a cry. His head spun around. It was Jo. Crying out, devastated.

Dan looked down at the face of the old man. For a shameful moment he wasn't sure if he was actually grateful that the dead body belonged not to his father but to Ira Gottlieb.

Dan and Jo carefully carried the body into the room at the back of the deli. It was the room in which, only the day before, Ira Gottlieb had been so full of life, drinking vodka.

Dan went to the front of the shop, his heart twisted with a mixture of relief and a profound sadness for old Ira. He quickly phoned the emergency services, then paid the taxi driver and asked him to unload the luggage. Returning to the back room he found Jo kneeling next to Ira, stroking his head, smiling. But Ira's eyes were shut, the characteristic glint of the vivacious old man no longer visible.

'Any hope?' Dan asked.

'Plenty . . . for him now.' Jo looked up and Dan could see the tears in his father's eyes as he pursed his lips, refusing to allow them to fall.

'Why would he kill himself?'

'This ain't suicide,' Jo said, continuing to stroke his friend.

Dan looked at his father, amazed.

'There are easier ways to kill yourself. There *are* easier ways.'

'Do you know who did this?'

'What if I do?'

'Then you've got to get involved.'

Jo shot to his feet and grabbed the front of Dan's coat. 'I *have* been involved for fifty years. Don't you understand?'

'How can I understand? I know nothing about you. About the war. The fifties.'

'Leave the past alone for Chrissake.'

'Say something. Tell somebody.'

'Then the next dead Jew will be me.'

'Who killed him, Jo?'

He said nothing.

'Look, I only just met Ira. But I liked him. Either you tell me about this or I'll find out myself.'

'Then your daughter will grow up without a father – just like you did.'

'At least she will know that I was trying to do the right thing.'

'And I wasn't trying to do that? In 1945?'

'That's the point. I don't know. You won't tell me. And I really *need* to know. Why you left us.'

'No.'

'Who you are.'

'Why? So you can hate me? So that you can be ashamed to be my son?'

'So I can understand who I am, Jo. And why my mother lived alone. Why she died alone.'

Outside, Dan could hear the screaming siren of the ambulance rushing to the scene. When he looked at his father, Jo was lost in thought. The old man appeared to hear a profusion of sounds and voices, but these were echoes from a different, earlier time.

'You know who killed him, don't you?' Dan whispered.

Yuri observed the chaos outside the deli from the relative safety of Brighton Beach Avenue. There was by this time a cluster of police vehicles on the scene, and a woman officer was already cordoning off the area with scenes-of-crime tape. He fought back a smile when, a little later, he saw Dan Becket emerging from the building, arguing with a detective. Dan was screaming about police insensitivity, the fact that they treated everyone as suspects.

A crowd of ethnic Russians gathered around Yuri, pushing him from all sides, fighting to get a better view. He hated crowds. He hated the small-minded sheep mentality of them. So there was no surprise when the name Ira Gottlieb was whispered mouth to mouth like an ancient incantation. All around him various theories were propounded as to how the popular Ira had died, but they faded away as soon as the next person thought of an even more incredible explanation.

If only they knew. Ira didn't know what he was meddling in and it had cost him his life. The old man was foolish and careless and proud; he was almost asking to be killed. It was as simple as that.

Just then Yuri spotted Dan Becket again. He knew Becket was returning to London, and this fact pleased him. London was where it would all happen; it was where history would be fought for, where only the victors would decide the truth. Like it or not, Dan Becket would be part of that battle.

PART II

APRIL

Chapter 1

Chrissy awoke with a sense of excitement for the first time in days. Ever since she had been in Devon, the routine had been the same: her grandfather would put his head around the door to her bedroom at seven o'clock, although he would never say a word; a Spartan breakfast; piano practice; pages of long division and geometry; a 'bracing' one-hour walk; a timed essay on a current topic of her grandfather's choosing; a discussion on the merits and demerits of the arguments over dinner; and then more piano followed by game after game of chess before bed. And it was supposed to be the holidays, she moaned to herself.

She glanced at the old carriage clock on the mantelpiece above the fireplace. It was five to seven and she decided that this morning she'd give the old man a shock and be out of bed before he was. She jumped out from under the blankets and edged back the curtains, smiling widely as she did so. Thank God: it was raining. Finally, April had done its job and had delivered a belated shower. Surely he couldn't expect her to walk out in the rain? That wasn't bracing – that was downright barmy, she thought. She winced at the accidental alliteration of 'bracing barmy'. He Who Must Definitely Be Obeyed would have crossed it out in an essay and scribbled 'journalese' in the margin. Yet the teenager forced the smile back on to her face; nothing was going to dampen her spirits. As her grandfather had said, today her father was picking her up from London – or as Chris thought: Dad to the rescue – and about bloody time. She was thoroughly sick of this teenage Siberia. Since he had returned from New York in January, Chris had spent most of the time in Devon while her father continued his lecturing around Britain and Europe.

She quickly brushed her teeth with the disgusting anti-tartar powder stuff her grandfather insisted on, splashed her face, and pulled on a pair of reverse-fit jeans and a sweatshirt with the slogan Save the Planet. This was to be her life's work, she had already decided, and as far as she could see it had bugger all to do with long division.

Suddenly she heard the regimented footsteps creaking along the corridor of the Tudor house. Time for action. Before the steps had reached the door, she had dashed to the bed and put the pillows beneath the sheets, then dived full length behind the door.

Slowly, the handle turned, but from where she was on the ground, she could not see anyone. The door stayed open a few inches for a full ten seconds until she heard the voice.

'Christine?' the old man whispered.

She did not reply.

'Christine,' he said, now edging into the room. 'It's gone seven o'clock.'

This was the moment. She breathed heavily. She could see the astonishment on his face as he saw her lying on the floor.

'Phew,' she gasped. 'Just doing my sit-ups, Grandpa.'

He examined her, first with a certain suspicion and then with not pleasure but satisfaction.

'Quite,' he replied, pulling his cardigan around himself.

'I was thinking of perhaps a quick jog before breakfast,' she said, springing to her feet.

'Good idea, bad timing.' He pulled back the curtains. 'Rain, you see.'

'Oh no,' she sighed.

'Still, more time for mathematics.'

Chrissy froze. 'Er . . . what time is Daddy coming?'

'Who knows,' the old man replied curtly. His silver hair was parted precisely, his cheeks pinched. Not an ounce of fat could be found anywhere on his body, but in stark contrast to all this he had large brown eyes, softer and more gentle, she felt sure, than he would have wished. They were her mother's eyes.

'He'll come,' Chris said softly.

'Breakfast,' he replied.

When the door was closed, Chris padded quietly across the room. It was always at the moments she least expected it that she was reminded of her mother and the bad feeling between her grandfather and her father. She flung herself face down on the bed, feeling miserable.

The morning dragged. Mornings were always a drag. Chris had the inklings of her first law of speculative philosophy: the only thing worse than long division was piano recital. Antony Thorpe, her grandfather, had regaled her with tales of his years at the Royal Academy, how he had played to adoring crowds and had gone on to tutor several famous concert pianists, and how his most promising pupil – by far – had been his daughter, Vivienne. As she sat at the piano stool, Chris's attention had wandered to the silver-framed photograph of her mother sitting at the same piano in the same austere living room. In the photo, her mother was a teenager.

'Discipline, Christine,' Antony snapped, tapping the top of the piano with his pipe.

Chris knew she had played some false notes but was past caring. 'I'm trying to feel the music.'

'Discipline first. Feelings second.' He put the pipe in his mouth, half chewing the stem. 'From the top of the page.'

Chris's heart sank. She had been struggling to get off this wretched page for the last twenty minutes but couldn't concentrate. Her gaze crept to the right, and with her peripheral vision she could see the long hand of the grandfather clock on nine. Quarter to. But quarter to what? Her fingers were tired and her back ached; she couldn't be sure if she had been going two hours or three. If it was three, then she would have the temporary release of lunch at one o'clock. That would be only fifteen minutes more. But if it was two hours . . . she couldn't bear to think about it. It was just too much, and when she looked at the page of music the quavers and semiquavers danced before her eyes.

'After four,' Antony insisted. 'One and two and—' But then there was barking from outside. The two dogs, Rhodesian ridgebacks, Winston and Churchill, were going crazy. Someone was driving up to the house.

'Must be Dad,' she smiled.

'Or the postman,' Antony huffed. 'Always late.'

'The postman?'

'Both of them.'

The oak door to the lounge opened slightly and across the half-lit room came the fragile voice of Chris's grandmother.

'Antony, it's Daniel.'

Chris started up from the chair then, realising that her grandfather still stood above her, glanced up at him plaintively. 'May I be excused, Grandfather?'

He nodded, saying nothing, and attempted to relight his pipe.

Chris sped out into the corridor, making little sound on the thick green carpets. She overtook her grandmother just as she was going to open the door, and she was out in the rain before her grandmother could finish her sentence.

'Christine, you'll catch your death—'

'Dad,' she shouted, seeing Dan emerge from the driver's door of the Volvo.

'Hi, Princess.'

The dogs advanced on Dan, standing flank to flank, huge, muscled beasts, baring their teeth and barking incessantly. Chris ran between them.

'Winston! Naughty,' she scolded.

Instantly, the guard dog's ears dropped and it retreated, tail between its legs.

'Churchill, bad dog,' she shouted, grabbing the still-barking dog by the collar until he, too, retreated.

Dan had his raincoat above his head and sheltered Chris under it as she leapt towards him and kissed him again and again.

'Miss me?' he asked.

'Nah,' she smiled.

'No?' They began to walk back to the imposing Tudor façade of the house. 'What's one thousand divided by twenty-seven, then?' he asked.

'Sod knows.'

'Chris, don't swear.'

'Then don't leave me here, OK?'

'Deal.'

'Deal,' she said.

The dogs had regrouped under the porch and, seeing Dan approaching, began to snarl again.

Dan put his mouth to Chris's ear. 'I'm sure they're trained to bark at me,' he said.

The door was fully open, revealing both grandparents in the doorway.

'They are,' Chris whispered back. Then, more loudly: 'Grandpa, Grandma, Daddy's here.'

'How are you, Annette?' Dan said to the old lady as she smiled back at him.

'Right. Lunch,' Antony huffed, spinning on his heels and disappearing into the darkness of the hall.

Lunch at the Thorpe household was the main meal of the day but was still a simple matter, high on fibre and low on taste. As all four people sat around the dining table, the meal – cold salmon from the previous day, boiled potatoes, some kind of boiled green vegetable matter – was as miserable as the April rain outside. For Dan, the experience was all the more painful as arrayed around the dining room was image after image of Vivienne, photographs of his wife as a girl, sitting on cushions at a stool to reach the piano keyboard. Opposite him was a chalk drawing of her at a piano on her twenty-first birthday, shortly before she met Dan. Worst of all was a photograph of her holding baby Chrissy in her arms. This was an environment over which he had no control, unlike his home where every image of Viv had been removed from the living areas of the house, although he still kept their wedding photograph by his bed.

'Didn't think the salmon would stretch two days,' Annette said, trying to smile. No one replied. She had a roundish, plump face, in contrast to her husband, and her right eye was very weak, appearing almost glass-like.

'Antony,' she continued, 'did you ever think the salmon would—'

'Can I ask,' the old man interrupted, totally ignoring his wife, 'just what you are doing with yourself these days, Daniel?'

At that precise moment, Dan had his mouth full of cold fish and suspected that his father-in-law had chosen the moment on purpose.

'More potatoes?' Annette asked her husband, sensing the tension.

'I've had three potatoes, Annette. You know I only eat three potatoes. Now, Daniel—'

'I'm working,' Dan replied.

'Yes, but working at what? Christine says—'

'Whatever Chrissy says is true . . . Tony.'

Dan knew perfectly well that the abbreviation of Christian names was a misdemeanour bordering upon a felony in the Thorpe household.

'So is it true you are no longer a barrister?' Antony asked.

'One is a barrister for life. But if you mean am I practising, then the answer is I haven't taken a case for some months.'

'Ah,' the old man said, tapping his knife on the tabletop as he had earlier with the pipe.

'This is my point. How do you intend supporting my grand-daughter when you are not working? I hear piano lessons are very expensive in London. And Chris is slipping behind—'

'*I am* working,' Dan insisted. 'Only not at the Bar. I've written a paper on Abuse of Process and have received several invitations to lecture.'

'Which pays how much?'

'We'll get by,' Chris interjected, immediately seeing the fury on her grandfather's face. For a moment she hesitated, and then continued, 'Daddy and me will—'

'Daddy and I,' Antony snapped. 'And getting by isn't good enough for my granddaughter, Daniel. You know that . . .' He waved his fork briefly towards the bowed window. '. . . that all this will only pass to Christine when we both die. And I have no intention of dying.'

Annette spluttered with embarrassment. 'We . . . I mean, we could lend Daniel some money, couldn't we . . . er, Antony.'

'If we were asked . . . I would consider it.'

'I don't need your money,' Dan said.

'You see?' the old man declared, but it was unclear whom he was addressing. 'It's useless. He's too proud.'

'I'm trying to make a life for Chris,' Dan said.

'Like you made one for Vivienne?'

There was a sudden silence. Tears welled in Chris's eyes, but she fought them back with all her will. Annette studied her plate intently as the two men stared each other out. When it was clear that Dan was not about to respond to the recriminations, Antony stood slowly and neatly placed his knife and fork together.

'You'll excuse me,' he said.

He left the room silently, not bothering to close the door.

Each of his footsteps could be heard as they advanced further and further down the hall. Finally, the door to his study shut quietly.

'Where are your things?' Dan asked Chris.

She stood, as did he.

'You can't go yet,' Annette pleaded. 'You haven't had dessert. We've still got some of yesterday's trifle. Christine, didn't you like—'

'I loved it, Gran.' She was only allowed to call her Gran outside the acute, trained earshot of her grandfather. She now went and hugged her grandmother, who rested her greying head on her shoulder.

'Go to him, Chrissy,' Annette whispered.

Chris nodded. She went around the table and took her father by the hand, leading him out of the dining room and up the stairs. Before long she had taken him to a room on the first floor that he knew all too well.

'You're never staying in here?' he asked, pausing before he entered.

'I don't mind, Daddy, really.'

But Dan was about to explode. It was Viv's room. It was a ten-bedroom house and crazy old Antony Thorpe had made Chris stay in her mother's old room. He rushed in and saw his daughter's suitcases open against one wall.

'Really, I don't mind,' she repeated.

He pulled open the mirror-fronted wardrobe and saw Viv's old clothes hanging neatly inside. There was a powerful smell of mothballs.

'Grandpa makes Gran keep washing them, Dad.'

He didn't reply.

'It makes me feel Mum is . . . here,' she said.

'Help me pack,' he replied, beginning to toss the clothes into the cases at all angles.

'I've . . . I've got to see Grandpa.'

'Chris!'

'Please.'

'Two minutes.'

She dashed out of the room and took the winding stairs two at a time. She slowed down only when she arrived at the door to the study. Raising her left hand, she was about to knock when she heard a strange sound from within. She slowly opened the door.

Her grandfather's desk blocked off the far end of the room in front of the window. On each wall, climbing right up to the ceiling, were banks of books, first editions, monographs, the type that Chris expected to see smeared in dust. These were pristine. Behind the desk, a swivel leather chair had been turned to face the window and the high wings obscured most, but not all, of Antony's head.

Chris whispered, 'Grandpa?'

She scared herself, for the sound came out far louder than she intended and echoed faintly in the room. There was no reply. Instead of repeating his name, she took a deep breath and moved slowly towards the desk, step by step, growing more concerned as there was no movement from the chair.

Now she was at the edge of the desk and could see the parting in his hair, so absolute that she could discern a clear, straight line of scalp. She reached towards him, her fingers trembling, then pulled back. How can I be afraid of him, he's my grandfather, she thought, and scolded herself. But her chiding did not prepare her for what she now saw.

When she stepped around the desk, she sank to her knees and saw her grandfather's head propped on his palm. He made no sound. But two tears rolled slowly down his face.

He gazed through the glass, over the lawns and hedges outside. Chris touched his hand.

'Vivienne?' he said.

'Christine,' she whispered.

He looked at her with doleful, large eyes, not those of a strict tutor, but eyes that belonged to a proud father gazing upon his child for the first time.

'Chrissy,' he said quietly.

'Grandpa,' she replied.

By the time Chris returned to her mother's room, Dan had packed and forced shut one of the two suitcases, though bits of clothing stuck out from one side. For a moment she glimpsed her reflection in the mirror on her mother's wardrobe. There was something about herself she did not totally recognise.

Perhaps, after all, her father was right, and she was finally growing up.

'I've got to stay,' she told him.

He nodded and went to her, hugging her so tightly that she could hardly breathe, but she loved every second of it.

Chapter 2

Dan and Chris drove to the nearest town just over an hour later. It was a mile and a half towards the coast, through narrow lanes with high brush hedges on both sides and blind corners. The town itself lived for the tourist season and was now beginning to show the first flickers of life after the winter.

'Remember the shopping list?' he asked her as they reached the outskirts of the town.

'There are only about three things on it.'

'So what do we need?'

'Depends how long you're staying, Dad.' She pointed to a sign indicating the public car park. 'You've got to follow the one-way system.'

Dan indicated right and filtered into the traffic as it sped around a corner.

'So how was your trip?' she asked.

'Lecture went well. But Brussels was a bore.'

'Brussels is always a bore.'

'You've never been there.'

'You need to go there to know this?' she smiled.

'Don't be smart.'

She did not reply. A thought or a memory clouded her features and the smile vanished.

'Chris, what's the matter?'

'We want the short-stay car park.'

'Chris?'

She said nothing but wound her window down slightly, allowing a trickle of rain to creep into the car. Dan found a spot in the second row of cars, having waited until a Range Rover pulled out. It was as he put the handbrake on that Chris spoke.

'Grandpa doesn't think I'm smart.'

'You don't know that.'

'He's always going on about how brilliant Mummy was. By my age she was practically composing sonatas and I haven't even got Grade Five.'

'He's an old man, Chris.'

She looked at him squarely, the odd scattered droplet on her left cheek.

'He misses Mum more than you.'

Dan was shocked by the comment. But it wasn't just the import of the words, it was the utter conviction with which his daughter spoke them which upset him.

'I miss her, Chris. But ... people grieve in different ways.'

'Why don't you cry? It's OK to cry.'

'How do you know I haven't.'

''Cause I know everything about you, Dad. And I just know you're being strong for me. But you don't need to be. Not for me, I mean.'

He took her hand and she squeezed his back. Within him, in the vulnerable centre he struggled to conceal from the world, there was a release, a kind of dissipation of pain locked away so completely he sometimes forgot its cause.

'We do have enough money, don't we, Dad?' she continued. 'Because if we don't, I could take a job. A paper round and something on Saturdays. Remember I told you Clare Humphries works in that posh boutique in Turnham Green Terrace? And if she can get a job there ... God, she looks like the rear end of a—'

'We're fine, Chris.' He was reluctant to let her work. He remembered well that as he grew up he swore to himself that his children would not have to work as he had been required to do.

'Only I don't want anyone else's money. It was sweet of Gran to offer. But we'll do it, Dad, you and me. We're a team.'

Dan took the keys out of the ignition.

'I'm probably going to be doing a case anyway,' he said.

'At the Bailey?'

'Yes.'

'Murder?'

He paused, but knew that she was likely to find out soon. 'War crimes,' he said.

'So I won't need to do a paper round?'

'You stick to your piano practice.'

She sighed in an exaggerated way. Then, as they got out of the car, she smiled as sweetly as she could, cocking her head slightly to one side. 'But I can get a job on Saturdays?'

'Absolutely not,' he said. 'Right, where's the chemist?'

'D-aa-d. Just Saturdays.'

'Remind me: when is your Grade Five exam?'

'All right, after the exam, then?'

'Only if you pass.'

'No problem.'

'And only Saturday mornings, Chris.'

'And all day when I get Grade Six?'

He look at her and smiled. 'God, you drive a hard bargain.'

'That's why I'm the boss.'

'Oh, you're the boss?' he said, tickling her under the arms. 'We'll have to see about that.'

They began to walk into the sodden high street of the town. It had changed so much, Dan reflected, since Viv had first brought him here almost two decades previously. Now the town centre looked very much like all the others in the south of England – the same chain stores, the odd video rental, the same pizzerias.

He had not been able to sleep the night before he was first due to meet the formidable Antony Thorpe, he remembered. Even though Viv had assured him her father had promised to be on his best behaviour. In fact, to his surprise, Antony had been extraordinarily hospitable, opening a treasured bottle of Château Haut-Brion from 1961, the best vintage since the war, he lectured Dan. It was only when Dan opened the bin in the kitchen as he and Viv were doing the washing up later that he saw the empty claret bottle, upside down, without the cork. It was from 1962. Dan didn't know what to make of Antony's behaviour, but he was prepared to give him the benefit of the doubt.

The next day, when Dan went into the old man's inner sanctum, the intimidatingly dark study, to ask for Viv's hand in marriage, there had at first been no response. Antony drew deeply on his pipe twice as if to invite Dan to convince him, and when Dan was talked out about his prospects at the Bar, there was still no reply. Finally, Antony stood up and said – Dan had never forgotten the words – 'Of course, it's Vivienne's bed, she is the one who has to lie in it.' When Dan slowly climbed the stairs to her bedroom, the same one in which Chrissy had now been billeted, Viv was having kittens. He opened the door and, before he had even uttered a word, the expression on his face said everything. She burst into tears. He tried to hug her, but she shrugged him off and hurtled out of the room, leaving him standing rather foolishly, he felt, staring at himself in the wardrobe mirror. He was still standing there when he heard Viv's increasingly hysterical voice downstairs as she pleaded with her father. It was a largely one-way conversation, Dan remembered, except for three simple words from Antony repeated at regular intervals: I forbid it. This incantation was then replaced by the words: the piano, your studies; your studies, the piano. Finally, father and daughter were silent.

Dan and Viv got married regardless, and although Annette joined Dan's mother at the register office in London, Antony boycotted the event. The old man did, however, attend Chrissy's christening a couple of years later. He left an envelope of money for the child in Viv's handbag, but did not even shake Dan's hand. It was something Viv never admitted, but almost as an unspoken protest she never played the piano seriously again. The one thing Antony sought to protect by forbidding the marriage was, by his own hand, unwittingly destroyed.

These memories turned slowly through Dan's mind as though he were a silent witness walking through each scene; oddly, on another level, he could also make out Chris asking him questions and telling him about her time in Devon, and he was able to manage the appropriate positive or negative grunt as he wandered through the past.

They were now in the chemist's and Dan looked around men's accessories for some shaving equipment.

'So you'll stay all week?' Chris asked, handing him a larger packet of disposable razors.

'We'll see.'

He couldn't find his regular shaving foam and grabbed one that was on special offer instead. He looked at her, noticing faint rings under her eyes.

'Aren't you sleeping properly?' he asked.

'He won't let me go to bed when I want.'

'There's nothing wrong with an early night.'

'No, Dad. He keeps me up. Every night. Playing chess – game after game.' She paused. 'Until he wins.'

'So let him win.'

His daughter looked at him with set features until a mischievous smile broke out on one side of her mouth.

'Never,' she said.

He took the small tub of dental powder she gave him. When he examined it, he saw that it was the old-fashioned anti-tartar stuff.

'You trying to tell me something?' he asked her, smiling.

'Dad!'

'Whatever happened to Colgate?'

Chris put on a mock Gestapo accent. 'It vill be confiscated by ze dental police.'

'Fair enough,' he said.

After they had paid, Dan got the sense that there was something of importance she wanted to ask him. It was the way she hung on to his elbow, how she would begin a sentence and then stop. Only when they were back out in the high street did she come out with it. She stood squarely in front of him and conjured up her sweetest voice.

'Dad?'

'No.'

'Did you see that shop—'

'No, I didn't.'

'There's a shoe sale over there.'

By the time they returned to the house, Annette had laid out a tea for them, including the half-eaten trifle. There was an expensive-looking china teapot on the dining-room table which was immaculate save for a small chip in the spout. But despite the cosy she had placed around it, the tea was merely tepid. Dan suggested to Chris that they should retire to the lounge where he had spied Antony reading by the fire, his cardigan neatly folded over one arm of his designated armchair. He was one-third of the way through *War and Peace*.

The only noise that could be heard above the crackling of the fire was the even tick-tick of the grandfather clock near the piano, lending the room, with its ageing wallpaper and faded fabrics, a timeless quality. The old clock had a warped face with gold-leaf numbers that had begun to fray. Circling slowly about them were two heavy ornate hands which, Dan always thought, somehow slowed down time.

'Antony, may we?' he asked on entering.

The old man looked up briefly and nodded. While Dan sat on the chesterfield, Chris moved steadily over the thick carpet to the armchair facing her grandfather.

'Gran?' she asked.

'Resting,' he replied.

'Is she—'

'Thank you, but she's resting, Christine.'

Dan put his cup down on the coffee table and stood. 'Antony, if it's not too much bother, I was wondering if—'

'Please,' he interjected.

'Thank you. Just a day or—'

'Long as you like, Daniel.'

Dan glanced at Chris, just briefly, catching the satisfaction that lit up her eyes before they rejoined the rest of her face in a serious mask. He thought of his own father on the other side of the Atlantic, a man as much a stranger to him as Antony Thorpe, and made a silent vow to himself that one way or another he would get to know Jo, and such precious moments as they might have together would not be punctuated by these awkward silences.

'What are you reading, Grandpa?' Chris asked.

The old man held up the book.

'I hate things about war,' she frowned, screwing up her nose.

'It's not about war. It's about men. War is just one of the things men do.'

'Why?' she asked, leaning forward.

Antony paused for an instant, using the time to take his pipe from the outside pocket of the folded cardigan. He glanced briefly at Dan. 'It's in their nature, Christine.'

Not being able readily to refute this statement, the teenager sat back in her chair. 'How many more pages?'

'Oh . . . about a thousand,' he said.

'That's a lot of war.'

Antony couldn't help but smile at the comment and the smile turned into a grin when Chris continued.

'Well, if there's a convenient break – you know, in hostilities – would you mind giving me a game of chess?'

The old man put the book on the mantelpiece as he stood up. 'I feel peace breaking out already.'

Chris leapt from her chair and took the chess set from the top drawer of the sideboard. 'Daddy, are you going to watch?'

'In a minute, Chris. Antony, I was wondering if I could use your phone?'

'Be my guest. It's in the—'

'Yes, thanks.'

'Grandpa, before chess ... can I play some piano?'

The old man looked at her incredulously.

'No,' she said, 'I meant with you. A duet?'

Antony smiled and held up his right hand. 'Arthritis,' he whispered.

As Dan left the two of them setting up the pieces on the coffee table, he heard Antony say quietly, 'You know, in 1957 I played at the Albert Hall. The Queen was there, Christine.'

Dan walked the short distance into the study and sat at the desk he had remembered so clearly in his thoughts earlier in the day. Now that he was going to spend the night in Devon, he needed to check for messages on his answerphone. He lifted the receiver and dialled his home number. Soon he heard his own voice on the outgoing message, and he spoke the code word activating the recording. First there was a loud beep. Another beep. Someone had hung up twice. Then a female voice.

'Er ... hi, Daddy. Where are you? Just me ordering you to rescue me a.s.a.p. Love, the boss.'

Another beep. Another hang-up. Then a male voice.

'Mr Becket? Peter Grail. You probably know there's an application in the Montford case tomorrow at the Bailey. You shouldn't know – but there aren't secrets at the Bar, are there?' Grail laughed. 'Neville Neale really wants you to be involved and your clerks said I could ring you direct. If you're still interested, Old Bailey after lunch.'

Dan decided that he would at least hear what the prosecution QC, Neville Neale, had to say.

There was another hang-up. And then another male voice.

'Uh ... it's me. I'm ... landing tomorrow. I need to ... well, look, can we meet? This is my hotel.'

As the details were spelled out, Dan's mind raced. It was Jo.

*   *   *

Dan waited until Chris was ready for bed before he told her that he would have to return to London.

'But you promised,' she complained.

'I know, darling. I'm sorry.'

'You're sorry?' She rolled over and faced the wall, pulling the pink blanket tightly around her shoulder.

'Chris, look—'

'Is it important?' she asked quietly.

'Very.'

'So you won't come back?'

'Not immediately.'

She rolled over again and sat bolt upright. 'Well, then I'm coming up.'

'Of course you can.'

'In a day or two, I mean.' She hesitated. 'You know ... Grandpa.'

Dan hugged her tightly, then asked, 'Who won the chess?'

'Who do you think?'

'The Beckets triumph again?' he asked.

'But I think the Thorpes might just wipe the floor with us over the next few days.'

They both laughed, and Dan kissed her as he reached for the bedside light. He saw an open book illuminated by a yellow crescent of light on the side table. It was *War and Peace*.

'Wake me up before you go,' she whispered.

He nodded and then kissed her again.

Chapter 3

Dan left Devon at just before 6 o'clock the next morning. In contrast to the previous day's rain, the skies were practically clear, save for a scattering of cloud low to the east. As the sun rose slowly, he spent the journey with the sun-shield down, thinking alternately of his father and the strange world Chris had volunteered to remain in back in Devon. It pleased him that she had such generosity of spirit, for her appreciation of the complex agonies of her grandfather belied her years. He only wished he could so easily tune into his own father's emotions. After he left New York in January, he had tried to phone Jo twice. The first time the phone was clearly off the hook. The second time the line was dead.

The traffic was relatively light until he hit the M4 outside Heathrow, but turning off at Kew he skirted through the West London back roads and was able to pick up a croissant, a pint of milk and the *Guardian* in Brackenbury village.

He parked two doors down the street, snapping up the spot an irritable neighbour considered her own. Just as he reached the front door at nine, the phone rang. He rushed inside, leaving the milk and croissant on the stairs by the phone.

'Dan Becket.'

'Ah, Mr Becket. It's Peter Grail. Hope you don't mind—'

'How'd you get my number?'

'Your clerks gave it to me,' Grail said. 'I was wondering . . . if we can expect to see you today.'

'Why is it your business, Grail? Surely that's between Neville Neale and—'

'Look on me as the unofficial quartermaster,' Grail said, with an undertone in his voice that could either have been sarcasm or vanity. 'My job's to rally the troops.'

'Are we going to war?'

'We already are at war. The phoney one ended today.' He paused. 'I know you've been busy lecturing and things. I saw a profile on you in the Sundays. Brussels, wasn't it?'

'The ethnic cleansing trials are starting in Europe.'

'You see?' Grail exclaimed. 'You're the man for the job.'

'Perhaps we should let Neville Neale decide that.'

'So you're still undecided?'

'Mr Grail, you'll be the first to know.'

Grail paused and then said goodbye quite irritably, as if Dan's equivocations were a personal vote of no confidence. Perhaps, Dan thought, Grail took exception to the fact that matters were being decided above his head, on a counsel-to-counsel basis, but in his experience this was precisely the way things invariably happened. Why should this trial be so different?

While at the telephone, he replayed his messages on the answerphone. He smiled again when he heard Chris referring to herself as 'the boss'; he skipped past Grail's message and then memorised the telephone number of Jo's hotel. It was in the very centre of London, so could have been very good or very bad indeed – he suspected he knew which it was likely to be. For a moment he toyed with the idea of making a cup of tea and getting the croissant inside him before he faced his father; he had, after all, been up since around five. But he also knew that where his father was concerned one procrastination readily bred another by some inexorable family law that had been created even before he was born. He dialled the number.

At first there was an unusual ring – almost like that of an internal phone – then suddenly an answerphone cut in declaring the name of the hotel and inviting 'the caller kindly to call the emergency number – if . . . er . . . it was an emergency'.

He glanced at his watch. It was past nine. This was ridiculous; there had to be someone on the desk. He was just about to dial the emergency number when a heavily accented male voice spoke over the recorded message.

'Sorry, but our phones are up the spout,' was the explanation Dan received.

'Well, I'd like to speak to . . .' He hesitated. What name would Jo be staying under? It was a simple matter, but where his father was concerned he could not count on these little things.

'Do you have a Josef Rosen staying?' he asked.

'Who?'

'Josef,' Dan said patiently.

'Can you spell that?'

'J-O-S—'

'No, no one by that ... oh yes. There he is.'

Dan breathed out in relief. 'Right, can I speak—'

'No.'

'No?'

'Left a note. No calls.'

'But I'm ...' He paused for an instant. It still felt so strange saying this, especially in his own home where for so many years he had lived as a fatherless child. 'I'm his son.'

'Is it an emergency?'

'No ... I just ...'

'He's sleeping. Jet-lagged, I'd guess.'

'Well, can you take a message?'

He left instructions, twice, about exactly where Jo was to meet him, but he had no confidence whatsoever that his father would appear. When he had finished, he asked the receptionist to read back the message.

'Is that a "super" with an A or an ER?' the man asked.

The only discreet place Dan knew where it was possible to meet for lunch near the Old Bailey was a hamburger joint called Super Burger. He realised that most, if not all, of the other eateries around the Bailey were likely to be populated by solicitors, barristers, court staff and CPS representatives, bored with the fare put on by the Bailey's canteens and messes. None of this would matter except for one fact: he was not sure he wished to be seen with Jo. It was not necessarily that he was ashamed of the old man, he was just uncertain how other people would take it: Dan Becket, barrister of the Middle Temple, formerly one of Her Majesty's Treasury Counsel, and ... Jo, baseball cap and all. There was a logic to his thinking on this point which he did not question until he arrived in the vicinity of the Ludgate Circus hinterland where the burger bar was situated. Perhaps the truth was very simple: he had become a snob.

As he turned off the main road, the walls of grimy concrete shielded the air from the roar of the traffic. The side road was in shade, and given the narrowness of the street and the height of the bordering office blocks it remained in shadow all day. There was a large neon sign identifying the burger bar. Dan paused. Suddenly a thought rushed to the forefront of his mind: what if Jo wasn't there? In fact, what if his father did not come at all? The discomfort of another rejection began to unsettle him, and he remembered how he had waited, not daring to breathe, when he had phoned Jo from London. Again and again he had said to himself: just one more ring, no, two more. He's an old man, give it another ring. And when he had tried again a couple of days later, the line was dead. He had written a brief letter to Jo asking him to get in touch. There was no reply.

So when Dan walked in, a little self-conscious in his court suit among the workmen in overalls and the backpackers, he was at once relieved and surprised to see Jo sitting at a table in the dark corner furthest from the door. His New York Yankees baseball cap was on the yellow moulded plastic table. Without the faded cap to tame it, his grey hair was as wild as ever.

'They no have decent delis round here?' he asked as Dan sat down.

'This is Britain, Jo, not Brooklyn. You said you wanted someplace discreet.'

He examined the stand-up plastic menu with suspicion.

'Well, aren't you going to say it's great to see your father?'

'Why are you here, Jo?'

'To have lunch with my son.'

'No, why are you here in England?'

'Stopping over. There's a service commemorating the liberation of the camp in Germany.'

'Camp?'

'Neuwelt. It's where Ira was at the end of the war. The week before he died, he asked me to go with him to the service. Now . . . well, I feel I owe him.'

'You flew in this morning?'

'Morning, evening. I don't know. My jet's lagged. Can't tell you if I'm coming or going.'

Dan looked at his watch. He had to be at the Bailey by 2 p.m. They had under an hour together. 'Look, we'd better order. Doesn't matter what you choose, it all tastes the same, all fried in the same fat. Let's just get two super specials: two cholesterol burgers and Cokes.'

Jo nodded.

Dan went to the counter, pointed to the two shrivelled buns wrapped in greasy paper, and tiptoed his way back to Jo, trying not to spill the two regular Cokes, each the size of a window-cleaner's bucket.

'You thirsty?' Jo asked, as Dan put the drinks down.

'Forgot regular means regular for a camel.' He unwrapped the burger and frowned at the unmelted slice of processed cheese that poked out on all sides. 'When's the service in Germany?'

'Next week,' Jo replied, munching into his burger.

'I see.' But Dan didn't see at first. It was only after he had taken a slurp of the Coke that he understood. 'You're in England a week?'

Jo nodded. But Dan saw something else in his father's eyes, nothing much more than a flash, a glint, but something that hinted at a further agenda. Jo looked away and scratched his left wrist.

'Why a week?' Dan continued.

''Cause I love the weather. What you think? 'Cause I want to see—'

'Me?'

'My granddaughter.'

Dan was determined to rationalise the situation. Why should Jo want to see him? He had hardly been the unquestioning, devoted son.

'Chrissy isn't in London,' he told him.

'Where is she?'

'With her grandparents.' And then he realised what he had said. 'With her *other* grandparents, Jo.' He tried to change the subject. 'How did the inquest into Ira's death go?'

'What do you think? One more crazy old Jew kills himself. Who cares?'

'Would it have made a difference if I'd come back to New York to testify?' When there was no reply to his question, he continued, 'But you thought it wasn't suicide.'

'I *said* it was murder.'

'So why don't you do something about—'

'Wanna go over this again?'

An awkward silence descended on them, and they both pretended to concentrate on digesting the gristly meat. Jo scratched his wrist again. Finally, Dan could bear it no more. Almost despite himself, he understood that he needed to do something for Jo. He put down his burger. 'Jo, it's none of my business really, but you could always stay with—'

'It ain't your business.'

'I was only asking.'

'You really want me to stay with you?'

Dan paused. 'Yes.'

'So who you told about me, then?'

'Why are you giving me a hard time? Do you want me to dislike you, is that it? Well, I'm not going to, Jo. I'm going to like you so much you're going to puke.'

Jo tried to fight back the beginnings of a grin that was finding its way to the corners of his mouth. 'No one in England knows who I am?'

'No.'

'No one knows that your father lives in New York?'

'No one knows that my father is alive.'

Jo looked around the restaurant. 'Where you living?'

'Shepherd's Bush.'

'You bringing up my only granddaughter in Shepherd's Bush?'

'Viv sometimes used to pretend that it was Chiswick borders, but the Bush is the Bush, I'm afraid.'

'I remember Shepherd's Bush in the fifties. Back then it was—'

'Now it's worse.'

Jo squashed the uneaten third of his burger into the table and took out a packet of cigarettes. He lit up quickly and, before Dan knew it, toxic vapours were being blown his way.

'You *smoke*, Jo?'

'I survived the Nazis and I ain't going to survive the anti-smoking lobby?'

'What about cancer?'

'What about it?' Then he paused, his voice calmer. 'So what time you home?'

'About six.'

'Just write down your address again, will you?'

Dan took out one of his professional cards and scribbled on

the back. It was then that he saw what it was that Jo had been scratching on his arm. Just below the skin, almost in 3-D, like an implanted hologram, were six numbers carved into the wrist.

'Oh God, Jo,' he said.

The old man said nothing at first but took another drag on his cigarette. There was a pause until Jo said, 'Nazi doctor knocked that up for me . . . let's see – 1943? 'Course, when I moved camps in '45 they wanted to give me another number and I just said "Fuck you". Can you believe that? The Nazi quack just laughed – he must have known the war was about to end – things were beginning to slip.'

Dan looked on miserably. Suddenly the worries that he had had about the forthcoming war crimes trial were put into an entirely different context.

'Hey, cheer up,' Jo said, getting to his feet. 'I'm proud of it. Every time I see it, I say to myself: Jo, you bad-tempered old Jew, they did this to you and you survived.'

Just then an assistant came up to them and, straightening his absurd yellow and red uniform, said, 'I'm afraid it's a non-smoking restaurant, sir.'

Jo puffed again. 'So sue me.'

Dan got up, taking his father's arm gently. 'We'd better go,' he said.

Out in the spring air, with the lunchtime traffic rushing about them, Jo stood by his side, half a head shorter with his slightly curved back. Here was his father standing beside him, his grey hair blowing in the wind that breezed through the centre of London. It all had an ephemeral quality.

'Trick is,' Jo said, 'not to get mad. Just get even.'

'What do you mean?'

'There's all kinds of justice.' He paused and then added, 'You do yours, I do mine.'

'I never understand what you say,' Dan replied.

'That's a mutual kind of feeling.'

At that moment, an image of Antony Thorpe sitting alone in his study, fortified on all sides by books, came into Dan's mind. 'Please,' he said to his father, 'can we try to get on?'

'For Chrissy?'

'For us, Jo.' He looked into the older man's eyes. 'I don't want us to have secrets.'

At this, Jo laughed.

'Look, there's something that's been bugging me,' Dan said. 'Will you tell me the truth?' When there was no response except Jo stamping out his cigarette on the pavement, he continued. 'Why didn't you reply to my letter?'

'What letter?'

'You know.'

Jo shook his head slowly. 'Yeah,' he said. He took a shallow breath and added, 'I just had nothing to say.'

'I thought you didn't want to know me,' Dan replied.

Jo took his baseball cap and adjusted the peak marginally. 'You should never think that,' he said.

Chapter 4

Dan went to the security entrance of the Old Bailey alone. The lunch with Jo had disorientated him in the sense that it had made him think of the world outside the narrow confines of the case he was about to discuss. But even more, it had made him feel like a son. So when he had taken the lift to the fourth floor and had left his coat in the robing room, he walked down the stairs towards Court 1 in something of a daze. He so wanted to believe Jo's parting comment. Did his father finally want to get to know him?

When he was outside the public canteen on the second floor he heard someone calling out from above him.

'Wait there, Dan, will you?' Sophie rushed down the stone stairs, her white wig bobbing as she moved hurriedly towards him. 'Haven't you heard of this brilliant new-fangled contraption? It's called a lift.'

'Just wanted some exercise.'

'Well, I suppose it will be good for my cellulite. Of course, you New Yorkers probably call it an elevator or something.'

'I was only there for about a week.'

'So why haven't you bothered to see me since you got back, then?' she asked, trying to keep up with him.

'I've been all over the place. Devon. Brussels – don't go to Brussels.'

'And there I was thinking Dan Becket must have found himself some fancy woman in New York.'

Dan saw that she was finding it hard to keep up with him and slowed down. He did feel guilty about not seeing her in the three-month interim, but the time he had spent with Chrissy both in London and in Devon had recharged his batteries and had given him renewed strength.

'So did you?' Sophie breathed, as they arrived on the first floor.

'Did I what?'

'Find some woman.'

'Come on, Soph. I don't ask you about your personal life.'

'Why not?'

He smiled at her, but was unsure what to make of her last question. Her blond bob was just visible around her wig and her eyes, those almond-shaped eyes, smiled and at the same time hinted at some secret agony. He liked Sophie more than he cared to admit, but he couldn't deal with any more complications.

'My spies tell me that Lisa Hartman is absolutely beautiful.'

'Is that what they say?'

'And I bet she doesn't have cellulite.'

'Are you and Lancing still an item?'

'None of your business, Dan.'

'But I thought you said . . . about your personal life—'

'We're not an item. We're history. We're a detail in the chronicles of mismatched affairs started because . . . the woman couldn't have the man she *really* wanted.'

Suddenly Dan found that the conversation made him feel uneasy. If there was one person at the Bar with whom he could discuss more personal matters, it was certainly Sophie Chase, but his relationship with Lisa was not fair game – mainly because he could not understand it himself. Had he just been swept up in the magic of New York? He had one hundred times tried to convince himself that he had ended up in bed with the beautiful Manhattan attorney for reasons other than loneliness, a loneliness that plagued both their lives. These questions had become all the more acute as Lisa had arrived in Europe six days earlier. Having been stuck on business in Frankfurt and Berlin longer than she had foreseen, she would reach London the next day.

By now Sophie and Dan had reached the lobby on the first floor. There was the usual post-lunch bustle as witnesses, lawyers and court staff stretched their legs and their vocal cords before another half-day in court.

'So why are you here?' Sophie asked.

Dan hesitated before he replied. The prosecution's application, a P.I.I. application, was supposed to be a covert proceeding;

effectively the prosecution were sneaking off behind the backs of the defence to see the judge in private.

'I could ask you the same,' he replied, hoping it was a sufficiently nebulous response.

Sophie moved closer towards him and whispered, 'There's a P.I.I. in the Montford case.'

Dan stared back at her, surprised that she knew, but also amused. 'If it's a secret application, how'd you find out, Soph?'

She looked from side to side and then moved even closer. He could now smell her perfume: light, delicate, barely noticeable.

'The list office,' she said. 'Some dozy old sod only goes and faxes the notice of application to the defence solicitors, not the pros.'

'And I hoped you'd infiltrated the secret state.'

'There's always time,' she smiled.

They now stood under the high dome of the oldest part of the Bailey.

'They'll never let you in,' Dan said.

'Don't care. I'll hang around embarrassing the lot of them.'

They stood outside Court 1, where police officers in flak jackets and automatic weapons stood guard. The doors themselves had been cordoned off with high grey barriers.

'So where are you going?' she asked him again.

'Court One,' he replied.

The news stunned her into silence. She spent the next few seconds examining him with deep suspicion. 'What are you up to, Daniel Becket?'

'Job interview.'

She spun around in front of him and prodded him in the chest. 'They're never getting you on the pros team?'

'Neville Neale wants me.'

'Well, I want you – on the defence, I mean.'

The two policemen looked at the barristers with increasing interest. One officer had his automatic cradled across his chest and caressed the barrel.

'I'd better go,' Dan said.

'Tell them I'm outside and I know what they're up to.'

'What's that?'

'Well, I don't sodding know. Just tell them.'

He nodded once and then approached the armed police.

*   *   *

Robert Lancing sat in the front row of Court 1 with his wig
on the bench beside him. He was engaged in a frantic, hushed
conversation with two men in neatly pressed grey trousers and
blue blazers. They looked up anxiously as Dan reached the front
of the dark wooden court with its antique ambience. One of them
was Grail.

The prosecutor smiled to himself. 'I've been hearing all sorts
of things about you.'

Dan froze instantly, wondering whether Lancing's comment
was an oblique reference to the bombing case fiasco the previous
year. Grail smiled but did not say a word.

'Sophie Chase has been telling me all sorts of good things
about you,' Lancing continued. 'She said you'd been in the Big
Apple ... the Land of the Free ... the Big—'

'Brooklyn, actually. So what can you tell me about the
case?'

It was now that Grail began to speak. 'Have you decided to
accept our offer, Mr Becket?'

'The jury's still out on that one,' Dan replied.

'The trial will go ahead. Neville Neale wants the best juniors he
can get.' Grail suddenly looked towards Lancing, embarrassed.
'Including, er, Mr Lancing, of course.'

'Do shut up, Grail,' Lancing hissed. 'Point is, Becket, Neale
for some reason rates you. So what is it? Yes or no?'

Dan took in the competitive edge to Lancing's voice. 'Maybe,'
he said.

'You've got to decide now.'

'Sophie Chase is outside,' Dan added mischievously.

Lancing and Grail looked at each other, astonished.

'She says she knows what you're up to,' Dan continued.

Lancing was by now fuming. 'Well, we'd tell the defence in
due course anyway.'

Grail looked at Dan and winked. 'So can we tell Mr Becket
now?'

Lancing huffed mightily. 'We're doing a bit of vetting, that's
all.'

'Of the jury?' Dan asked.

'Of the jury panel.'

'Why?'

'All we'll do, for heaven's sake, is check their MI5 files.' Dan looked on aghast as Lancing continued. 'Amazing what you find. Now, if we had been allowed to see the MI5 files of the barristers in the case, *that* would have been interesting.'

'Does the judge know?'

'He was the first person we vetted.' Lancing again smiled to himself. 'Only joking. We have to eliminate any subversives, social workers from Hackney. Ex-members of CND, that sort of thing.'

Dan looked around the empty courtroom. 'Are there any nuclear missiles hidden away in this case that I have missed?'

'Metaphorical ones, Becket. Metaphorical missiles, that's all.'

'I don't understand.'

'Yours is not to reason why, Becket. It will just depend on how the defence is run as to how much of the background to all this will come out.'

'Defence?'

'Montford's defence. He could keep his head down, his mouth shut, and walk out of here. Or he could ... be awkward. That would be MAD.'

'As in crazy?'

'As in Mutually Assured Destruction. Of Montford and the ministry and good old Mother England.'

'You're exaggerating,' Dan said.

Robert Lancing shuffled in his seat and crossed his right leg over his left, exposing hideous red, white and blue socks. 'Am I?' he said.

Chapter 5

A short silence descended upon the three men, only broken when the court door was opened. An armed officer led the way with an elderly barrister, greying, with a gentle face, trailing reluctantly in his wake. It was Neville Neale, QC. Neale whispered something to the young officer which caused the constable to troop out of court with a look of annoyance.

Once he had disappeared completely, Neale approached Dan. 'Boys with toys,' he said, grinning.

'He was just doing his job,' Lancing retorted.

'And I'm just doing mine. This is a court of law, not a battlefield. No guns inside, thank you.'

As Dan watched the banter between Neale and Lancing, he remembered that it was in this very court that he had conducted his first murder case. Neale had led him in the prosecution of a vagrant who was accused of abducting a young girl and then leaving the defiled body in a golf course bunker. The tabloids had been baying for blood, the police had cut corners to get the conviction, and there was a hostile crowd outside court. But Neale had risen above it all. He had been scrupulously fair and the man was acquitted. At the time, Dan had been terribly disappointed, but Neale was as composed as ever. The prosecution wins no victories and suffers no defeats, he reminded Dan. It was his favourite phrase. Five months later, a member of a paedophile ring confessed to the golf course murder.

All this had happened in Court 1. And as Dan sat in counsel's row again, he was filled with contradictory emotions: the satisfaction of professional success, the pain of the victims he had seen, men wrongly accused, others rightly accused and walking free, the hours of work he had put in, the cost, the sacrifice of his family life. Sleepless nights. Did he want to go through it all again?

But the great drama of the courtroom again allured him. In theory, Court 1 was the most hallowed hall of criminal justice: it was here that Crippen was sentenced to death; from the ageing rows of dark oak the great Sir Edward Marshall Hall defended Victorian murderers in the days when the defendant was referred to solely as the 'prisoner'.

Towards the rear of the court the dock rose like a cage of wood and wrought iron. Counsel's row and the jury box ran down opposite walls so that the Bar and its audience sat in direct confrontation. Between the wooden jury box and the Bench was the witness box. This layout was no longer fashionable in courtroom architecture, but the result was that the jurors had to look up and to their left to see the witness, only a matter of feet from them; so near, Dan felt, that they would instantly smell the defendant's lies.

The public was excluded from the well of the court as if it were unclean. Spectators had to make do with a gallery twenty feet above proceedings, from where they could look down on justice being done in their name. It was a space of dark wood, worn leather and cloth, reverberating with the majesty of the law as depicted by the royal coat of arms above the judge's chair: *Dieu et mon droit*. It was beautiful and terrible and magnificent and cruel. It was the only place in which to be seen for a criminal barrister who aspired to the heights of his profession.

Neale put down his brief, a muddle of papers haphazardly folded, half hanging out of the pink legal tape that was supposed to bind it neatly.

'Now why are we here today?' he asked Lancing.

The junior barrister's face clouded with irritation. 'The P.I.I., Neville,' he said, as if speaking to a small child.

Dan had never been able to work out if Neale put on his eccentric Englishman act deliberately. It certainly annoyed the hell out of his opponents and endeared him to juries. He simply appeared too dotty to be pulling the wool over people's eyes. So he was invariably trusted.

He turned slowly to Dan and said, 'How are you keeping, Daniel?'

'Fine.'

'And little Chrissy?'

Dan was surprised that somewhere in Neale's cluttered mind he had stored away his daughter's name. 'Fine too, Neville.'

'Must be grown up?'

'Nearly.'

'At nursery school yet?'

Dan smiled to himself. 'She's thirteen, Neville.'

The elderly barrister looked at Dan in great confusion. 'Are you sure? 'Course you are. Your daughter and all that.' He returned Dan's smile, having apparently convinced himself that Dan's daughter was allowed to be thirteen and he hadn't misplaced a few years. 'Now, Daniel, can I assume you'll come aboard the good ship War Crimes?'

'No.'

'Ah.'

'Yes, ah,' Dan said.

Neale paused and looked at him intensely. 'Little Chrissy's really thirteen?'

'Really.'

Neale turned to Grail. 'Now, Detective, what can your boys do to persuade Mr Becket here to join our happy crew?'

'We'll think of something.'

'Well, while you're thinking, Lancing and I'd better go see the judge. And perhaps the CPS should come to court, too.'

Neale picked up his mess of papers. Lancing tutted under his breath but followed to the back of the court behind the bench where the judge's clerk was now waiting. Just before Neale disappeared, he turned back to Dan.

'Little Charlotte's really thirteen? I mean, I was at the christening.'

Dan didn't have the heart to correct the name. 'Yes, she is,' he replied.

Once the two of them were alone, Grail moved very close to Dan.

'We're meeting in chambers tomorrow,' he said. 'Will you be there?'

'Maybe,' Dan replied.

Grail showed no sign of emotion at the answer and busied himself inspecting a file of case documents. Dan, for his part, took the opportunity to leave court as a CPS rep entered.

Outside, Sophie was pacing up and down impatiently. When she spotted Dan she rushed up to him.

'So what's going on?'

'They'll tell you shortly, Soph.'

'So you can tell me now.'

Dan stared at her, shaking his head.

'Jesus,' she said. 'Why do you always have to be so bloody perfect?'

'Lancing wouldn't agree.'

'He's jealous.'

'Jealous?'

It was more than she had wished to say. Of course, she had told Lancing before Christmas that it was Dan who she really was interested in, and no doubt part of Lancing's hostility towards him stemmed from that fact. But Lancing was the past. Dan, she had a vague inkling, could be the future. If only she knew how to create the right situation.

'What are you doing tonight?' she blurted out. She couldn't understand why where Dan was concerned her buried feelings seemed to bypass her brain and spew themselves out in a torrent of embarrassing words.

'I'm washing my hair,' he replied.

She wanted to laugh, but was unsure if he was simply snubbing her. 'Look, there's a party on HMS *Belfast* tonight, a chambers one,' she said.

'Who will be there?'

'Me.'

'Anyone else I might know?'

'Oh, barristers, I guess.'

'Name some.'

She knew that this would be the stumbling block, that once she mentioned what it was really about, Dan would refuse. But he had a right to know. She half closed her eyes and blurted it out rapidly. 'It's technically to celebrate Julian Waugh being made up into a QC. I know, I know, you're not exactly in love with Waugh, but I'll be there and—'

'I'm seeing someone tonight – as well as washing my hair.'

Her head dropped. She gazed up through her eyelashes, trying to look a little sheepish. 'I know it's not any of my business, but is it someone from New York?'

'Yes.'

'Oh.'

'It's not a woman, Soph. It's just a family commitment, that's all.'

'Well, can't you come along just for a while?'

'I'll see.'

'Promise?'

'I said I'll see, Soph.'

She watched him as he opened the glass doors and disappeared into the first-floor lobby. She could faintly see the muscles of his thighs rippling under the material of his midnight-blue suit. Shortly after that, she went up to the robing room alone. She'd corner Lancing later, she decided, and then well and truly embarrass him about his sneaking around in court. She took off her wig and folded her gown. As she stood before a mirror, examining the traces of lines around her eyes, she wondered what her friend Vivienne would have thought of her invitation to Dan.

Chapter 6

In the early evening, Dan heard the front doorbell ring twice. Even through the wooden frame he could hear the idling engine of a black cab outside, and he knew that it was Jo.

He hesitated for just a moment before he opened the door. He took two deep breaths to compose himself, telling himself that he had lived all his life without a father and if things didn't work out with Jo, then he would be back where he had started. But just as he clicked the double lock, he glimpsed himself in the mirror on the left-hand wall.

The ceramic frame was painted with tiny blue and yellow flowers, cascading down each side of the reflective glass. Vivienne had haggled her way into an outrageous bargain in the Portobello market the month before she died, and consequently the mirror was her pride and joy. It seemed odd to him that this one item, out of all the other accumulated flotsam of a marriage, reminded him most of his wife.

Undoubtedly it was an overstatement to say that Viv, like the mirror, had let him see himself more clearly, but she had taught him to appreciate beautiful things in a way that his Catholic mother, who saw the world as a cesspit of sin, could never do. And the most beautiful and the most important thing in life, Viv believed, was the family. Perhaps this was why this mirror, surrounded by family coats and scarves, barely above the handlebars of Chrissy's bike, was so important to his wife. Now, as his eyes met those of the Irish-Jewish-Catholic widower in the mirror, he knew that he had just deceived himself. He *desperately* wanted to get to know Jo, to get to like him, to be liked – loved? – back. He wasn't prepared to go back to being a fatherless son.

Jo stood at the bottom of the four worn steps that led to the door. And Dan thought that, a little like a salesman, he must have rung the bell and then retreated down the steps awaiting a response. Perhaps he, too, was nervous? He stood with hunched shoulders, a battered leather suitcase in his left hand, the hand with the camp numbers. In his right, he held a small pot plant wrapped in cellophane which he thrust towards Dan.

'Hi, Jo. Thanks—'

'It's not for you. You got change?' Jo replied, not advancing a single step.

'Change?'

'Only this joker in the cab don't take credit cards. Don't even take American Express. Can you believe that one? I offered him fifty dollars but—'

'I'll take care of it,' Dan said. 'Come in. Can I help you with your—'

Jo clenched his left fist, raising the suitcase three or four inches. 'It ain't heavy. I ain't staying that long.'

As his father passed him on the top step, muttering a short sentence in a language Dan didn't understand, Dan reached for the wallet in his jacket pocket. He found a twenty-pound note and went to pay the cabbie, leaving the plant on the floor beside Chrissy's bike. Then he mounted the steps in two bounds on his way back and, once through the threshold, caught himself again in the painted mirror. There were five droplets of sweat on his forehead and his breathing was short and irregular. So much for composure.

Jo had dumped his grubby suitcase in the middle of Vivienne's cherished white lounge carpet. He sat, half disappearing in the cushions of the sofa, his feet crossed on the wood and glass coffee table in front of him.

'Well,' Dan said, 'here we are.'

Jo did not answer and stared resolutely at the scuff marks his tatty shoes were making on the erstwhile pristine glass tabletop.

'Home,' Dan said.

Jo looked up with tired eyes. 'Your home.'

Don't get rattled, Dan told himself. Be cheerful, think happy thoughts, above all don't let the miserable old git get you down. 'Come on, Jo,' he smiled. 'England used to be your home, too. For ten years after the war.'

Jo made a muffled clicking sound and again muttered to himself in his private tongue. 'You just don't understand, do you?'

'Understand what?'

'I ain't got no home. Haven't since the camps.'

'Come on.'

Dan felt a cool trickle of sweat tracing the line of his spine. This was the room in which Vivienne and he had argued, the room in which he had seen her alive for the last time. But through all the devastation and the pain, this house, this building was still home. It was where he and Chris felt safe; he wasn't going to let his father ruin it.

'When Viv died,' Dan began, 'I thought about moving. But why should I? This is the place where my daughter grew up. It's where she's been happy and loved. It's her home.'

Jo softly kicked the table away from himself and walked with small, rolling steps to the bay window that gave on to the street.

'That's just it,' he said. 'Since the camps, there's been no place I felt safe. Or happy. Or ... loved, I guess. But that last one is simple. Since I left your mother, I ain't had nobody to love me.'

Dan stared at the gentle curve of his father's back. There was pain in the old man's voice, though he tried to hide it, and Dan was determined to reach him. 'It needn't stay that way, Jo.'

There was no reply.

'Jo, I said ... I mean—'

'I know what you mean, but I'm just trouble. I've had a whole lot of bad things done to me and I've done a load of bad things back.' Finally, he turned around, and there was the hint of a smile in his eyes. 'But anyway,' he said, 'I'm glad you invited me to your home. Now where's your john?'

'John?'

'Bathroom, restroom, toilet, lavatory, loo. Yeah, loo, that's what your mother used to call it.'

Dan smiled. 'She used to tick me off if I called it a toilet.'

'You too? Now there's a thing.'

'Would you like something to eat?'

'Bathroom and bed, that's about all I need. Think you can manage that?'

'I think so,' Dan said. 'I'm going to go out to a legal function

tonight. I might be back for dinner. But there's food in the fridge,'
he continued. 'Will you be all right?'

'Where'd you put my plant?' Jo asked.

'In the hall.'

'Needs watering.'

'I can water it,' Dan said.

Jo shook his head. 'It's one of them temperamental ones. Fuss
too much and you kill it.'

Dan felt that there was a warning in the comment that was
aimed directly at him, but he didn't have time to agonise over
it. He persuaded himself that he was just being over-sensitive.
'Who's looking after your plants in New York?' he asked.

'One of the guys,' Jo said. There was a sad look in his eyes,
though his mouth sketched a faint smile. 'Ira used to do it. If I
went down to Atlantic City for a few days.'

'You must miss him terribly,' Dan said.

'He was a drunk.' Jo scowled. Then his features softened again.
'A God-fearing, crazy, decent drunk. The best kind.'

'When I found him . . .' Dan began, hesitant about raising so
delicate a matter, although he wanted to show his father how he
felt. 'I was sad about Ira. Relieved it wasn't you.' He paused, then
decided that he wanted to say it. 'Could it have been you?'

Jo looked back at him intensely. 'You mean, should it have been
me?' He laughed aloud, but it was clear that he was laughing at
himself, at what he was. 'Why would anyone want to kill me?
Why'd I want to kill myself? I'm a . . . goddamn saint.'

By the time Sophie got home that evening, she was already
behind schedule. The Tube from Temple had dawdled, and for
a reason that was not explained for ten minutes had come to
a grinding halt just outside Victoria station. Just as the tempers
of her fellow commuters had reached boiling point and people
were muttering about the Citizens' Charter, the driver cleared his
throat over the intercom. Someone, he said, had fallen under the
preceding train.

Next, the lift in her block of flats had decided that it preferred
to operate without residents actually inside it – a sound decision,
Sophie thought, considering how obnoxious most of her neighbours were – and was to be seen hurtling up and down between
floors while the concierge hammered away at the control panel.

On an average day, this chronicle of setbacks would have washed over her without trace, part of the supposedly rich tapestry of living in London, but ever since Helen had come to stay with her – in fact before that, since the dreadful night in hospital – the world had evolved for Sophie into a sinister place full of ominous signs. For example, why was it, she wondered, that as the Tube finally crawled through Victoria station, she had briefly glimpsed ambulancemen standing helplessly around a stretcher on which there was a body covered with a blanket? This morbid sign combined with the saga of the lift made her shudder. Not for herself, but for Helen. Consequently, she charged up the staircase even though she was weighed down with an awkwardly shaped bag containing her wig and gown, another containing Archbold, the ancient criminal text now as heavy as several telephone directories, and a brief bag tenuously clutched by a couple of spare fingertips. As she went round and round, up and up, she fought against fleeting pictures in her mind that returned her to the Victoria platform; but now her Tube had stopped and she was being led to the stretcher. She saw herself struggling against the ambulancemen, but they forced her to the side of the body, only inches away; from here she could see the blanket like a soft, red shroud over the face of the victim. She imagined her fingers trembling as they crept towards the edge of the blanket, and she held her breath as she pulled it back. The hair she saw was the colour of Helen's hair, yet the skin had a bluish shine from the electrified tracks. And when she finally saw the face, it was that of her sister, not as she was now, but in her youth.

The sound of Sophie's footsteps thundered louder in the stairwell as she rushed up the final flight. Her eyes misted with panic; her bags rattled around her body, knocking out of her such strained breaths as she had managed to draw. She stumbled on the last step and her shin scraped painfully against the rough concrete, but she could now see her front door. Throwing her bags down, she rang the bell twice, three times, but got no answer. Then she smelt burning.

From inside her flat emanated a strong smell of burning flesh. A sweet, sickly smell that made bile rise in her throat as she struggled to find her keys in her bag. She dropped them once, and cursed between clenched teeth as the key-ring made a strange tinkling sound on the floor. When she bent down, the stench was even stronger. Finally she managed to slide the key into the lock and the door flew open with her weight pressed against it. Confusion instantly filled her mind. It was totally dark within.

'Helen?' she cried. Then louder, 'Hel-en?'

She advanced further inside, knocking her leg, the same shin, against a side table.

In the darkness, the smell of burning felt like a physical barrier against which she had to fight. But before she could call her sister's name again, or even reach for the light switch, the room was flooded with light.

Helen appeared in the doorway between the living room and the kitchen, the sequined black top she wore shimmering in the sudden brightness.

'Dinner is served,' she exclaimed like an over-excited child.

'God, Helen,' Sophie cried. 'Something's burning.'

'Something was burning. The main course. But it's in the bin now. Panic over?'

Sophie ran across the lounge and pushed past her sister to get into the kitchen. Once there, an acrid smell tore at the back of her throat, causing her to cough painfully. She grabbed a dish-cloth and put it over her mouth as she saw two charred hunks of meat on top of the bin, still exuding black smoke like dirty flares. Grasping them in one hand, she momentarily dropped the cloth and forced open the kitchen window. It jammed. She had been meaning to get the concierge to have a look at it and now, of all times, it jammed. The meat, what was left of it, was still warm in her hands, but she used all her strength to squeeze it into a tight ball and then, bending over slightly, flung it out of the three inches the window had opened. Helen watched from the door.

'You've thrown that on Mrs Collins' roof terrace,' she said.

Sophie did not reply. She hurried into the lounge and opened all the windows. Finally, when she felt fresh air pouring through her nostrils and into her lungs, she slumped on to the sofa exhausted.

'Not hungry?' Helen asked. 'Well, I'll start anyway.'

'Where's Marie?' she demanded, referring to the home help.

'I sent her away. I wanted to surprise you.'

At the word surprise, Sophie couldn't help but burst out laughing, principally with relief. 'Darling,' she said, 'I don't like you being alone.'

'And I don't like people.'

'Why not?'

'They're all bastards.'

'Thanks.'

'You're not people,' Helen said. 'You're my bossy little sister.'

Helen now sat at the dining table that was shoved against one wall in the lounge. It rarely saw action, being relegated to the status of a convenient spot for junk mail and old newspapers while the two sisters ate TV dinners on the sofa. But this night Helen had set the table with long blue candles shoved crookedly into the pair of silver candlesticks their grandmother had left them.

'You eating?' Helen called.

For the first time since she had arrived home, Sophie thought about the chambers party on the *Belfast*. But now that the nanny had been sent away, how could she go?

'I'm meant to be going out tonight,' she said.

'You can still eat.'

'I'm not going.'

Helen began tapping gently with the back of a teaspoon on an egg in a plastic eggcup in front of her. There was another egg set at Sophie's place at the table.

'You know,' Helen mused, 'I used to love the nursery teas Nanny used to make.'

'We didn't have a nanny,' Sophie tried to explain patiently.

Helen put down her teaspoon carefully. She paused for a couple of seconds before she spoke, ensuring than Sophie looked directly at her. 'So why do I need a nanny now?' she asked.

Suddenly there was a different mood in the room. Sophie got up immediately, surveying her sister's face as it stared back defiantly at her.

'What are you trying to prove, Helen?'

For a moment, something deep inside Helen choked her and she was unable to speak. Then she said softly, 'I . . . I'm not a child, Soph. I wanted to show you I could cope.'

Sophie was at her side and took her hand. 'Of course you'll be able to cope, it just takes time.'

'I'm frightened, Soph.'

'I'm here.'

'I'm afraid of what I've become.'

Sophie hugged her as Helen began to cry, and she felt sick with grief as her elder sister wept on her shoulder.

'You're still my Helen,' she said. 'You're still my big sister.'

'So you don't hate me?'

'I love you.'

Helen pulled back so that she could see into Sophie's eyes.

'You do?' she asked.

'Of course, I ... I can't say I love your cooking.'

They both burst out laughing.

'You always were better at domestic science,' Helen said.

'And I was crap.'

Helen stroked Sophie's hair. 'Please go out. I know you want to see Dan.'

'I ... I can't leave—'

'I phoned Carol Lowry. She's coming over.'

'But you hate Carol Lowry.'

'Exactly. I've invited her for dinner.'

Again Sophie laughed, hoping that this was the first sign of real improvement. After all, this was the first time that Helen had arranged for one of her old girlfriends to come around.

'I'm not leaving till Carol comes,' Sophie said.

'You can trust me.'

'Bollocks.'

'Good point.' Helen smiled.

'I'm going to take a shower.'

'You need one. You stink of smoke.'

Sophie grabbed a linen napkin and flung it at her sister. Not to be outdone, Helen flung one back.

'Do you like me living here?' she asked.

Sophie ducked as another napkin flew at her. 'Like is not the word for it.'

'Well ...' Helen said, suddenly stopping. 'I ... like living with you, Soph. I mean, you're a bossy cow, but I like living here. I always want to live with you. Even when you marry Dan.'

'Who says I'm going to marry Dan?'

'I can be like ... the dark family secret. The crazy old woman who lives upstairs in the attic.'

'I live in a block of flats. I don't have an attic.'

'Well, get one.'

*   *   *

The HMS *Belfast* was anchored off the South Bank of the Thames between London Bridge and Tower Bridge. The vessel was painted predominantly battleship grey, but the deck was lit by a multitude of party lights, creating a multi-coloured apron in the water below. The huge guns were blocked at the ends.

The party to celebrate Julian Waugh's elevation to the ranks of Queen's Counsel, his silking party, consisted of two hundred barristers with a comparable number of spouses, partners and significant others, six hundred bottles of cheap German hock and a mountain of uneaten, inedible canapés of the type that would be swept up at the end of the evening and used by the caterers at the next do.

Sophie spotted Dan immediately he came aboard. 'Glad you managed to walk the gangplank,' she said, rushing up to him.

'I'm not so sure Waugh will be delighted to see me.'

'Rubbish. The invite said Miss Sophie Chase of counsel "plus one". Well, you're the one. Besides, he's sloshed somewhere amidships boring everyone with his court martial stories.'

'It's nice to see you, Soph.'

'Didn't think you would come. I thought you said you had a visitor.'

'He's asleep.'

'A long-lost cousin?'

'I think the operative term is definitely long-lost. Talking about relations, how is Helen?'

Sophie tried to smile bravely, but knew instantly that he would see through it.

'I'm sorry,' he said.

She took him by the hand and led him through the ranks of half-inebriated revellers to the stern of the ship. It was already dark, and the lights of an all-white steamer shone brightly as the vessel slid towards Tower Bridge.

'I'll get us a drink,' she said when they reached the rails. He could see that she was determined to put on a brave face. 'All they've got is German, I'm afraid. Will that do?'

'It'll have to.'

'Back in a sec. Don't talk to any strange men.' She turned with an exaggerated toss of her blond bob. 'And don't talk to *any* strange women.'

Dan found himself alone at the stern of the ship. As he surveyed the eddies in the water, he tried to decide whether the tide was coming in or going out. Five or six miles up the river to the west, he knew, Jo would be in bed asleep. As it flowed in the opposite direction, the Thames opened out past Greenwich and Tilbury until it reached the sea. Beyond that was the Continent and, finally, Neuwelt concentration camp. He watched a branch caught in an eddy spin around and around. Then he heard someone calling his name from the river bank.

It was Yuri.

Chapter 7

Yuri stood in the half-light, a silhouette more than a shadow, looking to all the world like someone innocently walking along the South Bank. He had a card or a slip of paper held tightly between the fingers of his right hand, and his raincoat was loosely tied. He did not repeat Dan's name. Dan quickly calculated that he could ignore Yuri, pretend maybe that he was someone else, but it wouldn't work. Yuri had found him and could undoubtedly find him again. But, of course, this was London. Around Dan were dozens of members of his profession. He felt somehow safer than in New York, and for better or for worse this was an opportunity to resolve the matter once and for all.

He glanced around twice and, seeing no sign of Sophie or the drinks, he moved unobtrusively to the gangway. When he arrived on the bank, Yuri said nothing but began to walk upriver towards the landing stage for the Thames ferry. They passed the deserted shops of Hays Galleria in silence. It was only when they were in the covered passages darkened by the shadows of London Bridge that Yuri began to speak.

'I'm sorry it's taken me so long to get back to you,' he said.

Dan decided not to reply but surveyed the deeply hewn lines across the man's face.

'Mr Becket ... I said—'

'Why are you here?'

'I'm here to protect you, Dan.'

'From what?'

'From yourself – I'm here to protect your *daughter* from a stubborn streak in you. Something ... wilful in you, Dan, that will get her hurt.'

Again Dan was grateful that Chrissy was out of reach, at the western end of the island, in one sense closer to New York, but a safe distance from London.

'Have you accepted the Montford war crimes case yet?' Yuri asked, half turning his head, accentuating the chiselled profile of his forehead.

'I haven't decided yet.'

'*We* have decided for you.'

'Why do you need me?'

'Montford will be prosecuted for what he did in the war. That must happen. But he will also be acquitted – unless other steps are taken.'

'But why me?'

'It could have been someone else. A barrister with a son instead of a daughter. Someone with a mistress or a – what's the word? – a rent boy, instead of a past.'

'A past?'

Yuri took two precise steps away from Dan and then spun on his heels. 'Do you often think of the two Kurds, two innocent men rotting in prison?'

Dan should have guessed that this secret would have been dug up, unearthed and dusted off for use against him.

'Just as they *had* to be convicted, so Montford has to be acquitted. It is just the way the Establishment wants it to be, Mr Becket.' His voice hung on the last phrase. 'But not the way it *must* be. Not with your help.'

'And if I refuse?'

'You won't refuse.'

Yuri examined the card in his hand with great deliberation, holding it eighteen inches from his eyes, changing its angle two, five degrees, until it caught the light coming from the top of London Bridge above.

'I understand you have a very beautiful country, not that I've seen all of it, any of it, really – busy as I've been with our case.' There was an ominous certainty in the way in which he asserted that the impending war crimes trial was something he *already* shared with Dan. 'But,' Yuri continued, 'I may well see the West Country. Cornwall or Dorset or . . . perhaps Devon. Which would you recommend?'

He gave Dan the card. It was the postcard Dan had sent Chrissy from the hotel in New York. The postcard with the

Devon address of her grandparents on it. Written in Dan's hand.

'Do you remember Dmitri?' the man asked. 'Friendly young man, started at your hotel the same time you arrived?'

Dan looked on, sickened.

'Russian,' the man continued. 'But there are so many Russians in New York these days. Difficult to know. Who is a friend and who is ... I'm told you gave him the postcard to frank ...'

His voice trailed off as a police barge shot the central arch of the bridge, sending dark, thick waves, topped with off-white foam, towards the shore. They lapped against the stone walls rising vertically from the water.

'How many times, I wonder, have you thought of going to the police once I approached you? They might be able to help and then all this trouble would go away. But then again, they might not. Is that a risk that you can afford to take?'

Dan had prosecuted two cases in which his star witness had gone to the authorities, told them everything, been taken into protective custody, made part of the witness protection programme. One of them had been fine. Resettled. Safe. The tongue of the other was neatly wrapped in a cardboard box and sent to the presiding judge at the Old Bailey. Dan wondered now which way he would end up if he went to the police. But it was not just his own safety that was at risk. Yuri had located Dan's weak spot, his daughter, Chris.

'You will prosecute the case. You will use our evidence. And you will win. Montford has everything at stake. And so do you.'

'But why are you so determined to get Montford?' Dan asked.

Yuri looked into the Thames once more. The waves were rapidly settling and soon there would be no trace of the police barge at all. 'In 1945, Simon Montford ordered an execution,' he said. 'Of a Russian.'

From the deck of the *Belfast*, Sophie saw Dan Becket walking slowly back towards the ship. His head was hanging and both hands were buried deep into his trouser pockets. He looked as if any moment he could jump off the river bank and disappear without trace beneath the surface of the

Thames. She couldn't remember ever having seen Dan like this.

Well, she said to herself, you certainly have this *great* effect on men. First date – he doesn't realise that it's our first date, but that's not the point – and he cannot decide whether to do a runner or commit suicide.

As Dan reached the bottom of the gangway, he was challenged by the two bouncers at the bottom. They wore the black jackets and bow ties that seemed to be *de rigueur* for those licensed to threaten GBH with impunity.

Sophie called down, 'He's with me.'

'Sorry, luv,' the smaller, marginally less Neanderthal of the two called. 'He hasn't got an invite.'

'He *had* an invite,' she called. 'Let him up or I'll personally ask the Assistant Commissioner of the Met over there to run a CRO check on all members of the security staff. I'm sure you'll both pass with flying colours.'

There was a stereophonic gritting of teeth at this threat to examine their criminal records, and Dan was let on to the ship. He had a lost, wounded look in his eyes, one that made him appear more vulnerable.

'What's the matter?' she asked.

'I miss my daughter.'

'So bring her up to London.'

He stared at Sophie, his head slightly tilted to one side and a look of genuine enquiry on his face. 'Do you really think I should?'

'Look, Dan. Girls can get into a lot more trouble away from home than they ever can under your own roof. Believe me, I've been there.'

Of course, Sophie had her own agenda. If Dan brought Chrissy up to London, Soph would have the opportunity to see him more.

'I think you're right,' he said, but he still seemed miles away. 'I think she'll be better off with me.'

'There's a jazz band downstairs.'

'Some other time, Soph.'

'So there'll be another time?' She cringed and held her breath; what if he said no?

'Another time for what?'

You were too pushy and now look what has happened. Regroup. Change the subject. 'Dan, as you were walking along the embankment, there was someone – I know this must sound weird – but there seemed to be someone following you.'

She saw him looking across the water as waves rhythmically struck against the stone walls, then his gaze wandered up the river to the black arches below London Bridge.

'Just shadows,' he said.

'No, but—'

He suddenly took her wrist. 'Listen, Sophie. It was just shadows. Do you understand?'

She nodded when she saw his eyes again. Now she was certain that he was in some kind of pain, but for the moment the hurt was somewhere beyond her reach.

Chapter 8

Jo was sitting in the lounge when Dan returned home. His feet were up on the glass coffee table as before, but there was a delicious smell of cooking onions and lightly spiced meat that emanated from the kitchen and warmed the house.

'Smells great, Jo,' Dan said, walking towards the matching armchair that faced the sofa. 'What is it?'

'Goulash.'

'One of your Russian specials?'

'Never made it before. And goulash is Hungarian,' Jo said, picking up a book from the small pile next to his shoes on the table. 'Saw a recipe on the notice-board in the kitchen, buried below all those fast-food flyers.'

The realisation that this was something Vivienne had carefully cut out from a Sunday supplement shortly before her death filled Dan with a dull pain that started at the back of his head, where the connection was made, and then seeped downwards, taking with it the last dregs of his energy.

Jo put down the book. 'Your wife's recipe, huh?'

Dan nodded. He found that he had sat down on the arm of the chair in a way he constantly scolded Chrissy for doing.

'That's tough,' Jo said. 'Just when you thought it was safe, huh?'

'Something like that.'

'You still hurting?'

'I've never really got over it.'

'Think you were meant to?'

'No.'

'I think us Jews and you Catholics are pretty much the same on that one.'

'How do you mean?'

Jo shuffled his feet on the table and said, 'We both understand suffering, that's all. Now this is going to sound a little crazy, but sometimes ... you know, sometimes when I'm alone, I think it was worse to survive the camps.'

Dan gazed across the white rug at his father's intelligent eyes. He noticed how they were still young and alert, perhaps as they had been when he was first captured by the Nazis half a century before. He was relieved that he could not see the numbers scratched into his arm.

'You see,' Jo continued, 'we saw things in those camps no human beings that *ever* walked the planet had seen. This was a new kind of killing and no one could tell us what we should make of it, you know, what we should think. We didn't have names for what they were doing.'

He paused and half closed his eyes, as if trying to connect the time and place in which he found himself with the distant time of the camps.

'There was this one fellah. He tried to escape. Caught trying to claw his way under the wires. So the guards let the dogs chew most of the flesh from his leg. I remember it sort of hung down like stringy meat. Then they brought him back to the square where we used to have the roll-call, and they brought us all out. They made a big fire in the centre and roped him up to some gallows above it. The more he struggled from the flames, the more the rope strangled him. Eventually, you know, he couldn't fight any more. The flames crept up his body and I saw him burn before my eyes ...'

The pungent smell of simmering meat from the kitchen made Dan want to throw up. Warm odours wafted into the lounge, cloying and sickly. He walked slowly to the bay and forced open all the windows.

'Should be about ready,' Jo said, heading for the kitchen.

'You can *eat*?'

Jo smiled and a myriad of wrinkles appeared on his face. 'You know, I figured a long time back, life goes on. I don't think too much about why all my friends in the camp died. But I can't work out why – out of the whole lot of them – it was me who was allowed to live.'

'Any idea?'

'To make amends. For what I did. But most of all for revenge.'

'Revenge? On who?'

'On all those bastards at Neuwelt,' Jo said, wiping his left shoe on his right trouser leg. 'D'you mind me wearing my shoes all over? But if you took anything off in Neuwelt, it was gone. A habit I can't seem to—'

'You were at *Neuwelt*? Oh my God, Jo. You never said.'

'You never asked. Look, I better check dinner – don't want the thing to burn.'

Dan was left alone in the lounge. As the door slowly closed behind Jo, the light faded from the room. Opposite him, his father's impression was still left in the cushions of the sofa. Dan smiled to himself when he saw the scuff marks from Jo's shoes clearly visible on the coffee table.

But he was convinced that the exchange had cast a new light on things. Yuri's comment that any barrister could have been chosen to prosecute the war crimes case suddenly appeared to be the nonsense Dan had always suspected. But he had never guessed the reason. His own father was at Neuwelt.

That night, Dan was lost in a deep sleep, having allowed himself to relax for the first time in weeks. He had put clean sheets on both Jo's bed and his own, and the smell of the fresh linen combined with the relief he felt, sensing that now he had a way to rid himself of the trial, caused him to lapse into a series of vivid dreams.

But at four in the morning, he suddenly awoke with a start. He looked around quickly in the half-light, unsure whether he was now asleep or awake. All he knew was that he had heard a scream.

He felt uncomfortable. His hair and the pillow were drenched with his sweat. Around the bottom edge of the curtains, there was a vague halo of yellowing light from the streetlamp outside the house, and he heard the muted drone of a car along the Uxbridge Road, fading into the stillness of the night. Again the house was silent. Dan told himself that he must have had another of his intermittent nightmares about the case. He ran his hand through his hair and shook off the excess sweat, then took the spare pillow from the other side of the bed, the left-hand side on which Viv had always slept, and tried to get back to sleep. He remembered the branch slowly spinning in the vortex of water by the *Belfast*, and as the branch began to disappear under the water, so he began to plunge into sleep. Then he heard the scream again.

This time there was no mistake. Adrenalin pumped through his body, causing the drowsiness to vanish in an instant. At first he was confused, for he knew Chrissy was down in Devon, but then he remembered: his father. Jo was screaming.

Dan raced out of his bedroom, giddy with the rush of blood to his head, stumbled along the corridor in the darkness and came up against Jo's closed door.

'Jo?' he called. 'Jo?'

There was another scream. Dan barged through the door and was stunned to see his father, not in bed, but squatting by the dressing-table, shivering and mumbling to himself.

He didn't know what to do. He remembered a decade before when Chrissy had gone through a period of sleepwalking. Then the doctor had advised Viv and him not to rouse her but to ensure she did not harm herself. Now before him his father was babbling in a tongue Dan did not recognise, his back to Dan, facing the corner. He had something in his hands.

Dan edged forward, desperate to get a better look. There was something wooden, like a stick, protruding out of Jo's fists, but although Dan couldn't be sure in the half-light, he didn't dare turn on the lights. He moved still closer. He was merely inches from his father when the torrent of words stopped. Jo calmly looked round at him.

'You all right?' he asked his son.

Dan squatted beside him and saw that he was in fact cradling the plant he had brought to the house.

'Couldn't sleep, huh?' Jo asked.

'No,' Dan whispered.

Then Jo appeared to realise where he was. He shook his head, and half grinned, half winced. 'Those Neuwelt nightmares,' he said. 'Get you every time.'

'Do you want to talk about it?'

'Yeah, sure,' Jo said. But he slowly, deliberately, stepped across the room and got into bed without saying another word. He placed the plant on the bedside table, adjusting it precisely as he wanted it.

'Goodnight,' Dan said.

But his father was already asleep.

Chapter 9

The next morning, Sophie was woken by the sound of the television at 6.30. Her alarm was not due to go off until seven, but as she buried her head under the square French pillows, she knew exactly what had happened: Helen was up.

She dragged herself out from under the duvet with her eyes still jammed closed, slid her feet into the furry slippers at the foot of the bed and pulled her thick towelling bathrobe over her nightshirt. Her well-practised autopilot had honed in on the curtains; she braced herself. Suddenly searing light flashed on to her retinas through half-closed lids; instinctively her hands went up to protect her eyes, but she forced herself to open them. She knew she had to check on her sister.

Next, the mirror, and her ritual anti-wrinkle inspection. It was an absurd affectation, she realised. After all, how could a mass of wrinkles appear on her face overnight? But this was routine. It was part of the black magic: if she stayed vigilant and purchased jars and jars of moisturisers, then perhaps she could delay the inevitable.

She manoeuvred herself to the dresser. There, on the left-hand side, next to a vase of dried red roses that had faded into a gorgeous rust, was a photograph in a heavy silver frame. It was of a happy moment in her life, her call night, the evening on which she was officially admitted into that mysterious brotherhood of barristers. And it was a *brother*hood, which just about tolerated the odd compliant sister. Five years previously, no crow's feet around her eyes then, she had worn her very own black gown for the first time. She was photographed in an ancient hall in the Temple, full of long wooden tables, with the heraldic shields of medieval knights on the walls. The face of the

twenty-four-year-old she once was beamed a little drunkenly from
the picture frame, for standing to her right was her pupilmaster,
Daniel Becket.

Now Sophie's tired eyes dwelt on those of Dan for a moment
before she dared to look into the wooden-framed mirror. Think
beautiful, she told herself, think *beautiful,* ah yes, pretty things:
jasmine, Botticellis . . . *shit.* She looked like death. That was the
greatest benefit of not living with a man, she decided, you had
the absolute right to look like a sack of shit in the morning and
no one – correction: no one male – would know.

There was raucous laughing from the lounge.

Sophie opened the bedroom door and gazed into the darkened
room. None of the curtains had been drawn, but the blue electric
light thrown by the television screen illuminated the face of her
sister, inches away from it, sitting cross-legged and naked on
the carpet.

'What's so funny, Hel?' she asked.

Helen giggled childishly at the weather forecast. 'It's going to
piss down,' she said. 'So you're going to get drenched on your
way to court.'

'Thanks.'

But Helen didn't seem to hear. Sophie took off her robe slowly
and inched towards her sister in the way you might approach a
frightened bird with a broken wing. When she was at Helen's
back, she carefully draped the warm, comforting material over
her bare shoulders.

Helen didn't seem to notice. She continued staring at the screen
and said, 'You're going to get *soaked.*'

Sophie kissed the top of her head. Ever since Helen had left
hospital, she had withdrawn into herself and her mental state had
been unpredictable. The psychiatrist whom Sophie had consulted
said that this was not unnatural after the trauma of a stillbirth.
It was some kind of healing process, a reaction. For Sophie, who
had volunteered to put up with Helen's daily tantrums, tirades of
abuse and weeping, there was a simpler explanation. Helen was
living out the childhood denied by that cruel death to her baby.

'I love you, sis,' she whispered above Helen.

There was another giggle. 'See? An inch of rain in Manchester
yesterday and it's moving south.'

'Darling, I've got to go to the magistrates court.'

Helen could not hear anything to do with the strange, distant world of adulthood: she was never an army doctor, she was never pregnant, she had never even grown up.

'So it means,' Sophie continued, 'that I'll have to leave before the au pair arrives. Can you manage?'

This attracted her attention. 'I *hate* her. She's a fucking Nazi.'

'Helen, Marie is half-French, not German.' It was a conversation they had had a dozen times.

'I don't trust her. She steals things.'

'No, she doesn't. She's here to help.'

'I don't *need* any help.'

'But I do, sis. I can't keep the place clean, cook, and run these trials at the Bar. Ask her to clean up in the kitchen, will you?'

Helen was in fact absolutely correct to smell a rat. Sometimes she seemed to understand that Marie was not an au pair. She really was a Norland nanny undercover, reluctantly agreeing not to wear the usual uniform, but to dress like one of the vast army of teenage Euro au pairs that had invaded London. Sophie had wanted proper supervision for her sister by someone qualified in – she hated to admit it – childcare. She had begged her clerks for extra work – boring civil pleadings, anything she could do in the evenings to finance it.

'Want some coffee?' she asked. But there was no answer. 'I'll make you some anyway, sis,' she said.

As she walked to the kitchen, she reflected again that Helen had refused to speak to her about the cause of the stillbirth. But one way or another, Sophie was determined to find out. In the meantime, she was grateful for every piece of work she could grab, since she had been forced to discover just how expensive nannies could be. But none the less, she was determined to honour her less lucrative commitments. That morning, for a measly guinea brief, she was to defend her Kurdish client at the East London Magistrates Court.

Sophie's Tube had been stuck for twenty infuriating minutes in a dripping tunnel somewhere near Mile End. Owing to the depth underground, her mobile did not work, so she was unable to call ahead to the court to warn them that she would be late. Then, just as she was about to scream, the train moved off.

There were perhaps twenty journalists milling around the

court lists in the foyer of the building by the time she arrived. It quickened her pulse: all were trying to find out in which courtroom the Kurd's trial would take place.

A heavy April shower had drenched the streets outside, forcing people to rush into court, holding newspapers above their heads and shaking out umbrellas. The evaporation from their bodies misted up the vast expanse of glass fronting the building, and then ran in vertical streaks towards the floor.

In the intervening months Abbas Bicak's trial had become something of a *cause célèbre*. Sophie's stay of the deportation order in the High Court in January had set the press grapevine buzzing with the promise of a scandal. One report in a tabloid sported the headline 'Refugee Sent to Saddam?' The story had then been picked up, exaggerated, distorted and reported elsewhere, resulting in a pack of journalists sniffing around for a sensational headline.

By the time Sophie arrived in the courtroom, the prosecutor was already seated with a piece of paper in his hand. All his files were closed. The CPS had wheeled out its heavyweight: it was not the woman who had prosecuted the case initially but the senior branch prosecutor, a big man with a small balding head.

'I'm for the defendant,' Sophie said, putting down her briefcase on the front row.

'Will he plead *guilty*?' The prosecutor's voice was surprisingly high-pitched and tinged with sarcasm.

'No,' she replied.

'Accept a bind-over?'

'No.'

'It's a good deal.'

'My client's not in the mood to do deals, not since his entire village was gassed by the Iraqis, who happen to be the people he was demonstrating against. Now call me a bleeding-heart liberal, but I think he's got a right to be a bit miffed about that.'

The prosecutor ran his fat hand over the bald part of his scalp, which, she noticed, was adorned with scattered droplets of sweat. The strip lighting flashed briefly in the beads of liquid when he moved his head.

'How about,' he said, glancing over his shoulder to ensure that for the moment they were alone in court, 'how about a letter to the Home Office, you know, to explain that it was all a bit of a storm in a teacup, no real harm done, shouldn't really affect the Secretary's decision to deport or not to deport, you know the sort of thing?'

'Yes, I know,' she forced herself to reply confidently. But it was an offer that she did not understand at all. Were the CPS really going to prosecute someone for an imprisonable offence and then write to a Cabinet minister to say that it really wasn't up to much anyway?

'Well?' he said, smoothing a few strands of sweaty hair from above his left ear to the top of his scalp.

'I'll have to speak to my client,' she replied.

'You've got ten minutes.'

'I'll only need five.'

Sophie buzzed at the reinforced glass reception to the cell area below the building and was let through the system of alarmed doors and into the cells. From there it was a short walk through a narrow, urinous-smelling corridor until she reached the door of her client's cell. His name had been scribbled in chalk on a board outside.

When she looked through the tiny wicket gate two-thirds of the way up the door, she saw him hunched up on the bench at the far end of the cell.

'Are you all right, Mr Bicak?' she whispered through the tiny hole in the metal door. She had to crook her neck to speak into the gap.

'My heart, the doctor say it breaks.'

'Breaks?'

'The pipes, the arteries, hard, brittle, the gas kill me,' he said, raising his head. He looked at her with huge, doleful eyes.

'I'll ask the court for more time.'

'No,' he insisted. 'Reporters, upstairs?'

'Yes.'

'The community centre contact everyone. Press release.'

Sophie thought she could see tears welling in the man's eyes, and she wanted to go in and at least touch him, comfort him, if only for a moment. 'They won't let me in the cell.'

'I know.'

'They've offered me – offered you – a bind-over and a letter to the Home Office, helping in the deportation.'

'Will it do some good?'

'I'm afraid I don't know. All I know is that it cannot do any harm.'

'I die anyway. This way, I make the news. Let them know about British government and Iraq.'

'But I thought Britain supplied arms to Iraq in the eighties—'

'Saddam rearms.'

'What?'

'War is business. Business go on. War go on.'

'So we fight the case?'

'We fight.'

He tried to stand up as he said this, and his shirt front billowed a little when he moved.

As she was let back through the security doors, Sophie could not stop worrying about the stricken man, doubled over in his darkened cell, being offered a lifeline and refusing it for a moment's publicity in court. She knew that something more newsworthy could easily steal the headlines from him: an actor might be caught in a red-light district with his pants down, a lottery winner might have been identified thanks to his former friends, a royal might be photographed skiing. Then the coverage of the Kurd case would amount to no more than a couple of filler paragraphs on an inside page – and who would read it?

When she arrived back in court, the crowd of journalists, mainly young-faced reporters, probably second-stringers, had still not been let into the courtroom. She wanted to grab each of them in turn and scream: This is a human story, a tragedy, now use it, but use it properly. However, she said nothing as she went into court.

Inside, the prosecutor was standing for the first time; there was an envelope in his right hand. 'Here it is,' he said.

'We don't want it.'

'Is he mad?'

'Maybe – but also very brave.'

'So it's a fight?'

'It's a war,' she said.

The prosecutor let out a huge sigh, puffing out his small cheeks as though he had a billiard ball in each of them. 'Very well. I suppose I'd better tell you.'

'What?'

'We're dropping the case.'

'You're doing what?'

'Not proceeding, letting it go. But no letter for your courageous Kurd. Bravery has its price, you see.'

Within three minutes, the bench of magistrates had been brought in, the journalists had been allowed to fill the public gallery, and the prosecutor was on his feet, with the drops of sweat once again sparkling all over his head.

As he read, Sophie turned slowly and looked at her client, barely visible as he sat alone in the dock, doubled up in pain.

'The prosecution has taken the decision, on the advice of counsel and having consulted with the appropriate authorities, that it would not be in the public interest to proceed with this case against Mr Bicak.'

Sophie got the distinct impression that he was addressing the press as much as the bench of magistrates.

'We take this opportunity to quash some of the unfounded rumours that have surrounded this case. In the eighties, the government created guidelines restricting the trade of chemical and biological technology to Iraq. These guidelines followed United Nations concern about the use of poison gas by Iraq against Iran in the Fao Marshes campaign of the Iran–Iraq war. However, the delegation in the instant case was a purely peaceful team of pro-democracy Iraqi exiles visiting an industrial site at Tilbury outside London. We wish to stress that they had no link with chemical or biological weapons at all and any suggestions to the contrary are totally without foundation and irresponsible.'

He finished his homily as suddenly as he had started it. The lay magistrates disappeared behind a door at the rear of the courtroom; the journalists trooped out muttering among themselves, scribbling as they walked. Before long, Sophie was left alone at the front of the court. She went to the dock where her client was still hunched up.

'It's all over,' she said to him. 'Well, this case.'

He did not look up. He seemed lost in a distant, private place, where all he felt was pain. She leant over the smooth wooden edge of the dock and took the fingers of his right hand.

'Now we have to fight the deportation itself,' she said, trying to smile, but in doing so she was absolutely aware of the hollowness of her words.

'The Iraqis have killed me anyway,' he replied, his eyes still fixed on the floor. 'The gas kills me anyway.'

She felt his fingers momentarily squeeze hers, but there was no power in the grip – it was like the first grasp of a baby, or the last grasp of someone resigned to die. A jailer led her client back to the cells beneath the court and, though she walked back into the fresh air and freedom, Sophie felt sick.

Chapter 10

Dan and Jo left the Hammersmith and City line exit of Paddington Underground and walked down the steep metal stairs that led to the mainline station. Ahead of them were the sleek carriages of three InterCity trains, their dark tops visible, three long, parallel carcasses of steel. Chrissy's train was due in five minutes.

Dan was on a very tight schedule. He would meet his daughter off the 11 o'clock train, have Jo take her home, and then get to Neville Neale's chambers in the Temple in time for the prosecution conference before lunchtime. And on top of all this, there was something important he had to say to Jo. He knew it was likely to be painful to his father, and for that reason he had not been able to confront it. But he knew also that it could be delayed no longer.

As they reached the landing halfway down the staircase, he lightly took the sleeve of his father's fraying overcoat. High above them, the rain pounded on the metal roof of the station concourse, echoing around the vast hangar. It blocked out other sounds: people passing nearby were in conversation, but their words were drowned out, isolating father and son further.

'Jo, I've got to tell you something. I was going to mention it last night.'

'You don't like goulash?'

'I'm afraid it's going to make me sound a little like a hypocrite.'

'So sound like one,' he smiled. 'Be my guest.'

Dan looked into the eyes of the older man. The traces of Jo's laughter had not faded – but soon they would. 'I haven't really told Christine about you.'

Jo looked down at the trains. The nearest one began to creak and groan out of the station. 'I see.'

'I just figured that the last thing she needed was to know that she had a grandfather, and then to lose him when he went back to New York.'

'I got you.'

'And Jo, believe me, the last thing Chrissy needs in her life right now is to have someone close and then lose that person. After Viv . . .'

A group of students pushed past. Their backpacks bumped into Dan, forcing him closer to his father.

'So who am I?' Jo asked. 'One of your criminal clients?'

'No.'

'So who?'

'I don't know. I thought . . . maybe a long lost great-uncle sort of thing.'

'Yeah, perfect,' he replied, sharply turning. He stared into Dan's eyes intensely. 'I'm your Great-Uncle Buck.'

'Come on, Jo.'

'I came to see my granddaughter.'

'You can see her.'

'I came so that she could see me.'

'She can see you, too.'

'For who I am.'

Dan wanted to say that this was precisely the point. Who was Jo? Who was his father, really? The metal in the staircase began to vibrate as the train slid further out of the station.

'Feel that rumble beneath my feet, Jo? That's the slipping away of my moral high ground, I suppose. But I'm doing this to protect Chris.'

He saw his father grip the ageing metal rails with such determination that he drove the blood from his knuckles.

'When I was in Neuwelt, I thanked God every day for one thing. That I had no children. I said to myself, this thing, this suffering had to end with me.'

He turned his face towards Dan, and his eyes followed a line that Dan could not see, as if he were trying to find a route to the past.

'There was this man,' he continued. 'A Russian. In the army, a brave man, stood up to the camp guards – they would hit him with rifle butts but he wouldn't be bowed. This same man, proud, a hero like I could never be, he cried like a baby every night because he had a child and he didn't know whether the child was captured or was free, whether he was alive or dead. And though his sobs, you know, wrenched my heart, I felt like sad . . . and happy . . . happy 'cause I said to myself, that can't happen to me. No way. This pain, this ends with me. It was like this unspoken . . . pact I had with them Nazis. So you kill me, a Russian Jew, but that's the end of it for me.'

There was a blast from a whistle and the growl of a train coming into the station. The rails alongside the platform creaked as the mass of the train ground to a halt.

Dan looked at his watch. 'That must be her train.'

By the time Dan had fumbled in his pockets to find a pound coin for a trolley, passengers had already begun to disembark on to the platform. The first-class carriages were at the front of the train and he knew that Chris wouldn't be in them, so he wheeled the trolley to the beginning of the standard section.

In the mass of faces, luggage trolleys and suitcases, Dan could not see her, and he had a twinge of panic. What if he had left it too late to bring her up from Devon? All Yuri would have to do would be to board the train, follow Chris between carriages and . . . He felt the smooth yellow grips of the trolley brake begin to slide under his palms with his sweat. The sudden fear caused the blood to pound in his head. But when Dan looked at Jo, he was smiling.

'There she is,' Jo said.

'How do you know?'

'Looks like your mother.'

Dan saw Chrissy emerging from behind a group of business-men, wheeling her own little suitcase; her hair was tied back in a ponytail and she looked tired.

'Now remember what we discussed,' he whispered to Jo.

'Sure.'

Dan left the trolley and ran the length of two carriages and took her in his arms. He tried to lift her off her feet, but had forgotten again how much she had grown.

'*Dad*,' she hissed, 'people are watching.'

'Let them watch.'

'It's embarrassing.'

'So how's *War and Peace*?'

'Nine hundred to go.' She paused and smiled. 'I wish it was nine thousand.'

By this time, Jo had reached the two of them and he stood to one side, looking at his granddaughter, smiling. Dan saw her smiling back at him.

'I want you to meet someone,' Dan told her.

'Hi,' Chris beamed.

'Chris, this is your—'

'Uncle Buck,' Jo interrupted. 'But you can call me Jo.'

Chris broke free of her father's grip. She looked between the two men uncertainly. 'What's going on?'

Jo looked directly into her eyes, but at the same time he played with the fraying cuffs of his coat.

'I'm your grandfather, Christine. But you can still call me Jo.'

She spun around and stared up at Dan. He paused for a moment and then nodded, not knowing whether to scold Jo for breaking the agreement, or to hug him for lighting up his daughter's eyes.

'This is my father, Chrissy.'

She went up to Jo as he held out his right hand. He resolutely put his left one, with the numbers carved into his wrist, into his deep coat pocket. But Christine put her arms around him, ignoring the outstretched hand, and for the first time in his life, Dan saw his father cry, if you could call it crying, for at first there was just one tear, then two more.

'I've wanted to meet you for so long,' Jo said.

'I miss my mum,' she replied, as if this was the perfect reply to his statement.

For an instant, Dan felt like an outsider, otiose, unneeded as grandfather and granddaughter embraced beside the carriages of the InterCity train. He couldn't remember when Chris had shown him such unbridled affection, certainly not since Viv had died. And he and Jo had always kept each other at a certain distance. But suddenly he saw the line that Jo was searching for on the staircase, the link between the present and the past, between the generations, and as he looked at them, he realised that *he* was the connection: a grandfather's son, a granddaughter's father.

They finally walked along the platform, together, three generations of the family. Cleaners were boarding the train to prepare it for the journey back to the West Country.

'Didn't we agree I'd stay in Devon with Grandpa?' Chrissy asked as they approached the taxi rank to one side of the concourse. Dan was caught unawares and was unsure what to say.

The three of them had travelled in the cab all way across London, with Jo and Chris chattering away in the comfortable back seats, while Dan perched on one of the fold-downs.

Grandfather and granddaughter talked, Dan reflected, as if they had known each other for ever. But Chris refused to go straight home, and Dan finally relented, agreeing to meet the two of them for lunch at the National Film Theatre after the morning conference and before the afternoon one commenced. Eventually, the cab pulled up outside the Temple. Dan kissed Chris on both cheeks as he got out, but she wouldn't let him go, and he had to climb back in and hug her.

Dan walked along Middle Temple Lane, the thoroughfare that divided Inner from Middle Temple, and ran from Fleet Street in the north to the Embankment in the south. An illegally parked car was being fitted with a yellow wheel clamp, while ahead of Dan a motorcycle courier was desperately trying to understand the labyrinths of cloisters and barristers' chambers.

Neville Neale's chambers were one of the established prosecution sets. They were known as a 'Division One' chambers. This place was the top of the tree – people aspired to it, young hopefuls did what they could to scheme their way in. But Dan was heartily sick of the whole legal set-up. He no longer wished to sacrifice quality time and the rest of Chris's growing up to win success within this arcane world.

As he reached the outer door to chambers, Dan was confronted by a man. He said nothing, though he clearly knew Dan. It was Julian Waugh. Dan held the door open, though he dearly wished to slam it in Waugh's supercilious face. For this was the man who one year earlier had compromised Dan's integrity in the Kurdish trial.

'Good morning, Julian,' Dan said. He smiled as widely as

his rage would allow, calculating that politeness was the best weapon against Waugh, just as a cross was against a vampire.

Waugh's stare, lucid, intelligent as ever, penetrated deeply into him. Still Waugh remained silent. He had the trim figure of someone who still worked out regularly. He was just over six feet tall, and despite being into his fifties he still had a full head of dark, thin hair that was always greased straight back.

'I hear you're for Montford,' Dan said.

Waugh stared back. He was going to say something but appeared to change his mind. 'This is out of your league, Becket,' he said instead.

'I haven't taken the brief yet.'

'You will. You'll want to have another crack at me.'

'There's more to life than cases.'

'Really?' Waugh mocked. 'I was so sorry to hear about your wife.'

As Waugh glided into the next courtyard and out of sight, Dan remembered in a flash that this was what he hated about the Bar. This vitriol. This personalising of the legal struggle. He had once admired Waugh's advocacy skills, the devastating cross-examinations, the riveting speeches, but now he saw them for what they really were: conjuring tricks, conjuring tricks by a forensic magician, who didn't care whether his magic was white or black.

He took the steps up to the chambers reception and told the junior clerk that he wished to see Neville Neale. Although he was then shown to the waiting room, he could not sit down. He paced up and down, back and forth until Neale arrived, a couple of minutes later.

'Ah, Daniel,' Neale beamed. 'Welcome aboard?'

'No,' was all Dan replied.

Dan deliberately used the pavement nearest to the river as he walked away from the Temple. He was in no mood to chat with other barristers and the risk of meeting someone was too great if he walked along the high black railings that separated the opal lawns and privileged cloisters of the Temple from the rest of London.

To the left and below him, the river was agitated with the mud and debris that had been washed into it miles upriver by the rain. Pleasure boats were permanently berthed off the north bank, and between them he spotted floating plastic bottles, supermarket carrier bags, newspapers fanning out and floating just beneath the surface, the decayed carcass of a dog. There were dirty heads to the waves, with grey frothing peaks, and he could hear the groaning of the rusting moorings as the boats struggled against the strong tide, a treacherous body of water than could rise by as much as twenty feet in six hours.

It seemed incredible to him that five or six miles up this same river, on his part of the Thames in West London, people would row in small canoes, youngsters – no older than Chrissy – would sail in boats the size of a single mattress.

When he reached the dank arches of Waterloo Bridge, the traffic echoed loudly. It was here that some tramps sought shelter from the elements, and the unfortunate stench of their rags filled the air. Dan was about to climb the steps that led to the top of the bridge and then on to the National Film Theatre on the South Bank when he saw Cleopatra's Needle a short way along the curve of the river. Inevitably, it reminded him of its pair in Central Park in New York.

A couple of minutes later, he paused as he reached the base of the monument, inspecting the carvings made millennia earlier. Then an array of other marks swirled before Dan's eyes: those carved into Jo's wrist, marks that would last the rest of his father's lifetime. But he had no time to make sense of any of it, because somewhere behind him he heard Yuri's voice.

Chapter 11

'In April 1945,' Yuri began, 'the British tanks crossed the Rhine and entered the *Konzentrations Lager* of Neuwelt.'

His voice, Dan noticed, was not emotional, the voice of a passer-by asking you the time, barely audible above the traffic that sped along the Embankment on its way to Westminster. Dan turned away from the water and inspected Yuri's face. The weals were once again strongly evident and the Russian's eyes were trained on him. He wore a virtually pristine Barbour jacket and to all the world looked like a middle-aged English gent up from the shires for the day.

'Why are you telling me this now?' Dan asked.

Yuri ignored him. 'When the tanks entered the various camps of Greater Germany, the inmates thought that the Holocaust was at an end – and it was. Except at Neuwelt. For here there was one final atrocity. An atrocity, Mr Becket, unlike all others. An atrocity committed by the *British*. By Major Simon Montford.'

Dan stared down into the river, not wanting to hear any more. This was not going to be his problem. When he told Yuri about Jo and the Neuwelt connection and how it made it professionally impossible for him to conduct the prosecution, he would be free at last from the trouble.

'You already know that Montford killed a Russian,' Yuri said. 'A Jew called Ivan Basarov, but the name is not important for the moment. Montford got Klaus Keller to *gas* him. The fact of this Russian's death is important. The method of this Russian's death is important.'

'Can you prove this?' Dan said, daring to look at the Russian again.

'That will be your job.'

'I mean, have you the evidence against Montford?'

'We have some evidence.'

'Do you have enough for a conviction?'

'That will be ...' Yuri paused as a luxury coach thundered past. 'That will be your job.'

There was a rush of air as the forty-foot vehicle accelerated perilously close, leaving a wake of diesel exhaust. This was the moment, Dan knew, to tell Yuri about his father.

'I can't take the case,' he said.

'Cannot does not come into it.'

'Look, I mean, I will not be *allowed* to take the case. I have a connection with Neuwelt.' He hesitated, not wanting to reveal too much about Jo.

'Oh, you're talking about your *father*,' Yuri said, a hint of sarcasm lending a stress to the last word. 'Josef Rosen, Russian. Jew. Various camps. Auschwitz. Bergen-Belsen. Neuwelt.'

'It will disqualify me from prosecuting the case. Professionally ... ethically.'

Yuri smiled and walked right to the embankment wall, grimy, greasy brick sullied by years of traffic fumes.

'The words of a lawyer. The Final Solution, that was professional. But was it ethical? I suppose it was, in its own terms. But when the ethics are so repugnant to the weight of history, there is another word for them, Mr Becket ... evil.'

Dan turned his back to the river and again looked up at the Needle and its ancient carvings. At the foot of the monument were two black metallic sphinxes. 'I agree with what you're saying, any sane person would agree with what you're saying, but—'

'Six million Jews killed, was that ethical?'

'No.'

'Six million more Slavs and gypsies and dissidents, was that ethical?'

'No, but—'

'One Russian. A soldier. An honourable man. Survived the Third Reich, Hitler's dream, Himmler's orders, Eichmann's camps, survived it all and is gassed on the instructions of a British officer. Is that ethical?'

'You have a strong case, but I am not the man to prosecute it. If anyone discovers that I have concealed my personal connection to Neuwelt, I will be struck off.'

'Then you must ensure that discovery is not made.'

'If I am exposed during the trial, the jury will be discharged. Montford will be released. He might never again come to trial.'

'Then *you* will be held responsible.'

Yuri paused as a pair of Japanese tourists posed in front of Cleopatra's Needle and offered him their camera. He shook his head, but the immaculately turned-out lady smiled sweetly, tilting her head to one side, and he had no option but to take the camera. He shot them once and fooled around, pretending to ask Dan to stand between them. The male of the couple thanked Yuri very politely and bowed shallowly before they left.

'How is your father?' Yuri asked.

In an instant, Dan remembered why it was that he was walking along the Embankment in the first place: Jo and Chrissy. Lunch. Across the river.

But Yuri had come from the other direction, perhaps he didn't know, perhaps he was just trying to scare him. And anyway, what in fact had the totality of Yuri's threats come to? None of his family had been hurt, no one had even been approached. It was easy to raise these spectres, but what had actually been done? Dan still had his back to the river, and watched Yuri move a pace nearer the traffic. On the other side of the roadway the impressive façade of the Savoy faced the Thames.

'What is the next bridge called?' he asked Dan.

'Westminster.'

'No, the one before that, the one that goes to the National *Film* Theatre?' Yuri smiled. He knew.

Dan spun around and stared up at Waterloo Bridge. Just visible towards the South Bank was Chrissy.

She stood right against the white metallic railings that were all that divided the top of the bridge from the air fifty feet above the river. She was gesticulating with her arms, pointing out something to a man who stood directly behind her. His legs, Dan calculated, must have been virtually touching the backs of Chrissy's. His head appeared from above her right shoulder, his hands hovered behind her, but of course this was something she could not see. With one movement he could dump her over the side and into the water.

Suddenly Dan recognised the youth. It was Dmitri. From the Manhattan Hotel. He began to shout out desperately.

'Chris, Chrissy, for God's sake, *Chrissy*.'

But his words were drowned out by another tourist coach that rumbled past. He began running back along the river towards the cold, grey arches of Waterloo Bridge.

He screamed at people to get out of the way. They looked at him as if he were crazy as he barged past them, and he was, crazy with fear for his daughter.

As he ran nearer to the bridge, now directly underneath the arches, he lost sight of her, but he had to press on. He ran across the road. A taxi screeched and skidded past him, hooting, the cabbie bawling an obscenity out of the window. They wouldn't do anything to her, would they? They were frightening him.

Yes, he shouted inside his head, I'm frightened, I'm *terrified* for my baby. I'll do your case. Just leave her alone. But still he could not see her.

He charged up the dark, winding stone steps on the other side of the road. They smelt of urine and he slipped, skidded in something foul, crashed against the wall painfully, but couldn't stop. He had to keep running, though his hand now bled and a fold of skin hung from his right palm with dirt from the wall in it. What if they were going to make an example of her? One death? Control him. Crush his will.

He ran to the top of the bridge and into the light as London spread out on both sides, the dirty river far below, the dull sky merging with it on the horizons east and west, but he couldn't see his daughter.

'Chris,' he cried out, '*Christine*.'

He pushed past the astonished faces of people trooping over from the South Bank. The blood from the cut on his palm was now on his suit. He was fearful of looking into the water in case he saw her body carried by the muddy waves. He felt dizzy; nothing was clear.

It was then that he saw her.

His daughter Christine walking nonchalantly back towards the NFT, casually unwrapping a stick of chewing gum. She wore her latest pair of shoes, the type of clumpy footwear fashionable among teenage girls, and moved as though she had not a single care.

He rushed to her side. 'Why were you talking to that man?' he shouted, gasping for breath.

'Dad?' Her expression was confused. She looked him up and down, becoming embarrassed as passers-by stared. 'Dad, what's the matter?'

'That man, where is he?'

'Crossed the road.'

Dan looked behind him and saw Dmitri getting into a non-descript grey car that had pulled up beside him. 'Where's your grandfather?'

'He's reserved the table at the NFT.'

'*Why* did he leave you? Jesus, Chris—'

'I left *him*, to get some money from that cashpoint over the bridge. We wanted a cup of tea.'

'Jo had no money? For Christ's sake.'

'Dad, you're bleeding,' she said, chewing nervously.

'I told you *never* to talk to strangers.'

'He wasn't a stranger, that boy was a tourist. Said he was lost. I was just showing him how to get to Charing Cross. Dad, why are you bleeding?'

'He didn't say who he was?'

'No. He wasn't a psycho or anything. A student, on an exchange from Russia or somewhere. I quite fancied him – but I don't suppose he'd be interested in someone as young as me.'

Dan tried to breathe deeply but a stitch bit into his side and increased the feeling of nausea.

Chrissy took a large white tissue out from under the left sleeve of her jumper and started to wrap it around his bleeding hand. 'You mustn't worry about me, Dad. I'm a big girl now,' she said, still chewing away. 'I was only getting some money. The cashpoints south of the bridge were closed or vandalised.'

'I know, I'm sorry, but you didn't know who he was.'

'He was very sweet, offered me a stick of gum.'

Dan's eyes shot to her face. He could see the pale pink gum in her mouth as she chewed. 'Spit it out,' he demanded.

'Dad—'

'Spit it *out*, Chris.'

'But Dad, it's—'

He grabbed her face, one cheek in each hand, the blood from his right palm smudging on her left cheek. But he forced her to spit out the gum. Then she began to cry.

He tried to take her in his arms but she shied away. 'Chris, I'm sorry, you just don't understand.'

'No, *you* don't understand,' she said, tears running down her face. 'It was my gum—'

'But you said—'

'I said that he *offered* me some gum, but I had my own. I never accept sweets from strangers – my *mother* taught me that. I want to go home.'

Dan did not know what to say any more. His emotions had raced through shock, terror, relief and now embarrassment. Was he wrong? Would she have been safer in Devon? Yuri knew where she was. This could have happened – something worse could have happened – in the West Country. He just didn't know what to do.

They walked inches apart towards the South Bank Centre. Dan glanced over his shoulder and saw the swirling waters of the river. He traced the waves across to the other bank and to Cleopatra's Needle and the lone figure standing at its foot in a green Barbour, a figure to whom no one in London would give a second thought.

The tables outside the glass façade of the NFT were totally in the shadow of Waterloo Bridge. Since an icy wind had begun to blow off the Thames, all the tables were empty.

Dan and Chris walked slowly down the stone stairs that led from the top of the bridge. They passed open-air bookstalls at the river's edge, most of which were shut. Two tramps huddled together at the side of the building and covered themselves in cardboard boxes; a woman jogger with headphones ran by in her bright yellow Lycra outfit.

Jo was already inside and had secured a table on the left-hand side of the door. Dan saw that his father had taken off his old coat and had placed his Yankees baseball cap on the table. He smiled at the two of them.

'Best table in the house,' he said to Chris, his eyes wide with pride.

Dan sat down opposite him without saying a word. Christine sat next to her grandfather in silence.

'Did I miss something here?' Jo asked. 'What's the matter? You wanted no smoking or something?'

Dan took a deep breath. He desperately wanted to control himself; he certainly didn't want to say something he knew he would regret later. But as he stared at his daughter, who was not even willing to sit next to him, he noticed her puffy, sore eyes and the vestige of a tear track. He couldn't help himself.

'What the hell were you thinking of, Jo?'

'What d'you mean? Thinking?'

'No, Jo, I mean *not* thinking. Not thinking about Christine.'

'Come on, Dad,' she pleaded, but still did not look at him, staring resolutely at the tabletop.

'You can't leave her alone in the city, Jo.'

'But it was *my* idea to get some money,' Christine protested.

'I done nothing,' Jo added.

'Quite,' snapped Dan. 'How on earth can you have no money?'

'Spent it on the taxi. We dropped you off and it cleaned me right out.'

'Haven't you saved anything over the last forty years?'

Jo played with the rim of his cap. 'Sure I have. But I spent it on the ticket to see the two of you.'

'Dad, it wasn't Jo's fault,' Chris added, pleading with her father.

'Be quiet, please, Christine.'

'I'm not a child.'

'And you're not an adult. And until you are, I'm responsible for you.'

'Then why did you leave me in Devon?'

'Chris, we're not going to have this conversation here.'

'Then when? You never talk to me. Unless you feel guilty when you're working all the time, or if you're telling me off.'

Jo now played with a salt cellar. 'Your father's right, angel. I should never have left you like that. I did wrong. Not your father.'

'Jo,' Dan said, 'I just wanted to make a point.'

'Yeah, you made it. I don't know how to look after a child, I never even knew my own—'

'Jo,' Dan said, 'please—'

'No, I got to say this. I don't know what it is to have someone you got to care for. I'm just an old man who has forgotten how it is to be with a family.' He turned to Chris. 'Don't blame your father, sweetheart, it was my fault.'

There was a brief silence in which Dan avoided the eyes of his father and daughter. He glanced over to the metal and glass serveries in which a variety of salads, quiches and thoroughly wholesome meals awaited.

'What happened to your hand?' Jo asked.

'Nothing.'

'Looks like a bloody kind of nothing to me.' Jo sprinkled a few grains of salt into the palm of his hand and licked them. 'I *was* going to ask both of you, you know, if I could stay with you for a while.'

'Of course you can,' Dan said. 'You're very welcome to—'

'It wouldn't work,' Jo said. 'Not yet.' He looked deeply into Dan's eyes. 'You better wash that blood off.'

Chapter 12

Lisa had flown in that afternoon from Berlin. In one sense, she had saved Dan any awkward decisions by taking a room at the Knightsbridge Sheraton, but she had nevertheless made it clear that she wished to see him before she returned to New York. Dan could not refuse.

So while Jo again cooked goulash for a delighted Chrissy, now claiming that it was one of his tried and tested specialities from the 'old country', Dan met Lisa at a restaurant. It was an Arabic place in the Brackenbury village part of Hammersmith and had been reviewed ecstatically in all the food guides.

Lisa arrived before him as he had forgotten until the last moment that this was a restaurant where you brought your own wine and then paid a small corkage fee. She sat at a table in a half-lit corner, but he saw her immediately when he entered. She looked stunning. Her hair framed her face with curls, she rested her delicate chin on her hand, and the flickering candle on the table illuminated one side of her face with a soft yellow glow. She smiled coolly as he arrived and offered her cheek, which he duly kissed.

'It's perfect,' she said.

'Why?'

'Arabic restaurant. Two screwed-up Jews.'

He held the wine bottle towards her. 'Californian Chardonnay.'

'I hate Californian,' she smiled.

The meal consisted of *couscous aux sept légumes* – a mound of cracked wheat covered in steaming vegetables – and Dan was relieved when the wine actually complemented the food tolerably well. Soon the two of them were talking away as they had done in Manhattan. It was as if the three months between January and April had vanished.

When Dan paid the bill, Lisa made no efforts to enquire about cabs back to the hotel. Instead, she nonchalantly dropped into the conversation the fact that she had finally ended her on–off relationship. With this revelation, the talking momentarily came to a halt until Lisa spoke again.

'Live far?'

'We can walk,' he replied.

An hour later, Lisa and Dan were alone in the lounge, the dimmer switch was right down, and each had a glass of whisky. Jo had gone to bed, still sullen over the argument at the NFT, while Chrissy was up in her room surfing the Internet on the multimedia package Dan had bought her before Christmas. It had begun to worry him that Chris had increasingly withdrawn from her real friends and spent her evenings scouring the world's superhighways for electronic chums. She had been very polite in greeting Lisa, but there was an underlying coolness to his daughter's behaviour, almost as if she didn't trust Lisa.

The wind had swung around to the north and the icy chill in it had persuaded Dan to draw the curtains, turn up the central heating and make a fire in the grate. Lisa sat cross-legged on the carpet in a polo-neck that Dan had lent her. Her hair had been recently brushed and shone brilliantly in the firelight before her.

Dan took her shoulders, wonder again spreading from the tips of his fingers at the fragility of her frame. He considered whether to tell her more about his father, knowing that if the relationship was to continue, he needed to tell her.

But then the phone rang.

From upstairs, he heard Chris call, 'I'll get it.'

Dan shot to the door in an instant. 'Leave it for me.'

'It's all right, Dad, I'm almost there.'

'Christine, *leave* it for me.'

Dan rushed to the hall table and picked up the receiver just as Chris picked up the one upstairs.

'Hello?' she said.

'Put it *down*,' Dan shouted down the line.

'And what is your name?' the voice asked her. 'Is it as beautiful as your voice?'

Dan heard her giggling.

'I can see you,' the man said.

'Put it down, *immediately*,' Dan insisted, hearing the click as Chrissy's receiver was replaced. 'Who is this?' he shouted.

'You know who it is,' Yuri said. 'Is your daughter well? We hope she is well, and unharmed, and a joy and a blessing to you, Mr Becket, for as long as fate allows her to be.'

'It's *me* that you want,' he shouted back. 'I'll do the war crimes case, just leave her alone.'

The line went dead.

Dan kept holding the receiver so tightly that the muscles in his forearm trembled. He tore the telephone from the socket and smashed the casing against the wall, the brittle plastic cracking in a dozen places, the wires tangling in the wheels of Chris's bike. He stopped only when he saw Lisa in the entrance to the hall.

He gathered her in his arms and pushed her into the lounge, slamming the door after him. He switched off the lights, so that her body was silhouetted by the glow from the fire. Then he realised his mistake. *What* was he thinking?

I can see you.

Chris. Yuri could see Chris.

He ran up the stairs shouting at her to get away from the bedroom window. He took her by the hand, more roughly than he intended, barged open Jo's door and dragged him out of bed. He ordered the two of them to stay together and away from the windows. Christine was silent with shock and appeared too frightened to cry. Jo was still half asleep and confused.

Dan ran back down the stairs, taking them two at a time, and checked the front and the back doors. All locked; no sign of entry.

What more could he do?

He stormed back to the lounge and saw Lisa still waiting in front of the fire.

'We need to talk,' he said, breathless.

'Yes.'

'Someone has been threatening me. And Chrissy. And I don't know what to do.'

'Have you called the police?'

'And what could they do?'

'Nothing.'

'Nothing has actually happened.'

'Do you know who it is?'

'He says he's Russian. I think he's telling the truth about that.'

'When did it start?'

'When I was in New York.'

'And what does he want?'

'He wants me to prosecute Montford in the war crimes case.'

'And is that what you want?'

He took hold of her thin wrists, his fingers wrapping themselves around her fine bones. 'Oh God, Lisa, I just don't know what to do.'

She pulled away from his grip, speaking quietly. 'What do you want to do, Dan?'

For ten agonising seconds, as he looked on helplessly, she was silent and merely stared into the glowing orange ashes.

Then she spoke in a voice that was cold and distant, a voice he had never heard before. 'Yuri was my lover. Yuri was the man I had an affair with.'

Dan tried to compute the facts in this new light, but he couldn't make sense of it.

'I met him at the Bar conference when I met you. He was listening to you speak about abuse. I told you I was trouble,' she said coolly. 'I told you to keep away from me. But you wouldn't. Yuri's found out everything about you and Chrissy ... from me.'

His heart felt strangely still, even when she had uttered these crushing final words. What sickened him most was not the betrayal, but the defiant, proud way in which she confronted him.

'How could you jeopardise Chrissy?' he demanded.

She showed no shame, was even angered by the question. 'My mother had a picture. Of her and her sister Anna. Anna must have been about the age Chris is now.' She hesitated. 'Anna died in Birkenau.'

'That's not my fault.'

'Nor hers.' Lisa moved closer to him now, her lips lingering inches from his. He could feel her sweet breath on his face, but now it made him nauseous. 'This case ... your case—'

'It's not mine,' he protested.

'*Make* it yours. For fuck's sake, be a man, Daniel. Find out what happened at Neuwelt. How many people – just like us – do you think Keller tortured there?'

'Why does it always come back to Keller?'

'Because he was captured at Neuwelt. By the British. By . . . your people.'

'They're not my people.'

'Then who are?' She moved closer. 'Keller disappeared. He never faced trial. He never paid for what he did.'

'But what has Montford to do with Keller?'

'Montford has to know what happened to him. Convict Montford. Then he'll talk about Keller.'

Dan stared at her, furious that she could be so certain about these unpredictable things. 'So that's what Yuri thinks, is it?' he asked.

'That's what I think,' she snapped back.

'Whose idea was it? Don't tell me Yuri forced you to do it?'

She paused and said coldly, 'No one forces me to do anything.'

'So I won't have to force you to leave?'

She tutted so hard it was virtually a grunt. 'You always have to have a smart answer. But this case is more important than you or me. You're going to have to do it.'

He was about to reply when he heard Chrissy coming down the stairs, calling his name. 'What's Yuri's surname?' he whispered.

Lisa stared back at him defiantly.

'Yuri what?' he insisted.

'How do you know Yuri's his real name anyway? Everyone calls him by a different name. Take your pick.'

Her face broke into a cruel smile and he lost control, grabbing her roughly, intent on shaking the arrogance out of her.

'That's it,' she cried, struggling against him. 'Be angry. Be violent. Use it.'

At that moment Chris rushed into the room and the two adults froze.

'Dad?' she said, wide-eyed with amazement.

'It's all right,' he said.

'What's going on?'

He let go of Lisa. 'Nothing, baby,' he said. 'Nothing.'

PART III

SEPTEMBER

Chapter 1

Dan found that, despite himself, he had a growing fascination for war crimes cases. But on beginning to research the subject, it was immediately clear to him that the truth of those murky few months around the time of the Allied invasion of Germany was buried away from the view of the general public. In the books he read, there were numerous competing theories as to why the spring, summer and autumn of 1945 should still be so shrouded in secrecy. But at every turn, Dan's investigations were obstructed. Files at the Public Record Office were still sealed; books of memoirs were out of print; witnesses to the liberation of the camps were dead or untraceable; archive footage was either rotting away or lost. It was all the more frustrating to him since he hoped, through his researches, to find out more about those turbulent years in which his father had grown up.

Then, in early September, Dan had his first break. He found a reference in the British Library to Klaus Keller. The book was out of print, but a first edition still languished in the vaults of the national library, available at three days' notice once Dan had obtained a clearance pass to examine it. He had already arranged to meet Sophie for lunch that day in a wine bar just outside the Temple, but calculated that he could spend the morning delving into the book before moving on to meet her.

Once he arrived at the library and had confirmed who he was, he was led to a reading room. He fancifully imagined that the book, which was called *Medicine and Chemistry of the Third Reich*, would be a dusty volume, with cobwebs from the vaults binding the spine and the pages. But the hardback was in fact still in good condition with its original green dust jacket only a little creased. One of the library staff had run a cloth over the shiny surface, and there must have been a trace of moisture on the duster as the jacket was now slightly streaked. Dr Frederick Wiseman, Dan read, had written his largely academic tome in 1949.

If the author was, as Dan suspected, a Jewish academic, it was extraordinary how he could describe some of the greatest abominations dreamt of by mankind in so neutral a way. There was, for example, a chapter on Racial Hygiene and Purity; another on Miscegenation; still another on Toxicity of Gases. At first, Dan could not read more than a page at a time without putting the book down, getting up from his chair in the semi-dark alcove, and wandering back into the body of the library. He needed to see that ordinary life went on, that he was in London five decades later and the war had been won; and despite the certainty of the scientific theorems he had read, the Nazis had lost and the Allies, for all their faults, had defeated the Third Reich. He smiled when he saw two self-important-looking boffins arguing in stage whispers at a desk piled with books, especially when a young librarian, a thin, delicate Asian woman, gave them a severe telling-off. At another desk were two students: a girl in jeans and a red sweatshirt busily compiling notes; next to her was a preppy-looking boy, pretending to read with his head cupped in his left hand – he was really asleep. Dan felt reassured by these signs of normality. If this was what victory had meant, it was fine by him.

He returned to his small alcove with renewed determination and opened the chapter on Chemists. There was a short biography of several leading practitioners: Klinsberg, Beckman, Zilling, and finally Keller. On the latter there were just two paragraphs.

Keller, Klaus. Born Heidelberg, 11 August, 1920. Brilliant academic career. Youth League Scholarship. Studied chemistry under Beckman. Original research. Awarded Führer's White Cross for contribution to Racial Purity.

1942 volunteered to join Mengele at Auschwitz. Argued about efficiency of M's methodology. Sought controlled conditions to develop Final Solution (*die Endlösing*). Given Neuwelt sub-camp. Captured by British 1945. Disappeared.

It was the abrupt way in which Keller's whereabouts after capture were dealt with that took Dan's breath away. Disappeared.

Simply that. He supposed that as far as the academic content of the book was concerned, that was sufficient. But for Dan, this fact opened up a whole world of possibilities. It suddenly fitted in with other previously disparate strands of his research into chemical warfare and created in his mind an almost incredible hypothesis. But the methods of proof in the law and science were worlds apart, and he knew that an extract from a book could not readily be evidence in a criminal trial.

Consequently, he rushed to a computer upon which he hoped to discover more about Frederick Wiseman. But once the librarian had showed him how to move around the database, all he found out was that there was a later edition of Wiseman's book. This edition was on the shelves and, after five minutes, Dan found it. He calculated that if he found Wiseman's most recent publishers, he could ring them and perhaps discover the author's address. If he could get this information, Dan swore to himself that no matter where Wiseman was, he would track him down and interview him. He pictured himself finding the greying academic in a beautiful cottage in the Cotswolds, where despite the old man's frail body his mind still had the acuity of his youth. He would make the perfect witness. Dan took the book down from the shelf, his fingers trembling with excitement. But confusion soon set in. This later edition was edited by another academic, not Wiseman. On the inside back cover there was a brief note: Dr Frederick Wiseman died in Jerusalem in 1956. The references to Klaus Keller had been deleted from the newer book.

Lunchtime around the Temple was usually a hectic affair. Across the Strand, barristers in winged collars and white bands could be seen dashing over from the High Court, with pupils and solicitors in their wake. In the clerks' rooms, the nerve centres of the numerous sets of chambers, the telephones rang constantly, as counsel in far-flung courts called in to report the progress of their cases. In the overcrowded rooms, young barristers hovered expectantly, waiting for a frantic call from solicitors to dash to a magistrates court to pick up a last-minute afternoon brief.

Amongst this activity and chaos, Dan sat quietly at a table in the notorious legal watering-hole across the road from the Royal Courts, the Judge Jeffrey. He still felt subdued after his discovery that Wiseman had died in 1956, the year after he was born. But his mood improved a little when he saw Sophie walk through the doors.

'Been waiting for me long?' she asked, smiling at him.

She wore a designer suit with an unmistakably expensive sheen, but Dan had always thought that the more she tried to look like a typical barrister, the more her youthful enthusiasm stood out. She also wore a severe white court shirt with buttons right up to the throat, but even this accentuated her delicate mouth and the warmth of her smile. The suit hugged her contours tightly, and despite himself he could not help noticing the curve of her hips and the high swell of her breasts.

'Glad you could make lunch, Soph.'

'I'm glad – *surprised* – you asked me. As for tonight?'

'You and Helen can make it?'

'Dinner at Dan Becket's? I'll be there.'

'Excellent,' he said, but then paused. 'But weren't you going to hospital with Helen tomorrow morning?'

'Her help group? It's the first meeting so I want to be there, but it doesn't mean I can't be nursing a hangover from hell.'

'So you'll miss the Montford hearing tomorrow?'

'Oh, Waugh can cope without me holding his hand. Nothing's going to happen tomorrow anyway.'

They sat at a dark wooden table, within a line of discreet booths that hugged the wall of the wine bar. Through the grimy casement windows, they had a view of the hectic traffic hurtling around the RAF church that formed an island in the Strand.

'Helen's more important than this stupid case,' Sophie said, raising the subject again as if she needed reassuring.

'A help group? Sounds promising.'

'It's a major improvement. I mean, once they ask for help and all that.'

'What do they actually do?'

'It's not just tea and sympathy. Some new Californian method. They exchange stories, photos.'

'Photos?'

'Of the few babies that did survive. Even . . .' She hesitated as she searched for the right word. '. . . deformed.' She looked at him. 'To tell the truth, Dan, I don't know about Helen, but it scares the shit out of me.'

He leant across and put his hand on hers. 'It'll be OK.'

She smiled the kind of brave smile people force out when they are frightened. 'So what's for dinner?'

'Oh,' he said, 'state secret.'

He examined the handwritten wine list. The stock changed frequently as one line after another was swallowed by the legal profession. 'How about a glass of whatever, Soph – and I don't see why you were surprised I asked you to meet me. Chrissy's having kittens counting the hours to see you.'

'White whatever is fine. I just thought that your spare time would be occupied with—'

'Lisa?'

'Only half a bottle, Dan. I've got to drive down to the West Country. Car's outside on a meter, and there's a Panzer division of traffic wardens waiting to pounce. Yes, Lisa Hartman. Still seeing her?'

She took the wine list and Dan saw her examining it with an intensity that was not justified.

'It's all over between me and her, Soph.'

'How about half a bot of the dry white Italian thingee? My treat. Any reason I should know?'

'What?'

'Why you split up.'

'It happens. I had a past, she had a past, we just didn't seem to have a future together.'

'Shame.'

'I suppose two pasts do not a future make.'

As Dan got up to get the wine, he saw the trace of a smile around Sophie's lips. She put her hand lightly on his arm and it was sufficient to stop his progress.

'My treat, I said,' she whispered.

'Sure?'

'I'm sure. But when I get back, we've got to discuss the war crimes case. Look, I'm junior for Montford, you're junior for the Crown ... it's ridiculous that we haven't even talked about it yet.'

'Did we agree on dry white thingee?' was all Dan replied.

He watched her move through the crowds of dark-suited lawyers, squeezing past nimbly, avoiding the maze of glasses of wine, smiling at some people, avoiding the approaches of others. Dan realised that Sophie felt at home in this place, surrounded by people from her class and her background, in a way that he never really did.

The wine bar had a low ceiling from which snatches of other people's legal discussions bounced. There was one overriding topic of conversation: the forthcoming war crimes trial. Suddenly Dan understood what the Allied bars around Nuremburg in 1946 must have been like, for everyone had an opinion about who was really to blame for the Holocaust and how they should be prosecuted.

When Sophie returned, she poured him a large glass of white wine and half a glass for herself.

'I did ring you,' he said. 'You know, in April. A couple of times in fact.'

'I know.'

'You didn't ring back.'

'I know that too, Dan.' She took a sip of the wine and winced. 'Bit cold,' she said.

'Can I ask why—'

'I figured one woman in your life was enough. Of course, that depends on the woman.' She smiled and looked into the body of the bar where at least half a dozen beautiful, successful, professional women stood around chatting with the easy assurance of those who have found their place in the world. 'In fact, I've been out of London for two months. Doing a trial in Manchester.'

'Your clerks told me,' he said. 'What were you doing?'

'Paying off my mortgage.'

'Pardon?'

'Well, it was a long-firm fraud, boring as shit, but paid enough to stop my bank manager from sending me threatening, abusive and insulting letters. Helen came up and stayed with me. I've got a stack of other work. None of which – hard to believe – involves war criminals or Winston Churchill.'

Dan smiled and sipped more of his wine. The September light was diffracted by the accumulated grime on the windows and fell softly on Sophie's face. He sensed that there was something troubling her, causing her forehead to crease and her mouth to set more firmly than was normal.

But before he could say anything, she said, 'I'm worried about Helen.'

'How is she?'

'I just don't know what to do, she won't talk to me about Jenny's death. She just sits watching television all day.'

'What about the father?'

'Pig. Typical bloody man.'

'Thanks.'

She quickly took his hand. 'You're not a typical man, Daniel Becket, or I wouldn't give you the time of day.'

'So what's wrong with Helen's bloke?'

'Ex-bloke. Decidedly ex. The bastard ordered her to have an abortion.'

'Ordered?'

'Army, wasn't he? Bloody army doctor, too. Gulf vet and all that. When Helen did the decent thing and told him to go forth *et cetera*, he would have nothing to do with the birth. And now . . .'

'What?'

'He hasn't been to see her once. And whenever he phones, Helen locks herself into her bedroom to take the call.' There was a glaze of profound sadness in Sophie's eyes, as if she were shedding internal tears she wouldn't allow anyone else to see. 'Dan, tell me I'm an interfering bitch, but I'm going to confront the bastard.'

He looked at her silently, not knowing what to say.

'Speak to me, Dan. Am I interfering—'

'You love your sister, Soph. And if this man is causing her pain, then I think you have a right to persuade him to stop.'

'That's what I thought. It is the inalienable right of any sibling to cut the bugger's balls off.'

Sophie raised her glass and Dan clinked it.

'OK, enough of the Chase family sagas, what have you been up to?'

'Preparing crazily for the war crimes trial.'

'So the preliminary hearing is definitely tomorrow?' she said to him. 'We were wondering whether the prosecution would be ready.'

'I've got a con with the whole pros team this afternoon.'

'Can I tell you the truth?' She looked evenly into his eyes as she took a small sip. 'I'm surprised you took this case, Dan.'

'Why?'

'After the Kurdish bombing case last year and everything, I thought you had had enough of prosecuting.'

'I had.'

'So why change your mind?'

He desperately wanted to tell her about Yuri and the threats, about the whole fiasco, but it would not have been fair to her. It would complicate things. It would achieve nothing except embroil her in something that was already out of his control.

'Sometimes,' he said, 'we have our minds changed for us.'

'You don't mean you've been persuaded by that burnt-out copper, Grail or whatever his name is?'

'Not by Grail.'

'Then by who?'

He paused, looked carefully at her and then said, 'Since I got the brief, Soph, I've done a lot of reading.'

'That makes a first for a barrister: actually reading his papers. Christ, don't tell anyone else or the rest of us will have to do it.'

'No, I mean reading *around* the case. Did you know that after the British tanks first entered Belsen in April 1945, they moved on, leaving the camp in the partial control of a Hungarian detachment.'

'So?'

'So it was a detachment of the Hungarian SS. In two days over seventy Jews were shot by the SS.'

'I don't believe it.'

'Nor did I. But there's more to the liberation of the camps than most of us know.'

He noticed a darker mood wash slowly over her face. Little wrinkles suddenly appeared at the corners of her eyes and her body tensed. 'All right. Let's say that's true. It could have been a mistake.'

'True. But how do we know that there were not other atrocities like that?'

'*Dan*,' she insisted, an undercurrent of desperation in her voice, 'think about what you are saying. The camps were created *by* the Nazis. We fought them. We won the war.'

'So we were the good guys?'

'Yes.'

'Exclusively? Without exception? You can guarantee that not a single one of the Allies ... misbehaved?'

'I didn't say that.'

'What if there was a rotten apple in the British forces? Someone who used the chaos and the butchery at the end of the war for his own ends.'

'Montford?'

'Not necessarily. Let's say for the moment it could be anyone.'

'But what ends?'

Dan drank down most of the wine in his glass in one gulp. He looked around, not so much concerned that he might be seen or overheard, but because what he was about to say felt sacrilegious, blasphemous, disloyal.

'I went to the British Library,' he told her. 'There was this book. It said Keller disappeared at the end of the war. And I skimmed another before I came here. It said the Normandy landings were . . . not just an invasion.'

'Then what?'

'They were part of a race.'

'What race?'

'Everyone knew that there was going to be a confrontation of some kind between the West and the Russians. Both sides were racing for Berlin, trying to dictate where the Iron Curtain would fall. But they were also competing for German technology. The Germans were very advanced in rocket technology and weapons of mass destruction—'

'Nuclear?'

'Biological, chemical. They were the future. Remember those documentaries? The Americans recruited Nazis for their own nuclear programme – the Manhattan Project or whatever it was called. Well, what if other teams from the American Army and British Military Intelligence were hunting down Nazi chemical scientists? Not to arrest them – but *recruit* them?'

'But why?'

'If nothing else, to stop the Russians getting them. The book said there were also teams from the War Office, I think it was, special prosecution teams tracking down war criminals.' He paused; he had reached the end of his speculation. 'What if whether or not a war criminal was recruited or arrested depended on who got to him first.'

'Can you prove any of this?'

'Not a thing.'

'What has this to do with Montford?'

'Montford was at Neuwelt. So was Klaus Keller. Keller *disappeared*. Coincidence?'

'But what has this to do with Montford murdering that Russian soldier, Ivan Basarov?'

Dan looked at her and, in the relief of articulating his researches and thoughts, he grinned. 'I haven't got a clue,' he said.

'A British officer killing a Russian prisoner? That's totally absurd.' Sophie looked at her watch and frowned. 'I think I'd better go,' she said. 'I can see you haven't wasted your summer.'

'I don't know what to make of this case.'

'Just don't make a mess of it. That's all.' She hesitated as she stood at the end of the table and brushed non-existent crumbs from her dark suit. 'Can I ask why you're telling me all this?'

'In case I don't do the trial.'

'But you're junior counsel for the prosecution.'

'In case I *don't* do the trial, Soph.'

'I haven't got the foggiest what you're on about, but I've got to go.'

'Where?'

'I'm driving down to Montford's estate.'

'Montford?'

'I'm the enemy, remember? He's presumed innocent and someone's got to prepare his defence.'

She lightly took his right hand. In the intervening months, the fold of skin that he had sheared off against the dirty stone of Waterloo Bridge had largely healed, but had still left a rough ridge.

'Can I tell Montford any of this?' she asked.

He looked at her face, at the blond hair so neatly cut. 'That's up to you, Soph. If I'm wrong, then he has nothing to worry about. But if I'm right—'

'What?'

'He'll know all about it anyway.'

Chapter 2

After Sophie left, Dan walked down the Strand towards Charing Cross where he had to meet Jo.

On the way, he passed the increasing army of homeless people – mainly they were hardly more than children – who squatted on flattened cardboard boxes in the alcoves and archways of one of London's main thoroughfares. He reflected that Chrissy might have lost her mother, but at least she still had a home. He saw again how important these simple things were: home, family, parents, love. No matter what pressure was put upon him in the weeks leading up to the trial, he was determined to defend these things for Chris. A young girl wearing fingerless gloves and a moth-eaten grey overcoat emerged from a shadowy alley near the Savoy. She asked Dan for a cup of tea. He gave her a pound coin.

Jo was sitting in the window of a cheap café on the steep road that led from Charing Cross mainline down to Embankment Tube. He wore his old coat with the collar turned up and his Yankee cap, in spite of being indoors. Dan pushed open the glass door and in doing so set off a rusty bell. It brought out a diminutive lady with tightly pinned hair.

'You're late,' Jo said as Dan sat opposite him.

'I'm sorry. But you're not going to be late tonight?'

'This dinner thing? It ain't in my honour, is it?'

'It's just a simple thing, Jo. Family and friends. You'll be there?'

'Long as I can cook,' Jo said.

They were separated by an old-fashioned wooden table that wobbled when Dan rested his hands on it. The surface was covered in a mosaic of fossilised tea rings. In the dark, narrow room there were ten or so tables and at the far end a stainless-steel serving counter. Behind this was the kitchen. There was only one other customer, a man even older than Jo who was reading a Cyrillic newspaper.

'This place is disgusting,' Dan said.

'It's Jewish.'

'No, I meant—'

'It's Jewish and it's disgusting, OK?' Jo said.

In front of him he had a glass cup with a metal handle. Dan could see dark tea within, melting two sugar cubes, placed one on top of the other. 'They're Russian Jews,' Jo continued. 'My kind of people.'

There was the sudden crash of a plate breaking somewhere inside the kitchen. The accident produced an outburst of Russian from the woman, who stormed back into the rear room, leaving the swing-doors creaking back and forth in her wake.

Jo laughed but said nothing to Dan. Instead he picked up his cup and drank noisily.

'I didn't get a chance to ask you properly last night,' Dan said. 'How was Europe?'

Jo continued drinking until the level of liquid reached the top of the upper cube. At the beginning of May, he had left for what he called his 'European Tour'. Dan was decidedly unclear as to how his father could afford it, but every couple of weeks over the summer Christine would receive a postcard from another country: Russia, Poland, Slovakia, Hungary, Austria, Germany. In all Jo had been away close to three months, visiting the haunts of his youth and such of his friends as were still alive. He never once addressed a postcard to Dan but asked Chrissy to say 'hi to her dad' at the bottom of each card.

Jo put down his cup and moved it around in small circles, annoyingly. 'Countryside around Auschwitz is still pretty. But Europe's changed.'

'Of course it's changed. It's been forty years since you left.'

'Yeah, but deep down? It's just the same.'

'What do you mean?'

'Still hate Jews. Ain't no Jews left in Poland to speak of. Russia? People gone to Israel or the States. And *Germany* . . . you know, I went to this Jewish cemetery in Berlin and the tombstones have been painted with Swastikas. Can you believe that one?'

Dan didn't know quite what to say and scolded himself when he blurted out the first platitude that came into his mouth. 'Some people never learn, Jo.'

'Hey, they learn fine. One Germany's better than two. In my day they called it Greater Germany, now it's called Unified or something.'

'Oh, stop living in the past, Jo. Germany is one of our main allies.'

'Then why do they have to guard the synagogues? You tell me that, Mr Lawyer.'

'I don't know. But doesn't there come a time when you have to – not forget, not for one moment – but forgive. At least that. Forgive.'

'Right. Like you've forgiven me for leaving your mother.'

After a couple of minutes, during which an awkward silence had descended upon father and son, the woman came back out through the swing-doors. Her features were still full with rage, contorting nose, mouth and forehead into one frown. She patted down her hair instinctively. Jo held up his hand, said something in Russian or Yiddish that resulted in a steaming glass of tea being placed in front of Dan. Only when she had disappeared once more did Dan begin to speak to his father.

He took a breath. Above the noise of muted squabbling in the kitchen he could hear the hooting of cars around Trafalgar Square; this was London, ordinary, everyday London, the place he knew and had been brought up in. But he also knew that his life had been overtaken by far from ordinary events and he had delayed things long enough. He had to tell his father.

'Jo, I'm in trouble.'

'That runs in the family.'

'No, serious trouble. At least I think it is. Someone is threatening me – well, threatening Chrissy really. They're not going to do anything to me, but if I don't do what they say, then they're going to hurt Chris.'

'What do they want you to do?'

'Prosecute the Montford war crimes trial.'

'Can't you do that? It don't seem that much.'

'I'm not allowed to do the trial – because of you, Jo. You were in Neuwelt.'

'Not all the time.'

'It doesn't matter. Your presence at Neuwelt gives me a personal interest, so I'm not allowed to do the case professionally.'

'So do it unprofessionally – who's going to know?'

'What do you mean?'

'Who have you told that your father is a Neuwelt survivor who owns a stinking deli in Brighton Beach?'

'No one. But the man who's threatening me, he knows.'

'And who's he?'

'A ... Russian. His name is Yuri.'

'Yuri? Yuri what?'

'I don't know. He's a lawyer of some kind. He says the British Establishment will protect Montford.'

'Is he wrong?'

'Probably not, but he wants me to use some dodgy evidence.'

'What?'

'He hasn't told me what. I haven't seen him for a couple of months. Not since that time at Waterloo Bridge. I tried to tell you, Jo. But after that argument we had, you wouldn't speak to me before you left, and I didn't push it because ... well, I didn't want you to get involved too. I thought it might put you in trouble or something.'

'Has he hurt Chris?'

'No.'

'Not yet, you mean. Why don't you take her and go some place.'

'Jo, I'm not running. You know, at first I thought about it. But I'm not running.'

'So what changed your mind?'

Dan glanced to his left then to his right, into the body of the café and was satisfied that the other customer continued to read his Russian newspaper, paying him no attention.

'I've been reading up about the end of the war. You know, sort of background research.'

'Yeah?'

'Jo, this Yuri, I know he's crazy, but the more I find out about it, the more I think that he might have a point. About Montford and Neuwelt.'

'So?'

'So I need to know what I'm dealing with. I need to know what you know, Jo.'

'About Neuwelt?'

'Yes.'

Jo was silent. He rapidly stirred the remaining tea and sugar in his glass, the dark solution swirling round and round with brilliant crystals suspended in it.

'Jo, I said I need to know—'

His father struck the table fiercely with his left hand, causing it to shake violently and Dan's tea to spill on to the greasy surface.

'You people, think you can come into my life, mess me up, get me thinking to back then and all. Listen, it's taken me fifty years to forget about that place – and still I dream about it at night. No matter I'm happy or sad, I see the rotting bodies in the pit. Yeah, I can still see the ash floating down covering everything like snow from when they burnt them. Piles of them. And you want me to tell you all about it? Well, fuck you. And fuck your friend, Grail.'

Dan was stunned. 'Did you say *Grail*?'

'Fuck you.'

'Jo, I—'

'You know what I'm talking about. Don't try and kid me now that you dunno. What is this? Second bite at the goddamn cherry? I told Grail to take a hike, now you going to try again?'

Dan tried to remain calm. 'Jo, I promise, I *promise*, I didn't know Grail spoke to you.'

'Sure, and I'm Saddam Hussein.'

'What does Grail want?'

'You really don't know?'

'No. When was this?'

'When you was in New York. Said he was interviewing Neuwelt survivors. Wanted me to talk about Neuwelt. Well, I ain't going to—'

'Who does he think you are?'

'An old Jew who owns a stinking deli in Brighton Beach. Well, that's what I am, ain't I?'

'He doesn't know that I'm your—'

'Not unless you told him. No one knows. You told him or what?'

'I didn't tell him. So what's he got on Montford?'

'Zilch.'

Dan let the breath ooze slowly out of his body. No one else knew all the details of the connection between him and Jo – except, of course, Yuri. But that was out of Dan's control, and Yuri also had a vested interest in not disclosing the fact.

'Jo, I've got to stress to you, I'm going to have to do this case. Give me something, anything, to work with. I've got to know what I'm dealing with. Not for me, but for Chrissy.'

Jo hesitated. He glanced out of the window and the light fell on to his fine profile. Once more his eyes focused, not on the objects and scenery immediately before him, but on a time now forty years distant. 'In 1955,' he began, 'you know I had graduated in chemistry and went to work for the government.'

'In Stamford—'

'Yeah, Stamford Grange. Place was meant to be a research centre for chemical fertilisers, pesticides, to increase yields, that sort of thing. I wanted to be involved. When you been as hungry as I was in the camps, believe me, growing food, it was like . . . God's work, a miracle or something.'

'I can understand that.'

'But there was something else going on.'

'They weren't doing research?'

'Oh, they was researching, all right. But not just pesticides. There were soldiers and airmen. They would come in the gates, and then be taken to some restricted place at the back of the camp. No one would see them again. Sometimes we would see military ambulances driving quietly to that other place, never with their lights or sirens on or anything.'

'Did you find out what they were researching?'

'Wasn't supposed to.'

Dan smiled at his father. 'That's never stopped you.'

'Chemicals.'

'What chemicals?'

'Weapons,' Jo said.

Chapter 3

It took Sophie over three hours to drive west out of London and reach Montford's estate. The wind was getting up as she drove through the outskirts; the clouds began to break up, the drizzle giving way to heavier showers and then intermittent bursts of sunshine.

As she passed blankets of fields on each side, divided artificially by the dull sliver of tarmac, she thought about the bizarre theory that Dan had disclosed to her. She weighed in the balance the reluctance with which he had told her about his researches, and the sincerity of his tone, against the scandalous nature of his theory. She hoped – for all their sakes – that it could be dismissed as the over-analytical speculation of his undoubted intellect.

But when her lime-green 2CV turned on to a narrow B-road, Sophie felt a shudder of disquiet. What if Dan was right? Who was this man she was representing? She had appeared on behalf of people – men, almost always men – who had committed virtually every kind of abomination and atrocity imaginable in a Western country in peacetime. But if Dan was right about Montford, and he was a war criminal, what sort of monster was he?

There was a queue of traffic at an automated rail crossing. Her car grumbled into a lower gear as the barrier swung down. Lights flashed before her and warning bells rang loudly. While she waited, she tried to imagine the position of the Russian, Ivan Basarov. A soldier, perhaps a brave man, who had survived the war on the Eastern Front, the German invasion of the USSR in 1941, Operation Barbarossa, said to be the most ferocious battle in history; this man had then survived the degradation of the camps, was liberated, and then killed. On the orders of one of his liberators. Before her, the train suddenly screamed past, no more than a blur of blue and red metal, the speed of its progress causing the windows of her car to shake.

Fifteen minutes later, the tyres of the Citroën crunched on the gravel driveway as she entered Montford's estate. There was a long avenue of ancient oaks that led up to a formal-looking Georgian house, in front of which a perfect circle of grass was surrounded by the drive. The coldness of the perfectly symmetrical windows unnerved her, staring at her like one-way mirrors, a line of six windows for each of the three floors. She parked to one side of the royal-blue front door.

Montford came out in a well-worn cardigan and a cravat, waving an expensive fountain pen in his hand. 'Miss Chase, you are perfectly punctual.'

'No traffic, really. Got stuck for a bit at the railway crossing, that's all.'

'Ah, the crossing. Last month a young woman was caught between the tracks. Her car wouldn't budge. Of course, the train couldn't avoid her. Nasty mess. Still, you got here safely.'

'Yes.'

'I wish my solicitor was as efficient as you. He's just phoned to say that something's come up, something urgent, you know – *royal*.' Montford whispered the last word and laughed almost playfully. 'Some housekeeper or other wants to sell her memoirs. Same old story. Where can you find loyal staff these days?'

'I'm sure I don't know,' Sophie said.

'Once upon a time loyalty counted for something.'

From far across the fields, in the distance, she could hear a dog barking, but she could see no other sign of life as she stood alone outside the intimidating house of Simon Montford. She glanced towards her car, and calculated that it was only ten yards away. The wind gusted loudly around the side of the house as a cloud scudded across the sun. She chided herself not to be so silly: here was Simon Montford, the debonair Englishman, tall, ramrod backbone, distinguished grey hair, charming smile – what did she have to fear? Yet her flesh crawled when she looked back at him; suddenly her teeth were on edge and her palms sweated.

'Would you like to come in?' he asked. 'Tea? Or something

stronger? Or are you young lawyers like policemen and refuse all intoxicating substances on duty?'

'Is your solicitor definitely not coming?'

He shook his head but smiled, causing dozens of lines to trace their way across his face. 'Apparently Douglas tried to ring you in chambers before you left London, but you were out to lunch with someone. Then they tried your mobile but apparently it wasn't switched on.'

For an instant she imagined Dan's face as he told her about the unknown war crimes and atrocities in the camps. She wished he were right there, with her, as Montford moved closer, the shadow of his head across her face as the sun again emerged. She felt herself shivering, even though sweat now broke out on her forehead.

'You see, Mr Montford, we – that is, I – am unable to speak to you alone without a solicitor. Rules and all that.'

'What? You can't speak to me at all?'

'Well, we can't speak about the case.'

'So we won't speak about the case. We won't talk about me.' Montford paused, wrapping his cardigan around his still-trim waist. 'We could talk about you.'

'What is there to say?'

'Julian Waugh tells me that you are a great ... friend of Daniel Becket.'

Sophie was taken aback by the nonchalant intrusion into her personal life. If it had been any other case, any other client, she was sure that she would have declined to comment at all. She knew that she had begun to feel increasingly protective towards Dan, and Waugh would tell her nothing about his secret strategy for the trial. But if she humoured Montford then perhaps she could find out something to Dan's advantage. A few minutes with Montford was surely worth that. She tried to cheer herself by thinking of the dinner party Dan had invited her to that evening, but suddenly Montford's pristine garden seemed a million miles from London.

'Dan Becket was my pupilmaster when I first went to the Bar,' she said.

'Shall we take a walk, just around the formal gardens, give you a breath of fresh air before you head back for London?'

She felt she couldn't refuse.

'I'm sorry you've had such a wasted journey.'

'It's not entirely wasted. There's someone I've got to visit about ten miles from here. I'll just have more time with him, that's all.'

'A him?' Montford asked.

But she didn't answer. Her mission was far from romantic. It was to confront Helen's ex-boyfriend.

As they walked their feet crunched over the uneven gravel drive, and they soon rounded one side of the house, past the garages; from here regimented lawns and carefully trimmed hedges spread out from the rear of the house.

'What was it like at the end of the war?' she asked Montford.

'I thought we couldn't talk about the case.'

'This isn't about the case specifically. Just a general picture. Background colour.'

Montford stopped at a perfectly weeded flowerbed into which the branch of a nearby apple tree had fallen, blown by the gusting wind. 'What you young people cannot understand is the chaos that reigned towards the end there. It wasn't just the end of the war. It was the end of ... of a civilisation.'

The word jarred against all Sophie's concepts of World War II. Was he really saying that the Third Reich was a civilisation?

'Nineteen forty-five, you see, saw the dropping of the atom bomb and with it the dawning of a new world. We all knew that things would be different. Europe was going to be divided, boundaries redrawn, countries would disappear – well, as we knew them. Imagine seven million people on the move throughout Europe, many without homes or families or possessions.'

'It must have been easy for mistakes to have been made.'

'What sort of mistakes?'

'You know, trying to decide who was innocent and who was guilty.'

'Now you sound like the prosecution, Miss Chase.' He grinned, exposing his teeth which were still immaculate, but there was no warmth in his words. 'Is this going to be Mr Becket's approach?'

'He's only junior counsel for the pros. I don't think junior barristers are really allowed to have an approach. Let's just see what happens at trial.'

Montford began walking back to the front of the house. His

step had a military briskness with which she found it difficult to keep up.

'If there is a trial at all,' he replied.

'What do you mean?'

'Hasn't Julian Waugh told you? At the preliminary hearing tomorrow, he's going to get the whole farce thrown out as an abuse of process.'

'But I'm not going to be there.'

'Yes, Julian mentioned you had a hospital appoint—'

'It's not me,' Sophie snapped, angry that this private matter had been revealed to a client.

Montford smiled at her regardless. 'Julian said he would just about manage without you.'

Chapter 4

As she drove out of the Montford estate minutes later, relief suffused her body even more quickly than the jets of lukewarm air from the car's prehistoric heating system.

What had been wrong? Montford was perfectly courteous – in fact, more courteous than the vast majority of her criminal clients. Nothing he had said, including that strange comment about civilisation, was anything other than totally consistent with his complete innocence of the war crimes allegation. Yet she perceived an aura of malice, some kind of climate of corruption, that lurked around him, and that gave credibility to the allegations. She turned on to the rutted B-road, full of potholes, and began applying the first test Dan had taught her about assessing a client.

Could he have done what he was charged with?

The 2CV accelerated through the gears with all the enthusiasm of a man with a hangover getting out of bed in the morning. The tall brush hedges on both sides of the road made her feel claustrophobic, and it was already getting dark as she asked herself the question again.

Could Simon Montford have ordered the execution of a camp survivor?

Yes, she thought. Yes.

The clouds had gathered, draining the last of the afternoon's light. She squeezed her eyes, straining to make sense of the indistinct countryside beyond the smudge of her windscreen wipers, but not noticing the huge pothole until she hit it.

The chassis bounced back on to the uneven road surface, making her lipstick and purse fall out of her handbag. As did her mobile phone. She braked sharply and snatched up the mobile, realising that she hadn't actually called Captain Clive Harris of the Army Medical Corps, Helen's ex-boyfriend. She had wanted to take him by surprise. But now she had her doubts about the whole trip. She knew that it would take time that evening to get Helen ready for dinner and it would make sense to drive directly back to London. But when she momentarily imagined herself back in the hospital in January, when she again saw the tangle of small legs and arms being placed upon her sister's chest, Sophie knew there was only one thing to do.

She got out of the car to improve the reception on her phone, pulling the narrow collar of her suit jacket up to her neck, although part of the flesh was still exposed to the cold wind. She cursed the day she had cut her long blond hair into the neat bob she thought people – men – would take more seriously. No one takes women with long hair seriously, Julian Waugh had told her when she joined chambers. Of course, that didn't stop him from recruiting, bedding and then rejecting a string of long-haired young women pupils over the years.

At first she stood at the rear of the car by a drainage ditch on the side of the road, but the black branches of an overhanging tree dribbled a stream of raindrops on to her. So standing directly in front of the lime-green bonnet of the 2CV, she checked the number she had scribbled down on a page of *Cosmo* from Helen's room. The line crackled and then clicked. It was ringing.

'Hello, Medical,' the female voice at the other end said.

'Good afternoon, can I ... er ... speak to Captain Clive Harris, please.'

'Certainly, madam.' There was then the noise of the woman's hand being put over the phone. Sophie could hear the muffled words. 'Clive, another one of your chicks.' The hand was removed. 'He'll be right with you, madam.'

Sophie waited tensely. Her breath was short and her palms began to sweat. Relax, she told herself, you've met this so-called man, remember? And if your memory serves you correctly, he was overweight, overfed and a complete and utter plonker.

Suddenly there was a voice at the other end, patrician, curt – army. 'Harris h-here.'

'Hi, this ... look, I don't know quite how to put this—'

'Who is this?'

'Sophie.'

'Sophie who?'

'Sophie . . . Chase.'

'H-Helen,' he said.

There was a brief pause. Sophie took the phone away from her ear to check that the battery was still working.

'How is Helen?' he finally asked.

Sophie could control herself no longer. 'Clive, you bloody idiot, if you had ever bothered to see her after the birth—'

'It wasn't a birth. Wasn't that the point?'

'You are a fucking shit.'

'Yes, I am. I'm a fucking shit. But can I ask what you want with me?'

'We need to talk.'

'Haven't we been doing that?'

'No, I mean face to face, Clive. My one face to your two faces.'

'Christ, I ended up going out with the right sister, didn't I? Helen always said you had a bit of lip on you. You're a solicitor, aren't you?'

'A barrister.'

'That's even worse, isn't it?'

'Much.'

'Look, where are you now?'

'In a fucking pothole.'

'Which particular pothole? We have quite a few in the West Country as you've probably noticed.'

Sophie told him the name of the B-road.

'You can be here in fifteen minutes,' he said, giving her directions. 'There's a chapel outside the security fence. It's normally pretty quiet. Meet me there.'

It took Sophie double that time to find the place. She took two wrong turnings, ending up in a dead end, then on someone's farm. But eventually she saw the perimeter. As Clive had instructed her, she parked the car on the main road and walked.

The road up to the fence was two hundred metres long but the thick woods on either side afforded some shelter from the wind, if not the rain. The fence stretched in both directions, and was electrified. At regular intervals along its length were signs proclaiming:

This is a prohibited place
within the meaning of:
THE OFFICIAL SECRETS ACT
Unauthorised intruders
WILL BE PROSECUTED

The main establishment was set back several hundred yards from the fence. The complex of buildings had whitewashed walls and green lawns and a plethora of aerials and communication devices arranged chaotically on the roofs.

Suddenly, from behind her, emerging from the woods, Sophie heard a huge rumbling sound, the deafening purr of a massive diesel engine. She ran off the road and tried to merge into the wet thicket which immediately showered huge droplets on her.

A khaki lorry drove past slowly, spraying stagnant water and fine road chips towards her hiding-place. It was irritating rather than painful, and she wanted to shout out as abusively as she could, but she managed to bite her lip. On the side of the lorry was a logo:

GCC
The GLOBAL CHEMICAL CORPORATION

The drone of the tanker slowly faded as it crawled to the far side of the perimeter where there must have been a concealed entrance. But she did not move until it was out of sight. She traced her way in the opposite direction to which the vehicle had gone.

She walked perhaps a quarter of a mile before she saw the lights burning in a small building. As she approached, it became clear that there were candles in the windows of the chapel. The sign outside the half-open doors said simply 'Parish of Stamford Grange'.

A man in a khaki uniform several sizes too big for him stood in the doorway. 'You're late,' he said, retreating immediately back into the chapel.

He was gaunt and dangerously thin, with hollow cheeks and bulging red eyes. She barely recognised him as Clive Harris from the one photo of him that Helen had shown her. It had shown a tanned and healthy man outside a tent in the Saudi desert as Desert Shield had become Desert Storm.

The chapel was the type of hastily constructed prefab structure that mushroomed all over Britain after the war. Once inside, it was obvious to Sophie that the roof had begun to leak. An all-pervading dampness suffused the air. There were seven parallel rows of tatty wooden pews leading to an altar which had a raised pulpit on its left-hand side. On the other side of the altar was a red bucket which caught the steady drips from the leaking flat roof. Harris ushered her to one of the central pews and sat down after her. There was a dirty yellow light by the door, but the main illumination came from the banks of candles, stuck carelessly into wax-covered candlesticks made of wrought iron. Some dead white chrysanthemums drooped miserably in an urn along the wall.

'I have to say, you're looking in fine f-fettle, S-Sophie,' he said. He held the back of the pew in front as he spoke, revealing his sinewy hands stripped of excess flesh. 'I know what you're thinking. Wish you could say the same for me. When was the last time we met? Three years—'

'Four years ago,' she interrupted.

'Ah,' he said, nodding once. 'Shortly after I returned.'

'Returned?'

'From the Gulf. Heroically serving Queen and Country. Desert Storm. What a *joke*.'

His voice had risen inadvertently and he glanced over both shoulders swiftly. No one was there.

'Clive, what exactly is it that you do in this place?'

'You saw the sign on the gate, didn't you?'

'Yes, but—'

'Then you know it's a secret, Soph.' He put his left index finger up to his mouth and said, '*Shhh*.' Then he burst out laughing so hard that by the time he had finished he had begun to cry. 'Oh God,' he sobbed, 'I'm ... going to—'

'What?'

'Look at me. *Look* at me. I am going to die and there is nothing anyone can do about it. And even if they could, they would not be allowed to. I am an experiment, a bloody guinea pig. They let me run around my cage a little so that they can watch the progress of the illness.'

She took his hand gently. It felt like the scrawny foot of a chicken. 'What illness, Clive?'

'And to think I volunteered for the *fucking* Gulf.'

She looked into his eyes and watched the tears fall. Then she repeated as softly as she could, 'What illness?'

He sniffed deeply and wiped his face with the back of his hand. It made Sophie wince, the skeletal fingers rubbing against the protruding cheekbones and temple. Ten yards ahead of them there was the drip-drip of the leak into the red bucket. Candles shone brightly and flickered slightly from the draught.

'Before we went to Saudi,' he said, 'we were given all these injections. Some of us got very ill even before we took off. Of course, it was all hushed up. For the rest of us, the effects were slower, more protracted, more bloody painful. I'm a casualty of war and my death certificate was signed before I even left my own country. What kind of a war do you call that?'

'So what were these injections for?'

'Nerve gas. Amongst other things.'

'Such as?'

'Look, I shouldn't be telling you all ... *any* of this. But where did Saddam Hussein get fucking *nerve* gas from, that's what I want to know.'

Suddenly the very walls of the chapel began to shake; molten wax spilt from the various candles and formed small white pools on the floor.

Clive's eyes were wide with fear. 'It's another of the tankers,' he said.

'GCC? Global Chemicals. What chemicals?'

'I've got to go.'

'But you haven't told me—'

He hauled himself up and rocked on the balls of his feet. 'Tell Helen ... I'm sorry.'

'Does she know about your illness?'

'Of *course* she does,' he insisted. The red rims of his eyes became even more evident. 'Why do you think the baby died? Poor bugger. Passed down from parent to child, father to daughter – it was a girl, wasn't it? Bet they've got a file or two on that over there.' He waved dismissively towards Stamford Grange. 'Said the injections were a vaccine. But they were just one more experiment. One more in our nation's proud history of chemical warfare.' Then he paused, his strength withering. 'Will you tell H-Helen I'm sorry?'

'Look, why are you still here?'

'This place has taken over from Porton Down as the centre for chemical research. I'm trying to help find an antidote to the injections and the gas. Bit bloody l-late.'

He began to walk to the door of the chapel before she could question him further. His gait was the faltering one of an eighty-year-old man, hobbling on rigid knees as if he were about to topple over at any moment. Outside, as she followed him, the last glimmer of light barely lit the gravestones on either side of the path that led from the chapel door to the perimeter road. He paused at the little white chain-link fence and looked at the two dozen or so grimy stones. Grass grew wildly around them; no one had bothered to weed the place.

Sophie gently put her hand in the small of his back. 'Is there anything I can do for you?'

He shook his head.

She stared at one of the gravestones. 'Who are these people?'

'Not who, what. Experiments. Accidents.' He hesitated before adding, 'Worse.'

She went up to a stone that had commanded her attention and assured herself that her eyes had not played a trick. There was no name on the gravestone. The only marking was a year: 1955.

Captain Clive Harris once again laughed ironically. 'They don't exist. They are not here. You did not see them.'

Chapter 5

Dan had been asked by Neville Neale to meet him in his room in chambers before the prosecution conference actually began.

Neale's rooms were at the very top of the chambers building, accessed by a narrow winding stairwell with no natural light; the dusty bulb that remained cast a dull glow over a grey stone landing with no carpets. Dan knocked once. He then heard a high, thin voice from within and entered.

'Daniel,' Neale said. His suit jacket was hung over the back of a chair, and he wore a beige cardigan over his waistcoat.

'You're looking well, Neville.'

Neale smiled slightly. 'Don't bother lying, Daniel. You have absolutely no talent for it.'

Neale offered him a seat in front of his huge oak desk, but instead of sitting behind it, he brought his chair next to Dan's. Dan surveyed the old man's face; the skin was now blemished with liver spots and had lost its lustre. But the eyes still occasionally had the cheerful glint that Dan remembered from his early days at the Bar.

'I've known you now for . . . what?' Neale whispered.

'Years.'

'Quite. So I hope you won't mind me saying that you were – are – the best junior I have ever led.'

Dan looked back at him, warmed, touched by the comment.

'So I thought it was about time I got you this, Daniel.' Neale then picked up a small black plastic bag next to the desk. Dan recognised it immediately.

'Neville, you really shouldn't—'

'Nonsense.'

Inside the bag was another bag. But this was made of heavily embroidered red cotton. Dan's initials had been sewn on the front. It was a wig-bag, known at the Bar as a 'Red-bag'. This was the ultimate professional courtesy that a QC could bestow upon a junior he had led. The value was not in the hundred pounds it had cost, but in the accolade it signified.

'Really, Neville, you shouldn't—'

'I need you on the case, Daniel.'

'Why me?'

'Because waiting downstairs for us is a nest of vipers. Police, CPS – and others. Wouldn't know justice if they trod in it.'

'Is Lancing there, too?'

'I'm afraid he's got stuck in a rather nasty buggery in Exeter. But I wouldn't *dream* of putting him in the same category as the others.'

They both laughed at Neale's irony.

'When's Lancing back?' Dan asked.

'ETA tomorrow evening.'

'So he'll miss the prelim?'

'Oh, *dear*.' Neale smiled. 'But he assures me that he has to be back for some tiresome wardship election tomorrow night.'

'He's never dabbling in politics.'

'I hear a blue bag would be more apt than a red one.'

They laughed again. Dan didn't have the heart, however, to tell Neale that he had bought Dan such a red bag almost a decade earlier. You never bought a second. Neale's once acute mind was slowly disintegrating, he realised. He felt it all the more sharply because he did not know a more honourable man at the Bar.

'I'm a bit tired,' Neale said. 'Of the law.'

'Never thought I'd hear you say it.'

'Nor me, old thing. But recently I find the idea of sitting on a quiet riverbank pretending to fish immensely attractive.'

'So give up. God knows you deserve a rest.'

'Can't do, I'm afraid.' He stood up and began to usher Dan out. 'We can't leave it all to the barbarians.'

As Dan opened the door, the red bag under his arm, Neale did something unusual. He held out his hand. By rigid convention, barristers never shook hands. But now Dan and Neale did so.

'This is my last case, Daniel.'

'What a one to pick.'

'Complete and utter bugger.' Neale laughed. 'Oh ... how is young Charlotte?'

Dan lightly touched his shoulder. 'Young Charlotte's fine,' he said.

As Dan sat in the conference room of the plush chambers in Middle Temple, he thought about what Jo had said about Stamford Grange. Was it really likely that there had been chemical warfare tests there in the 1950s? And if there were, why was it all shrouded in secrecy? What did the military establishment have to be ashamed of? The Cold War was on. The Russians were developing chemical weapons. What was the problem? It didn't make sense.

Around the perfectly polished mahogany table sat a number of men, all with one thing in mind: convicting Simon Montford of war crimes. At the head of the table, by the formal Georgian windows, was Neville Neale.

There were two extravagant candelabras above the table and the carpet was a thick, opulent blue. The chairs had high, intricately carved wooden backs which made them extremely uncomfortable.

'To begin,' Neale said, 'perhaps it would be a good idea if we all introduced ourselves. I'll start.' He looked around the table. 'You all know who I am.'

'Dan Becket, junior counsel,' Dan said as quickly as possible.

The other men identified themselves in turn. There were two men from the Crown Prosecution Service, three members of the Met's war crimes squad, including Grail, who did not acknowledge Dan. Then an historian from Cambridge University who was an expert consultant, a female note-taker from the CPS, and a female pupil from Neale's chambers who would provide the same service for the Bar.

At the very end of the table was a lanky man, in his early forties, wearing a cheap suit and an even cheaper pageboy haircut and knitted tie, who only spoke when prompted by Neale. The man lounged back in his chair. He was unique in that he had no notes or papers in front of him.

'Andrew Short,' he finally conceded as if he were divulging a state secret. 'Just observing.'

Dan found the man's languid indifference offensive, especially after all the trauma the war crimes case had caused his own family. 'Yes, but who are you observing for? You see, "just observing" covers a multitude of sins.'

There was a silence in which other people around the table gazed intensely at the untouched notepads in front of them.

It was Neale who finally spoke. 'We don't need secrets around this table. Andrew has been sent along by the DPP's office.'

Dan knew that any war crimes prosecution could only be brought to court with the consent of the Director of Public Prosecutions, so he wondered why there was this reticence.

'What exactly would you like to observe?' Dan asked him.

Short leant forward for the first time; as he did so his hangdog jowls became evident. He spoke in a confidential way, his voice barely above a whisper. 'We are monitoring the progress of this case. The Director's office is at all times acutely aware of where the public interest lies.'

'And where does it lie in this case?' Dan asked.

'In the truth, or as much of it as is consistent with . . . national security.'

The words national security set off alarm bells in Dan's mind. He thought again of the Kurdish bombing case, and how the two innocent defendants were sacrificed to the overriding interests of this so-called national security. He knew that national security was a trump card that the unscrupulous Executive could play whenever things became embarrassing.

'Are you saying that some evidence has not been disclosed to the defence?' Dan asked.

Neale tried to smile. 'That's what we will all be discussing, Daniel.'

'Surely there should be full and frank disclosure?'

'*Consistent* with the interests of national security,' Short insisted. He ran his nicotine-stained fingers through his mousy hair. 'I know I don't need to remind Mr Becket that the DPP's office can take over any prosecution at any time and do with it—'

'Anything?' Dan asked.

Short sighed, as if he had been compelled to explain the blatantly obvious yet again to this backward child. 'We are the guardians of the public interest, Mr Becket. It's a dirty job,' he smiled, 'but someone's got to do it.'

It was dark outside. In the ensuing silence, Dan stared out of the casement windows on to the courtyard below. Huge trees towered out of sight, dwarfing a fountain in the middle of the courtyard. He could see other barristers in chambers opposite.

Then Grail coughed loudly. 'Can I say something?'

'Of course, Peter,' Neale beamed.

'I'm just a policeman, sitting among all you distinguished lawyers and civil servants and academics. But to me it seems as plain as a pikestaff. This is a *war* crimes case. It concerns the Second World *War*. And in a *war* you don't go around giving the enemy your secrets.' He looked up and down the table, having reached his conclusion. 'Have I missed something?'

'Only one small thing,' Dan said. 'Justice.'

Grail stared at Dan viciously. For a moment his bumbling-policeman demeanour slipped. 'You are happy for Montford to be acquitted, Mr Becket?'

In his mind, Dan instantly saw Yuri on the Embankment, staring up at Chrissy on Waterloo Bridge, while the tide raced through the arches beneath her. Perhaps, he thought, he should keep quiet. Let Montford be convicted, no matter what the evidence might show. That would satisfy Yuri. That would save himself and Chrissy from further trouble. That would be the safest thing to do.

'Are you happy for Montford to be acquitted?' Grail repeated.

Dan thought again of the two Kurds languishing in prison, innocent men with no chance of reprieve. He had done nothing then. True, he had left the prosecution team, he had resigned as a Treasury Counsel. He had argued about it with his wife, and then he had buried her and still had not told a soul – until he met Lisa Hartman. But he had done nothing, was *told* that he could do nothing, to help the Kurds. How was this different?

Neale tried to regain control of the wayward meeting. 'Of course, we are just the prosecution. We all know, as the time-honoured phrase goes, that we are mere ministers of justice. We win no victories and we suffer no defeats. If Montford is acquitted on the evidence, it is a matter of complete indifference to us, isn't it, Dan?'

'Yes,' Dan said.

But he wondered where Yuri was at that precise moment. He wondered whether the room had been bugged. Of course, if someone sitting around that table was leaking information to Yuri, there would be no need for bugs.

Neale continued to talk in general terms about the thrust of the prosecution case, but Dan was not listening. Instead, he allowed himself to think again about whether there was anywhere that he could hide Chris. Was there a safe place to which they could run? If you were watched and followed and bugged, where could you be safe? Or had he done the right thing by just staying where he was? He looked at his watch. Chris would be home from school by now. Alone in the house with Jo, but that's how she wanted it. She wouldn't have been any safer with her grandparents in Devon, she wouldn't be safer anywhere else at all. He desperately wanted to see her.

'So,' Neale concluded, 'I have been assured by Julian Waugh that he does not anticipate making *any* applications at the preliminary hearing tomorrow.'

'But couldn't he apply to have the case struck out as an abuse of process?' Dan asked, roused from his thoughts by the mention of Waugh's name.

'He could,' Neale replied. 'But I am told that he won't, at least not tomorrow. That's why I'm leaving tomorrow's hearing in your safe hands, Dan. I've got a case in the Court of Appeal.'

'Of course that takes priority, but what if Waugh tries to strike—'

'Dan, I have confidence in you. There's nothing Waugh can do tomorrow that you cannot handle. Relax. He is not applying to strike out the case.'

Two hours later, having spent the Tube journey strap-hanging, Dan arrived home.

The wind had a razor edge, forcing other people to turn up their collars and do up their jacket buttons. But Dan sweated, as he always sweated, on the short walk from the station to his house. What if Chris wasn't there? His pace quickened. He wondered if it was sensible to have planned the dinner party for that evening, but the day was a special one to him and he needed to have those he cared for around him.

Having turned off the Uxbridge Road, he could see the light burning through the gaps in the lounge window curtains. It was a warm light, something he used to find comforting when Viv was alive – his personal image of home. But now he could no longer be sure what was going on behind those curtains. He fumbled for his keys. Once he succeeded in opening the door, a blur, like a bat flying out of the darkness of the kitchen ahead, shot at him. It was Chris. She rushed up and threw her arms around him.

He gripped her tightly as she talked about her day, and he drew comfort from the smell of her clean hair and the warmth of her hug.

'Dad, I said the soles of my shoes have worn through, and I know, you're going to think I'm just angling to get another new pair of those *divine* ones with the clumpy heels that you hate—'

'Are you all right, Chrissy?'

'What do you mean?'

'Here, with Jo. Are you sure that you don't want someone else around – a housekeeper or something – you know, who will always be there when you get back from school.'

'I do want someone else around.'

'You do?'

'You. I want *you* around, Dad. But I understand, your work and all that. I boast to my friends at school, Mandy White – remember, the one with the pony and the acne? – anyway, she said her father was the most important because he was a doctor. But I said my dad was, because he put the bad guys away.'

'Do you really think that?'

'Well, I suppose you don't always get the bad guys, but mainly you do. Can I have that new pair of shoes?'

Dan couldn't help smiling. There was no need to do any work on the war crimes case that evening. The preliminary hearing the next day would be a simple matter, sorting out time estimates and witness orders. There was no need to stay up until the early hours preparing arguments against the dismissal of the case.

He could spend the evening with his daughter.

'Where's Jo?' he asked.

'In the kitchen, making dinner. Said he was making goulash, and it's *definitely* a lot gooier than Mum's.' She paused and let go of him. 'Than Mum's used to be.'

'Chris—'

'You miss her, don't you, Dad?'

'We both do.'

'I'll look after you.' She smiled.

'We'll look after each other.' This time he hugged her first and gripped her tightly. In the painted mirror by the door, he could see the back of her head, her hair tied in a neat ponytail, her slender neck. Viv's neck.

'Go and change,' she said. 'I don't want you looking like a barrister at dinner.' She surveyed him slowly, pausing and putting her right index finger to her lips. 'I think ... yes, I think that trendy blue shirt I bought you at Christmas.'

'I bought that,' Dan pretended to protest.

'Yes, but I chose it. Choosing is so much more important, don't you think?' she said with the effete air of an Oscar Wilde character. 'Now run along and wash behind your ears.'

'Yes, boss,' he said. It was one of the simple pleasures in life that he hadn't realised he would miss: being bossed around by a woman.

Chapter 6

When Sophie finally battled her way through the early evening traffic, she braced herself, wondering what state she would find her sister in now. To her relief, immediately she opened the door, she saw Helen in the lounge. But far from being ready to go out that evening, her sister was still undressed, save for a pale pink T-shirt. Around her, cocooning the rest of her body, was the duvet that she had dragged from Sophie's bed, her bedroom being slightly nearer the lounge. Her hair was held up tightly in a clip, but this could not mask the fact that it had not been washed for several days. The television was on in the corner, commanding her attention.

'Get wet?' she said to Sophie, not taking her eyes off the screen.

'Pardon?'

'Weather forecast. Squalls.'

Sophie ignored the comment, checking the answerphone for messages instead. There were none.

'Hels,' she said, 'you know what night it is tonight.'

'Brookie?' Helen mumbled, still engrossed in the television.

Sophie walked slowly in front of her, obscuring her line of vision as Helen craned her neck to see past her. 'Come on, don't play dumb. You know we're going—'

'I *don't* want to go to any silly dinner.'

'Hey, you know the deal. You come to dinner and I come to the help group.'

Helen nodded once. In the last month or so, Sophie had increasingly had the impression that the mist in which her sister's mental faculties had been engulfed since the birth was lifting. She suspected, although as yet she could not prove it, that Helen could be selectively vacant to suit her moods. On the one hand this was an improvement, since it meant that she was exercising some positive control, but it still worried Sophie that she refused fully to return to the life that had been in suspension since January.

'And it isn't any silly old dinner,' Sophie said.

''Tis.'

'Hels, you like Dan.'

At this, there was the first real reaction. Helen now tossed off the duvet and hit the remote control, switching off the television.

'Yes, but you . . . love him,' she taunted Sophie.

Sophie was caught in two minds. Since the birth she had been vigilant in keeping her personal ups and downs away from her sister. It seemed cruel and selfish to burden Helen with her relatively minor traumas. But she dearly wished that she could have discussed her feelings for Dan with someone, and her big sister had been her chief confidante as the two of them had grown up.

'You love Danny,' Helen chanted in a sing-song voice.

'I never said.'

'You don't need to say.'

Sophie smiled and joined her on the sofa. 'I don't?'

Helen put her feet up on the coffee table, deliberately defying one of Sophie's house rules which she could no longer be bothered to enforce.

'You could never keep secrets from me,' she said.

'Nonsense.'

'Oh yes? What about . . .' Helen proceeded to look out of the window and screwed up her face, trying to grasp the memory. Her nose and lips creased with the effort, and just as Sophie was about to say something, they relaxed. She turned round. 'What about when you came back from Sonya Clarke's party when you were thirteen?'

'So?'

'So I said to you, you've been kissed.'

Sophie immediately remembered. She smiled and blushed at once, astonished at the recollection, aware that for a few months at that awkward age Helen had teased her about it mercilessly. But now she was not altogether sure why. 'First time I'd been kissed?' she ventured.

'Second. As you later admitted. But first time I'd caught you.'

Now Sophie trawled through a host of teenage memories in an effort to remember the name of her accomplice. 'Ben Russel,' she finally announced.

'Whatever happened to him?'

'Became an accountant or a porn baron. Depends who you believe. How did you know . . . about the kiss, I mean?'

'I told you how.'

'I've forgotten.'

Helen moved over and stroked the side of her face, her fingers lingering on Sophie's neck. 'A lovebite, my dear.'

'The disgusting little boy.'

'You were a willing victim, Soph. You were always wearing scarves the day after parties in case Mum or Dad—'

'Yes, thank you,' Sophie said, standing up. 'I think that's quite enough humiliation to be going on with.'

'Oh, I've got loads of stories.'

'Right, then, tell me one.'

'Which one?'

Sophie looked down at her sister's eyes which had become brighter than she could remember for months. She hated herself for what she was about to do, but knew it was a matter of too great importance to ignore.

'Which one . . . which one?' Helen beamed.

Sophie sat down again slowly. 'I . . . I went to Stamford Grange,' she said.

The brightness vanished from her sister's eyes as surely as if someone had thrown a blanket over a lamp. Helen's features lost their animation and she again appeared very small, shrivelling, curling up, as she retreated into a strange but safe world which no one could penetrate.

'I saw Clive,' Sophie continued.

But Helen's eyes were now fixed on the television screen and, barely perceptibly, she was humming the signature tune to some programme.

'Hels, he told me about . . . about it all. The chemicals, the injections, the—'

'Did he also tell you how to make me well?' she snapped.

'No, but—'

'So what did you achieve?'

'I . . . I understand better now.'

'You understand what? That I have every reason to be mad? Or . . .' She paused, fighting with the emotions and the words, her face shaking fractionally as the pain overtook her. 'Or that I killed my baby.'

'Darling—'

'No. I joined the army. I slept with a Gulf vet. So I killed my baby. You could make that case in court, couldn't you, Soph?'

'Helen, please—'

'I . . . I killed Jenny,' Helen cried, finally succumbing to the tears.

Sophie held her tight, ridden with guilt for having provoked the situation. As Helen cried uncontrollably, Sophie remembered a time, over a decade before, when the roles had been reversed and she, whose heart had been broken for the first time, sought consolation in the only place she was certain it could be found: with her sister.

Helen finally looked up, her eyes now raw. 'Jenny was the only thing I ever really wanted,' she whispered.

'I know.'

'Sometimes I dream about her, Soph. She . . . calls to me in the night. She asks me what happened and . . . and I can't tell her. Because I don't really know. I sometimes dream that they gave her to me in that room. Just for a moment.'

'They did.'

'And for that moment she was alive.' Helen looked Sophie directly in the eyes. 'Was Jenny alive, Soph?'

What should she say? Helen, as she had so recently reminded her, could always tell when she was lying, and yet to lie now seemed so unspeakably cruel, even if it was what her sister desperately needed to hear.

'She was stillborn,' she said quietly.

Helen half smiled and nodded. 'So it was a dream?'

Sophie kissed her gently on the forehead.

'I went to the doctors again,' Helen continued. 'Said if I . . . there was no guarantee it wouldn't happen again.'

'We'll get a second opinion,' Sophie protested.

Helen smiled and wiped a tear that had welled in Sophie's eye. 'We don't need one,' she said. 'I've got one daughter. No one will replace Jenny. But . . .'

'But what?'

When Helen spoke again, her voice was firmer, older, and her almond eyes were the soft and strong ones Sophie remembered from her childhood.

'If . . .' Helen began. 'I mean, when you have a child, you will let me look after it, too?'

'Of course, darling—'

'I know . . . I know I'm still ill, Soph. But I'll make myself better. You'll see. You get that Dan Becket to love you and I'll get myself better.'

Chapter 7

By the time the doorbell rang, Dan, who had beaten Chris to the shower, was ready. He actually felt rather less than his thirty-nine-plus-one years when, regaled in the famous blue shirt, he clambered down the stairs.

'I'll get it,' Chris called from her room, the blast from her industrial-strength hairdryer suddenly stopping.

'You won't beat me,' Dan shouted, now more than halfway down.

The jibe brought Chris scurrying to the top of the landing. She huffed and put her hands on her hips in mock petulance when she saw her father at the bottom.

'Am I the hostess or what?' she said sternly.

Dan returned the severe stare. Then stuck his tongue out at her.

Chris shook her head and said in a world-weary way, 'Men.'

Through the glass of the front door, Dan could see two shadows waiting outside. He opened the door slowly to see Sophie and Helen standing at the foot of the steps holding hands; or rather it appeared that Sophie was keeping hold of her sister's hand, squeezing it reassuringly.

'Party time.' Sophie smiled.

'Come in,' he replied.

The sisters walked up the steps slowly, Helen first. She was much thinner than Dan remembered. She carried her head with exaggerated care, her neck muscles strained in the way they might be if she was in a deportment class with a book balanced on her head.

'Hi, Helen,' Dan said.

'Good evening, Dan,' she replied. She offered her cheek for him to kiss but no sooner had his lips reached the vicinity of her face than she withdrew fractionally, but sufficiently to let him know that this was enough.

'Oh, cut the Jane Austen routine,' Sophie teased her. 'Dan's practically family.'

Helen looked fully round at her sister and smiled.

'Hi, Soph,' he said.

'Well, you can peck me on the cheek,' she replied. 'We're not wearing wigs and gowns.'

Behind Dan there was a scampering of feet as Chrissy, now with a headband in her hair, raced down the stairs. The band was practically the same blue as Dan's shirt, a fact that made him chuckle to himself. It was these little touches he remembered so well in Vivienne: she would ask him before an evening out what colour shirt he was wearing and then she would wear a small item of jewellery, a bracelet or a brooch, to match; or she would choose his tie and it would match her dress or her shawl. He wondered now as he looked at his daughter whether she was even aware of what she had done, or whether this imitation of her mother was something innate.

'Helen,' said Sophie, 'you remember Christine, don't you? I know it's been—'

'Five years,' Helen said.

Prodded by Dan behind her back, Chris held out her right hand for Helen to shake. But instead Helen moved forward and hugged her tightly.

'Hmm, something smells good,' Sophie said.

'Goulash,' Dan said.

'He cooks, too?' Helen whispered to Sophie, who scowled back at her.

'No, that's Jo. Daddy burns everything,' Chris said.

'Jo?' Sophie asked. 'What's a Jo?'

Dan hurriedly took the guests' coats. 'Chris, perhaps you'd like to show Helen into the lounge and get her a drink.'

'Can I have one, too?' she asked.

'One now or one at dinner.'

'Oh, Dad.'

'Hostesses must stay sober. First rule of etiquette. Ask Soph.'

Sophie grinned apologetically. 'Whatever the man says, Chris.'

'Right,' said Chris, accepting her fate, 'I'll have wine with my meal.' She then began to lead Helen into the sitting room.

Helen whispered, 'Make sure you don't get a small glass.'

Chris beamed back at her.

Then Helen asked, 'Do you have an attic?'

'Yes. Why?'

Before Sophie could intervene, Helen said, 'One day I'm going to live in your attic.'

Sophie blushed as she remembered what Helen had said back in April, that she was always going to live with Sophie, and when she married Dan, she would live upstairs in the attic.

When Helen and Chris had gone, and strains of the latest boy band that Chris was obliged to worship were issuing from the stereo, Dan and Sophie were alone. She smiled up at him without speaking, causing him, through nerves or a desire for the evening to be a success, to feel embarrassed.

'Like my shirt?' he asked, feeling like a teenager on his first date.

'I love your shirt.'

'Matches—'

Sophie took his hand. 'I know. So what's the occasion?' she asked.

'It's a small family thing,' he said.

Just then there was the hissing of something being tossed into a scalding frying pan in the kitchen. The glass-panelled door misted up even more. Sophie looked deliberately in the direction of the noise, not needing to repeat her earlier question concerning Jo.

Dan made a false start, then began again. 'Jo is . . . a relative.'

'A relative what?'

'Well, he was . . . a kind of relative stranger, but now he's very important to me, Soph.' She continued to look at him, awaiting further amplification. Finally, he said, 'Jo is my father.'

He held his breath and could feel himself wincing. It almost felt like that moment before a wayward ball smashes into a pane of glass. He couldn't for the life of him give an adequate answer as to why this simple fact of his blood link to Jo should still cause such anxiety. But he was sure that her opinion of him would change once she had met him. Whether it would change for the better or the worse, he could not decide.

His concerns were not reflected in Sophie's face. She was gripped with curiosity and also unexpected happiness. If one

day in a distant century, she calculated, she and Dan were to
be married, this man would be her father-in-law. Nothing wrong
in making his acquaintance now.

Dan led the way and opened the kitchen door slowly. As he
did so, a mass of exotically fragranced steam rushed out at both
of them. When it finally cleared, an old man could be seen dressed
in an apron in front of the cooker. On the four gas rings four
saucepans of varying sizes bubbled away furiously.

'My God, Jo,' Dan said, 'how many are you cooking for?'

He did not reply but looked around and caught sight of the
woman next to Dan.

'Hey,' Jo cried, 'you must be Sophie.'

He put down a ladle that was covered in a thick, red-brown
sauce, and moved quickly towards her, shaking her hand. 'Only
Dan said how you was beautiful.'

'Helen's beautiful, too,' Dan added, embarrassed.

'Yeah, but you said Sophie was young and beautiful.'

'Pleased to meet you,' Sophie replied, already charmed that
somewhere within Dan Becket his father's eccentric blood had to
be lurking. She looked at Dan's face and loved the awkwardness
she saw there, knowing instantly that only a true parent could
create such public embarrassment as Jo had just caused Dan:
these two were definitely father and son.

'Here,' Jo said, tearing off a piece of bread and offering it to
Sophie. 'Try.'

'What is it?' she asked.

'Goulash.'

She accepted the bread and dipped it into the nearest pan.

'Oh my God,' she breathed, 'that is delicious.'

Then she started to cough.

'Yeah, got some kick, hasn't it? That's the paprika. You got
to use the real stuff.'

'Where,' she coughed, then took in some air, 'where ... did
you get the recipe?'

Jo looked down sheepishly and his voice was less strident.

'From the old country.'

Dan smiled to himself, but didn't have the heart to ruin his
father's moment. He looked momentarily at the notice-board in
the kitchen where the previous year his wife had pinned up the
recipe she had cut out from a Sunday supplement. He forgave

his father the small white lie, for he was sure that in his own way Jo was just trying to impress Sophie for his sake.

But as he watched Jo and Sophie discussing how this unique recipe had been passed down through the generations, a faint shadow began to cloud his memory of some of the stories Jo had told him, of the war, of his mother.

'How long till dinner?' he asked.

'Maybe ten,' Jo replied.

'I'll lay the table, then.'

'No, Chrissy did it when you was in the shower.'

Dan was touched by the seriousness with which his daughter had undertaken the duties of the hostess. She was always doing the best to fill the void left by Viv. He led Sophie out of the kitchen and back towards the lounge, but she stopped him in the hall.

'Well, you've got yourself nicely sorted out,' she said. 'Your father doing his galloping gourmet bit in the kitchen and your daughter doing her high society routine in the lounge.' She paused and looked at him head on. 'What more could a man want?'

He gazed at her, taking a moment to ensure that their eyes had met, but he said nothing.

Sophie had hoped that her flippant question might have produced a throwaway comment that she could have dissected over the goulash and decoded by the time coffee was served. But the stare he had given her was something far more, maddeningly more, profound. He appeared to her to be on the verge of saying something, but was being a typical man and was holding himself back. She pondered that if circumstances had been different she might have revealed her hand further. But as she looked around, she found herself not just in Dan's house, but in Viv's. Behind him, over his right shoulder, she could faintly see the mirror Viv had haggled for in Portobello market. She remembered that day well, for she and Viv had met for lunch in Notting Hill's Hillgate Village and Viv had struggled into the bistro under the weight of her new purchase. With these thoughts, the infectious gaiety of Dan's father slowly drained out of her and she briefly sat on the bottom stair.

'I assume you're not doing the preliminary hearing tomorrow?' she asked Dan.

'You assume wrong, Counsellor,' he said in an American accent. But his frivolity was short-lived when he saw her face.

'Hey, what's the matter?'

'I don't understand,' she said, 'how you can hold a dinner party when Waugh's going to try to strike you out tomorrow. I assumed Neville Neale must be doing it.'

Dan held up his hand. 'Whoa, there. Now just go back a step or two, Soph.'

'I said, Waugh's going to—'

'He's assured Neville he won't make the application tomorrow. That's why I'm going to . . .' But even as he was saying it the full force of what awaited him in court the next day struck him. 'I'm being set up,' he said, sitting down two steps above Sophie. 'Why would Waugh lie?'

'Why do dogs bark?' she said glumly.

'But why does this one bark so often?' he asked.

'If Waugh has lied, I'm resigning from the defence,' she said.

'It's not necessarily a resigning matter.'

'But it is necessarily a matter of principle.' She stood up, her anger suddenly making the confines of the stairwell appear claustrophobic. 'If I've been lied to, Dan, then . . .' She calculated as she spoke. 'Then it doesn't bear thinking about what else has been going on. Look . . . we can go home if you want to work.'

'Nonsense,' he said. 'I'll handle Waugh tomorrow. There's only so much he can say.' He smiled, almost as if he were trying to convince himself. 'Look, I haven't become the world's greatest bore on abuse of process without knowing a thing or two,' he added. 'Let's get a drink before dinner. I hope you like vodka.'

'Vodka?' she asked.

The conversation around the dinner table was just beginning to take off. The main topic of discussion was the cauldron of steaming goulash that Jo had proudly placed in the centre of the table. Dan, naturally, sat at the head, with his back to the French doors that opened on to the garden. He was nearest to the piano, upon which Chris had left a sheet of music. Jo was at the other end, nearest the kitchen door; on Dan's left sat Helen and Sophie – Sophie having whispered to Dan that she wished to sit next to her sister – and on his right sat Chrissy, halfway between her father and grandfather. Just above and behind Jo, Dan could see the archway that led through to the living area. It was a decade ago, he remembered, that he and Viv had finally saved enough money to be able to knock through the two rooms. As Jo now spooned out the goulash, he vividly saw his wife, dressed in dungarees, insisting to the builders that she wield the first blow of the sledgehammer on the dining-room wall. He had laughed, but she grabbed his hand and made him hold the hammer with her, almost as if they were cutting the first slice of a wedding cake. Viv had got a taste for it and had begged the builders to allow her to smash through almost a third of the wall. The next day, her muscles ached so much she lay in bed till noon. He was suddenly wrenched from these thoughts when the doorbell rang again.

Chris got up immediately.

'I'll get it,' Dan said.

He slid behind Chris and went to the front door. In the light of the hallway, he could just make out a figure outside. It was the figure of a man. It flashed across his mind that this could be Yuri, perhaps with some instructions for the next day's court proceedings. But warmed by the presence of his nearest family and friends, he didn't care. He opened the door.

There, in a raincoat that was damp from a light shower, was Antony Thorpe. Dan looked at his father-in-law, bewildered for an instant, before he made the connection. Then he said quickly, 'Antony, come in. Come in.'

'Well, it is tonight, isn't it?' Antony asked.

Dan stuttered out, 'Yes . . . yes, it is. But didn't you say you couldn't make it last week?'

'I couldn't make it until the concert was so terrible that . . . Honestly, trained chimps could have made a better fist of those sonatas.'

Dan glanced briefly outside the door. 'Annette?' he asked.

Antony shook his head. 'Won't drive up to London. Not since . . .' His voice trailed off as he looked around his daughter's house.

'It's lovely to see you, Antony,' Dan said.

The older man nodded. As Dan hung up the wet coat, he was grateful that Jo had made such a huge vat of goulash; there would certainly be enough for another guest. But suddenly the prospect of Antony meeting Jo and vice versa did not seem so appetising.

'My . . . my father is here,' he said.

'Father?' Antony replied. 'I've never really thought of you as having a father.' Immediately, he realised how these words might be construed. He looked at Dan quickly. 'I meant—'

They both broke into laughter.

When Dan ushered Antony into the dining room, the other guests were hushed with anticipation, as if someone had stopped the dinner in freeze-frame. Chrissy was the first to respond, her face breaking out into a joyous grin and her eyes narrowing accordingly as she hurried towards Antony.

'Folks,' Dan said, just before impact, 'this is Antony.'

Just then Chris flung her arms around Antony's neck as the old man braced himself.

'Grandpa,' she exclaimed.

'How's my Natasha?' he said.

'She's my favourite character. And I've finished *War and Peace*.'

'Excellent, go to the top of the class,' he said.

'That'll be a first,' Chris joked.

'Quite,' Antony replied.

'Chris's grandfather,' Dan whispered to the table. Sophie and Helen smiled at the sight of grandfather with granddaughter hanging from his neck. But Dan saw Jo's face as he observed the scene. On it was the falsest smile he could remember seeing. Jo was gritting his teeth so deliberately, and forcing his lip muscles upward so carefully, that the overall impression was something like a grimace. Dan tried to salvage the situation by adding quickly, 'Chris's . . . other grandfather, I mean.'

The spell was broken and the contortions on Jo's face melted away. But the old man saw with horror that the large serving spoon that had been dripping with goulash was now resting on Chrissy's pristine cream-coloured tablecloth. He grabbed his napkin and tried to wipe away the stain, but he just made the mess worse. Dan moved past Chris and Antony.

'I'll get a cloth,' he whispered to Jo.

Sophie had by now stood up, and she held out her hand towards Antony who approached with Chris at his elbow.

'I'm Sophie,' she said.

'Oh, God,' Dan blurted, 'I'm sorry, how rude of me. Antony, this is—'

'Just get a cloth,' Sophie whispered with a smile.

Sophie and Antony shook hands, Antony having said, 'Thorpe.

Antony Thorpe,' as if he were introducing himself on *Mastermind* or *University Challenge*.

Dan moved towards the kitchen, hearing over his shoulder that Sophie was introducing Helen. 'And this is my sister, Helen.'

'Pleased to meet you,' Antony replied.

'Her elder sister,' Helen added.

Once in the kitchen, Dan ran the cold-water tap, then hesitated, not knowing whether hot water would be better for the stain. Viv would have known. Before he could decide, however, the door behind him opened. Jo walked in slowly, totally silent, his eyes on the floor.

'He told me he wasn't coming,' Dan said. 'He had a concert or something.'

Jo, still examining the floor tiles, said, 'Chris's glad to see him.'

'Gladder than she used to be. Believe me.'

'No, he's the one she's grown up with.'

He took the dripping cloth from Dan. 'Look at the mess I've made,' he said.

'It doesn't matter.'

'You know, she's such a sweetheart. She so wants to do everything for you.'

'I know,' Dan said.

'But I ain't part of this.'

'Jo—'

'I don't know your friends. I don't know your family.'

'You can get to know them.'

Jo looked at him. 'When? I don't have that long left.'

He moved away slightly, towards the back door. Then he turned towards his son and said, 'I mean, I'm an old man. I think we're all biting off more than we can chew here. You guys got along fine before me. I'm not part of this.'

'But you can be,' Dan pleaded.

Jo moved a pace closer so that the half-light coming through the kitchen window struck his face. 'Yeah,' he said, but he shook his head at the same time.

At that moment Antony came into the kitchen, adjusting the knot of his single-striped tie. He considered the scene for a moment, the awkwardness between the two other men, but spoke regardless.

'Daniel, I was just wondering if there was a decent wine merchant in the vicinity.'

'It's Shepherd's Bush, Tony.'

'Yes, good point. Just as I, er, thought. So I hope you'll forgive me for not bringing any wine to the feast.'

Dan glanced at his father. His mouth was slightly ajar in reaction to the pomposity of Antony's comment.

'Antony,' Dan said, 'this is my father.'

Jo forced another smile and held out his hand. 'Jo,' he said.

Antony shook perfunctorily. 'And how long shall we have the pleasure of your company on these shores?'

'Till they deport me,' Jo said, looking at Dan and winking.

'Quite,' Antony replied. Then, looking quickly at Dan, he said, 'One more for dinner?'

'Chris will find you a seat,' Dan replied.

Then Antony hesitated, as though he had something to say and was unsure how to say it. He eyed Jo warily and then spoke haltingly. 'I . . . I hope you won't mind, Daniel, but I've . . . taken the liberty of mentioning Christine to one of the tutors at the Academy. And he really is a top man.'

He paused, waiting for Dan's response, and when there was none continued. 'He said . . . he'd be interested in hearing her play and if . . . he could bring out her full potential. He taught Viv just before . . .' Both men knew he meant just before Viv met Dan. 'Still, these things . . . run in the blood. What do you say?'

'You'd better ask Chris,' Dan replied. 'If she agrees – but I think she prefers the Internet to the piano.'

'Excellent,' Antony replied, not really listening. Then he came right up to Dan and took his hand. For the first time he could remember, his father-in-law shook hands with him. 'Dan,' he said in a softer voice, 'this is . . . well, you know, to make up for . . . that time.'

Dan remembered the day instantly: how Antony had appeared and had put money in Viv's handbag, leaving without even congratulating the father of the baby. He fervently hoped that Antony would not mention the occasion in Jo's presence, for when Jo had asked him the reason for today's celebration, he had pointedly avoided the question.

'Thank you,' he said. 'It was a long time ago. Things were . . . different then.'

'Yes, things change,' Antony replied sadly, 'but rarely it seems for the better.' Then he appeared to brighten up. 'Still, Christine – I can't believe how much she's grown. So much like . . . I remember how small she was above the font. She didn't even cry when the vicar anointed her. Do you remember?'

Dan nodded and cast a glance at Jo, who appeared confused.

'I think it's a touching gesture,' Antony continued. 'You know, a meeting of the clans and all that. A mini-anniversary. Splendid.'

He turned neatly and was out of the kitchen with a minimum of fuss. Dan found that he was still holding his breath, hoping that Antony wouldn't blurt out the fatal word in Jo's presence. When he dared look at his father, the confusion had disappeared from his face. He stood there calmly, muttering something under his breath in his private tongue.

Dan tried to smile. 'Well, the goulash will probably be soldered on the tablecloth by—'

'It's her christening?' Jo asked quietly.

'No one was meant to know. Chris doesn't even—'

'You have a party to celebrate the day my granddaughter was confirmed as a Christian?'

'Jo, it wasn't meant . . . it's just Viv and I used to have dinner together on . . . you cannot imagine how awful that day was. We made it a private thing. That's all. I didn't want to be alone.'

'Well, you ain't alone. You got your real family around you.'

'That's not fair.'

'Look, I can understand. Not wanting to be alone. Believe me. That I can understand. But I'm just not . . . part of this.'

'You can be,' Dan said. 'If you want.'

'Wanting's got nothing to do with it. It's just every time I think, yeah, you and me is doing fine, something . . . the past, comes up and stabs us in the back.'

'Do you think I don't feel it, too?' Dan asked.

'Yes. No.' Jo paused. 'Oh, I don't know for Chrissake.'

'You are . . . I mean, definitely . . .' He was summoning up the courage to say the words, to lay himself bare. 'You definitely are the best thing that's happened to Chris and me since . . .'

Suddenly Dan had run out of steam and his words couldn't find their way past the emotions that welled in his chest. The next few seconds weighed heavily on both of them, and Dan again became aware of the pans boiling on the stove.

Then Chris came through the door.

'Why do all the best parties end up in the kitchen?' she smiled.

Dan took the cloth and headed for the dining room, while Jo brushed a few stray hairs away from his granddaughter's forehead.

'What?' she asked, still smiling.

Jo winked at her without replying but, as he did so, the closure of his eyelid caused the shedding of a single tear.

'You're crying,' Chris said, suddenly concerned.

Jo pointed to the stove. 'Pa-paprika,' he said, waving his hands in front of his mouth as if it were on fire.

'Dad,' Chris called, just as Dan was about to leave the room. 'I just wanted to say ...' She paused to ensure she had both men's full attention, then she smoothed down her skirt almost regally as she spoke, in the way Dan remembered Viv doing countless times.

'I just wanted to say,' she whispered, 'how proud I am of my two boys.'

Chapter 8

At the Old Bailey, the judge who was to have conduct of the Montford case, His Honour Judge Constant, had invited counsel into his private chambers. Dan walked two paces ahead of Julian Waugh as the two of them were led through security-locked doors and the dark corridors behind the courts. They both wore their gowns and winged collars but carried their wigs in their hands. Dan did not want to see Waugh, to look upon him or even to speak to him, unless it was absolutely necessary.

When they arrived at the door to Constant's chambers, the clerk of the court, an irascible man with no hair, knocked loudly and announced them. 'Counsel in the case of Montford, M'Lord.'

Constant sat behind his vast oak desk with his wig of office placed on top of a pile of documents like a paperweight. 'Come in, Julian,' he said, beaming towards Waugh. Then almost as an afterthought, he nodded towards Dan. 'Becket, thank you for coming. Please, take a seat.'

He waved towards two low armchairs in opposite corners of the room. Dan sank into his. His knees seemed to be miles above his midriff. The room had dark walls covered in badly framed prints of nineteenth-century court scenes. A smaller frame contained a black-and-white etching of a hanging at Tyburn. The carpet was old, an indeterminate colour somewhere between rust and brown, and had worn through in several places. There were high windows out of which it was impossible to see anything except the changeable autumn sky. Overall there was a musty smell, occasionally sharpened by the faint perfume of alcohol.

'I just wanted a quick chat about the case,' Constant said.

Dan had never appeared in front of Constant before and, in truth, was surprised that this particular judge had been chosen for the case. Constant was a big man, whose mood, Bar gossip said, oscillated between affability and anger in an unpredictable way. He had the convex cheeks and rosy hue of someone who appeared to enjoy the finer things in life to the full. Without his wig, he was almost bald, and a port-wine birthmark stained the right-hand side of his scalp. On the small table behind the desk, Dan could see two bottles of sherry, one opened, and next to them an extremely old vintage port in a pitch-black bottle with a cork.

'How can we help, Judge?' Waugh asked, sitting comfortably in his chair.

'Just wanted to run a few things up the flagpole,' Constant said.

'Of course, Len,' Waugh responded.

Dan began to feel uneasy. He was always wary of these whispers behind the scenes, the off-the-record comments, things said between lawyers that were not for public consumption. He tried to avoid them, but an invitation into a judge's chambers could not be refused.

'Should we have a shorthand writer?' Dan asked. 'For the record?'

'No need, Becket. We're just having a chat between chaps, if you'll excuse the expression. Isn't that right, Julian?'

'I'm sure it is, Judge.' He turned towards Dan, raising his hawkish nose. 'But some people are unduly sensitive about these things. Perhaps we can undertake to repeat for the record anything that *Mr* Becket is worried about?'

'Is that acceptable?' the judge asked.

Dan nodded.

'Right, before we start, would anyone like anything? Julian, how about a little ... no, you're right, far too early.' Constant coughed nervously and turned away from the small table behind him with obvious regret. 'Really, there's one personal matter that I should mention. It involves *personal* involvement with the case.' He paused and looked at each barrister in turn.

Did he know? Dan wondered. Was this an oblique reference to Jo? Had someone tipped off the authorities?

'Of course,' the judge continued, 'in a high-profile trial like this, we cannot let *personal* considerations get in the way. We must all be seen to be completely objective. I see this as a getting-things-off-one's-chest opportunity, as the probation officers would say.'

Waugh looked at Dan in a hostile way, his eyes scouring his face for signs of reaction. Did he know about Jo, too? Dan wondered. All he could think of were Yuri's words: if Dan's personal connection came out then it would be Dan who would be held responsible.

'I'll start,' Constant said, taking up his wig and fiddling with it. 'I have no Russian blood, I have no English blood, and I have even less Jewish blood. My parents were both Poles who came over after the war. To be honest, I think that's why the powers that be chose me for this case. I mean, they could have chosen a proper High Court judge, but as I'm sure you both know, this case is something of a hot potato.'

He waited for a response but received none. There were a few difficult moments of silence until Waugh spoke.

'I know of no reason why I cannot appear as counsel in the case,' Waugh said, greasing back his hair and then smoothing out the bundles of paper he had brought into chambers.

'Becket?' the judge asked.

This was the moment. It had come up so unexpectedly. Dan sat for as long as he could, considering the permutations. Should he now say that he was disqualified by a personal interest, withdraw from the case, apologise, and be free of the trial?

But where was Chrissy? At school. How long would it be until Yuri found out about Dan's decision? Minutes? Hours? It would be obvious immediately that something was wrong since the hearing could not go ahead until Neville Neale was free to take over, or until Lancing returned from Exeter that evening. It wouldn't take long for word to get out. There were droves of reporters hanging on every nuance of the case; it would get out before Dan could get to Chris. And even if he got to her first, where would they go? Where would they be safe?

'Becket?' the judge repeated. 'Anything that you would like to share with us?'

'No,' Dan said. He decided that there was nothing that he *could* share with anyone. Way above him, he could see through the high bars of the windows that the weather was changing. It was beginning to rain.

Waugh handed the judge a half-inch bundle of stapled pages

and then held out a similar bundle towards Dan. 'I'm applying to have the case stopped as an abuse of process,' he said.

'Did you expect this, Becket?' the judge asked.

'I'm prepared to expect anything of Mr Waugh,' Dan smiled as his opponent scowled back at him.

Dan knew that the meeting in the judge's chambers was a turning point. Unless he could think of something else, he was stuck with the war crimes case. If his relationship with Jo came out, he was professionally ruined. If the case collapsed because of it, then . . . He didn't dare think what might happen to Chris.

But the bridge had been burnt. There was no turning back.

Julian Waugh's written submissions constituted the most impressive legal document that Dan had ever seen. In eighty-five pages, Waugh cited everything from the Magna Carta to the Yalta Agreement to the judgments in the Nuremberg Trials. His argument appeared unanswerable.

The case had been listed in the modern part of the Old Bailey, in Court 12, one of the bigger courtrooms, and the well of the court and the public gallery were packed with spectators of every description as Waugh began his submissions in his curt, assured tones. Dan sat at the right-hand side of the front row, not making notes, but trying to figure a way out of his predicament. He glanced up at the public gallery to see if Yuri was there, but he saw no one in particular as the panoply of faces blurred grotesquely the one into the other.

The judicial bench, counsel's row, and the dock itself were made of light, stripped wood which had more or less held its varnish. He felt that if Ikea were ever to sell DIY courtrooms, they would look pretty much like this one. Beneath the judge's high-backed leather chair was the clerk's table, with the shorthand writer to one side. The witness box was on the right and three rows of benches for the lawyers led back to the dock, in which sat the inscrutable Simon Montford. The public gallery was way above and to the right. It had a separate entrance at the side of the Bailey.

Dan sat in the front row even though Waugh was a Silk and he was not. He was damned if Waugh was going to get an easy psychological advantage by having Dan one row behind him.

'My submission falls into three parts,' Waugh said, glancing at

Montford, who sat very still in the dock. 'They are each given a chapter in the written skeleton and I repeat only the bare bones of the submission here. There is objection to this case proceeding to trial as a matter of substance, of fairness, and of principle. I shall deal with each in turn.'

People all around Dan began to write, even the judge started to annotate the skeleton argument, but Dan could only think about Chrissy. What if they left and went abroad? The States would be too obvious because of Jo, but what about Europe or Australia? He had no inclination to run – but was this just his pride? And anyway, how long could they keep running? When would they know they were safe? Then there were practical things. Chrissy's schooling. Her friends, her settled life. He wondered what Viv would have done.

Waugh's first argument was ingenious, almost diabolically so.

'The War Crimes Act provides,' he said, his voice even, matter-of-fact, as if he were discussing a shoplifting in Oxford Street, 'that murders committed broadly between 1939 and 1945 can be brought to trial in this country if they were committed in – and the wording is precise – *German Occupied Territory*.' He paused to allow the judge to catch up. 'Now the case Mr Becket would have the court believe is that the murder ordered by Simon Montford took place after Neuwelt concentration camp was liberated by the British Army. It was consequently no longer *German* Occupied Territory, it was *occupied* by the British.'

Dan heard an ominous murmur around the court, the sort of penny-dropping that occurs when a devastating point is made. Had everyone missed this legal technicality which Julian Waugh had now exposed?

'Perhaps my friend would like to reply to that before I move on,' Waugh said, casting a challenging glance Dan's way. He momentarily stroked his long sideburns and sat down.

'Mr Becket?' the judge asked. He crossed the long sleeves of his robes of office.

Dan slowly, reluctantly, got to his feet. Within the folds of his gown, he felt the muscles in his right leg tremble.

'Mr Becket,' the judge continued, 'this is a point of grave importance, is it not? If Mr Waugh is right, that is the end of this case? In its entirety.'

Dan looked swiftly around the courtroom. At the height of his powers, when he was confident that he was a barrister acting in the interests of justice, when he believed in what he was doing, he would have acted precisely as he did now: pause, build up the suspense, make them wait. But now what he sought was inspiration, some thought or sentiment that would salvage the case.

He thought of Chrissy.

'A young girl is brutally murdered,' he began. 'Jewish, half-Jewish, it doesn't matter. She is murdered an hour before the British tanks arrive – that is a war crime. She is murdered an hour after the British tanks arrive – that is a murder this court must now ignore? That is what *Mr* Waugh would have you believe.'

There was another, louder murmur as Dan sat down. He noticed that his leg had stopped trembling.

Waugh continued remorselessly with his other submissions, but he seemed to Dan to be in another courtroom, in another country, in another time.

'This statute, this case,' Waugh opined, his voice rising, 'is a case of what some people in Parliament called, and I use the word not offensively but as a technical description, *Hebraic* justice. What is sought here after all these years is not a fair trial or the due process of the law, but a platform to air political views, the stirring up of the past, in fact, *vengeance.*'

There was a murmur in the public gallery, but Waugh ignored it.

'Your Lordship will see from the magistrates court depositions that a certain witness testified against Mr Montford. That witness, a so-called informant, was thought to be crucial to the Crown's case.'

'What did he say?' the judge asked.

'Nothing in court. But his original statement – let me be blunt – claimed the defendant had made certain admissions. Concerning Neuwelt. And 1945.'

'But isn't that damaging?'

'If true.'

Dan saw how Waugh hesitated just enough to sharpen everyone's curiosity. Suddenly the QC held up a handful of documents.

'I have here a retraction statement from this witness. He claims – on oath in this affidavit – that he lied about Mr Montford with a view to a reward.'

The affidavit was handed up to the judge and an almost illegible photocopy passed to Dan.

'I should like to hear this from the witness himself,' the judge said.

'So should I,' Waugh snapped quickly. 'But none of us shall. Your Lordship will see that he is now in ... suffice to say, a country from which he cannot be extradited before the trial.'

With that final volley, Waugh sat down to Dan's left, his black silk gown wrapping itself around him like the folded wings of a resting crow.

'Mr Becket?' the judge asked. 'Would you like time before you respond?'

Dan got up, aware for the first time in his life of his Jewish blood boiling in reaction to the taunts concerning Hebraic justice.

'Murder does not cease being murder just because the years have passed,' he said.

If it had been up to him, he would have left it there. However, the judge clearly did not want to make the crucial decision about stopping the trial so quickly. Constant asked Dan to remind him of what the prosecution case against Montford was. Dan had no written notes, he needed none, for the details of the strange death of Ivan Basarov fifty years before were crystal clear in his mind.

'In spring 1945,' he began, 'the British Army crossed the Rhine and the Germans were in retreat. Simon Montford, a major in the British Army, was in one of the advance tank battalions that first penetrated into the heart of Germany.

'The tanks reached a little known sub-camp between the two more infamous camps of Belsen and Buchenwald. The camp was called Neuwelt.'

The words were coming quickly now, and he did not have to think about what he was saying. To his surprise, he found that he was convincing himself almost as he spoke that this was a case worth prosecuting, not because of the threats, or Yuri, or because of Dan's Jewish blood, but because someone had to speak up for Ivan Basarov – because it was the right thing to do.

'Neuwelt was full of Russians – soldiers, prisoners of war, as well as civilians, all of them Jews. They had been specially selected and brought from the Eastern Front where the Red Army was advancing rapidly through Poland.

'They were brought on what are now known as "Death Marches", walking hundreds of miles. The stragglers were immediately shot. Sometimes they proceeded on open train carriages without food or water. Up to eighty per cent died on the way.

'Neuwelt was special. For it was here that chemical gas experiments were carried out on prisoners. Terrible, unspeakable experiments. But the chief scientist, someone known as the Mozart of Murder, Klaus Keller, disappeared after the British arrived.

'But before he vanished, Keller put on a demonstration. He gassed a Russian soldier by the name of Ivan Basarov.' Dan looked around the court, aware that his next words were the ones that the mass of people was waiting for. 'Basarov was gassed by Keller on the orders of . . . Simon Montford.'

There was uproar everywhere. The noise seemed to circle around Dan's head, and then spin into his ears. Through all this he was determined to speak on, unsure how loud his words were, or whether anyone at all could hear them.

'It was a *war crime*,' Dan said, trying to ignore the din. 'No matter how many smokescreens Mr Waugh puts up, it was a war crime. There is only one issue: does the evidence prove that Montford ordered the gassing? If it does, it was a war crime.'

He sat down, aware again that sitting in the dock not thirty feet behind him was a former minister of the Crown, a Privy Councillor, a Member of Parliament, an elected representative of the people. Someone who was a commissioned and decorated officer in the British Army, a member of the Establishment, an Englishman.

Under the cover of the chaos in court, Grail edged his way clumsily in. He had a dusty file in his hand.

Chapter 9

Shortly after Dan sat down, His Honour Judge Constant retired to consider his decision on the question of abuse of process.

It was only when he had stopped performing that Dan realised how exhausted the strain had made him. He desperately wanted to find a quiet place where he could seek sanctuary. But Grail followed him out of court with the battered file in his hand. He insisted that Dan joined him in a conference room on the third floor.

Inside the room, sitting as languidly as before, was Andrew Short, the representative from the DPP's office. The room had no natural light and was a square, dirty space with a dim pearl bulb and one chair.

'You know the judge's real name?' Grail began. 'He isn't English, he's—'

'Polish. Yes, I know,' Dan said wearily.

'Born Leonid Konstanowicz, or something like that. One of those names with loads of Ws and Zs.'

Short let out an irritated huff. He took a long drag from a vile-smelling cigarette and opened his mouth to form a series of smoke rings. 'You're missing the point, Grail. Lenny Constant is *Polish*. It's not the name, it's the nationality. Does that fact mean anything to you, Mr Becket?'

'Germany invaded Poland to start the—'

'The Russians had a non-aggression pact with Nazi Germany before the war, agreeing to divide up Poland between them. When the war began, some Poles welcomed the Nazis, preferring them to the communists. And then, of course, there was Katyn.'

'The Katyn massacre,' Grail said, reciting the fact as if it were something he was reading off the back of a cereal packet. 'The

Russians massacred four hundred – or was it four thousand? – still, loads of Polish officers and then tried to blame the Germans.'

'So,' Short interrupted, clearly annoyed by Grail's interference, 'old Len Constant is unlikely to be a great fan of your dead Russian, Mr Becket.'

Dan looked from one man to the other, from Grail standing guard at the door, to Short holding court from the chair. 'Do you want me to object to Constant as trial judge? Is that the purpose of this little . . . chat?'

'Oh, no,' Short said. He coughed violently and stubbed the cigarette into the filthy carpet. 'Constant is perfect. He's . . . manageable.'

'We have files on several judges,' Grail blurted. 'But then you'd expect that, wouldn't you?'

'I wouldn't expect anything less,' Dan said.

Short lazily got to his feet and began to lean against the graffiti-strewn wall at the far end of the room. He straightened his knitted tie. 'Constant's first instinct will be to help Montford at every stage. We have to usher him away from that. Is that the report?'

'What report?' Dan asked.

Grail held out the file that he had not let go of since Dan had first seen him that morning. 'Took us ages to dig it up, and we only came across it by accident, really,' Grail said, but his words did not ring true.

It was a distinctly old-fashioned document, with fading cardboard covers that had lost their original colour and firmness. There was a fraying Treasury tag in the top left-hand corner, and once Dan opened the file itself the paper inside was almost sepia. It was headed:

POST HOSTILITY ANALYSIS
COMPARATIVE VIABILITY OF CHEMICAL CAPACITY

There were three minutes of silence as Dan skimmed through the report.

The fifty or so pages were filled with indecipherable calculations and cross-sections of specialised equipment. Dan saw the plan of a rectangular room with pipes that fanned out from the

central housing like the roots of a great tree. There were arrows
with strange codes alongside them, and a shaded track outside.

'What is it?' Dan asked.

'Couched in sanitised mumbo-jumbo, of course,' Short replied,
without looking at the file. He examined the nails of his left
hand before running his fingers through his oddly circular
haircut. 'Turn to page twenty-seven. But can't you guess? That
cross-hatching is a narrow-gauge railroad track.'

In an instant, the appalling truth of what he was holding in his
hand sickened Dan. He felt the bile rise in the back of his throat
and his hands suddenly felt unclean.

'The main gas chamber at Neuwelt,' Short said, in a casual
fashion. 'Those openings around the rectangles are gas-tight
doors, the arrows point out the flow of Tarin A gas through
the pipes, the special railway outside is *supposed* to take the . . .
processed bodies to the mass graves. Nazi efficiency at its best,
worst, whatever the word is.'

Dan imagined how it had started. A few lines scribbled on a
piece of scrap paper: the bodies go in here, the gas comes out
there. A ruler, a pencil, rubbings-out, make the chamber bigger.
Finish the first draft. Pin it to the drawing board. Work on it.
Six million dead.

'Who made the report?' Dan asked.

'William Querry,' Short replied.

Dan thought he recognised the name.

'Professor of Modern Military History at one of our great
universities,' Short continued. 'Problem is, Bill Querry, bless
his cotton socks, when he examined the blueprints for Neuwelt,
concluded that they . . . well, wouldn't have worked.'

'How do you mean?'

'I mean the chamber wouldn't, couldn't, *didn't* gas people.
The pressures are all wrong, or the flows go the wrong way
or something. All technical, but conclusive. The point is that
Querry deduced in the 1950s that Neuwelt was not an active
death camp. And that fits with the broader picture because most
of the extermination camps were in Poland and not in Germany
itself, where Neuwelt was.'

Dan put the file down and saw that fine traces of the dust
from the covers had ingrained themselves into the grooves in
his palms.

'You've just been touching an official secret. A dusty, old one – but still a secret,' Short said. 'You'll have to sign some form or other, but you're bound to secrecy anyway.'

Dan looked at Grail, who looked down; it was clearly Short who was in charge. 'Why is this a secret?' Dan asked.

'Because of what else is in the file.'

Dan picked up the faded document and leafed through, seeing further blueprints, annotations and calculations.

'The key word in the title is *comparative*,' Short said.

And then Dan saw it, a plan of a facility in England. At Stamford Grange.

'We were doing a little research into chemical gases after the war,' Short said. 'Nothing too sinister but all a bit hush-hush. Wouldn't do to let the cat out of the bag after all these years.' He took four slow steps towards Dan and stood before him, smiling cynically. The stench of tobacco on his breath was obscene.

But by now Dan had appreciated the thrust of the impromptu meeting. 'You want me to bury the report, don't you?' he said.

'We don't want you to do anything that would offend your conscience, Becket,' Short said. 'But if you disagree with us, you will be sacked immediately.' He grinned, exposing more nicotine-stained teeth. 'Anyway, you're not so much burying the report as putting it back to rest, shall we say?'

'But if Querry's analysis is correct, then Montford *must* be innocent,' Dan insisted. 'We've got to disclose it to the defence.'

'It is an official secret. We have a duty to protect it. Let the jury make its own mind up from the evidence they will have.'

'I am not letting an innocent man go to prison.' Dan was about to add: I'm not going to let it happen again. But he controlled himself. He knew it was the same kind of off-the-record conversations, the same phrases in the same windowless rooms, which had led to the Kurds being sacrificed before.

'Do you understand the . . . implications if Simon Montford is acquitted?' Short asked.

Dan studied his eyes intensely. Did Short know? Was he in on Yuri's plan, too? That would explain why he wanted to bury the Querry report. But there was something that didn't quite fit. Dan just *knew* that Yuri would not have used a patronising pain in the arse like Short. But, of course, Andrew Short had asked the correct question. What would be the implications if Montford was acquitted? Yuri had said that Dan would be held responsible if Jo's connection to him came out, and Chris would be in danger if he refused to do the case. He was trapped: he had to do the case and he had to win it.

'Listen, Becket,' Short continued, 'this case is your big chance. Danny-boy's big comeback. Especially after he fucked up his promising little career last year by crying into his Guinness over a couple of Kurds.'

'I don't drink Guinness.'

'Isn't that what working-class Irish boys drink? And before you ask, of course we check on you. The Lord Chancellor has a thick file on all you hot-shot barristers. Do you think they would let a half-Paddy like you become a Treasury Counsel, licensed to prosecute terrorist cases, without an MI5 check? What do you think MI5 do all day? Play fucking cards?'

Grail looked up.

'Yes, all right, Grail, they do play cards. But they also check out subversives. People like Becket, here.'

Dan let the tirade of prejudice wash over him. It was no worse than he had encountered day after day as a boy. He always knew the Establishment held these views; in a perverse way it was somehow reassuring to hear Short articulate them, for they confirmed his hatred for the man. Short continued to whine on about the security services, while Dan read Querry's report.

'I want to do this case as much as anyone,' he said. 'You heard my speech in court.'

'Very touching,' Short mocked. 'A little melodramatic for my tastes, but it shut Julian Waugh up.'

'I'm going to do all I can to convict Montford,' Dan continued. 'But I'm not going to bury evidence. I'm going to disclose this report to the defence.'

'I'm afraid you can't do that.'

'I'm afraid I can do anything I want consistent with my lawful powers as *your* legal counsel in this case. You instruct counsel, but we are independent, we form our own views. We advise *you*. And my advice is that the Querry report must be disclosed. If it's leaked and we haven't disclosed it, the whole trial will be terminated for good. You've got to hand it over.'

'I can't do that,' Short said, his pallor being replaced by a rising flush.

'But I can,' Dan said. He looked at Grail defiantly. 'And I'm going to. You've instructed me and—'

'We can always withdraw those instructions. You are not indispensable, Becket.'

'I am going out of this room and I am going to tell the defence about the existence of this report.'

'We'll prosecute you under the Official Secrets Act. Half-Paddy or not.'

'Let's see how far you'll get. You want to bury a report that might well prevent an innocent Englishman from going to jail. I haven't looked at the Official Secrets Act recently, but I think there is a chance a London jury might think I was justified in breaching the Act.'

'You insist on doing this?' Short asked.

Dan stared at him resolutely.

'You're sacked. I shall tell the senior prosecutor from the CPS.' Short stormed out of the room, leaving an invisible wake of stale nicotine odour. Grail ran along behind.

About thirty seconds later, through the open door, Dan heard the message over the Tannoy summoning all parties in the case of Montford back to Court 12. He had been sacked. He had not withdrawn, he had been sacked. He could not be blamed by Yuri; if the report were not disclosed, the whole war crimes prosecution would be infected with illegality and Montford would walk free without even a trial. But though he repeated this chain of logic again and again to himself like a mantra, it gave him no comfort.

When all the parties had assembled ten minutes later, there was a buzz of expectancy around the court.

Dan heard whispered asides, he saw two court ushers in black gowns pointing at the clock, more jailers than were necessary had come up from the cells, police officers chattered conspiratorially, and the public high above the body of the court crammed into the available seats in the public gallery.

At the end of the front row, Julian Waugh sat wrapped in his silk gown, motionless. He stared down at the bench in front of him, avoiding eye contact. Montford, too, sat quietly in the dock, and kept his own counsel. Then there were three loud knocks at the judge's door. There was a shuffling of feet as the court rose for the judge's entrance, and one of the ushers to Dan's left shouted, 'All rise.'

Len Constant sat down solemnly and flicked through the pages of his large red notebook. He scanned the packed court nervously, and Dan wondered if the Polish judge had ever played to such a large stage.

'In this case,' the judge said, 'the defence makes an application to stay these proceedings as an abuse of process. Julian Waugh, QC, who appears for the defendant, Mr Simon Montford, has submitted an extraordinarily impressive skeleton argument and has backed that up with, if I may say, his characteristic eloquence. In summary, he contends that this war crimes prosecution is not founded in the wording of the War Crimes Act, is unfair due to prejudice, and is an affront to the fundamental principles of British justice.' The judge paused and made brief eye contact with Waugh. 'These are all formidable objections.'

Dan's mouth was totally dry, but he didn't reach for the carafe of water in front of him. If the judge was going to throw the case out, he wanted to hear every word of the judgment; perhaps there would be some morsel that he could throw at Yuri. Look, I did my best. This is what the judge said. It was beyond my control.

'But there is one sentence that has persuaded me above all else,' Constant continued. 'It is this: murder does not cease to be murder just because the years have passed.'

Dan was incredulous.

'I have been dissuaded from stopping this case by the passionate arguments of Mr Becket. Accordingly, I reject all Mr Waugh's submissions. This case will go to trial.'

People milled around outside the doors of the court after the judge had left. The show was going on: there would be more headlines, more juicy revelations, more intrigue. Reporters talked in whispers to policemen, the support staff from Montford's solicitors spoke among themselves, but Dan left the scene alone, sick with worry about what would happen now.

When he reached the lifts at the end of the third-floor landing, he saw Grail.

'So you're out of it?' the policeman said to him.

'Wish I wasn't.'

'Would you have disclosed the Querry report?'

'Wouldn't you?'

Grail inspected the scuff marks on the tips of his carelessly polished shoes. 'Think we'll convict Montford?'

'There's a chance. Depends how many witnesses you can dig up, Mr Grail.'

The lift to the robing room had arrived and Dan ventured to get in.

'I already got a few,' Grail said. 'You want to try finding them after fifty years.'

Then Dan tried to say casually, 'I understand that you approached some old deli owner in New York.'

'How did you—'

'Lisa Hartman, a Manhattan attorney. She has a contact who has a contact – the Russian Jewish grapevine isn't that big in New York. Are you going to use him, the deli man?'

The lift doors began to shut and Dan put his left hand in the way, causing them to reopen.

'He wouldn't speak to us,' Grail said. 'I hear he knows nothing anyway. Just because he was in Neuwelt doesn't mean—'

'Quite,' Dan said, and allowed the door to shut.

Julian Waugh disappeared through the double glass doors of the men's robing room. From outside, he could be seen throwing down his wig in disgust even before he reached the further door reserved for QCs. But Sophie wasn't about to let him stew in peace. She was breathless, having rushed from the hospital back home, where she dropped off Helen, then to the Old Bailey. But despite her haste, she had arrived just after the judge's ruling. Violating all convention, she stormed into the men's area, even though in one corner a junior barrister's naked torso could be seen as he changed his sweat-stained shirt. The man was startled by Sophie's intrusion, but Waugh was not.

He sneered, 'I know they say you have balls, Sophie—'

'You lied to me, Julian.'

'Ridiculous.'

'You bastard, you lied to me about the abuse argument. You said you weren't trying to strike it out. You never even asked my advice. How could you?'

'Seen Becket recently?'

'I'm not trustworthy? Is that it?'

'Not where Becket's concerned.'

'Well, I can't trust you, Julian.'

'No. You can't ... trust yourself.'

She hated Waugh's patronising tone, his patrician looks, all of it. In a flash, she knew what she wanted to do. 'I'm returning the Montford brief. If you've lied about this, God knows what you'll do when things get sticky.'

'Briefs like this can make you, Sophie.' Waugh paused again. 'Or break you.'

He stood still and waited until the other barrister had left the room. Sophie, too, watched his departure, and then let her gaze return to Waugh's face. But his eyes had changed; hardened, narrowed. They penetrated right through her as he spoke.

'You stand on the very brink of disaster, Sophie.'

She tried to interrupt but he was relentless.

'The eyes of the Bar will be on you. A word about the Montford defence and ... I will ruin your career. I liked you, Sophie. I thought you could have gone far in the law. But I will ruin you. And Becket. Believe me.'

She did not reply.

Chapter 10

That evening, Chrissy was due to go to the theatre. The Marlowe tragedy, *The Jew of Malta*, was playing at the National Theatre, and since the trip was supervised by the school, Dan had decided to let her go. He would pick her up after the performance. Of course, after he had been sacked from the prosecution, he considered calling up the school and fetching Chris home. But was that the alternative? Going home? Sitting and expecting ... the worst? He wasn't prepared to do that, even though he constantly felt as if he were holding his breath, waiting for everything to explode. All his senses became more acute, noises were amplified – a closing door became a slamming door, shapes became shadows, everyone he encountered, he imagined, was talking about him.

He returned home from the Old Bailey in the early afternoon and not long after that Sophie called him. They agreed to meet in the Judge Jeffrey for a drink, after which he could travel the short distance across the river to the National.

The Judge Jeffrey was packed by 8 p.m., by which time the courts and chambers were empty. There was special excitement in the wine bar as there were to be hustings in a City of London wardship election in the small hall near the wine bar, at which a notorious right-wing candidate was due to stand.

Dan and Sophie managed to get a table by the window. She was still in her sombre court suit, whereas he had changed and wore a sports jacket and an open-neck shirt Chris had recently bought him to 'liven him up'.

'You look ... different,' Sophie said, pouring out the first glass from the bottle of white.

Dan glanced at the weary features of his companion and smiled.

'I know what you're thinking,' she said. 'You wish you could say the same for me.'

'Bad day at the office, Soph?'

'I've withdrawn from the Montford case,' she said. She waited for a response from him, but he just smiled back as if it were something he knew would happen. Then she paused and shook her head before continuing: 'Would you believe we paid our own servicemen one shilling a time for the privilege of being poisoned?'

'Yes.'

He did not want to engage her in a discussion in which he would undoubtedly agree with her every sentiment. The problem, as so often, was Jo. He would be constantly aware of having to skirt around Jo's links to Stamford Grange.

'Yes?' she said. 'Is that all you can say?'

'Yes.'

'That's what I've always liked about you, Daniel Becket, you keep the art of conversation alive.' Then she paused, a more sombre mood catching up with her. 'The guy Helen slept with, he was injected with an anti-gas serum before the Gulf. I don't know, something went wrong.' She took a sip from her glass. 'All right. Now you. Why have you been sacked?'

So it was already out, Dan realised. He wasn't surprised.

Sophie said, 'The jungle drums around the Temple are resounding with the news. Clerks from all sorts of chambers are trying to grab your return brief for one of their out-of-work barristers. It really is like a pack of hyenas closing in on a wounded lion. You're the lion, by the way.'

Yuri must know by now, Dan thought. Perhaps it *had* been a mistake letting Chris go to the theatre. He just didn't know.

'Everyone's talking about this legal sensation and you sit in front of me, your friend, your confidante, your . . . most beautiful pupil by far—'

'The rest of them were men.'

'Thanks . . . and you tell me *nothing?*' She finished her glass, clearly expecting that Dan would disclose a juicy morsel of gossip. 'Well?'

'Nice wine.'

'Sod the wine.' Then she modulated her voice and softened her expression. She whispered, 'Is it true you've been sacked?'

As he looked into her intelligent eyes, he wished that he could tell her the truth. She tilted her forehead slightly to the right, so that the neatly cut bob slid away from the side of her head, exposing the smallest pair of ears he had seen on a grown woman.

'Don't look at me like that,' he said, smiling.

'Like what?'

'With *those* eyes. And don't pretend you don't understand what I'm talking about. Christine gives me the same look and I always end up buying her another pair of shoes.'

Sophie glanced over her shoulder and whispered, 'So what *can* you tell me?'

There were perhaps eighty other lawyers in the low-ceilinged bar, and every now and then one of them would indicate Dan with a nod or a meaningful glance. Dan beckoned Sophie closer with the crook of his finger and she leant forward, her ear inches away from his mouth.

'What?' she whispered.

'Nothing,' he whispered back.

'Nothing?'

'I can tell you nothing, Soph. Except that rumours of my demise are not for once exaggerated. I've just returned all the war crimes papers. Actually, I'm going to pick Chris up in the car later.'

'So that's that,' she said. 'We're both off the case.'

'Apparently.'

'And you're saying no more?'

'Nope.'

'Shit.'

There was a distant round of clapping and cheering emanating from the hall across the road.

'All right, then. Want to go?' she asked.

'Go?'

'The hustings for the wardship elections.'

'I think I've had enough of politicians.'

'Come on, there's this right-wing nutter standing against Lancing. Poor Robert's standing on this sensational election platform, something to do with more parking permits for the Bar around the City, and the painful execution of those wheel-clamp cowboys.'

'And the other guy?'

'He's a lecturer. A revisionist historian. You know, addresses New Right rallies in Germany.'

Dan took her arm. 'OK,' he said.

He looked at his watch. Either he could sit in the foyer of the theatre for over an hour or he could hear for himself some of the lies propounded by the ultra-right. It was no real contest, for since he had met Jo, notwithstanding Lisa's extremism, the 'Jewish question' had become so much more important to him. He drank the rest of his glass of white wine and savoured the warmth of the alcohol as it burnt in his throat. They left the rest of the bottle behind the bar for later and headed across the road.

The hall was gaudily lit, with an arched roof and high narrow windows as are seen in Gothic churches. There was a block-wood floor and rows of fold-away seats, although no one sat down. The walls were decorated with dark oil paintings of severe-looking men standing in gowns of office and mayoral chains.

Between Dan and Sophie and the stage, a raised platform twenty yards away, was a swath of people. But these were not the City types in suits and ties that Dan had expected. The audience consisted mainly of students, in jeans and denim and leather jackets. Some of them were decidedly unkempt, with long hair, ponytails, and a variety of badges. Others had very short haircuts and serious expressions that verged on the menacing.

'Can you see Robert?' Sophie called to him above the din that echoed around the room. She tried to stand on the tips of her toes to see over the shoulder of the short-cropped man in front of her.

'Lancing's at the back of the stage,' Dan replied. 'Looks a bit overwhelmed by it all.'

He saw a movement in the crowd, a surge towards the stage, as a man in his forties, wearing a jacket but without a tie, got to the podium to address the crowd. There was a mixture of cheering and booing. The man in front of Sophie cheered loudly.

'Is that him?' she asked.

The man in front turned and said in a threatening manner, 'Who did you think?'

'Oh,' she said, '*that's* Gordon Wilson. Thanks. Wow.'

Dan picked up a flier from the floor and looked down the

list of candidates. The paper was badly soiled and had a large footprint down its length. But he saw the name Wilson G. The man was a lecturer at the City and Guildhall University. He was also a member of the New English Nation Party and used every platform, stood in every conceivable election, as a pretext to spout his ultra right-wing views.

On the stage, Wilson cleared his throat and waited for the shouting to die down. He was very patient, and by the time he began to speak one minute later, Dan felt the acute tension around the hall.

'The Holocaust,' Wilson began, 'is a *lie.*'

With that one simple sentence, pandemonium broke out in the crowd. Flour bombs were thrown on the stage, a couple of scruffy youths climbed up and tried to get at Wilson, and fights broke out between the factions around Dan and Sophie. He could see her caught between the large man in front and two long-haired youths who were being pummelled to the floor, her eyes wide with fright.

He dived under the exchange of blows, but was knocked to the floor. He lost sight of her but heard her cry out that she would meet him outside.

The press of the crowd was now in the opposite direction as people who did not want to fight scrambled for the door. Dan got to his feet and had his jacket grabbed violently from behind by someone he did not see.

He struggled to break through the mêlée and ended up sliding through the door with the crowd, his feet barely touching the ground. He crossed the narrow side road that led into the Temple, thinking he would be safer in there. He didn't dare turn around but kept moving forward. Suddenly he saw the black-painted wood of the side entrance to the Temple itself.

Out of nowhere, a woman appeared in front of him. She was no one he recognised; he didn't see her clothes, just the blur of her face and then a flash. A flash of yellow as she raised something level with his eyes.

A searing pain instantly bore into his eye sockets. The world disappeared. He was aware of liquid dripping down his face, acidic liquid, seeping into his mouth. He spat, not seeing anything, staggering he didn't know where.

He must have been within the grounds of the Temple by now,

he calculated, but he couldn't see. All he felt was the pain, tearing away at the lining of his eyes, from the inside, an uncontrollable heat inside his head, as if someone had taken a needle and was thrusting it slowly through the centre of his eye socket.

Suddenly his elbow was taken as someone led him down stone steps. He heard the splash of water from a fountain, then felt the water cooling his face. There was still pain but it was no longer increasing, as if the needle were stuck halfway through his eye.

Nothing was said, but his knees begin to buckle and he was helped to the floor. More water was splashed on his face, and the cool-hot, painful-soothing liquid traced the outline of his chin and neck.

Slowly the world, blurred and painful, appeared. As did the face of Yuri.

'Crazy woman,' he said. 'I saw it all. Perhaps I could be your witness, Mr Becket.'

Dan struggled to focus on the man's face, but the effort created waves of pain like further small shards of glass being driven into his pupils from the other side.

'If you're *lucky*,' Yuri said, with genuine concern in his voice, 'she will only have used watered-down lemon juice and not acid. You might not lose *all* your sight. Isn't that good news?' He tried to get Dan on to his feet. 'Now why do you suppose she was *so* annoyed with you? Could it be that you have *miraculously* been sacked from the war crimes trial?'

Dan could hear someone else approaching, and through his pain he tried to make out who it was, but his eyes were now soldered together.

'Maybe you will be just as miraculously . . . reinstated into the Montford trial. But what do I know?'

The other person, a man arriving on the scene, now said something that Dan could not properly make out. There was too much pain. There was too much fear.

'Thank you very much,' Yuri said to the other man. 'But he's with me. I'll look after him from here.'

Dan felt himself placed on a bench that he knew overlooked the Temple lawns and the river. He saw nothing.

'You know,' Yuri said, 'I'd never even heard of *The Jew of Malta*. So I bought a book. Said it was an anti-Semitic play.

I'm surprised at you, Mr Becket, allowing your daughter to go to something like that.'

'Chrissy,' he gasped. 'Don't do anything to—'

'Oh, this is just a warning. Not even that. A piece of friendly advice: do what we say. Don't disappoint us.'

'So you won't—'

'Her fate is entirely in your hands. Now how many parents can truly say that?'

'If you touch her—'

'What? How will you know? You know, it reminds me of another play in which a beautiful young daughter leads her blinded father around.'

'You bastard.'

'Of course, Cordelia dies at the end of *King Lear*. Doesn't she, Mr Becket? I remember when the RSC toured Moscow. The benefits of glasnost.'

'I'll kill you.'

'Someone must be punished for what the British did to Ivan Basarov. There are only two candidates: you and Montford. It's your choice.'

'Why can't you just kill Montford?'

'Fine sentiments from a lawyer. Of course we've thought of that. But death is only part of the process. First the whole corrupt British system must be exposed.'

'Exposed as what?'

'As offering a haven to some of the architects of the Final Solution.'

'Keller?' Dan shouted. 'Do you mean Keller?' he repeated more loudly, but there was no reply.

Chapter 11

Dan heard Yuri's footsteps receding.

The Russian left with an unhurried pace, as if he were taking time to admire the fauna in Temple gardens. Dan remained on the wooden bench and tried to think past the pain. He cupped his head in his hands as he had seen many a barrister do in the late evening, after they had staggered back into the Temple having consumed too much South African Chardonnay at the Judge Jeffrey. He focused all his energy on listening out for Yuri, until finally he could no longer hear the clip-clip of his metal-rimmed heels on the ancient flagstones. What should he do? Shout for help? What if Yuri were just standing there watching him? He tried to get up but his knees immediately gave way and he crashed back on to the wooden seat. He felt his face burn, and now the sensation was as if someone had him by the back of the head and was forcing his head into a raging fire.

But he knew that he couldn't just sit there, however bad he felt. He had to reach Christine. Slowly, he tensed the muscles in the tops of his legs, the same muscles that had trembled just hours before when he was in court. He put his right hand on the cool, slimy wood of the bench and tried again. But he froze. There were more footsteps. He saw lights in his head, each one a different kind of pain.

The footsteps approached more rapidly.

'Oh, my God. *Dan*,' Sophie cried.

He didn't have the energy to call back before he felt her slim hand on his shoulder, and even through the acrid smell of the liquid that had violated his eyes and had seeped into his nose and his mouth, he could smell Sophie, that soft, sweet smell he would recognise anywhere.

'Where are you hurt?'

'My eyes,' he said.

'Acid?'

'Lemon juice or—'

'I'll get some water.'

He reached for where he thought her hand would be but grasped her wrist. 'Chrissy,' he gasped.

'What?'

'She's in danger.'

'Who did this to you?' There was a moment's hesitation in her voice. 'You *know* who did this, don't you?'

'We've got to get Chrissy.'

'Why is she in danger?'

Silence.

'I'm going to call the police.'

He tightened his grip. '*No*. My way.'

She lifted him off the bench. 'There are some chambers at the bottom of the stairs. We'll wash your eyes there.'

'No, we've got to—'

'Dan, you can't see. What use are you to Chris like this? Just lean on me.'

He heard her breathing quicken as she took the strain of his body. His feet would not move properly, his left foot scuffing lazily behind.

Someone grabbed Dan's other arm and hoisted him up, spreading the load.

'Just an accident,' Sophie explained to the other person. 'If you help us to those chambers down the stairs, we'll be fine.'

Dan heard a voice to his right and smelt the cigarette on the other man's breath. But he couldn't see him.

'That all right, luv?' the man said, when they had negotiated the stairs.

'Thanks.'

'Want me to call anyone – ambulance, police—'

'*No*,' Dan insisted as they put him down in the covered passageway outside the reception doors to the chambers.

'I'll just get them to open the door for us. There's a light on, the cleaners are probably still in the building,' Sophie said.

As the other man disappeared, Dan could hear her speaking over the intercom, persuading the suspicious contractors to open the front doors. There was a rattle of keys and the sound of Sophie's frantic voice as she barged her way in.

He lay on the cold stone floor of the outer lobby, trying to ignore the throbbing in his eyes, regular as the blood pumping through his body. How long would it take to get to the National Theatre? But hadn't Yuri said it was only a warning? He couldn't take that risk.

Sophie came back and he instantly felt a relieving splash of water in his eyes.

'This might hurt,' she said. 'Actually, it will hurt. It will hurt one hell of a lot. But it will hurt me more than it will hurt you, Dan.'

He tried to smile. The odd blurred shape and colour appeared, as though he were opening his eyes for the first time in a heavily chlorinated swimming pool. But at least it was an improvement: he was seeing through the pain instead of seeing into it – and he had someone looking after him.

'She's at the theatre,' he said, wincing.

'Where?'

'National.'

'What time does it end?'

'Ten.'

'What is it?'

'*The Jew of Malta*.'

'Shit, she *needs* rescuing.' He heard the material of Sophie's sleeve crease as she pushed her cuff back to look at her watch. 'We've got thirty minutes.' There was a pause, as if she were calculating. 'Now here's what we're going to do.'

'But you don't know what's going on.'

'Then why don't you tell me?' When he did not reply, she continued, 'See? Right, I'll wrap something around your eyes.'

'Thanks, Soph.'

'Didn't you drive?'

'Yes, but—'

'Where are you parked?'

'Bar car park.'

'Keys?' she said, rummaging in his pockets. 'Here we are.'

'Sophie, you're not insured—'

'Fuck the law. I'll drop you at Accident and Emergency at St Thomas's and then get Chris. I'll have her back to you before they've taken the bandages off. Tommy's is just along the road from the South Bank Centre, isn't it?'

When they walked out of the chambers doors, he felt the sudden blast of cool night air over his face like a fan on a summer's evening. He held his face into the breeze as Sophie led him towards the relentless rumble of the traffic along the Embankment.

He knew that they were now beyond the inner metal grille and into Temple Place near the river. As she deactivated the alarm on his car by pressing the button on the key-ring, he squeezed her arm.

'Soph, I just wanted to say—'

'Save it. I can't take you seriously with a dirty tea towel around your head.'

Dan sank into the worn rear seats of the Volvo.

'Right, you got three minutes,' Sophie said, crunching the gears. 'Bloody family cars.'

The wheels spun as she accelerated out into the Embankment. There was a large blast of a horn as what sounded like a truck braked sharply to avoid her. 'Piss off,' she yelled out of the window.

'I'm in serious trouble, Soph.'

'And there I was thinking your contact lenses were playing up.'

'You can't say anything.'

'I won't.'

'*Promise?*'

'I promise, Dan.'

'Christine's life has been threatened if I don't prosecute the case. All this,' he said, indicating his face, hoping she would see in the rear-view, 'is punishment for getting myself sacked.'

'You *got* yourself sacked?'

'I provoked an argument with the DPP's office.'

'So who's threatening you?'

'I'm not sure.'

'You must have some idea.' She braked sharply. 'Shit. Red light.' Then the vehicle accelerated even more violently, provoking more hooting. 'Bugger that,' she said.

'The man Montford is supposed to have murdered is Russian,

right?' he called over the din of the straining engine. 'Well, there is this Russian, calls himself Yuri, who fronts some part of a Russian organisation. I don't know what it is – the Mafia, a splinter group from the KGB, it could even be the government itself. I don't know. They want me to ensure that Montford is convicted.'

'How can I help?' she asked.

'Get Chris. Bring her to me. Make sure my baby is safe.'

'Anyone in a fur hat comes near us, I'll kill him,' Sophie said. 'We're crossing the river.'

They did not speak again until the car screeched to a halt and someone Dan presumed to be a porter or an orderly opened the door.

'Someone sprayed an acidic solution in his eyes,' Sophie explained. 'I've washed them with water and wrapped them in a clean towel.'

'You said it was a dirty tea towel,' Dan whispered.

'The truth didn't sound so funny,' she said. Then to the hospital staff, 'Can you take him from here?'

'Yes, madam.'

'I can't stay,' Sophie said. 'I've got to go and collect his daughter.'

'Are you his wife?'

Sophie paused and he felt a kiss on the side of his face. 'He can answer questions like that. I've *got* to go. See you in a few minutes, Dan.'

It all happened very fast after that: he was led into Casualty with a nurse he could not see firing questions at him. Then he was taken to a bed and put on it. Moments later the doctor arrived, and the towel was removed, revealing the painful blur of lights from the ward. Next there was the more painful penetration of the doctor's small torch and the application of some kind of solution.

Dan tried to concentrate on other things: he felt the smooth, even surface of the mattress beneath him; he heard the scream of a child in the next cubicle; someone was wheeled in on a trolley as a female doctor fired orders to the nurses; an old man groaned loudly from the cubicle opposite. He didn't know how long it all lasted: five minutes, ten, twenty. He measured time by the regular stabs of pain. He thought of Montford and Yuri and Jo. His poor Chrissy.

Suddenly he heard the voices of Christine and Sophie outside his cubicle; there was a male nurse with them explaining the situation.

'Can we come in?' he heard Sophie ask.

The room was still a multi-coloured blur. He tried to get up but fell back against the elevated pillow end of the examination table.

'Are you his wife?' the nurse asked.

'This is his daughter,' Sophie replied.

'I'm not sure she should see—'

'I *want* to see my father,' Christine insisted.

'All right, but just for a moment.'

Dan heard a swish as the curtain was pulled. He felt the rush as Chris moved towards him.

'Daddy, are you all right?'

'I'll live, sweetheart.' It was a phrase he had picked up from Jo. He liked it.

'And you'll see?'

'It'll just be a bit blurry for a day or two, the doctor said.'

'I can't believe you were using that paint-stripper in chambers. You never do any DIY at home.'

Dan was confused and didn't answer.

Sophie quickly explained. 'A lot of barristers enjoy doing up their rooms, Chris. It makes a change from locking up criminals.'

'And saves money they can spend on new shoes for their daughters,' Dan said, smiling.

'Dad!'

'Well, you wanted those clumpy monstrosities. See? Sophie doesn't wear things like that.'

'She doesn't need to. She's beautiful already. Mr Grant—'

'*Christine,*' Sophie hissed.

'Mr Grant, our English teacher, said he didn't realise I had such a young *and* beautiful aunt.'

'Aunt?' Dan said, smiling.

'I had to say something. You can't just collect a girl from a school trip, Dan. So I told a little white lie.'

Dan laughed. He could just see that another nurse had come in. She asked them if they would like a cup of tea. Chris volunteered to help.

'I can't thank you enough,' he said to Sophie.

'She's a great kid.'

'I know.'

'And I bet you're a great father.'

He could discern the contours of her face, and her sweet smell was unmistakable. 'I've put Chris in danger with this case.'

'Didn't sound like your fault to me.'

'Wait till I tell you the full story.'

'You want to tell me?'

'You got a few minutes?'

'I've got the rest of the night.'

Dan tried to sit up again. 'I suppose you could stay ... you know, the night ... if it got too late.'

She pretended to be shocked. 'Why, Mr Becket, are you propositioning me?'

'No.'

'Shame. We can stop off at my place along the way. I just need a few things. Check Helen's all right.'

'Can you leave her alone?'

'Recently, she's been improving. I've left her before, so ...' She paused. 'Dan, we can't call the police in on this?'

'No,' he said.

'So what do we do?'

'Wait.'

'For what?'

'Yuri said that I would be miraculously reinstated to the case. Well, let's just hope miracles happen in Shepherd's Bush. You don't have to do this, Soph.'

'I want to.'

'It could be dangerous.'

For the first time his vision cleared sufficiently for him to see that Sophie was smiling.

'You know,' she said, 'I went straight from school to university and from there straight to the Bar. Then straight into practice, and the most dangerous thing that has ever happened to me is my car breaking down on the M25. I think I could do with a little action. But what do you think?'

'I think you could do with a little action.'

Chapter 12

Dan woke up the next morning when his alarm went off at ten.

Both Sophie and Christine had insisted that it not be set any earlier, and when he had protested, they had ganged up on him: Chris held his hands down, while Sophie fiddled with the timer. Jo had not come home. He had left a note saying that he was staying with a 'guy from the old days' and that they 'should not worry'. Of course, Dan did precisely that, but he could do nothing about it.

When he awoke there was no pain. But his eyes would not open. He knew that he was well rested, and his body had not moved once in the bed overnight. But the world had disappeared along with the pain in his eyes. What had the doctor said? Your sight should be undamaged, not definitely, not certainly, but at least you have a fighting chance.

Thirty seconds later, he heard the soft padding of feet from the door. Someone trying to hide their presence, hovering somewhere at the foot of the bed. He tensed under the sheets and pretended to be asleep. He mumbled something quietly. More footsteps, nearer. The scrape of something metallic. Nearer. He clenched his right hand into a fist; his left was hanging out of the bedclothes. Still nearer, directly above him. He reached out and caught a leg right next to the bed.

There was the crash of metal and china.

A cry. '*Dad*, what *are* you doing?'

It was Chris. The bed was suddenly wet, and the sweet, perfumed aroma of Earl Grey tea rose from the sheets.

'I was only trying to get you breakfast in bed,' she cried.

Then she pulled away from his grip and padded to the window.

'I'm sorry, sweetheart.'

'Look at the mess.'

'Don't worry about it.'

'The teapot is broken.'

'We'll get another.'

'I don't *want* another,' she sobbed. 'This was Mum's favourite.'

'Chris, come here. Please, come here.'

'There's tea everywhere.'

'Yes, but it's Earl Grey. You *love* Earl Grey. You must drink . . . what? Six cups of it a day?' He sensed the tension sliding out of her voice as she moved around to the other side of the bed.

'Dad, what's going on?'

'What do you mean, what's going on? A daughter is bringing her old dad breakfast in bed and he's behaving like a bit of a psycho, that's all.'

He felt the mattress give as she sat on the bed.

'That's not what I mean. What *is* going on?'

For a moment, he wondered what Sophie had told her. They had talked together late into the night and he had told Sophie everything he knew. For long periods she had just sat on the edge of the bed silently. Then, when he had finished, she asked the same questions he had asked himself: Could he run? Why was *he* chosen? But he had made her promise not to tell anyone else. Or did she assume that Chris would know something by now?

'Why has Sophie slept over?' Chris asked.

'Oh,' he said with relief. 'That?'

'Are you seeing her?'

'Chris, just at the moment I'm not seeing anything, or haven't you noticed?'

'Sophie's coming with those drops. The gunge has just hardened on your eyelashes, that's all. Are you and Sophie going together?'

'Would you be angry if we did?'

'I'd be angry if you didn't.'

The phone rang loudly somewhere to Dan's right. He could feel the twisting of the duvet as Chris reached towards the bedside table. He tried to stop her, to get there first, but he was just lunging in the dark. Before he could do anything else, she had the receiver in her hand.

'Hello?' she said. 'No, my name's Christine . . . no . . . not Charlotte. Yes, he's here. But you can't speak to him just at the—'

'Give me the phone,' he said.

'Dad, you're not well—'

'Give me the phone please, Christine.' He could hear her huffing but she carefully placed the receiver into his right hand. He felt the warm stickiness where she had held it.

Down the line he heard a man's voice. 'Is that you, Daniel?'

'Hi, Neville.'

'How are you doing?' Neale asked.

'Oh, I've been better.'

'So have we all.'

He was aware of Chrissy right next to him and didn't want her to overhear anything further. He put his hand over the receiver as Neale continued to talk at the other end. 'Can you go and get Sophie?' he whispered to her, not turning his attention back to Neale till he heard the bedroom door pulled to. 'Can you repeat that, Neville?'

'I said, I hear you did a brilliant job at the prelim hearing – and then got yourself sacked.'

'It was their decision.'

'Well, I want it to be mine, Dan. And I want you back on the case.'

So Yuri was right. Here was the offer of reinstatement. Right on cue the miracle had happened. Was Neale also in on the whole charade? Dan couldn't believe it, but the timing was just too convenient.

'I understand that the disclosure of the Querry report was the real bone of contention, Dan.'

'It wasn't just a bone, it was the whole skeleton.'

'I take the point. But I think we might be able to resolve this. I'm having a meeting with that horrid man from the DPP's office—'

'Andrew Short?'

'That's the fellow. What a little turd. Can say that now – off duty and all that. Grail should be coming, too. Someone has sent me further documents concerning the case.'

'Who?'

'They were sent to me in chambers anonymously. I think Grail is using his legendary powers of detection to trace the source. So I suppose we'll never know.'

'What do the documents say?'

'Amazing stuff ... if they are genuine. They link Klaus Keller to Montford and England. If Montford was in on Keller's disappearance, perhaps it would provide some sort of motive for the execution of Basarov. I'm not sure exactly how, but think on it. Could you come over? I'm just in Chiswick, it's only a mile or so from you, I understand.'

'I'm afraid I've had a bit of an accident.'

'Nothing too serious, I hope.'

'Nothing too serious.'

'I'd really like you to come, Dan. Before it's ... too late.'

Perhaps Neale *was* in on it after all. 'Too late for what?'

'They will almost certainly appoint your replacement next week and you'll be off the case for good. It will be your last chance to get reinstated.'

If the eye-drops work, Dan calculated, aside from blurred vision and looking as though he'd gone ten rounds with Mike Tyson, he should be able to make the meeting. 'What time, Neville?'

'Shall we say one o'clock? Only I'm going fishing later.'

'One o'clock's fine.'

He heard the click as the phone was put down at the other end. But he still couldn't see anything. He reached over to the bedside table and tried to feel his way back to the cradle of the telephone.

'One o'clock is fine for what?' Sophie said as she paced into the room.

'Nothing.'

'Dan—'

'Neale wants me back on the case.'

'Will you do it?'

'What choice do I have?'

She did not answer but sat close to him on the bed. She fluffed up his pillows and then eased his head back onto them. Her slender fingers caressed the small of his neck. 'Now be a brave boy while Nurse Sophie puts in your eye-drops. Anyone ever tell you how sexy you look in pyjamas?'

By one o'clock Dan was suffering only occasional double vision, but double vision, he thought, was better than no vision at all. So when the taxi dropped him off in Chiswick, the painted white fences and Dutch gables of Bedford Park looked perfect; the grey sky over London had never looked duller but he had never before appreciated just how wonderful dirty grey clouds could look.

Neale lived in a detached mansion in a curving tree-lined avenue, somewhere in the heart of a conservation area. There were expensive cars parked in front of the houses and an unmistakable appearance of wealth everywhere. It was out of Dan's league, the sort of place that a QC could afford. He pushed open one of the large iron gates directly in front of the garage and to the right of the house. He walked up the gravel drive and saw that the garage door was slightly open. He thought back to his own house and Chris and Sophie cooking lunch together, a scene that seemed to him so right. They had also decided to bake a cake that afternoon and were negotiating about just how chocolate-infested it would be. It was Chris who was trying to control Sophie's excesses. Helen was coming over to join them.

Neville Neale's huge wooden front door appeared to be bigger than the whole of Dan's own garden patio. It was painted an opulent blue. There was no bell but rather a brilliantly shining brass knocker. He did not need to use it immediately: the door was on the latch. He was about to enter then thought better of it and used the knocker once. There was a hollow echo from within. He knocked again, this time harder, and the force of the impact opened the door properly.

'Neville,' he called from the doorstep. 'It's Dan Becket. Are you there?'

There was no reply.

He took a pace across the threshold and smelt the rich odour of freshly made coffee. His other senses had become more acute to compensate for his defective vision and he identified expensive newly ground coffee beans, probably Colombian. There was also the faint smell of stale tobacco. He called out again but there was still no response.

Then he remembered the garage door. It had been slightly open.

He spun round and jumped on to the drive, sending a small spray of gravel on to the perfectly cut lawn in front of the house.

He reached the garage in a few strides, not knowing what to think, but with a dreadful feeling of *déjà vu*.

The garage door was on rollers and opened to the right. Dan used his shoulder to force it back, not wanting to touch anything. The metal hinges cracked and groaned against their rusting housings. Inside the garage was Neale's blood-red E-type Jaguar, fishing tackle propped against it. But inside the car was Neville Neale.

There was a deep cavity in his chest.

His heart was mutilated. A hose ran from the exhaust pipe to the driver's door, but there was no smell of carbon monoxide or other fumes. Dan's eyes filled with tears for the gentle man who had never harmed anyone at the Bar.

'Don't *touch* anything,' a man shouted from behind him.

He turned around quickly to see Andrew Short. 'Call an *ambulance*,' Dan shouted.

'He's dead, Becket. I'll call the police.'

Dan pushed his way past Short and into the open air. His stomach churned at the sight of the entrails and blood, and he breathed deeply, taking in huge lungfuls of air. His mind raced. He couldn't get the thought of the fishing tackle out of his mind. Who could have wanted to kill Neale? All the elderly man had really wanted to do was go fishing.

Short walked in front of him and surveyed him suspiciously. 'And how long have you been here, Becket?'

Dan did not reply. He stared defiantly back at Short as the DPP's rep dwelt on the damage around his eyes.

'Looks to me like you've been in some sort of *fight,* Becket,' he said.

Chapter 13

Dan waited on the doorstep until the first police car arrived four minutes after Short's telephone call.

He had sensed Short moving within the house behind him, but the two of them had not talked to each other. He tried to piece together what had happened, the relevance of it all to the war crimes case, to Montford, to Keller. But his brain would not work logically and the diagrams he drew in his mind were constantly eroded by the image of Chris on Waterloo Bridge, and by the fleeting impression of the woman who had attacked him the previous evening.

Short strolled over to the front gates to meet the police vehicle. A young uniformed officer got out and then approached Dan, who was now sitting on the doorstep.

'This gentleman says he saw you by the body.'

'I discovered the body,' Dan said.

'I discovered him next to the body,' Short interrupted.

'One at a *time* . . . please,' the policeman shouted, clearly overwhelmed by the situation. 'Did you know the deceased, sir?'

'Yes,' Dan said. He paused, unsure how much he wanted to say in front of Short. But when he thought again of Neville, he couldn't contain himself. 'You'll find that the Jag engine is dead.'

'How did he know that?' Short asked.

'This was supposed to look like a *suicide*,' Dan said quietly, as the resonance between this scene and the one in New York began to trouble him. 'But the car engine didn't work, so the body was mutilated instead.'

'What's he talking about?' Short snapped.

The policeman paused. 'We might have to ask you some more questions.'

'Aren't you going to arrest him?' Short asked.

Dan got to his feet. 'Where's the weapon? Where's the blood on my clothing? Where do I have a motive?'

'No one's going to arrest you, Mr Becket.' It was Grail, striding purposefully up the gravel drive. He had a Burberry on, but it was not belted and fanned behind him as he walked. 'I'm DI Peter Grail,' he said to the relieved young officer. He flashed a card. 'I'll look after this one until CID arrives. Perhaps you should interrogate this other gentleman,' he said, indicating Short.

'I'd be happy to answer any questions,' Short said, indignant. He grinned, but it turned into a grimace full of tartar-stained teeth.

Short and the policeman went to the police car.

'Thanks,' Dan said.

'I've been watching you for a number of months, Mr Becket. And you're not a killer – well, not outside the courtroom.'

There was a brooding silence between them.

'Leaves us without leading counsel on the Montford case.' He paused. 'I was wondering—'

'No, Grail.'

'Just thought I'd try,' he said. 'What happened to your eyes?'

Dan hesitated and looked closely at him. But there was no sign of nervousness, no indication that he knew about Yuri, or that he wanted Dan to know that *he knew* about Yuri.

'Allergic to something?' Grail asked.

'Something like that.'

'Poor old Neale, wanted you back as junior. Will you agree to that much?'

Dan knew that he had no real option. 'Yes.'

'Good. Then you should know that you can sleep easy at night.'

'What do you mean?'

'Well, you know that you objected to us burying that report? The one about the gas mechanism at Neuwelt not working?'

'The Querry report?'

'We got permission from on high to disclose it to the defence. State secret or not. As we speak, Julian Waugh, QC, is probably reading it.'

This was the *worst* of all possible worlds. He was back prosecuting the case and the most damaging piece of evidence, the report that would probably lead to Montford's acquittal, had been sent to Julian Waugh. On *Dan's* instigation.

'So we're not hiding anything from the defence,' Grail said.

Further police cars and an ambulance had arrived at the scene and an Asian PC began cordoning off the premises with scenes-of-crime tape. By now neighbours were gathering: a man walking his Labrador, a woman returning with her shopping, two young boys sitting on their bikes.

'One more thing,' Grail said. 'We've got some more documents relating to Neuwelt.'

'Neale told me that someone had sent him some new documents,' Dan said.

'I don't know about that. These are old. They are old SS files or something. Look a bit dodgy, but they link Klaus Keller to Neuwelt.' Grail waved to a couple of CID officers before he carried on. 'The files have just been disclosed to me . . . by the Russians.'

Dan realised with a chill that this had to be the evidence Yuri would insist that he used. It was now September; the trial had been fixed for December. There was so little time until it all began again.

PART IV

DECEMBER

Chapter 1

The Covent Garden Donut Diner was the archetypal eaterie for people on the move. It cultivated the ambience of a set in a Quentin Tarantino movie, with sassy waitresses and a questionable clientele giving each other lip and taking themselves as seriously as they could given that the main item on the menu was doughnuts.

Insisting that it was a diner and not a café, it was situated one hundred yards from the Bow Street magistrates court. It was populated by motorcycle couriers with their radios still on low, and by taxi drivers, who parked their cars on yellow lines around Covent Garden and seemed to have divine immunity from terrestrial concerns such as parking tickets. Then there was a final group of aficionados, people who went there because of its proximity to the magistrates court: lawyers waiting to perform.

So at 9.30 on a frosty December morning, two members of this last group sat in the least cacophonous corner of the diner. They both wore sombre court suits made from dark cloth, with lots of buttons and faint pin-stripes.

'Don't look so glum,' Sophie said, sipping her scorching coffee from a stubby brown cup. The square wipe-clean table had not been wiped clean. 'What's the matter? Don't you like doughnuts?'

Dan surveyed the diner and frowned. The place was to him an unsavoury mixture of chrome, moulded plastic and glass, the sort of place his daughter would have adored.

'I love doughnuts,' he said. 'I think they are a fine, nourishing meal and that they are the best import from America – after my father.'

'Jo isn't so bad,' she said. 'I think he's quite a sweet guy. But you know what I like about him best?' she asked, chomping into a custard-filled confection. 'I can see so much of you in him, or the other way around, whatever.'

At times in the past three months, when Dan had seen Sophie with Chris, messing about in the garden, he had momentarily forgotten that another woman had once played with Chris in the same garden. He didn't know what to feel about this. The guilt was diminishing with each of Sophie's visits, and he knew that he wanted to move on. With Sophie. Now that he had put Lisa's betrayal firmly behind him, he saw with increasing clarity that it had been Sophie that he had wanted all along.

'Nervous about the trial?' she asked.

It was listed at the Old Bailey as 'not before twelve'. This was legal shorthand meaning that after that time the case could be called at any moment. Dan said, 'In less than three hours I will start the biggest case of the decade and here I am, eating doughnuts.'

'You haven't eaten yours.' She leant over the table and grabbed it. 'Hope you don't mind.'

'How can you eat it, Soph?'

'I just love this custard stuff. It sort of comforts me.' She smiled at him. As she did so her blond bob tumbled to the right as she tilted her head. 'If I was corny, I would say, like you do . . . But I'm not corny, Dan. I'm . . .'

'What?'

'I can't say it.'

'What, Soph?'

'Desperate,' she said. 'Desperate to be a part of your life. *Shit*,' she said, taking another bite. 'I can't believe I said it. God, now you're going to think that I'm some kind of crazed predatory woman who jumps out of baths with knives.'

'What?'

'You know, like Glenn Close in *Fatal Attraction*. Did you ever see the director's cut where the ending was different?'

'Sophie,' Dan said, trying to stop the flood of gabbling.

'Apparently the original ending was too dark—'

'*Sophie*—'

'Like the original ending of *True Romance*.'

Dan took both her hands, the one with the doughnut and the one with the coffee cup. 'You just said something very important and I'm not going to let you get away with it by discussing the finer points of dramatic theory.' He slowly released his grip, seeing the pink-and-white impressions his fingertips had left on her wrists.

'Why do I have to spell it out?'

'You raised it.'

'You really want to know?'

'I really want to know.'

Through the plate-glass window next to their table, the December light filtered into the room. There were smears on the glass surface where the window cleaner had not removed the detergent, and in the crystalline sunlight of a cloudless winter's day the rays were diffracted into a brilliant pattern of colours which fell across Dan's face. Sophie decided it was a sign, perhaps not quite as dramatic as in 1066 when William the Conqueror had seen Halley's Comet in the sky. But a sign for the nineties, for her life.

'Right, now I'm totally screwed up,' she said. 'I don't know what the hell to say. I've thought about it, planned what I wanted to tell you – what I wanted you to tell me back, Dan – but what with the trial coming up, I just thought that it would be better to leave it until all the verdicts were in and everything. But there you were sitting opposite me with the sun on your face—'

'The sun?'

'Don't interrupt. And here I was with a mouthful of confectioner's custard and a warm feeling in my belly and, well, it just slipped out.'

Dan was confused. 'Is that what you wanted to say?'

'No.'

'Then what?'

'I think we should be together.'

'Why?'

'We have common interests.'

'The Bar?'

'Sod the Bar.'

'Then what?'

'Chrissy. I love her, Dan. I know she's not mine, never could be. I mean, last week – no, two weeks ago – she cried when we talked about Viv—'

'She never talks about it to me.'

'She wants to be brave for you, Dan. She's a remarkable young person. I love her and I think – deep down – that's why I resigned from Montford's defence team. I don't want to go running around hiding things, I want to be with you and I'm not ashamed of that.'

'Do you know what you're getting yourself into?'

'I don't care what I'm getting myself into.'

There were a few moments of silence between them, neither taking up the burden of being the next to speak. Her eyes dwelt on the surface of the table, with its patterns of dried-on coffee rings. Surely it was his turn to speak? Or had she made a *total* spectacle of herself? He was quite old-fashioned on one level, she loved that about him. She couldn't bear it any longer. She had to speak.

'It sounds crazy, but I don't want to lose you, Dan, and I haven't even got you yet.'

'Haven't you?' was all he replied.

'Haven't you? What sort of macho shit is that?'

The brass clock on the wall next to the servery had ticked around to 10 a.m. Sophie glanced at it anxiously: the magistrates court would now be open. Yet again her profession was getting in the way of what she laughingly described as her private life.

'We'll have to call a time-out on this discussion,' he said. 'Shall we hit the courtrooms?'

'You're not going to watch me perform, are you?'

'Sadly, I'd better get to the Bailey.' He smiled. Then, teasing her further, 'But I'll come along the next time.'

'Don't you dare,' she said.

In a nervous reaction, she took her brief out of her bag. There was an inch of photocopied sheets bundled together with a pink ribbon. Typed on the right-hand side of the back sheet was the name of the case: that of a Saudi woman. Next to this was written the word 'Private' and a large brief fee scribbled in pencil.

'Shoplifter,' Sophie said. 'Her husband is the Sheikh of What-sit.'

'Not your type of case,' he replied.

'I'm being punished. For resigning from the Montford case. On Waugh's instructions the clerks are putting me out to graze in the mags court. Teach me a lesson.'

'What lesson?'

'Don't call a highly paid QC a lying bastard.'

'It's something worth bearing in mind,' Dan said, smiling. He stood up and took his first bite of doughnut from one of the two mutilated by her. 'God, that's disgusting.'

They fought their way through a group of leathered motorcycle couriers who held their helmets and sipped from Styrofoam cups of coffee. From inside the plate-glass door, Sophie could see bikes parked at various angles to the pavement. A traffic warden looked on suspiciously, a tramp slept in a doorway opposite. When she stepped into the open air she again felt the sharp chill of the morning. Dan followed her out of the door, but sped past her and turned on his heels, blocking her path.

He took her by the shoulders, held her face in such a way that she was looking into his eyes. 'Kiss me,' he said.

The first thing she felt was her nose crinkling up, and then her bottom lip quivering as a smile formed at the corners of her mouth. Her shoulders heaved slightly. She could hold it in no more and burst out laughing.

'I don't normally get this response when I ask women to kiss me,' he said.

'I'm sorry, Dan. It's just that you've still got custard on your top lip.' She reached up, standing on tiptoe, and put her arms around the back of his neck. 'Here, let me get rid of it.'

His kiss was warmer than Sophie would have believed. Perhaps it was the fact that they were standing on the icy pavements on a winter's morning. Of course, there was the fact that he had just been drinking piping-hot coffee, but he had an ardour, an enthusiasm for kissing her, which melted her remaining doubts. When they finally broke apart she was almost breathless. She saw the breath from his mouth and nostrils frosting in the air in front of him.

They walked together up the road towards the court. They did not hold hands, nor did they speak. Sophie was aware of a brilliant light in the sky high above them. No doubt astronomers would assure her that it was the sun, shining as it had done so already for 4.7 billion years. But for Sophie, for that morning, it was Halley's Comet. Even if she was wrong, the sun had a lifespan of 10 billion years. So, she calculated, that left 5.3 billion years – give or take the odd millennium – in which she would be with Dan.

Chapter 2

At five minutes to one, having spent the fifty-five minutes from noon hearing excuse after excuse as to why jurors could not sit on the trial, His Honour Judge Constant was finally able to empanel a full jury in Court 12 at the Old Bailey.

The procedure was a fraught exercise because the jurors who clearly wanted to sit on the case had followed the progress of Montford's war crimes prosecution in the media far too closely to remain impartial. Those who knew next to nothing of it suddenly got cold feet when they saw the gathered legal circus. The atmosphere was akin to the macabre carnivals that used to proceed to public hangings. For Dan could see around him in Court 12 the massed ranks of press, the crowded public gallery high above the court, and the rows of suited solicitors and bewigged barristers.

Having found the twelve jurors, the judge, with a puff of relief, adjourned for lunch. To his surprise, Dan felt better than he had anticipated. The previous weeks and months had conjured all kinds of spectres in his mind, but now on the first day he found himself in court on another case, facing another jury. So far nothing out of the ordinary had happened.

As the trial had drawn near, there had been increasing media speculation: profiles of Simon Montford, debates about war crimes prosecutions, raising the same sorts of argument as the one Dan had had with the Manhattan lawyer, Aaron Stein, way back in January. This enforced waiting period had reminded Dan of the agony the condemned man must have gone through as he heard the scaffold being built outside his cell. However, now the waiting was over and his private scaffold had been completed. There was only one question left: would they hang him?

Having taken the lift to the second floor, where he expected
to meet Sophie in the restaurant, Dan was confronted by Julian
Waugh in the corridor by the bank of lifts. Waugh's silk gown
swirled around him as he paced up to Dan, preventing him from
entering the canteen.

'So, Becket, you've finally hit the big time?'

Dan did not reply. He observed the waxy sheen to Waugh's
skin, the slight kink in his beaked nose; face on, Dan saw that
the man's long sideburns were uneven.

'And I thought you had given up prosecuting for good,' Waugh
continued. 'Still, you never were going to get a leading brief again
– until *poor* Neville . . . died. How does it feel trying to fill a dead
man's shoes?' When Dan didn't reply, Waugh continued, 'Do you
still think about your poor Kurds? I can see it in your eyes, Becket.
You're weak. You haven't got the stomach for the fight.'

He came very close to Dan and his stale breath felt unnaturally
cold upon Dan's skin, making it crawl. The two of them were
virtually touching the huge windows outside the canteen which
gave startling views of the London streets beneath. Waugh took
off his wig and revealed his greasy hair, swept back with such
severity that it looked as if there were streaks in his scalp where
the teeth of the comb had been.

'You ran out on me, Dan. And then what did you do? I thought,
let me be frank, that you had some *guts*, that you would blow
the whistle, tell someone, anyone who mattered that we buried
that evidence. I was waiting for the story in the press about how
we sent the second active service unit back to Iraq, that those
poor sods in prison were probably innocent.' He fixed Dan's eyes
coldly. 'You could have done that, couldn't you? And in a way,
I would have admired you for that. I would have made your life
a misery, I would have personally ruined your career at the Bar,
but I would still have admired you. But what *did* you do, Dan?'

Waugh paused as two suited men emerged through the doors
to the canteen. He even affected a smile at the elder of the two,
a man with greying hair and a Falklands campaign pin.

'Afternoon, Inspector,' he said. 'You're looking in fine fettle.'

The officer made some comment that Dan had no interest in
digesting.

'I'll tell you what you did, Becket. You *ran* away. As soon
as you said nothing, you became just like the rest of us. Only

worse. You pretended to be acting out of conscience. But it wasn't conscience. Do you know what it was, Dan? Cowardice. Plain and simple yellow-bellied cowardice.'

Waugh began to walk around Dan, as if he were a sergeant-major on a parade ground inspecting a slovenly soldier. 'If you were in the army, Becket, they would *shoot* you for cowardice of that magnitude. And they would be right to. Look at you now. Prosecuting a decorated war hero. A man who never ran away from the enemy, who did his duty, who has served his country in ways you cannot imagine.'

Dan looked hard into Waugh's eyes, trying not to give away how he really felt.

'I'm going to give you a last chance, Daniel Becket,' Waugh continued. He fired his words at Dan faster and faster. 'Drop the case. Consult with the CPS and the DPP, take your time, take instructions and all that *crap*, and then drop the case. Tell them the defence has a witness. A crucial witness – and we have, Becket, believe me – someone independent, unimpeachable, deadly, someone who will strike into the heart of your case. Drop the case, Dan, and then go home. Go home and . . . *mother* your poor little daughter.'

By the time Waugh had finished his tirade, he was breathless.

'I'm continuing with the case,' Dan said.

Julian Waugh smiled cynically and ran his left hand through his hair. 'Then it will be the last case you ever . . . continue with. Can't you understand how much is at stake here? For God's sake, don't think you can bring the law into it.'

As he watched Waugh's silk gown disappearing up the stairs to his left, Dan reflected on the one thing Waugh had said that was true. By keeping silent about the imprisoned Kurds, he had indeed become an accomplice.

He stepped through the glass doors of the canteen but Sophie was not there as she had promised. The two long rows of tables were filled with faces that stared at him silently as he stood at the entrance in his wig and gown. It felt as if he had walked into a bar in a strange town. What Waugh had said about mothering his daughter was unforgivable, but Dan had again done nothing – he had just kept quiet. He wondered if, for all his penchant for cruelty and exaggeration, Waugh had hit on some essence of Dan's being: cowardice. He shook his head, trying to clear it of

these negative thoughts. Surely he wasn't a coward. Was he not
standing to fight this trial? He had not run away.

He pushed his way back through the glass doors and turned
right towards the lifts. A bell sounded and silently, almost
magically, the doors to the lift in front of him opened. Montford
was inside.

Simon Montford stood upright, motionless but relaxed, showing no trace of the embarrassment both of them certainly felt.

'Going down?' he asked casually. Then he smiled. 'I suppose,
Mr Becket, you should be saying the same thing to me. But, you
see, I'm not going down.'

The lift doors shut, leaving Dan alone in the corridor on the
second floor. He looked at his watch. It was 1.17. In less than
one hour he would have to make the opening speech in the war
crimes trial.

At 1.30 Dan tannoyed Grail to come to the reception desk at
the entrance to the court. As he waited, the lunchtime comings
and goings played themselves out around him: new defendants
arriving for the afternoon cases looked for their solicitors; pairs
of barristers dashed out for a restaurant meal; a steady stream
of jurors negotiated the X-ray machine. The court staff, for their
part, stood behind the security windows, bored, challenging all
who entered the building. After four minutes, just as Dan was
trying to decide whether to tannoy him again or to abandon his
quest, Grail appeared. His cheeks were flushed and he sweated
slightly. His beige overcoat swung loosely around him and the
two ends of the belt hung unevenly from each side.

'Ah, it's only you, Mr Becket,' he said.

'I tried the police room. They said—'

'They know nothing.' Grail paused and wiped his brow. 'Now,
how can I help you?'

Dan ushered him away from the chaos in the lobby and up
the shiny stone steps to the landing beside the court lists. It
was quieter there, though occasionally a defendant passed them
to see in which courtroom his case had been listed.

'Neville Neale?' Dan asked.

'Ah.' Grail reached for the right-hand part of his belt, fumbled
and then found the buckle. 'Of course, it's not my jurisdiction.
Officially. It's a separate investigation.'

'So whose ... jurisdiction is it?'

'West London. Murder. There's no proof it's linked to the war crimes.'

'Is there any to rule it out?' Dan snapped. 'Neville Neale was about to prosecute Montford for a murder at Neuwelt and Neale is killed. A coincidence?'

Grail moved closer. 'Look, we're really worried. This is a top priority. We're devoting huge resources to it. But Montford has a cast-iron alibi.'

'So he hired someone.'

'Who? Don't tell me ... Klaus Keller?'

'Why not?' Dan asked.

'Because I've seen no proof that Keller is alive – or has been for the last forty years.'

'Fifty years,' Dan said. 'I thought he disappeared in 1945.'

'Whatever,' Grail replied more heatedly. 'What do you want us to do? Arrest an innocent man?'

'No.'

'Plant evidence on Montford?'

'Perish the thought,' Dan said. 'The police never, ever do such things, do they, Mr Grail?'

Grail paused and examined Dan closely. 'It has occurred to Homicide ... I mean, if people investigating Neuwelt are in danger, the next candidates are ... me – and you.' There was a more concerned note in his voice, an anxiety that gave an edge to his words. 'If you're worried, I could speak to the Chief about getting you protection. No promises. But—'

'I'll take my chances.'

'But what about your daughter?'

Dan stared back, surprised. 'How do you know I've got a daughter?'

'Neville Neale mentioned it. Remember? The Bailey. April?'

Dan instantly recalled a scene in Court 1 when Neale had ordered the armed policeman to remove himself from the court-room.

'Charlotte, wasn't it?' Grail asked.

Dan didn't reply.

'Look, I liked old Neville,' Grail said more solemnly. 'He was a decent man.' His cheeks were now flushed. 'And some ... bastard killed him. Brutally. The Murder Squad have promised me, if they catch the killer, to let me . . . speak to him. You know. Alone. Me and him. In his cell. One to one. We'll see what a hard man he is then.'

Dan did not know how to reply to this. He had condemned such strongarm police tactics so many times, but now, if he was honest, a part of him craved precisely the same thing. While he feared the damage Neale's killer could do, he also wished to meet him, on even terms, to make him pay for Neville.

'I'll try to keep you informed,' Grail said.

Dan nodded.

'And if you have any problems . . .' He reached into his jacket pocket with a chubby hand and took out his personal card. 'Really. Night or day.'

'Thanks.'

'Good luck on Montford.'

'Who needs luck when you've got evidence?'

Grail laughed loudly. 'Oh, yeah.'

The jury filed into Court 12 just after five past two.

Julian Waugh sat in the front row at the opposite end to Dan. Behind Waugh was his junior, someone who always wore red braces and who Dan had seen drinking copious quantities of Armagnac at the Judge Jeffrey. This man was invariably telling stories about the sado-masochistic punishments at his ancient public school. Then there were two young female pupils from Waugh's set, who sat with their pens and blue counsel's notebooks poised to take down every cough and stutter in the trial. Behind them again were the legions of lawyers from the firm that Montford had instructed, Wallace Howard, *the* blue chip firm, solicitors to the high, mighty, rich and famous. There were senior partners, including Douglas Wallace himself, assistant solicitors, articled clerks, outdoor clerks and paralegals. Together they had created ramparts and turrets of legal papers, box files and exhibits; they had installed laptop computers to cross-reference their information, and were able to provide Waugh with a simultaneous transcript.

Dan was heavily outnumbered. In the row behind him was Robert Lancing. Behind Lancing was the senior Crown prosecutor from the CPS, the man who, on the last hearing at the Old Bailey in September, had sacked Dan from the war crimes case. Andrew

Short sat on his own at the side of the court, low in his chair and with his legs crossed.

Finally, the moment had arrived when Dan had to speak. He had no files or trigger notes on his lectern. But he had a napkin, one from the Covent Garden Donut Diner, and on it he had written one word: *families*.

'This case,' he began to tell the jury, 'is about murder. It was a murder committed fifty years ago, during the war in Germany, and it concerned a gassing in a concentration camp. For that reason it is a murder that in law we call a war crime.'

He tried to take the jury in two at a time, as he had told Sophie to do, years ago when she was his pupil. These twelve strangers, the representatives of the public, sat forty feet away from him across the well of the court. There was one black woman, two Asian youths, an elderly white woman, two labouring types, assorted businessmen and housewives. Over the next few days, he would come to notice their every reaction. But it wasn't easy for him to concentrate as Julian Waugh sat between himself and the jury, almost standing guard over them. Further, Dan felt the great weight of anticipation in the courtroom. He knew that the next words to come out of his mouth would be on the front pages of national newspapers, would be quoted on the television news.

He was also aware that when he spoke directly to the jury, his back was to the public gallery. He didn't know who was watching him; whether Yuri was there, or whether there was someone else Yuri had sent. He felt exposed and vulnerable. He wished he could sit down and leave the court in silence; he wanted to go home and see Chrissy, but he knew equally well that there was one other option he was prepared to take: he had to go on.

The paper napkin again: *families*.

'The murdered man was a Russian. His name was Ivan Basarov. He was gassed to death on the orders ...' This was it, this was the nub of it. '... of a *British* commanding officer before many of you were born. No one in court will know the victim, no one will openly grieve, you will not see tears in the public gallery.'

Again an image: Chrissy's face, not smiling, but content and peaceful.

'Ivan Basarov must once have had a *family*, maybe even children, a daughter or a son. Perhaps he means nothing to us now. But wouldn't he have meant something to his family then?'

Dan turned his head fractionally to his left so that, with his peripheral vision, he could see the dock. 'Ivan Basarov was gassed on the instructions of Simon Montford in the Neuwelt concentration camp, Germany, 1945. It was a war crime and it was a murder. This case is about that murder.'

The courtroom was completely silent except for Dan's voice. He could have gone on. He could have opened the case for two or more hours. But he had said all that he had wanted. Now he needed to get on with the case. Lancing, who sat behind him, gazed up at him as if to say: That can't be it?

Dan slowly rotated his body to his right, towards the judge, who sat above the court in his heavy robes of office.

'With Your Lordship's leave, I shall call my first witness.'

Constant nodded.

Dan neatly folded the napkin and put it in his pocket. 'Call George Parsons,' he said.

Chapter 3

George Parsons stood in the witness box ten feet distant from Dan. The box itself faced the jury, and was accessed by three short steps. As the witness gazed at the twelve assessors of fact, his line of vision would have taken in the trial judge to the right and the first row of barristers to the left.

Dan saw before him a small man, undistinguished by life. A man who had, according to the police report, slipped quietly through dole offices and betting shops, sitting at a corner table in a South London pub, drinking alone, not interested in other people's business, making it obvious that he wanted no one to be interested in his own. This was a man who had resigned himself to living in the shadows since the Second World War. After everything he had seen in that terrible campaign, Parsons had lived by choice on the margins of things. He had shunned the limelight as would the nocturnal creature – a vole, perhaps – that he resembled. Now he was the reluctant star witness in the trial of the decade.

After Parsons had been sworn and had given his name, Dan said, 'I want to ask you about a time fifty years ago, 1945, at the end of the war.'

Parsons sniffed and pulled his corduroy suit around him. 'Oh yeah?'

He had untidy sandy hair that was thin and flyaway. His eyes were small and darted around the room nervously, as if it were not a witness box in which he found himself, but a cage.

'You were a private in the British Army?'

'Never made corporal. Should have.'

'And in the spring of 1945, the Allied armies were advancing through western Europe and finally into Germany.'

'Well, don't ask me, I was just driving the tank.'

There were sniggers from around the court, including from the public gallery. It was not a good sign. Dan had the first inkling that the witness's lack of co-operation might go beyond a mere reluctance to be in the spotlight.

'Can we set the scene?' Dan said. He thought of the months of research he had done, while hidden away from the world. 'Figures and personalities who have with the years assumed almost legendary status were involved in the Allied advance on the Rhine and beyond. Montgomery was commanding the Twenty-first Army Group. To his south, Lieutenant-General Bradley was commanding the US Twelfth Army Group, with the US Third under the command of Patton.'

'I was still just driving a tank,' the witness said.

More sniggers.

Waugh saw an opportunity to score off Dan and rose swiftly to his feet. 'What is the relevance of all this?'

'Is my friend saying that any of this is untrue?'

'But this is a speech, not an examination of a witness.'

'I'm setting the scene for the jury.'

'Perhaps my friend would like to play them footage from *Patton – Lust For Glory*?'

'My *friend*,' Dan said, using the professional courtesy as if it were the most foul term of abuse, 'is objecting when these basic facts are not in dispute. I suppose he has his reasons for not wanting the jury to hear about them.'

Waugh subsided without any comment from the judge. Len Constant's full cheeks were flushed, through nerves, or a lunch-time medicinal, or both.

Dan turned back to the witness. 'Was there a major in your tank group?'

'Tank "group" is not the right word.'

Dan lost his temper. 'Was there a *major* with you when your tanks reached the Neuwelt camp in Germany, the Nazi *extermination* camp?'

Waugh was again on his feet. 'My Lord, I object. This is Mr Becket's *own* witness. He shouldn't badger him.'

Dan knew that he was wrong. But the pressure was getting to him – how could he keep perfectly calm? 'I apologise,' he said.

But there was something strange in the way in which Waugh

had said that this was Dan's *own* witness. It was an unnecessary stress, something that made him suspicious. He wondered if someone had already got to Parsons.

'Was there a major?'

'Yes.'

'What was his name?'

'Montford.'

'Major Simon Montford?'

'Yes.'

Dan took a deep breath. He had reached his first target. Now the camp, Neuwelt. 'You reached Neuwelt, a sub-camp on the east bank of the Rhine but still in western Germany, in April 1945?'

'I don't know when in April,' Parsons said.

'Well, the British tanks entered Belsen on April fifteenth.' Out of the corner of his eye, Dan could see Waugh itching to get to his feet to object. 'Perhaps Mr Waugh would like the Dimbleby documentary footage of Belsen played to the jury, if there is any doubt about that fact?'

Waugh retook his seat.

'We arrived about the same time as that,' the witness said.

'Can you remember the sight that confronted you?'

The witness did not answer. Dan noticed a change come over his expression, as if Parsons were suddenly looking out of the turret of a tank driving through Hitler's Germany and into the heart of the Third Reich.

'Can you *remember* the sight that greeted you?' Dan repeated.

'I haven't been able to forget,' Parsons snapped. 'I saw a programme, a documentary or what have you, the other day. A repeat of one of those programmes about the end of the war fifty years ago. Showed some Russians – no, Ukrainians. They talked about entering Auschwitz. Said it was like . . . falling into hell.'

He coughed roughly. The years of cheap tobacco had torn away at the lining of his throat.

'But Neuwelt wasn't like that. You know, hell – not at first. It was a spring day, and we came out from this long, dark track in the woods and suddenly there it was. I think the Nazis had let the trees grow right up to the wires so our bombers couldn't see it. There were neat rows of huts, bathed in sunshine, set in these green forests. It had been raining earlier and even over the reek of the tank diesel I could smell all that wood and foliage.

Then the majority of the tanks got the orders to pause so that an advance party—'

'Including Montford?' Dan asked.

'Yes. I saw them disappear towards the camp. But, you know, I thought nothing of it. Even over the ticking of the engines I could hear the birds in the trees, hundreds of 'em, big birds, with wings . . . beating the air. Well, that's how some Taff described it to me, but they have a way with words, those—'

'Welsh people?'

'They have a way with words, don't they? It was only when we got the order to advance to the electric fence that I realised what it was all about.'

'What?' Dan asked.

'The birds. They was crows. Big, black, bloody crows and they were flying down and pecking the eyes out of the bodies in this pit outside the perimeter fence.'

Dan thought about Jo. This was the reality of the place that his father had never properly talked to him about. Now he knew why. 'And that was Neuwelt?' he asked.

The man's voice was cracking as the images that had lived inside him for fifty years once more became real. 'Yeah, that was Neuwelt.'

The judge made his first intervention into the evidence. 'Would you like a break, Mr Parsons?'

'No, sir. I just want to get it over.'

'Mr Becket?'

'Thank you, M'Lord.' Whatever Parsons had been told, whatever threats or promises had been made to him, Dan felt that they would lose some of their force now that the dreadful image of Neuwelt on that sunny spring day was in his mind.

'Now, Mr Parsons,' he said. 'I'm going to ask you about an execution.'

Julian Waugh exploded to his feet. 'I *object*. The term execution is highly contentious.'

I *know*, Dan whispered to himself.

From behind, Lancing hissed, 'Don't overdo it, Becket.'

At first he wanted to retaliate with some barbed riposte, but he thought of Neville Neale. He knew that Neale would have underplayed the whole thing; he would have let the facts speak for themselves, for this truth still spoke loudly through the decades. Here in the Bailey, enmeshed in a trial, Dan realised just how much he missed Neville, and he was incensed that the murder investigation had been so dilatory. No suspect had even been arrested.

'I was put in this makeshift guard hut,' the witness said. He spoke to Dan with an earnest intimacy, as if the rest of the people in the courtroom had disappeared. 'I ain't proud of what I did, even now – what? – over fifty years later.'

Dan's eyes flicked from the witness to the jury. He was satisfied that their complete attention was devoted to the drama unfolding before them. 'Tell us simply what you did.'

'I heard – we all heard – that there was this store of Russian vodka in the SS staff room in the cordoned-off part of the camp. So later that day, I ...' He hesitated. It was clear that his embarrassment hadn't diminished with the passage of time. 'I sort of forced a back door and tried to steal a bottle. You know, for the boys,' he quickly added. 'We had fought our way through Europe on basic rations and we felt – I felt – that we were owed.'

'But you were caught?'

'By Major Montford. I didn't realise that he was in that SS place. Anyway they put me in the guard hut.'

Dan looked down at his copy of the thin statement that Parsons had made to Grail earlier in the year. 'Did you stay in that jail alone?'

'No,' the witness replied, glancing nervously at Montford in the dock.

'Who joined you?'

'This Russian chap.'

'What was he like?'

'A skeleton. He was one of the inmates of the camp. A soldier originally but by the time the SS had finished with him there was nothing left of him.'

'Did you ever find out his name?'

'He told me again and again. Ivan ... Basarov. He said to me over and over: they're going to kill me. My name is Ivan Basarov, my name is Ivan Basarov, they're going to kill me.'

'What had he done?'

'They said he had—'

'I *object*,' Waugh shouted. 'I object most *strongly*. This has gone on long enough. This is clearly hearsay evidence and inadmissible.'

Parsons didn't care. 'They said he had—'

'My Lord, I—'

'Killed a British officer,' Parsons insisted. 'They said he killed one of us.'

The judge tried to take control, but it was too late, the explanation was out. 'Mr Parsons, if an objection is taken to part of your evidence, please wait until I have ruled.'

The man looked down. 'Yes, sir,' he said.

'Now, Mr Becket, please try to control your witness,' the judge said.

Waugh had subsided back into his seat in the first row and Dan was aware that the atmosphere had changed again in court. Suddenly the events of 1945 seemed to be the most important thing in the world. But the allegation that Basarov had killed a British officer was a new one, not contained in Parsons' statement. It immediately worried Dan, for it was one of those elusive truths in a trial which both sides fear, unsure to whom it would cause the most damage. On the one hand, if Basarov had killed a British officer, the jury would lose sympathy with the prosecution. On the other, it lent a certain weight and credibility to Parsons' story. Perhaps it even provided some kind of motive for Montford's actions.

'What happened to Ivan Basarov?' Dan said.

'He disappeared.'

'What do you mean?'

'They took him in the middle of the night.'

'Who took him?'

The man looked defiantly at the dock. 'Major Montford and the others. An armed escort.'

'Did you see Ivan Basarov again?'

'No.'

'Thank you, Mr Parsons. Please wait there. Mr Waugh *might* have some questions for you.'

'We'll have a five-minute adjournment,' the judge said. He gathered his robes and the court stood as he rose from the bench.

Lancing whispered, 'Waugh's going to kill him.'

Once Constant had left, people formed clusters all around the court. The great blast of noise suddenly generated in the public gallery was as if someone had opened the door to a raucous party. Dan walked into the corridor outside alone. Lancing ran after him, asking which other witnesses he wanted lined up for the rest of the afternoon, but Dan brushed him away. He wandered along the third-floor corridor, past the dirty windows that gave on to the London rooftops, until he saw someone by the stairs. Sophie.

At first, she did not say a word, and he followed her down the stairs to the very well of the Old Bailey. They stopped outside the huge door to the cells area.

'Where were you at lunch?' he asked.

'I had to leave the building.'

'Why?'

'Waugh saw me in the canteen. Gave me a little bit of well-intentioned *advice*.' She had to force out the last words.

'Advice?' Dan asked.

'Such as if I showed my face during the war crimes trial, he would regard it as a breach of my duty of confidence to Montford and he would report me to the Bar Council. A tribunal, he assured me, where all his mates would sit in judgment. He still hasn't got over me quitting.'

She hoped that Dan would not see the puffiness under her eyes and the redness that stained the clarity of the iris.

'I told you things would get rough.'

'I can handle it,' she said, but once more she felt annoying tears welling in her eyes. However, now that Dan was with her, she felt stronger. She gritted her teeth and fought back.

'I don't want you to have to handle anything like that again,' he said.

'Look, they didn't let me in on any of their secret meetings when they were creating Montford's defence. And Montford's attitude has always been keep your head down and see what they can prove. I mean, he never said to me that he was innocent.'

'Did he say he was guilty? Actually,' he added quickly, 'don't answer.'

'No, he *never* said he was guilty,' she blurted.

'See?'

'Oh, shit, Dan. All right. Point taken. It's just that it's torture for me not being in that courtroom.'

'Oh,' he said, trying to affect a lighter mood, 'it's pretty boring, really.'

'Sure.'

'But, Miss Chase, I'm afraid exile is the price you have to pay.'

'For what?'

'For kissing me outside a doughnut diner,' he said.

She burst into laughter, and furtively touched his fingers. 'Is there anything I can do for you?'

'Oh, I've had one or two thoughts.'

'I mean about the *trial*, Dan.'

'The witness spoke about Basarov killing a British officer. Do you think Helen could check army records? Find out if that's true?'

'Doesn't it cut both ways?' Sophie asked.

'What doesn't in this trial?'

'True.'

'Take these,' he said. 'House keys. It would be great if you'd wait for Chris to come back from school. Maybe have some supper together. The three of us.' He faltered when he remembered that Jo was also at home. 'The four of us.'

'So how d'you think it went with the first witness?'

'He's the first link between Montford and the murdered Russian. But—'

'What?'

'Waugh will try to break him.'

'You never saw this Russian again?' Waugh demanded, five minutes later.

The witness looked carefully at the intimidating Silk, obviously trying to work out if it was a trick question. Finally Parsons gave up and answered simply, 'I never saw him again.'

'Dead or alive?'

'Dead or alive.'

'*Dead* or alive?' Waugh repeated.

'I never saw his body, if that's what you mean.'

'Oh, Mr Parsons, that's *exactly* what I mean.' Waugh paused to allow the jury time to absorb the point.

'There was a pit full of dead bodies outside the camp?'

'Yes.'

'And emaciated survivors, I imagine, barely alive, were within the perimeter fence.'

'Yes.'

'It must have been the most horrific spectacle you have ever seen in your life?'

'Yes.'

'By far?'

'Yes.'

'And you decided to *steal* a bottle of vodka?'

Once more Dan saw that the witness looked down. But this time there was something more; it was as if something inside him had crumpled, for his shoulders sagged and his arms hung loosely at his side.

'You had seen the Holocaust with your own eyes, and you decided to *steal* a bottle of spirits?' Waugh insisted.

'*Yes*,' the witness shouted. 'I'm sorry, but I was only a boy, I had never even left home and—'

Waugh wouldn't let him finish. 'As far as you know, this ... Russian could have been handed over to the field hospital. Couldn't he?'

'I don't know.'

'That's the point. You don't *know*. He could have been handed over to the Red Cross, couldn't he?'

There was no answer.

'*Couldn't* he?' Waugh shouted.

'What? After he had killed a British officer?' Parsons snapped back, trying to retaliate.

'Did you see a British officer killed? You didn't mention this in your statement.' Parsons looked down sheepishly.

'The truth is, you can't help the jury with this because you were still in jail for stealing a bottle of vodka.'

'Yes.'

'And it was Simon Montford who caught you in your dishonest act.'

'Yes.'

'It was he who caused you to be imprisoned.'

'Yes.'

'And you bore a grudge against him because of that?'

'No, I—'

'You felt it was the spoils of war?'

'Yes, but—'

'And that's why you've invented this *rubbish* about Montford taking a Russian in the middle of the night.'

'No. He did.'

'How do we know that the Russian existed?'

'I saw him, he was next to me. Ivan—'

'Prove it.'

'You have my word.'

'The word of a self-confessed thief.'

'I saw him. With my own eyes. *Ivan* Basarov. Ivan *Basarov*. They said the gas mechanism went wrong or something.'

'Hearsay evidence, Mr Parsons.'

'They killed him slowly.'

'But you don't *know*.'

'They gassed him. Montford and that Klaus Keller. They said one of them was Keller.'

'But you don't know. Do you? *Do* you?'

By the time the exchange had blown itself out, both men were breathing heavily, red and sweating.

Julian Waugh paused and then said in an astonishingly calm voice, 'You didn't see them gas him, did you, Mr Parsons?'

'No.'

'Did you ever see Klaus Keller?'

Parsons hesitated. Then he was forced to admit, 'No, but—'

'So Klaus Keller might just be a phantom? A ghost? A rumour?'

Parsons did not reply. As Waugh sat down, Lancing leant forward from the row behind Dan's shoulder.

'I told you,' he whispered.

It was Dan's turn to re-examine the witness. But he didn't know how far to go. For he was unsure what the jury would have believed, just as he was unsure himself as to where the truth of Parsons' account lay. However, his forensic instincts told him that he could not leave the evidence with Waugh having delivered so many crushing blows. Whatever the truth about Keller in the story Parsons had told, there was one thing that rang unmistakably true to Dan. The fact that Ivan Basarov was not a spectre, or a fantasy figure, but flesh and blood.

'Did Ivan Basarov exist?' he asked.

'Yes, sir,' the witness agreed. He tried to perk up but the stuffing had been knocked out of him.

'Did you see Basarov?'

'Yes.'

'Was he alive when you did?'

'He was as alive as any of you in this courtroom today.'

'Tell us about him.'

The witness again seemed to retreat into the secret pocket of history that he had carried around with him for fifty years. 'Of course, we could hardly understand each other. He spoke a little English but I . . . well, there's not that much cause for speaking Russian in Bermondsey.'

There was a short peal of laughter around the court, which Dan knew was motivated as much by relief as by humour, a release from the tension that had preceded it.

'But,' Parsons continued when the court was again silent, 'there was one thing, you know. Funny, I haven't thought of it all these years, but he kept saying something about his kid, in Russia. He wanted to see his kid back in Russia. He cried because he knew that he was going to die and then he wouldn't see him ever again.'

'*Him?*' Dan asked.

'His kid.'

'His son?'

'Yes,' said George Parsons. 'His son. He kept going on. My son. My son. Yuri. Yuri. *Yuri.*'

Chapter 4

The name caused no reaction that Dan could discern anywhere else in the courtroom. But to him it was as if someone had torn him from a nightmare, forcing him to look straight into the eyes of a still darker fear. Yuri. Yuri. *Yuri*.

At last, he knew.

Yuri Basarov, the *son* of the murdered Russian prisoner at Neuwelt in 1945. He remembered the only note he had made for his opening speech: families.

At the front of the court, high on the judicial bench that now seemed a great distance from Dan, the judge announced that there would be no further evidence that afternoon. To his surprise, Dan noticed that he had not sat down after the revelation of the name, so he did not have to stand as did the rest of the court when the usher formally closed proceedings.

She used the ancient formula which now sounded to Dan like a curse: 'All persons having anything to do with my Lords the Queen's Justices depart hence and draw nigh tomorrow morning at 10.30 in the forenoon. God save the Queen and my Lords the Queen's Justices.'

The dock was opened once the jury had been escorted from court and Simon Montford walked out slowly, pausing to exchange a few words with his solicitors, half smiling discreetly. How had he reacted? With nervousness? Confidence? Dan could not tell.

Having picked up a few case papers more or less randomly, Dan, still lost in thought, suddenly found himself outside the court. There was a fast-moving scrum of reporters, comparing notes as they disappeared towards the phones. Robert Lancing came up to him and said something he didn't hear. Then

Lancing repeated that Dan had been tannoyed to go down to reception.

He rushed towards the stairs at the end of the third floor. Pushing past two barristers on the landing, their wigs in hand, he took the stairs two at a time, accelerating down and around the stairwell until dizzily he reached the security door. It was here that he saw Lisa Hartman.

He did not speak to her immediately for he saw a different woman, one no longer obviously in her twenties, wearing more make-up.

'I flew in yesterday,' she said.

'How convenient.'

'Can we talk? I . . .' She hesitated, as though she had forgotten the lines of a well-rehearsed script.

'Talk.'

'I mean somewhere else. Outside.'

'So what is there to talk about?'

'There's someone I want you to meet. Or meet properly.'

'Who?'

'Yuri.'

Fifteen minutes later, Lisa and Dan walked into a wine bar down by the river. It was a place more influenced by the City than the world of the Bar, a sort of post-yuppie, pre-millennial place that made no statement except in here you can get drunk quickly, cheaply and quietly. The walls were without decoration, the lighting was muted; it was a large floor space with the tables sufficiently far apart to appear isolated from each other. It was a vacuum, a limbo.

Yuri sat in a corner next to a juke-box with its plug pulled out, the socket lying on the sawdust floor next to the wall. It was the first time Dan had actually seen him since September. He got up when they reached the table, but Dan knew that the courtesy was not intended for him. Just as swiftly, they sat down, with Lisa between the two men. The Russian wore the same heavy coat as he had worn in Central Park in January. His face was riven with lines that ran almost vertically, as if they were inlaid tracks of a hundred years of tears.

'So now you know, Mr Becket,' he said.

'I just don't understand why you didn't tell me that Ivan Basarov was your father.'

'It would have made a difference?'

'Of course.'

'You say that with great confidence. But what would my father have meant to you? After all, correct me if I'm wrong, but your father has meant *nothing* to you for forty years.' He turned to Lisa. 'Would you like a drink?'

She shook her head but did not say anything.

'So am I wrong?' Yuri asked. 'We have a saying – I think you have a similar one – that a chain is as weak as . . .'

'Its weakest link,' Dan interrupted.

'Your weakest link is your daughter, Mr Becket. Of course, it's your strongest one, too. That's the beauty of these family things. But as far as we knew, you had no link whatsoever with your father.'

Dan examined the man's deep eye sockets, then the sinewy body – hard, attractive, cold.

'But don't you see?' Dan replied. 'I would have understood why this case is so important to you.'

'You knew that Ivan Basarov was a Russian who was killed by the British. He was someone's son. Whoever that someone might be. You knew that. He also is *my* father, but that fact does not change the nature of this crime.'

Dan looked at Lisa, sitting with her hands neatly folded in her lap, not making eye contact, ashamed. Her hair had lost the magical lustre he remembered so vividly from the Rainbow Room. Now it appeared thinner and the ends had split.

'I want to understand,' Dan said. 'Were you in on this from the start, Lisa?'

She said nothing.

Yuri put his weathered hand on the table. The skin was rough, like canvas. There was a gash on his index finger. 'Lisa was someone who—'

'No,' Dan insisted. 'I want to hear it from you, Lisa. Were you just setting me up? Look at me, Lisa. Speak to me. *Tell* me.'

She stared at him with great determination, her eyes now burning. 'You are ashamed of being Jewish, Dan. But this thing we are doing, it's more important than anything else.' She paused. 'Too important to leave to chance.'

Dan half rose out of his seat. 'Chance? What else is there? You want certainty? The . . . Nazis, they wanted certainty.'

Lisa got up and rushed from the table, hissing, 'I wish we'd never met.'

'Let her go,' Yuri said, following her with his eyes as she stormed out. 'We have more important things to discuss. Tomorrow you will call the Russian consul as a witness. He will prove – through you – that Klaus Keller was at Neuwelt in 1945.'

'So what?'

'So it will prove that Montford had the most notorious Nazi scientist with him to gas my father.'

Chapter 5

By the time Dan arrived home, a fog was descending over West London. It shrouded the houses, filled the streets, and made the air thicker as the temperature plummeted. Black ice formed on the roads and streetlights more than twenty feet away disappeared save for the yellow orbs of artificial light they produced, suspended fifteen feet in the air.

When Dan finally stood outside the front door to his house, he paused for thought. Things had changed. The trial was now a different ordeal. It was no longer the incomprehensible mission of a mysterious Russian, determined to ruin one of Britain's foremost political figures. Now it was the vengeance of a son, pursuing his father's killers through the years, the decades, across continents and jurisdictions, and trying to fix the trial so that the guilty should not escape. Dan wondered this: would he have done the same if it was Jo who had been murdered? And if he would not, what kind of a son did that make him?

Having earlier given his keys to Sophie, he now rang the doorbell. From inside there was a scurry of feet and the catch was disengaged, but no sooner had he pushed the door open than he saw the rear of Chrissy's head disappearing back into the lounge.

Once in the hall, he could hear the familiar chatter of the television. He pushed open the living room door and was momentarily suffocated by the blazing fire, accustomed as he was to the evening chill outside. There he saw Chris and Sophie and Jo, all three sitting riveted to a dramatic scene in an Australian soap.

'Hi, Dad,' Chris said, getting up, pecking him on the cheek, and sliding back into her armchair, not having taken her eyes off the screen. 'Wayne's just proposed to Norleen.'

'But she went surfing and has disappeared,' Sophie added, getting up.

'And some guy's just sounded the shark warning,' Jo said. 'You know, Ira, bless his soul, once saw a shark off Brighton Beach, but I reckon it was just an old boot floating in the surf or a bottle of vodka floating in Ira's gut.'

Dan did not know what to do but laugh. Here were the three people he cared most about in the world, and all they could do was tell him about some soap opera. However, it was the very normality of the scene, its wonderfully banal nature, the feeling that the same ritual was being played out in tens of thousands of households around the country, which reassured him. It allowed him to believe that his was a normal family.

Sophie moved from the sofa and stood next to him, still watching the screen. 'Want to talk?' she asked.

'What, about Wayne? And his quest for Doreen?'

'Norleen,' Chris called, still watching. 'God, Dad, don't you know *anything*? Norleen Church is *only* the most famous soap character in the *entire* universe.'

Sophie smiled. 'Got to admit, it is exciting. But I think I'd prefer to talk.'

'Come into my office,' Dan said, pointing to the kitchen.

As he shut the door, he could hear Chris screaming hysterically from the other room, and Jo shouting, 'Swim, lady, swim. You want to be a shark sandwich?'

The light was already on in the kitchen and a granary loaf stood on the breadboard half demolished, with crumbs everywhere. Sophie knew that this was substantially her handiwork and wished she had cleaned up the mess before Dan had come home. But Chris had insisted on showing Sophie how to surf the Internet in her room and had then dragged her downstairs to watch the soap.

In the distance, through the dark square kitchen windows, Sophie could just see the skeletons of bare trees in the nearby garden as the fog descended. She had been so absorbed with Chris that she had not noticed the sudden deterioration in the weather.

'Peanut butter sarnies,' she said with embarrassment.

'How did your shoplifting Saudi lady fare?' he asked.

'Two hundred and fifty pound fine. Can you believe, she just laughed out loud. Said she'd paid more for a dog's collar in Knightsbridge. What do you think of that? Dan . . .' It took her a moment to realise that he had not responded. 'What?' she asked, examining his face.

'Any news from Helen? About the British officer?'

'She's going to try, Dan. Call in a few favours. But she's still not a hundred per cent.'

For a moment, Dan was silent. 'I was just thinking. You know . . . what I would do.'

'If what?'

'If a bomb – I know this sounds crazy – or a gas explosion or whatever took out the house before I came home. I couldn't bear to lose the three of you.'

'That's not going to happen, Dan.'

'You seem to get on so well, the three of you. I mean together.'

'It's your family, not mine.'

'Yes, but Chris gets on better with Jo than I do, and you – well, Chris tells you things that she doesn't tell me.'

'She's a young girl, Dan. She loves you completely, desperately – I can . . . understand why she does – but brilliant a dad as you are, she needs occasionally to talk to a woman. And if you hadn't noticed, being a woman is one of the few things I can actually do tolerably well. But that's all. You're at the centre of the family, Dan. You hold it all together. I don't know anyone who could have coped with what you've had to put up with.'

She saw Dan cut himself some crusty bread, unevenly, the slice collapsing in the middle.

'Here, let me do that,' she said, grabbing the knife.

'Thanks.'

'How did the case go?'

'It went. Where it went, I'm not sure.'

'Did you sit late or something? I mean, the time's now—' She looked at the clock above the kitchen door, in the shape of a papier-mâché pig, which Chris had asked her mother to buy the Christmas before she died.

'Actually, we rose early.'

'Went to chambers after?'

'No,' he said.

'Tubes? Central Line up the spout again?'

'No, ran perfectly.'

'Well, I can't think of anything else,' she said, handing him a geometrically cut peanut butter sandwich.

'I saw Lisa.'

She pretended to smile, but she knew that the falseness was obvious. 'Of course, you've got every right to see any woman you—'

'Lisa's not just any woman.'

'No, she was your lover. Before me. Well, of course, I'm not your lover. I mean, we've just tangled tongues outside a doughnut diner, so I suppose . . .' She paused for breath. 'So I suppose that doesn't count for anything.'

'Sophie.'

'Shit,' she said. 'I *hate* being jealous.'

'There's nothing to be jealous of. I told you, it's all over between Lisa and me.'

She spun away from him. He put down the plate and grasped her shoulders to turn her back.

'Look, Soph, I want to be with you. I've fought it for longer than . . . I care to admit—'

'You have?'

'Just listen. I want you to be around. To be part of what goes on here. I want things to be normal and boring and *wonderful*. But there are certain things I've got to do before we get to that. Seeing Lisa was just one of them.'

Sophie nodded, more to herself than to Dan. Right, she told herself, the situation is back under control. Don't get hysterical or suicidal. Try to be mature and intelligent. 'You haven't tried your sarnie.'

'It looks great.'

'I make great peanut butter sarnies, Dan.'

'They're the best.'

'I mean, it's a crucial social skill.'

'Absolutely.'

Then she paused. 'I want to . . . come to the trial.'

'No.'

'I want to be there.'

'Waugh will ruin you, Soph.'

'Fuck Julian Waugh and Simon Montford and the sodding Bar.'

'Look, you want to help? There's some research I might need you to do.'

'What?'

'It might come to nothing, but Waugh is bound to rely on the Querry report to show that gassings couldn't happen at Neuwelt. Think you could look at that?'

'Look where?'

'That's part of the fun. I haven't got a clue.' He picked up the plate and took an exaggeratedly large mouthful, speaking as he munched. 'Is this wholenut peanut butter?'

'Of course.'

'It's great, Soph.'

'So the critics tell me.' She wiped a couple of crumbs from the side of his mouth and their bodies touched gently, her thigh against his, his arm against her breast. She desperately wanted to kiss him, mouth full of peanut butter or not. But then there was a quiet knock on the kitchen door.

'Am I interrupting anything?' Jo asked.

'No,' Dan mumbled as the two of them sprang apart.

'Just wanted a glass of water,' Jo said.

'I need to speak to you,' Dan told him, opening the cupboard next to the sink which contained the glasses.

Sophie looked from father to son and neither seemed to be prepared to continue the conversation in her presence. 'I'll go see what happened to Norleen,' she said.

'Too late,' Jo said, deadpan. 'She's shark-meat.'

The strip light underneath the kitchen cabinets which illuminated the work surfaces began to flicker. It buzzed as though a fly were trapped within the neon tube. Then it fizzled out. There was silence in the kitchen. Dan could just make out Chris chatting away to Sophie in the lounge, filling her in on the gory details of the programme.

'So you like peanut butter?' Jo said.

Dan put his index finger to his mouth and whispered, '*Hate* the stuff.'

'What you want to speak to me about?'

He paused, thinking where to begin. 'Yuri is the son of Ivan Basarov.'

Jo winced. 'I could've told you that.'

Dan felt the muscles in the back of his neck tense with anger. 'So why the *hell* didn't you—'

'You never asked.'

'But I—'

'You *never* asked, all right? Tell me I'm wrong and I'll . . . you can't, can you?'

'The time for these *bullshit* games is over, Jo.'

'So you want to know, huh?'

'Yes.'

'What I did in Neuwelt?'

'Yes, Jo.'

'It'll change things.'

'I want to know.'

'It'll change *everything*.'

'I still want to know.'

Jo muttered to himself in his private tongue, the guttural words sounding to Dan like an incantation. 'All right,' he eventually said. 'Godammit, all right.'

Jo shut the kitchen door, ensuring that the latch clicked in the housing. Soft light came through the frosted glass panels. But the kitchen was otherwise in darkness, save for the yellow rectangles of light from the windows of the house opposite.

'Funny thing about families,' he said.

'What?'

'They fuck you up.' He leant against the sink unit, his head silhouetted. 'Three things you can do with them. You can live with them and loathe them. Love 'em and leave 'em. Or—'

'What?'

'Kill 'em.'

'Jo—'

'You telling me you never seen those stories on the news? Mr Joe Smoe sells carpets in Kansas, good father, good husband for twenty years, comes home one weekend, watches some ball, has a six-pack and then slices up his family with a hunting knife. Then goes and makes a nice barbecue.'

'I've seen cases,' Dan replied. 'Prosecuted them. But what's your point?'

'This friend of yours, Yuri, he's driven. But he can't remember his father, so he's in love. He's in love with the idea of his father, and that's a dangerous thing.'

'And you knew all this, Jo? And you didn't tell—'

'I didn't know it as a *fact*. But I knew it . . .' He paused and banged his fist on his heart. 'I knew it in *here*. This business was a blood thing. It was personal. This wasn't going to stop. He, Yuri, wasn't going to stop, he won't stop until the blood is repaid. This guy's driven . . .'

Dan began to pace the smooth kitchen floor, walking towards the rear door that gave on to the garden. He could see people – no more than shapes – moving in the houses opposite as their lights burnt through the fog.

'I need to know, Jo,' he said with his back to his father. 'I need to know what you did in Neuwelt.'

There was a pained intake of breath. Then a scraping of metal as Jo picked up the carving knife and drove it into the breadboard.

'I survived,' he said. He ran some water from the mixer tap into the sink. 'Now what you're thinking,' he said, 'is why did this old Jew survive and not some other one?'

'No—'

'Do you think surviving is a blessing? I did. I thought I was lucky and smart and . . . God help me, better than some of the others who just went into the chambers naked, clinging to each other, praying to a God who I knew, just *knew*, didn't exist. There I was, Josef Rosen, safe and warm and alive, and I was going to do what it took to stay that way.'

Dan was still facing the garden. Behind him, he could hear Jo pacing the kitchen with his careful steps, breathing heavily, getting nearer and nearer until he felt his arm being taken and Jo pulling him around. There was tension between them, as there always was when they confronted the past. Dan's heart raced. His palms were sweaty.

'I *only* did what I *had* to,' Jo said. His words almost choked him as they came out. 'Do you understand?'

'Yes.'

'No, you *don't*. No one does.'

'Come on, Jo. Don't do this to yourself.'

'You wanted to know, didn't you?'

'Yes, but—'

'Then you're going to know.'

'What?'

'How I survived. How this good-for-nothing old Jew survived when all those God-fearing people was gassed.'

Dan looked deep into his father's eyes as the lights from the houses at the rear sparked in the irises of the old man. This was the question that had troubled him for so long, and now he was on the verge of finding out he felt sick. It was that moment: the fractional hesitation before opening an important letter, the pause before opening a locked door. His imagination ran wild, but nothing could have prepared him for what Jo said next.

'I worked in Keller's labs.'

There was a moment of agonising silence between them.

Then Jo shook Dan roughly by both arms. 'I worked in Klaus Keller's labs. Do you *understand*? What that means? What that makes me? What that makes you?'

'Jo, you can't leave it like that.'

'I ain't saying no more.' He started to leave but stopped, and said without turning his head, 'And now you can hate me.'

When Dan was left alone, he leant for support against the kitchen units. His legs were weak and he felt dirty. A small voice in the back of his head chided him: this was why you ignored your father for years. He felt he had always known on some instinctive level. He remembered the Holocaust Museum in New York, the terrible photographs, children lining up outside the gas chambers, their eyes still hopeful, unknowing, even though their end was moments away.

He was unable to sleep for hours. Although he squeezed himself into every conceivable position it was possible for a grown man to adopt in a king-size bed, nothing worked for very long. Sometimes he stacked both pillows under his head; other times he buried his face in them, hoping somehow to shield his mind from the images of the camps which slowly turned through it. It was all useless. As the night wore on, the various shocks to which he had been exposed became interchangeable: Jo working in the labs, Ira's death, finding Neville Neale; he saw all these, the images of one occasionally superimposed on the other. He saw the garage in Bedford Park, Neville's fishing equipment propped by the Jaguar, and a body, the chest open, bleeding. But some secret knowledge or fear kept him from seeing the face of the corpse, though he struggled to. Then he saw what he suspected was his face. Someone was out there killing people connected to the case. Would he be next? He awoke with a start and saw someone at the foot of the bed.

His heart beat so hard that he imagined he could hear the blood pumping in his head. His face dripped with sweat, and though he tried to speak he could not.

'Dad?' Chris whispered.

Relief flooded through his body, though he still found it hard to breathe.

'Dad,' she repeated. 'I couldn't sleep.'

He tried to smile. 'C-come here, sweetheart.'

She crept forward in her nightshirt, but once she sat down on the mattress next to him, she cramped up in pain.

'What's wrong?' he asked, alarmed.

'You know,' she said. Then she whispered, 'You *know*.'

He had always imagined that he would find such a discussion embarrassing, for although he knew Chris had started her periods the previous year, it was not something they had discussed. This had been Viv's territory. But now he saw his daughter sitting next to him in pain.

'When Mum had a bad month,' he said, 'I used to get her a hot-water bottle. Want one?'

She smiled briefly. He got out of bed, aware that his T-shirt and boxers were drenched with sweat.

'Dad,' she said, 'you were muttering something in your sleep.'

'I was dreaming of you, angel,' he joked.

'Oh, thanks. It sounded like a nightmare.'

He smiled. 'Yes,' he said.

Chapter 6

Dan arrived at the Old Bailey weary from the avalanche of thoughts that had been set off by Jo's revelation. But despite his lack of sleep, he found to his surprise that it was with a sense of relief that he sat down in counsel's row in Court 12, even with Lancing behind him. This was familiar territory, for the courts had been his life for the last decade and a half.

'Do you think we're going to win?' Lancing asked. He was in his black gown but had his wig on the bench in front of him.

'I don't know,' Dan said.

Lancing stood up, checking all around to ensure that they were alone. 'Well, I know.'

'We win no victories and suffer no defeats,' Dan said.

'Total crap. That's the sort of old-fashioned . . . tosh that Neale used to spout.'

Blood rushed into Dan's head and the memory of Neale's prostrate body flashed before him. 'You'll never be half the advocate he was, Lancing.'

'Wouldn't want to be.'

'For Christ's sake, he's only been dead three months.'

'The past.' Lancing paused. 'The future. That should concern us.'

'Future? Your pathetic political future? Would a defeat blot your copybook?'

Lancing smiled falsely. 'You couldn't be more wrong. Look . . . Simon Montford . . . warts and all, he's one of us.'

'One of you.'

'Perhaps we should cut our losses. Offer no evidence. I mean, do we really have enough evidence, Becket?'

Dan paused as the court door opened and Waugh walked in. 'Why don't we let the jury decide?'

The second witness in the trial was to be a sergeant from one of the tank crews that had entered Neuwelt with Montford in April 1945. So just after 10.30, Dan waited for the bustle in court to die down. He bowed shallowly to the judge, and called out the name of the witness: Norman Turnbull. As he stood at the front of the court, his peripheral vision caught Lancing looking at Waugh glumly.

As the sergeant was sworn, Dan sized him up. Turnbull was a tall man, in many respects a contrast to the private who had testified the previous day. This man was impeccably turned out, with a regimental tie, a precisely pressed pair of trousers, a neat dark haircut and, despite his advancing years, he stood erect, refusing to allow the years to give him an excuse to slouch. He had a long nose and very thin lips. He held his chin out, with the effect, Dan noticed, that you were never sure whether he was looking directly at you or not. This man was the epitome of the adage you can take the man out of the army, but you can't take the army out of the man.

'What is your name?' Dan asked.

'Norman Turnbull.'

'And were you a sergeant in the Second World War?'

'I was.'

Dan looked at Julian Waugh to his left and received a nod from the defence counsel when he said, 'I intend to take you through the preliminaries very quickly. It is agreed between all parties, Mr Turnbull, that you were a sergeant in the tank unit that entered the Neuwelt concentration camp in April 1945, at a time when the defendant, Simon Montford, was also there.'

'Yes, I see,' Turnbull replied.

All at once, Dan lost his thread. It was the use of the word Neuwelt, which filled him with revulsion. For he felt an inherited burden of guilt that had been passed down from father to son, from Jo to himself. While the court waited, he recalled how in the early hours he had knocked on Jo's door and tried to talk to him. There was no answer, the door was locked. He knew Jo was up as the radio was on softly, and he could hear the pages of a magazine being turned over.

These recollections were interrupted by Julian Waugh, who had sprung to his feet to Dan's left. 'Does my friend have any more questions or is he just stretching his legs?' he asked sarcastically, obtaining a few chuckles from the jury.

'Mr Becket?' the judge asked. Constant's face was sallow, as it often was early in the day's proceedings.

'Yes, I'm sorry, M'Lord,' Dan said, trying to shake the cobwebs of thought from his head. He turned his attention back to the witness. Above him and to the right, the public gallery was packed once more, and dozens of unknown faces stared resolutely at him. 'Do you remember any incident in particular at Neuwelt?' It was a vague question, but all that he could manage for the moment.

'I remember many.'

'Any involving—'

'I *object*,' Waugh said. 'No leading questions, please.'

Dan knew Waugh was right. He had to find a way to get to the dead Russian without telegraphing it to the witness. 'Did you know anyone by the name of—'

'I *must* object. When will Mr Becket learn the most basic rules of examination. No leading questions.'

Dan's brain had turned to peanut butter. Here was a man who had been in Neuwelt at the same time as his father. He wondered whether the sergeant had seen Jo as the tanks rolled into the camp. If what Jo had said was true, then the relatively healthy Josef Rosen would have stood out from the living corpses elsewhere in the camp.

'Was there an impromptu jail?' Dan asked. 'Created in the camp?'

'Yes.'

'Who was in that jail?'

'A private. Name of Parsons. I believe you heard from him yesterday. At least, I was waiting outside court with him most of yesterday.'

'Anyone else? In the jail?'

'A Russian,' the sergeant said, as if it were the most obvious thing in the world. 'That's why I'm here, isn't it?'

Dan knew that it was an unfortunate answer, giving away a little too much. It suggested that the witness might have been rehearsed or tipped off. He was aware of Julian Waugh scribbling the reply down.

'Did you know the name of the Russian prisoner?'

'Yes, sir.'

'And what was it?'

The sergeant stuck his chin out a little further. 'Ivan Basarov. At least, that's what the man told me.'

'You spoke to him?'

'Yes.'

'Why?'

The witness straightened his tie, which Dan could see didn't need straightening at all. 'I was ordered to take the prisoner from the jail to the ... SS barracks. Or rather,' he quickly added, 'the barracks we were using as a temporary command post.'

'And who was there?'

'The defendant, Major Montford.'

'Anyone else?'

'A German officer.'

'What was the name of the German?'

'I was told—'

Waugh shot to his feet, 'I *object*,' he said. 'Hearsay.'

'Did the German tell you his name?'

Waugh shouted, 'I still object.'

'Was Montford present?' Dan asked.

'Yes.'

'Did you ever find out the name of the German officer?'

'Yes.'

'Who told you?'

The witness paused and looked directly at the dock. 'Major Montford told me.'

There was a murmur around the court. Waugh could no longer object, for if Montford was actually present the hearsay rule did not apply.

'And what was the name of the SS officer at Neuwelt concentration camp in April 1945?'

The sergeant brushed some fluff from his suit sleeve and looked at the jury. 'It was Klaus Keller. Major Montford told me it was Klaus Keller.'

There was an explosion of noise all around Dan. Suddenly the gallery high above the court was a mass of movement. He glanced up instinctively, craning his neck to his right; he saw mouths opening and shutting, and faces full of disbelief. There had been articles about Keller, Hitler's disappearing chemist, in the papers.

'What happened to the Russian?'

'I did my job. I left him with the officers at the SS barracks.'

'What *happened* to Basarov?' Dan insisted.

'I only did what I was told.'

'Did you see him again?'

'Yes.'

'Where?'

'I was following orders.'

'Where?'

'They took him to that place.'

'Who took him?'

'There was an armed escort. Soldiers I hadn't seen before. British soldiers.'

'Where did they take him?'

'To the chamber.'

'What sort of chamber?' Dan saw the reluctance in the man's face, a tightening of his features, the pressing together of his thin lips. 'What *sort* of chamber?'

'The gas chamber, I think.'

'You think?'

'I know.'

'Was there any other sort of chamber you saw?'

'No.'

'So Basarov was taken to the gas chamber at Neuwelt on the orders of who?'

The man was silent.

Dan continued, 'Ivan Basarov was taken to the gas chamber at Neuwelt on the orders of—'

'Major Montford,' the man said. 'And before you ask, yes, yes, *yes* to all your questions.' He turned to the judge. 'Can I go now?'

'No,' Dan said. 'I need to ask you more.'

'*What?*' the man shouted, spinning to his left in the witness box. He stared at Dan with menace in his eyes, the controlled violence of a man who had been taught to kill quickly and efficiently. Dan could feel his own chest rising and falling; his breathing was short and rapid. He took a moment to let the jury absorb what they had just heard. But he needed one more thing from the sergeant, one more painful betrayal of another British Army soldier. The hardest part.

He tried to speak as calmly as he could. 'Did you see Ivan Basarov later, Mr Turnbull?'

'Yes.'

'And what condition was he in?'

The man looked down, ashamed. 'He was dead.'

Chapter 7

Julian Waugh asked for a five-minute adjournment before he cross-examined Norman Turnbull. In consequence, the judge ordered that the jury be led out of court and into their waiting room.

Dan knew that five legal minutes constituted ten minutes of real time, once you took into account all the comings and goings and bowings and formalities. Chrissy had told him recently how her physics teacher had talked about relativity and how in theory time bends. But, Dan thought, all you had to do was come to court any day of the week and you would see time warp from five minutes into ten. Still, he was grateful that Chris had thrown herself into her studies in a way she had never done prior to Viv's death. He didn't quite understand his daughter's sudden obsession with science and computing: perhaps it was a search for things – unlike families – that were constant, knowable, immutable and safe. As a reward for her outstanding grades he had bought her the Internet multi-media package the previous Christmas, and she had made friends all across the globe – he only wished she would make one or two in London. But he rarely nagged her about the inordinate amount of time she spent in front of the computer screen, just as he had stopped reminding her about doing her piano practice. The events in Devon had shown him again just how resilient his daughter was. She would find her own level. He would just have to trust her.

For the duration of the adjournment, Julian Waugh sat motionless in his position at the front of the court, not taking any instructions from Montford or the battery of private solicitors behind him. Dan realised what he was after. It was an old, low tactic: he was sweating the witness.

By the time Waugh was on his feet minutes later, Dan could see the forehead of Norman Turnbull covered in perspiration.

'Sergeant?' Waugh began, softly, almost hesitantly.

'Yes,' the man replied.

'Well, should I call you Sergeant?'

'You mean after all these years?'

'*No*,' Waugh shouted. 'I mean after your dishonourable discharge.'

'I parted ways with the army after the war.'

'You were *booted* out?' Waugh shouted, pressing home the advantage. The man was silenced. 'Weren't you?' Still no reply. 'Weren't you?'

Again the eyes of the witness half closed. 'Yes.'

'And for what?'

'It was never properly proved.'

'What was this thing – this thing that resulted in you being *booted* out of the army, this thing that was never properly proved?'

'I disobeyed orders. But you've got to understand—'

'Oh,' Waugh said, interrupting, 'I think the jury will understand perfectly. You see, *Mr* Turnbull, there appear to be some orders that you obey and some orders that you disobey.'

'So?'

'So, if your evidence has a shred of truth, and I suggest that it has *not*, but if this fanciful account of yours is true, then you were prepared to deliver this poor, innocent Russian prisoner into the hands of a homicidal major in the British Army and his evil SS conspirator so he could be murdered.'

'I did what I was told.'

'It's too obvious to say that that is precisely the pathetic excuse the Nazis at Nuremberg used.'

'It's what happened.'

'So why have you only come forward now?' Seeing that the witness did not reply, Waugh repeated, '*Why?*'

'I've been asked . . . by the police.'

'Are these the same police who have paid you money to testify?'

'They've helped me with my rent.'

'On the understanding that you would come to court to tell this *monstrous* pack of lies against this man of impeccable character?'

'It's not lies.'

'And have they also helped you with a new house?'

'I've been relocated to a new council flat, if that's what you mean.'

'You know what I mean.' Waugh paused and glanced at the jury with a look of gross incredulity on his face. He was almost defying them to believe the witness.

'Can I go now?' Turnbull asked.

'Before you disappear,' Waugh said, 'to your new council apartment, I want to ask you this. Did you actually see Simon Montford kill this ... Russian?'

'No.'

'The man was frail when you took him from the jail?'

'Yes.'

'For all you know he could have died at any minute?'

'I don't know ... possibly.'

'And you saw him later. Sure he was dead?'

'He looked it.'

'Could he not have been just asleep?' Waugh paused and when there was no response to his provocation, he shouted more loudly, 'Could he not have been *asleep*?'

'People don't tend to take naps in a gas chamber. You don't tend to bury people who are asleep.'

The acidity of the reply stunned Waugh for a moment, and Dan saw him shuffle his papers nervously for the first time during the cross-examination. This was the first real sign of weakness that Dan had seen Julian Waugh show during his demolition of the two prosecution witnesses.

'One last thing,' Waugh said eventually. 'You say the SS officer was the infamous Klaus Keller?'

'Yes.'

'Apart from your bare allegation that Mr Montford told you it was Keller, can you bring to court any other evidence that the German you saw at Neuwelt was in fact Klaus Keller?' The man paused and tried to think, but Waugh, ever persistent, would not let him settle. 'Well? What other evidence is there that it was Keller?'

'None,' the man said.

In the most dismissive tone Dan had heard him use, the defence counsel said, 'I've *finished* with this witness.'

There was a buzz around the courtroom as Turnbull retreated from the witness box. He looked once more at Montford, who stared back defiantly. In normal circumstances, Dan would have glanced at the jury to gauge what they had made of the sergeant's evidence. But his mind was too preoccupied with the next witness. The Russian consul, who would give evidence after lunch.

Chapter 8

The judge adjourned for lunch shortly after the sergeant's evidence. Dan knew that he could not bear to be in the court building during the break, so he walked out into the chilly air outside the Old Bailey.

He ignored the bustle and the crowds thronging around Ludgate Circus, people dashing to sandwich bars, rushing back to their offices. Instead, he forced himself to use such determination as he had left to concentrate on the job in hand. There was one substantial witness left before all the formal evidence, most of which Dan would get Robert Lancing to read. It meant that there was only one more chance for the prosecution, for Dan, to produce damning evidence against Montford. This was Yuri's evidence. It was going to be crucial.

He walked up the incline towards the steps of St Paul's and then turned left into Old Bailey itself, passing the empty car dealership, the travel agent's, the sandwich bar and the misted windows of the pub. He was fifty yards from the revolving door of the court when he heard his name being whispered. At first he did not see the caller. Passers-by hurried with their collars turned up against the cold. A traffic warden argued with a delivery driver who was parked on a yellow line. But then he heard his name again, and in a passage near the *Reader's Digest* shop he saw Sophie.

'You in a better mood than last night?' she asked.

She wore a large college scarf high around her neck, ostensibly against the cold. Combined with a trendy black floppy hat, it made it difficult to identify her as Sophie Chase, barrister.

'What are you doing here?' Dan said.

'Coming to see you at the office, darling,' she said sarcastically.

The cold had made her lips dry and the tips of her bob were just visible below the hat.

'What if—'

'I'm seen? Waugh and all his cronies are always in the Bar mess over lunch. The rest of London is safe. Look, I just wanted to find out what the hell happened to us last night. One minute we were making peanut butter sarnies, the next—'

'Jo happened. Jo happened again. That's all, Soph.' He moved further into the half-shadows of the passageway as two taxis hurtled along the one-way street. 'Nothing's changed. I meant what I said. I still want you. Of course, you've probably gathered that our whole family is as nutty as a fruitcake.'

'A little screwed up, perhaps.'

Again he became aware of the press of time. 'Look, I've got to go back to court. I'm calling that Russian consul.'

'Be careful, Dan.'

'I've got to do it.'

'I know.'

'Wish me luck.'

'Luck.' She began to push him in the small of his back towards the court entrance, then she suddenly stopped. '*Shit*, I nearly forgot why I came. When is Querry testifying about the gas chambers?'

'Tomorrow. Found something?'

'Maybe. Don't get your hopes up. It's only a maybe.'

'What?'

'I cross-referenced his name with everything I could think of in the library. The Second World War, Eva Braun, the space programme – I mean everything. And I found a reference to him in a footnote to an appendix.'

'Soph, I'm going to be late.'

'He gave evidence in America.'

'America?'

'I'm going to get the transcript of his evidence faxed over, if they have a fax.'

'The Americans invented faxes.'

'Good point,' she smiled.

At a little after ten past two, Dan inspected the short, balding man standing in the witness box. He wore an expensive grey suit, with the sort of sheen that was more redolent of Milan than Moscow. He was the type of man who constantly had a five-o'clock shadow, though the skin under his chin had been scraped so vigorously with the razor blade that it was raw.

'My name is Levin Panchevsky.' The accent was heavy and deliberately overstated, each vowel and consonant enunciated to the full.

'And what is your occupation?' Dan asked.

'I am currently attached as a consul to the Russian Embassy in London.'

'And what is your field of specialism?'

'I was previously attached to domestic ... security.'

Dan noticed that the last word was said self-consciously, as if it were a stale secret finally released from the lips of a Cold War combatant, a secret that was no longer particularly important. He perceived a rustle of interest from the jury, but remembered his game plan: keep it short. Intriguing as the Russian's occupation sounded, he just wanted to get him in and out of the box. He reminded himself once again: this was Yuri's evidence; it could blow up in his face at any stage.

'Have you produced a document for us?'

The man nodded.

Dan was handed a clear plastic envelope by Lancing behind him. The envelope was about A4 in size and inside was a wallet-sized sheet of weathered card. He saw, before he passed it to the usher, that the card was sepia in colour and sported a photograph.

Panchevsky examined the document with great deliberation.

'What is that document?' Dan asked him.

'It is a *Dienstausweis*.'

'What is that?'

'It is a service security pass.'

'For which organisation?'

The witness held the envelope up towards the jury, but across the expanse of the courtroom it was impossible for them to make out the letters he indicated. 'You see? The two letters. The lightning strikes. The SS.'

Dan chose to ignore the whispers around the court, the short exchanges of conversation. 'So that there is no doubt, what was the SS?'

Waugh got to his feet. 'My Lord, must we have this evidence about the SS? It seems unnecessary. It is a little like asking a witness who Adolf Hitler was.'

There were some smirks around the courtroom, but Dan was coiled tightly with tension and was intent on rubbing Waugh's face in it. 'I wonder,' he said, 'if Mr Waugh would like to make an admission on behalf of his client as to who Adolf Hitler was? The saviour of the Aryan race? The Antichrist? A madman? All of the above?' He was pleased when he saw Julian Waugh slump back into his seat. 'It's a perfectly simple question, My Lord. Who were the SS? Unless Mr Waugh has any other humorous observations in this extremely serious trial, perhaps the witness might be allowed to answer.'

The judge nodded to the witness.

Panchevsky put one hand on the front rim of the witness box and stared at the jury, holding the pass in the other. 'The SS, the *Schutzstaffel*, started as Hitler's bodyguard. They ran and policed the concentration camps. They became an army within an army, under Heinrich Himmler. They organised the murder of about fifteen million people ... including five million Russians.'

It was interesting how this man mentioned the Russians first: it was the sort of thing Yuri would have done. 'And how many Jews?' Dan asked.

'Six million is now the accepted figure,' Panchevsky said.

Dan pointed to the document in the witness's hand. 'Who did that pass belong to?' he asked.

The witness again examined the card, as if discovering the answer for the first time. '*K*laus *K*eller,' he said, stressing the first letter of each word.

'And which camp was this valid for?'

'Neuwelt, Greater Germany.'

'What year?'

'1945.'

'What month?'

'April.'

That was about as much as Dan could get from the Russian, perhaps more than he had hoped. He sat down in counsel's row and watched Waugh get up to cross-examine. He wondered if Panchevsky knew Yuri at all. And if he did, what had they agreed? Who had given the orders? Who was controlling whom?

Chapter 9

Waugh asked to see the original exhibit before he asked any questions.

Dan knew that it was little more than a standard advocate's ploy. The tactic was to take the incriminating document out of the hands of the witness, handle it, show the jury that you were not afraid of it. So much was routine. But as Waugh looked at the document again and again, Dan sensed an uneasiness growing in the diminutive Russian witness: he started to rub the palm of his left hand down the side of his grey trousers; sweat appeared for the first time on his temple. Still Waugh continued to inspect the SS pass. The public gallery was silent and frozen. The tension continued to build.

'You were in the . . . security service?' Waugh asked.

'Yes.'

'Were you part of the communist secret police?'

The man feigned indignity. 'I find the term offensive.'

'Were you KGB?'

'No.'

'Something like it?'

'That is not relevant.'

Waugh raised his voice. 'Let's see what is relevant, shall we? This document miraculously appeared from KGB files?'

'The only miracle was that your Metropolitan Police requested it. Your *Insp*ector *G*rail requested it.' Again he stressed the beginning of the name, rubbing his chin uneasily where the flesh was raw.

'You understood that the Met wanted to establish whether Klaus Keller was in Neuwelt concentration camp in April 1945?'

'Yes.'

'And this proves ... what?'

'That Keller was at Neuwelt in April 1945.'

'What a *happy* coincidence,' Waugh said sardonically.

'Pardon?'

'Oh, nothing.' Waugh poured himself a glass of water from the dusty carafe in front of him. As he was pouring, without bothering to look at the witness, he said calmly, 'This document is a ... forgery.' He said the last word so softly that the witness had trouble hearing it.

'Is a what?'

'A *forgery*,' he shouted. 'A *lie*. A fake. A deception created by the KGB.'

'Nonsense.'

'Isn't it true that document forgery was an important part of KGB business? So much so that an entire division was dedicated to forging documents?'

'I cannot answer that.'

'You choose not to answer that, *Mr* Panchevsky, because it is true. Didn't the KGB fake reports to blame the Germans for murdering several thousand officers at Katyn?' Waugh looked at Len Constant quite deliberately. 'When really it was the Soviets who had murdered all those thousands of *Polish* officers?'

Dan's instincts as an advocate told him that he should object to this line of questioning. But Waugh was entitled to examine the credibility of the witness and the organisation that had produced the document. The mention of the Katyn massacre, this appeal to the second-generation Polish judge, was a very shrewd move on his part. But despite the damage it was doing to his case, Dan felt that the jury had a right to know the truth.

'My Lord,' Waugh said, 'the defence have provided an expert report on the authenticity of the so-called SS document. Does Your Lordship have a copy?'

The judge nodded.

Dan looked around in panic. He had not been given the report. Sitting two rows behind him were the senior Crown prosecutor and Andrew Short, the DPP's rep. Robert Lancing was directly behind Dan. He shrugged.

'What report?' Dan mouthed.

'Haven't you read your brief, Becket?' Short said, coming up to Dan's shoulder.

'I haven't got the wretched report,' Dan said.

'Grail was supposed to give it to you.'

With that, Dan was left alone in the front row. Grail had blundered again and now Dan would have to listen to Waugh demolishing the Russian. The duty of the defence was to serve expert reports on the prosecution, not the *prosecutor*. It was up to the prosecuting authorities to ensure that Dan had a copy.

'Forensic tests have shown,' Waugh said with absolute certainty, 'that this paper has been artificially aged to appear fifty years old. Any comment on that?'

The witness was silent.

'The face on the photograph, Keller's face, has been superimposed on to the print using computer-aided montage techniques. Do you see? The photo itself had faint marks in the top left-hand corner. These are likely to be staples that have been filled in. Staples attaching the photograph to another document entirely.'

Dan watched the witness fiddling with the cuff of his suit jacket, not fighting back, not daring to.

'The glue,' Waugh continued, 'is of a chemical composition unknown in Germany in the 1940s. Any comment on that?' He stared at the witness with total disdain. 'I could go on. But I can summarise this shortly. Your document, *sir*, is a forgery. It is not worth the paper it was fabricated upon.'

Dan knew that the small gains he had made throughout the trial had been destroyed in a few moments. The Russian forgery – Yuri's forgery – was likely, more than anything else, to ensure that Simon Montford was acquitted by a British jury.

For the rest of the afternoon, Robert Lancing stood behind Dan and read out evidence that was agreed between the parties under the Criminal Justice Act. These were typed statements agreed under Section 9. They spoke of the fact that Montford was indeed a major in the British Army in 1945, that he had been at Neuwelt and that the camp had chemical gas facilities. It saved much time and effort to be able to agree these uncontentious matters without having to call witness after witness whose testimony would not be challenged. Then there was a series of handwritten admissions of fact, under Section 10. Julian Waugh had scribbled these out on a perforated sheet of counsel's notepaper in his spiderish hand. Dan was required to sign and date them. The principal admission Dan was compelled to make was that Simon Sinclair Montford was a man with no previous criminal convictions. A man presumed to be of previous good character.

Later that afternoon Dan stood to close the prosecution case, torn to shreds as it now appeared to him. But Waugh had one final trick: he insisted that Grail be tendered for cross-examination.

In many criminal trials, the case officer was called at the request of the defence to tie up loose ends concerning the investigation. But as Grail walked nervously into court, this was precisely what Dan feared: where would the loose ends in this case lead? To Dan and his association with Yuri? To Jo? To a father who was at Neuwelt? A father who disqualified Dan from taking the case.

Grail no longer had the tatty coat with which he had first approached Dan in Central Park in January. Now he sported a cool grey cashmere double-breasted that was generous in its cut and swirled around him as he walked. He refused to swear an oath on the Bible, but affirmed. After that, Dan did all the talking.

'Your name is Detective Inspector Peter Grail. You are attached to the War Crimes Investigation Unit of the Metropolitan Police. You are the officer in charge of the Montford prosecution. Please wait there. The defence will have some questions for you.'

Waugh got up to cross-examine immediately, like a boxer coming out of his corner to finish off an injured opponent. 'I am not going to beat about the bush,' he snorted. 'You have been an accomplice in the production of fabricated evidence against Simon Montford.' When Grail did not answer, Waugh added, 'Isn't that *right*?'

'No,' Grail replied quietly.

The refutation was so understated that not even Dan was convinced.

'Well,' Waugh continued, mocking the witness, 'let's see how much truth there is in your *vigorous* denial.' He hesitated, allowed more tension to build, and then attacked once more. 'Isn't it right that it was you who liaised with the Russian ... security services to obtain this?' He brandished the plastic envelope with the supposed Keller SS pass in it.

'I was assigned,' Grail said, 'to—'

'Never mind that. Didn't you make any checks on the authenticity of this document?'

'No. We were in the hands of—'

'So you trusted the *KGB*?' Waugh said, full of scorn. 'Do you find, Mr Grail, that you are a naturally trusting person?'

'I just did my job.'

'That's the problem. Your job was to gather evidence to convict Simon Montford of this preposterous crime.'

'My job was to investigate whether there was evidence of—'

'And in your desperation you cut corners. Isn't it right that you paid Sergeant Turnbull, the second of the witnesses, to give evidence?'

'He would have testified anyway. But he was initially reluctant to give evidence against a former senior officer.'

'So how did you assuage his doubts?' Grail did not reply. 'How?' Waugh demanded.

'Money.'

Dan winced when he heard the barefaced way in which Grail spoke about buying the sergeant's evidence. There had been several cases in which Dan had been involved where the police had paid informers for their information, but these people had been career criminals, and money was no more than a professional gratuity. This was different. It was more desperate, dishonest.

'Do you think the money affected his performance in court?' Waugh asked.

'Do you think money affects *yours*?' Grail retorted, for the first time rising to Waugh's bait.

Dan could hear tuts from the jury box, saw the dismissive shaking of heads at the arrogance of the policeman. This, too, was disastrous. If the investigator was suspect, so too would be the investigation.

'One more thing,' Waugh said, appearing to be delighted to have provoked the outburst from Grail. 'Is it right that you wanted to bury evidence?'

'I find that accusation offensive.'

'Let me put it another way. Did you want to hide evidence? Withhold it from the defence? Unlawfully conceal it?'

'What evidence?' Grail said uneasily, but Dan knew what Waugh meant.

Waugh paused and glanced at Dan, as if to tarnish him as a co-conspirator. 'How about the Querry report? You wanted to bury that.'

'We disclosed it.'

'Only in September 1996, Mr Grail, and your investigation started ... when?'

'1994.'

'You wanted the Querry report withheld.'

'I didn't think it was relevant.'

Waugh handed a photocopied sheet to Grail via the usher. 'Read that to yourself. It is a highlighted passage of the report you say was irrelevant. Now tell the jury what it says.'

Grail looked up, embarrassed. He began to form words but then stopped.

'Well?'

'It says that the chambers at Neuwelt were *incapable* of conducting gassings,' he said.

Before Grail could recover from this blow, Waugh struck him again. 'One final point, Mr Grail.' He paused, stoking up the tension and anticipation. 'It's been said that the reason this man Basarov, if he ever existed, was in custody was because he killed a British officer. Have you checked the army records?'

'Yes,' Grail said.

Dan stared at him, astonished.

'Was any British officer killed at Neuwelt?'

'No,' Grail said.

There was an eruption of noise around Dan, and Waugh shuffled along the front row to his side.

'Drop the case, Becket,' he hissed. 'Querry's lined up for tomorrow. And we have an eye-witness. A final fucking crucial witness who will blow you out of the water.'

Dan stared defiantly into his opponent's hawkish face. 'Call them, Waugh. Call them *all*. We're going on.'

'Your funeral.'

'We're still going on.' Dan rose, turned to the judge and said, 'My Lord, that is the case for the prosecution.'

As the judge closed proceedings on the second day, Dan knew something with absolute certainty: Waugh had known that Grail had wanted to bury the Querry report. For this fact, there was only one explanation. There was a leak in the prosecution camp.

In the corridor, he collared both Short and Grail and penned them in a corner, barely able to contain his anger.

'What the hell happened in there?' he demanded.

'You lost our case for us,' Short sneered.

Dan turned to Grail. 'Why didn't you tell me you checked the army records?'

Grail hesitated. 'I told Mr Short.'

Short blushed, indignant. 'You stupid liar.'

'I left a message at your office this morning,' Grail protested. 'Have you checked your messages?'

Short was about to explode, then wavered. 'Well . . . I—'

'Jesus Christ!' Dan shouted. 'Can't you two sort yourselves out?'

'Like you've done so admirably,' Short said sarcastically.

Dan was determined not to be drawn into a slanging match, so he breathed deeply and tried to clear his head. 'Look,' he said finally, 'the defence know everything we're doing. How?'

Short crossed his arms tightly. 'Wasn't Sophie Chase once for the defence?'

Chapter 10

It was in the deserted lobby of the Old Bailey forty-five minutes after the court rose that Dan came across the woman. Or rather, she came across him, blocking his path and mouthing words with a desperation that verged upon hysteria.

'Why is Miss-ter Neale not prosecuting the case?' she asked. Her accent was very Middle European, *Mittel Europa*. She wore clothes that were exclusively black. Around her neck was a crumpled black headscarf which she had allowed to fall back, revealing thinning hair through which her scalp could be seen. A heavily laden bag weighed down her left shoulder.

'Neville Neale can't do the case,' Dan replied.

'Why not?'

'He's dead.'

He saw her muttering to herself, as if death were hardly a good excuse.

'So you are now the man in charge?' she finally asked.

'That's what they tell me.'

'Then why haven't you used my documents against that . . . that monster.'

'Montford?'

'I was at Belsen,' the woman said. She paused, looking up into Dan's eyes, fixing his attention. 'When I come to England I work as a cleaner. Thirty years I clean at the Foreign Office. No one notices me. No one cares.' Her eyes were watery, but the whole face, the creased forehead and the pursed lips, created an impression of great intensity. 'But then I see this. I sent to Neville Neale.'

Dan was about to ask: Which documents? But he remembered Neale's last call to him, when he had talked about a secret source.

'Was this in September?'

'Why haven't you used them?'

'They've disappeared.'

She took the bag off her shoulder and rummaged inside. Amongst the clutter Dan saw a bundle of documents held together with a fraying rubber band.

'These are copies,' she said.

'What are they?'

'My English is not good.'

Dan saw pages and pages of badly photocopied memos. Confidential documents. 'Can I copy these?' he asked, glancing at the clock. The court offices would be about to shut, but he might catch them.

The woman stood with her arms crossed near the noticeboard with the court listings. 'I wait here.'

Dan took the bundle and climbed the stairs to his left as fast as he could to the administration offices on the second floor. He knew that the photocopier to which the prosecution had access was broken and awaiting the visit of the service engineer. However, if he was lucky, the court staff might agree to help.

At the glass window on the second floor, he rang for attention. When there was no answer, he rang again and again until a surly young woman with brightly painted nails sauntered over to him.

'We're shut,' she said, trying to pretend she wasn't chewing gum.

'I need to photocopy some documents urgently.'

'We're shut.'

'I'm counsel in Court 12.'

'I don't care if you're the King of—'

'Never mind,' he said, for suddenly the argument seemed totally unimportant. He had looked down at one of the sheets of paper. The young woman was about to leave when he called her back.

'I want to issue a witness summons,' he said.

'We're still shut.'

'Just give me the forms, will you? It won't take more than a few seconds.'

She grumbled as she complied. When Dan had filled in the forms, she looked back at him in disbelief and asked, 'You want to summons the Foreign *Secretary* to court?'

'Or one of his cronies,' Dan said.

He took the summons and, as he walked slowly back down the stairs, looked at the sheet of paper again. It was headed '*Contact Note*' and was classified as '*Secret*'.

It was a report dated 1990, addressed Box 850, Whitehall. It was countersigned by the FCO, the Foreign and Commonwealth Office. The language of the note was neutral – but the contents were anything but that:

CONTACT NOTE – SECRET

1. *Sources from Iraq, including British businessmen recruited by this office, indicate that the Iraqi Ministry of Trade and Industry is purchasing equipment and heavy machinery from Britain, Switzerland and West Germany. It is for a high-velocity gun with extended range, certainly capable of reaching, for example, Israel. The weapon is comparable to the V4 rocket developed by the Germans in the period at the end of the war. (THIS INFORMATION IS HIGHLY CLASSIFIED.)*

2. *The warhead of the projectile will be capable of not only HE (high explosive) but CBW loads (chemical and biological warfare).*

3. *As is known, the development of the technology for Tarin A (the Keller chemical gas – HIGHLY RESTRICTED) at Stamford Grange and its onward sale to Iraq has been the most lucrative 'commercial' contract supervised by this office.*

Dan tried to keep calm as he approached the woman. He quietly asked her if she would come with him to the print shop in the arcade near Ludgate Circus. They would be able to photocopy the documents there.

Outside, the rush-hour traffic that piled up from St Paul's towards Fleet Street seemed unreal and distant. Suddenly Dan had a glimpse of what the case was really about. Tarin A. Keller's gas developed at Stamford Grange. Sold on to Iraq. And the British government knew. Montford, still a minister in 1990–91, *must* have known.

And there was a further question: did Jo know that they were developing Nazi chemical gases at Stamford Grange? And if he did, why hadn't he said? Dan needed to speak to his father.

Chapter 11

Dan returned to Shepherd's Bush by Tube, taking the Central Line from St Paul's. He paid for a single ticket and then squeezed into a packed carriage, full of City workers heading home. He was no different to them except for one thing: in his briefcase he had a bundle of photocopied secret documents. At Holland Park, he was able to get a seat between a youth with a skinhead haircut and an old lady with a walking stick. He cradled the bag on his lap as if it were an explosive. And in a sense it was.

People pushed past him as he left the station and walked along Shepherd's Bush Green, and he wondered what they would think if they knew the contents of the Contact Note, whether they would believe it at all. He passed an old man with a woollen black hat and fingerless gloves by the flower stall outside the station. The man repeatedly called out some indecipherable phrase than was meant to signal the availability of the late edition of the evening paper. Tomorrow, Dan thought, the contents of his briefcase would be on the front pages.

He walked past the green and then along the Uxbridge Road. The pavement was lit by the neon lights of the various pizza and fast-food restaurants, and Dan felt a thin sheet of ice beginning to form under his feet as the temperature plummeted. He grappled with the permutations: Keller ... Stamford Grange ... Montford ... Iraq. What was Box 850? Why had the Foreign Office countersigned the document? Lost in these thoughts, he passed the Hammersmith and City Line exit to the Tube and crossed several side roads leading north, unaware of the traffic. Soon he passed the Shepherd's Bush police station. He was only a few yards beyond the blue light outside the building when he saw Yuri.

'We need to talk,' Yuri said. His collar was turned up and his hands were buried deep in his long coat pockets.

'I'm cold and I'm going home.'

He continued to walk past Yuri, who was taken aback. He paced rapidly after Dan, but found it difficult to keep up with his insistent strides.

'The case has been a *disaster*,' he said, striding along at Dan's shoulder.

'Yes, it has.'

'You know what it means if the case is a disaster?'

'Montford will be acquitted.'

'And if he is found not guilty?'

'Then he will not be found guilty,' Dan said.

'And *you* will be responsible.'

Dan stopped and half turned, looking into the man's face, illuminated by the multi-coloured neon lights of a pizza delivery parlour.

'I will be responsible?' Dan said softly. 'I will be *responsible*?' His voice was getting louder, but he no longer cared about controlling his temper. 'You *dare* to hold me responsible?' He suddenly dropped his briefcase and grabbed the lapels of Yuri's coat. 'I'm sick and tired of your bullshit games. It's your bloody bent KGB evidence that is going to get Montford acquitted. Don't you see, you fucking *idiot*?'

Yuri tried to break free, but Dan held him tighter, forcing their faces only inches apart, the frosted breath of the one mixing with the other.

'So your father was at Neuwelt,' Dan shouted. 'Well, my father was there, too. I want Montford convicted and Keller, wherever he is, and I want all the other *bastards* who have evaded justice. I was this close, *this* close, to persuading the jury, I know it. I could smell Montford squirming, and Waugh. I could have had a shot at getting home with the evidence of the soldiers. And what do you do? Get me to call the evidence of that second-rate spy? For *Christ's* sake.' He took a deep breath and spat out the final words. 'So when the *fuck* are you going to stop threatening me with all this bullshit and start *helping* me to nail Montford?'

He let go. There was a stunned look on Yuri's face. His eyes were wide, his mouth slightly open. Clearly he had not expected the onslaught.

'How is your daughter?' he asked carefully.

A haze of blood red filled Dan's eyes and he lurched at the man. 'You fucking *coward*. Threatening a young girl? Well, come on, then. You want to kill me? So do it. Now. Here. In the street. What are you going to do? Shoot me? Push me under a car? Or have you got some phial of poison? If you want to do it, do it now. You have my *permission*. But what would that achieve? You want some more killing? Well, *do* you? Hasn't the time come to start working together on this damn case?'

'How?'

'Look, I know . . . I think I know what's been going on. It's to do with the gas Keller devised.'

'Tarin A?'

'The British, some part of the secret services, have been selling it to Iraq.'

'How do you know?'

'I've got a memo.' He ushered Yuri into a dark side road and stood between two parked cars. He bent down and opened the case, taking out the Contact Note. A wind rose and blew litter past the police station on the main road. He felt the note rustle in his hand.

Yuri looked at it carefully, and as he did so his forehead began to crease. 'Box 850,' he said. 'Do you know what that is?'

'Not a clue. For all I know it could be the Prime Minister's chiropodist.'

'MI6,' Yuri said. 'Military Intelligence 6. The Secret Intelligence Service funding black operations with arms sales to Iraq.'

'So now we all know.'

'It's perfectly legitimate in an illegitimate sort of way. One would expect no less of Military Intelligence.'

'Look,' Dan said, 'I've got to go.'

'Why?'

'Because I want to,' Dan replied. 'Is that all right with you or can we expect some more dirty phone calls later tonight?'

Yuri smiled. 'I could still have you killed.'

'I know. But before you do, I want you to do something for me.'

'What?'

'Dig up the post mortem reports on Ira Gottlieb and Neville Neale.'

'And do what with them?'

'Find an expert. An expert in toxicology or chemical poisoning or whatever it's called. Just find a doctor who can tell us whether they were both gassed. With Tarin A. I think that's the link. Get the information to me as soon as you can at the Old Bailey tomorrow. And after that,' Dan said, returning the smile, 'you can kill me.'

As he strode away from the Russian towards home, he realised that never before had he actually looked forward to seeing Yuri.

Sophie and Chris were watching television when he arrived. He shouted out hello and then hesitated by the painted hall mirror, shaking out the sparkling particles of ice that had formed in his hair, some of which were already beginning to melt in the cosy warmth of his home.

Unwittingly, his eyes caught their reflection in the mirror. It was not the hint of darkening bags which preoccupied him – those were an inevitability during a trial – it was something far more simple. For the first time for months, he was actually able to look at himself without his gaze being tinged with shame. Of course Yuri could still have him killed, that was still possible. In fact, now that he thought about it, he realised just how crazy he had been on the Uxbridge Road. But things had changed. Now, despite what other people might order him to do, he was going to take control: he was going to pursue Montford, hunt him down, and trap him. He didn't care that between them Grail and Yuri had messed up the prosecution case. The jury still had not gone out. There was still a chance of convicting Montford. He took off his coat and hung it over Chrissy's school mac, then went into the lounge.

'Hi, Dad,' Chris said. 'You're just in time. They're lowering Norleen's coffin into the ground. Isn't it exciting?'

He went up to her and tried to kiss her, but she shied away and said, '*Dad!*'

So instead he sat on the sofa next to Sophie and kissed her gently on the top of the head, smelling the soft fragrances of her blond hair.

'What's that for?' she asked.

'For your help.'

'What help? I've tried to get the transcript of Querry's evidence from America, but Christ, the red tape—'

'No, I mean the help you're going to give me tomorrow. How would you like to serve a witness summons on the Foreign Secretary?'

Sophie looked up aghast. 'Dan,' she said, 'have you gone completely mad?'

'Perhaps not quite completely.'

'What's it about?'

'I've just seen . . .' He lowered his voice and silently mouthed, '*Yuri.*'

'What?' Sophie started.

'Told him he was free to kill me.'

Christine huffed loudly. '*Hey*, you two. Wayne's jumped into the grave.'

Dan and Sophie looked at each other conspiratorially and giggled silently at the serious-faced teenager in the armchair. He took Sophie's warm hand and held it to his still-icy face. 'Did you miss me?' he whispered.

'What do you think?'

And then he realised: his father was not there. 'Where's Jo?' he asked.

'He went out,' Chris said in a deadpan way.

'When?'

But Chris did not reply. She continued watching the screen and then put her hand to her mouth. 'Oh my *God*. The coffin is *empty*.'

Chapter 12

Dan was awoken with a start from dreamless sleep at 3.37 a.m. Though his eyes did not focus properly, he could just see that the electric glow from the alarm clock numbers cast an eerie green light over a figure silhouetted at the window: Jo.

Still half drugged with sleep, he whispered, 'Jo, is that you?'

The figure moved away from the window and sat at the foot of the bed.

'Where the *hell* have you been?' Dan whispered.

'You got it in one.'

'Pardon?'

'Hell. I've been right down there.'

In the street outside a car raced past, braking noisily as it reached the Uxbridge Road junction. A thread of yellow light from the streetlamp crept around each side of the curtains, but otherwise there was darkness.

Dan hauled himself up so that the back of his head rested against the cold oak of the burled headboard Vivienne had haggled viciously for in Shepherd's Bush market. 'I waited until two a.m. for you. I was worried sick. You can't behave that way in *this* household ...' He halted the tirade. 'Are you listening to me?'

'You tell my poor little Chrissy off like that?'

'Jo?'

'But you're right. You're always right. I don't know how to behave in this household – or any goddamn household.'

'Oh, don't get all self-piteous on me, Jo. I'm not going to have you moping around all day.'

'No, you're not.'

'Good.'

'I'm leaving.'

Dan tried to take his father's hand but Jo started up and moved back to the curtain, pushing back the edges a little further, glancing out nervously.

'Look, Jo. I'm sorry if I—'

'No need to be sorry about anything. I fucked it all up. Even before you were born.'

'Did you know they were developing Keller's gas at Stamford Grange?'

'Do I look like an asshole?'

'So why didn't you tell me?'

'Same reason that I didn't tell you I worked in the labs at Neuwelt . . . I was ashamed. You know, sometimes we do stuff and at the time it seems right and then we look back on it years later and say "What a fuck-up." You ever found that?'

'All the time.'

'Yeah, well I ain't gonna fuck up this family no more. That's why I'm leaving. I'll just get my things from the room and—'

'You can't go in there. Sophie's stayed over.'

'It's your home, not mine.'

'It *is* your home too, Jo. If only you'd allow yourself to feel that way.'

Jo drew the curtains tight, excluding all the street lighting. 'I'll get my stuff some other time, then.'

'Jo, *please* don't go.'

'I loved your mother so much, Dan, and I left her. And I know it was the best thing I could ever have done for her.'

'Where will you go at this time?'

'I've got places to go and people to see. You don't hang around this planet for seven decades without having a few of them.'

Dan suddenly felt as though he were a young boy again, and that the ephemeral figure in his room was the apparition of his absent father he had conjured up throughout his youth, someone to love and to hate and then to love again.

'But I . . . I don't *want* you to go,' he said.

In the darkness, he could hear the old man padding softly across the room. For a brilliant instant, Jo's eyes caught the light from the alarm clock and his face, weathered, unshaven, weary, was illuminated in neon green. Then it passed into darkness and Dan smelt the tobacco on his breath.

'I don't want you to go, Jo,' he whispered.

'Sure you do,' the old man said.

And then, for the first time in his life, his father kissed him gently on the forehead. Seconds later the front door closed quietly downstairs and Dan rolled over, burying his face deep into his pillow.

At six in the morning, Sophie awoke with a shot. Suddenly she realised that she might be able to help crack the trial – but she couldn't do it alone. She needed Chris's help. She stumbled out of bed in the half-light, pulling on one of Dan's old dressing-gowns. The door creaked loudly as she slid into the corridor. Thirty seconds later she was beside Chris's bed.

'Dad?' Chris yawned, not focusing.

Sophie put her finger to her lips, and Chris's eyes opened wide with excitement. As she got out of bed, Sophie switched on the PC. The electronic glare of the screen flickered in the morning's semi-darkness, lighting up the two female faces in front of it and little else.

'Know any hackers in California?' Sophie asked.

'California's only computer geek heaven,' the girl replied.

There was then a blur of keystrokes and menus as the teenager accessed a list of her favourite candidates.

'What's the target, Soph?'

'Pardon?'

'Where do you want to hack into?'

'LA county court records. There's a trial transcript I—'

'Got to get in first.'

For the next twenty minutes, Sophie watched in amazement as Dan's daughter sped across the information superhighways until she found the best person. He was an UCLA drop-out who boasted that he had once hacked into a database similar to their target to erase a conviction for cannabis. He relished the challenge and said he would keep them updated every fifteen minutes.

Feeling totally useless, Sophie went downstairs to make a cup of tea. When she returned at 7.15 with two steaming cups, Chris turned to her.

'How'd you spell that name?'

Sophie smiled. 'Q-U-E-R-R-Y.'

* * *

A few hours later, Sophie was in the back of a cab speeding around the West End.

'Where are you now, Dan?' she called down her mobile.

'At one of the phones on the first floor of the Bailey,' he replied. 'I've checked at the court office, the CPS, everywhere, and the fax is not here.'

Down the line she could hear the crackle of interference on her mobile phone. 'The guy in LA was working into the night, Dan. God, it must be what? Two in the morning in Los Angeles.'

'Querry is going to give evidence any minute. I need to have some ammunition or the whole case gets blown away.'

'Hang on.' She opened the glass partition and spoke to the cabbie. 'Turn left and stop on the corner. Yes, there.' Her voice got louder as she spoke to Dan again. 'You still there, Becket?'

'Yes.'

'Taxi's just arrived at the Foreign Office. You really want me to summons the Secretary himself?'

'I don't care if it's the lavatory attendant. Just grab someone and drag them to the Bailey and tell them if they don't produce the files on the Iraq gas thing, I'm personally going to get them arrested for contempt.'

'I love it when you get mad.'

'You ain't seen anything yet.'

'When I finish here, I'll go to that Internet place in Soho. I'll speak to the computer geek from LA again. I'm afraid he was taking uppers or downers or something.'

'What do you mean?'

'Dan, it's the middle of the night there. Everything is shut. He's going to hack into the state law library or something.'

'I should never have got that Internet thing for Chris.'

'Oh, relax.'

'Is all this illegal?'

'Let me put it this way, I don't think it's very legal. Shit, my battery's running down. Look, try to ring me before you cross-examine Querry.'

'Soph,' he said, but his voice was now barely audible over the interference on the line. 'Be . . . careful.'

He said something else, but she was unable to understand what it was. Working its way through the traffic, her taxi passed Downing Street and the Cenotaph and stopped opposite

King Charles Street. Having paid the cabbie, Sophie walked towards the austere building that was the Foreign and Common- wealth Office.

William Querry was a substantial man. He rejoiced in the fact that he was unashamedly the sort of claret-soaked academic who was loath to leave his ivory tower for the real world. But he had such an awesome reputation that the real world could be depended upon to come to him.

He wore a brown tweedy suit with a silk handkerchief in the front pocket. The chaotic colours of the silk clashed with the tweed, which in turn clashed with Querry's necktie, but no doubt that was the intended effect. It was clear that he had a prodigious appetite for life, the kind of man equally adept at bagging a brace of partridge or debagging a pair of freshmen. He had curly ashen hair which looked as if it was a courtier's wig that had been mangled. His facial skin was blotchy, alternately ruddy and sallow, and his profile was dominated by a bulbous nose.

As he was a defence witness, it was Waugh who got to examine him first. He had sought the permission of the judge to take Querry's evidence out of turn. Querry was in a hurry: he was due to address a parliamentary sub-committee later that day.

'What is your field of specialism?' Waugh asked.

'I am currently Professor of International Military History at Oxford.'

'And before that?'

'I was a consultant to what is now the Ministry of Defence.'

'You have a wide experience of these matters?'

'I have addressed NATO, the United Nations, the European Court of Human Rights, and . . . even Cambridge.'

Waugh tittered sycophantically, but Dan noticed that the academic in-joke was lost on the Old Bailey jury, comprised of ordinary London folk.

'Let me get straight to the point,' Waugh said. 'Did you write a report after the Second World War on . . .' He scanned the pages of technicalities. '. . . put simply, the so-called gas chambers in the concentration camps?'

'I did.'

'Am I allowed to ask you why?'

'No has been the official answer for years,' Querry said, the appropriate parts of his cheeks reddening. 'But I understand the powers that be have authorised the disclosure of my report to the court. So I can now say.' He paused and moved forward in the witness box. 'In the postwar period, as is widely documented, Britain had an *offensive* chemical gas programme that was stopped in the 1950s. My paper was merely part of that.'

'And did you,' Waugh asked, his face alight with eagerness, 'inspect Neuwelt concentration camp?'

'Shortly before it was demolished, yes.'

'And your conclusions?'

'The gas chambers were not functional.'

'They didn't work? But you inspected the camp some years after the end of the war.'

'The gas complex had been carefully preserved by the occupying forces.'

'And?'

'And the gas chambers could not work. Not in the way envisaged by the blueprints. This was an experimental facility in construction. It was not operational.'

'Could gassings have taken place at Neuwelt?'

'In my opinion,' Querry said, looking slowly around the court and catching Dan's eye for a moment, 'no. *Definitely* not.'

Dan needed more time. He knew that not even a bulldozer would be able to budge Querry on the technicalities of the report compiled decades ago. Although he would not shy away from jousting with the man's intellect, he needed something more.

'My Lord,' he said. He stood up slowly and pulled his gown around his shoulders. 'I wonder if I could have some time before I cross-examine this witness.'

Julian Waugh leapt to his feet. 'Mr Becket has had *fifty* years to bring this prosecution. He does not deserve a moment longer.'

Judge Constant looked at Dan suspiciously. He crossed his arms defensively. 'And what would an adjournment achieve?'

'I might have some information,' Dan said.

'What information?'

'Information that might be relevant to the credibility of this witness.'

'Can't you be more specific?'

What could Dan say? He didn't know any more than that

on another occasion, years ago, Querry had testified about the Holocaust in America.

'Perhaps,' Waugh said, 'my learned friend could share with the defence the source of this information?'

Dan pursed his lips. He wasn't going to lie to the court. But how could he dress up the fact that his secret weapon was a doped-up computer freak in California who was illegally hacking into a law library?

'Well, Mr Becket?'

Dan was about to abandon the idea and take Querry on with what he had when a female usher opened the door of the court to his right.

'There is a fax coming in for Mr Becket,' she said. 'A big fax.'

Chapter 13

Dan rushed to the court admin office where he had told Sophie to send any communications. He knew that there was a leak somewhere in the prosecution team and he didn't want to tip anyone off by having the fax sent to the CPS office. When he was let into admin, he saw the document coming slowly through the machine. He tried to read the pages as they came off the press, asking a clerk in the office to photocopy the shiny fax paper for Waugh and the judge.

Five minutes later he was ready to deal with Querry.

'Have you been to America, Mr Querry?' he asked when the court had reassembled.

'Many times.'

'Any occasions when you have given evidence?'

'Yes.'

'In what circumstances?'

'I've addressed the United Nations on the proliferation of weapons of mass destruction.'

'Anything else?' Dan asked.

'No.'

'Let's see if I can jog your memory.' Dan looked at the transcript that he had been sent. 'Ever testified in a court case?'

'Years ago, perhaps, but it really is not relevant to—'

'You're *lying*,' Dan shouted. 'Now why don't you tell us the truth?'

The court was stunned into silence, and Dan knew that everyone was waiting on his next words. He just hoped to hell that there were not two British academics called William Querry.

'You gave evidence in California in 1971, didn't you?'

'Yes, but I don't see—'

'Just answer the questions,' Dan said. 'I'll finish with you much quicker if you do.' He scanned down the transcript and tried to decide on his best line of attack. Then he saw a way in. 'You were called as an expert?'

'Yes.'

'By whom?'

'The defence.'

'Just as you've been called by the defence today?'

'Well, I wouldn't . . .'

'Do you find that a difficult question to answer?'

'No.'

'You testified in America to establish what – precisely?'

'The viability of certain chemical facilities. It was a purely technical analysis.'

'I *see*,' Dan said. Again his anger spilt over into his words. He momentarily thought of Jo, fifty years previously, but the Jo he saw was still the old man Dan knew now, the old man who had kissed him in the early hours and had then left. 'You see, people might be *forgiven* for thinking that you are no more and no less than a racist and an *anti-Semite*.' Dan screwed up his face, expecting an eruption of outrage at his scandalous suggestions, but there was silence.

'I would not forgive you for such an accusation,' Querry said. 'I have a distinguished record. I've addressed the United Nations.'

'Was that when Kurt Waldheim was General Secretary?'

'What if it was?'

'Wasn't he proved to be an *oberleutnant* in the Austrian SS? Was it *Oberleutnant* Waldheim who invited you?'

Querry was silent.

'The man on whose behalf you were appearing was charged with disseminating material about the Holocaust.'

'He was.'

'And these . . .' Dan paused to replicate the witness's precise words. '. . . these *chemical* facilities you were opining about were what?'

'I don't understand the question.'

'I think you do. I think you understand it perfectly. But I'll make it easy for you. Name one of the facilities that you testified about.'

'There were several.'

'If you insist on doing this the hard way ...' Dan said, flourishing the fax for the jury. '*Auschwitz*. There's one. Is that right?'

'Yes.'

'In your opinion, were the gas chambers at Auschwitz capable of gassing all those Jewish victims?'

'Well—'

'Yes or no?' Dan insisted. 'Yes or *no*?'

'No.'

'So millions of Jews were not exterminated at Auschwitz?'

'Not according to the blueprints.'

'And that was your learned opinion to the American court?'

'Yes.'

Dan paused and looked at the jury. He repeated Querry's words. 'Not according to the blueprints?'

'No.'

'How about,' Dan shouted, 'according to the *survivors* who saw mothers and fathers, brothers and sisters go to their deaths naked? How about according to *them*?'

'All I'm saying is—'

'All? *All*? All you're saying is the Holocaust didn't happen, is that it?'

'Not as it's popularly conceived.'

'Oh, I doubt that there is anything very popular about the Holocaust, Mr Querry, except among revisionist historians like you.'

'I find that an offensive suggestion.'

'And I find your views offensive, Mr Querry.' Waugh was on his feet and the judge was shouting at Dan to stop, but all he could really think about was Jo, and he wasn't about to stop. 'What gas was said to be developed at Neuwelt?'

'It was *said* that Tarin A was being developed there.'

'By Klaus Keller?'

'I object,' shouted Waugh.

'Yes.'

'And is it right that in your capacity as consultant to the United Nations, you spoke about the proliferation of weapons of mass destruction?'

'WMDs? Yes.'

'Including chemical weapons?'

'Yes . . .'

Dan noted a hesitation in Querry's reply, almost as if he had guessed what Dan intended. 'You are aware that the United Nations has recorded chemical outrages by the Iraqis on, for example, the indigenous Kurd populations?'

'Yes.'

'And what gases have been recorded as being used by Saddam?'

'Sarin, then a type of mustard gas . . .'

Dan knew why the witness had broken off. 'Anything else?'

'Traces of Tarin A,' Querry said rapidly. 'On some reports.'

A few people in court had made the connection, but Dan wanted to ram the message home: it might be the only chance he got.

'So is this the position? Keller devised Tarin A at Neuwelt in the war.'

'Allegedly.'

'Neuwelt was captured by the British.'

'So I understand.'

'Chemical weapons were researched in Britain after the war.'

'Yes.'

'Particularly at somewhere called Stamford Grange.'

'Yes.'

'Iraq uses chemical weapons in the 1980s, including Keller's gas, Tarin A.'

'Yes.'

'So where did Iraq get Klaus Keller's Tarin A, Mr Querry?'

The man shuffled in the witness box. 'Perhaps you should ask Saddam Hussein.'

'But I'm asking you.'

'I cannot answer.'

'Did Britain recruit Klaus Keller?'

'I cannot say,' Querry replied.

'You mean you don't *want* to say. You know, don't you?'

Waugh was on his feet. 'My Lord, I object.'

'Was it Britain who sold these *murderous* gases to Iraq?' The witness was silent. But Dan's voice was rising with each connection he made. 'Well, was it? You know, don't you? We armed Saddam. Didn't we? *Didn't* we? We've recruited Nazi scientists, we developed their gases and we've sold these weapons to murderers.'

'I never said we did.'

'Are you saying we didn't?' Dan stared hard and long at Querry, daring him to divulge more, but when there was no further response, he summarised the position. 'Let us see whether you agree with a simple proposition. If . . . if government agencies – let's pick one at random: MI6, for example – if they have knowingly sold the tools of chemical warfare to Saddam Hussein, that would have been a shameful episode in our political history, wouldn't it?'

Querry gritted his teeth and wiped his forehead with his coloured silk handkerchief. 'Yes,' he said.

Chapter 14

After Querry left the courtroom, there was a frantic consultation at the back of the court between Montford and Julian Waugh. Their heads were inches apart and a steady unintelligible whisper emanated from them. Dan regarded this as an encouraging sign. From his experience of defending, he knew that these last-minute discussions at the dock looked inelegant and suspicious. They usually heralded one thing: a hiatus in the defence.

After one minute of whispering, while the jury looked at the spectacle in disbelief, Waugh sauntered to the front of the court and tried to pass the episode off as though nothing was amiss. He smiled at the judge as he began to talk. But Dan could see his hand, shrouded from the jury by his gown, opening and closing nervously as he tried to control the trembling in his fingers.

'My Lord,' he said, 'the defence will call Simon Montford.'

This was Dan's best chance.

He had assumed that Montford might not testify, but would rely on Waugh's formidable destruction of the prosecution witnesses, on the Querry report and on the fact that the prosecution – Dan – bore a very heavy burden of proof. Proof beyond reasonable doubt might not mean proof to a certainty, but on a charge of murder it was damn close.

Now Dan had flushed Montford from the cover of the dock by his routing of Querry. Despite the setbacks during the prosecution case, everything was once again up for grabs. He knew that in almost every trial in which the defendant gave evidence the verdict turned on his performance in the box. Soon Montford and Dan would be head to head: and that contest would decide the outcome of the trial.

The gate to the dock was opened silently by the dock officer

and Simon Montford picked his way past the rows of lawyers to
the front of the court. He walked slowly, but without reluctance,
treading as carefully through the court as he would no doubt
shortly have to tread through the past. Montford had, Dan
observed, long, delicate fingers, the fingers of a sculptor or
a violinist. When he arrived in the witness box, he placed
them around the black-bound Holy Bible and the plastic-coated
oath card.

The usher whispered to him.

In a clear voice, Montford said, 'Church of England.'

Dan noticed that there was just a hint of stress on the word
England, but that was to be expected. Stressing that he was 'one
of us' would be one of Montford's strongest appeals to the jury.
He stood erect and gave off an air of quiet dignity in his simple
charcoal suit and understated striped tie.

'I swear by Almighty God,' he said, 'that the evidence I
shall give shall be the truth, the whole truth and nothing but
the truth.'

Dan saw him hand the holy book back with a half-smile, but
no words. There was tension in his face, pulling his cheeks tight,
making him look down his nose a touch more severely than
normal. His features were unmistakably patrician, with high
cheekbones, a clean-cut chin, piercing cobalt eyes and neat hair
that had faded elegantly to grey.

'What is your full name?' Waugh asked.

'Simon Sinclair Montford.'

'And is it right that you have no previous convictions whatsoever?'

'None.'

'And where do you reside?'

'Near to Stamford Grange in the county of . . .'

Dan noticed Montford's attention divert towards an insistent
buzzing. It came from the internal telephone on the court clerk's
desk below the judge's bench. The clerk, a thirtysomething Asian
man also in a black gown, picked up the receiver and put his
hand over his mouth, talking into it rapidly. He was shaking his
head as he spoke, and looked from Montford to the judge, and
then at Dan.

It seemed to Dan that the court was suddenly suspended.
Montford had broken off in mid-sentence, Waugh did not speak,

and everyone looked at the clerk, who, aware that he was suddenly the centre of attention, reddened visibly. After thirty seconds, he put the phone down, stood and, turning his back to the court, whispered something to the judge. There was a shaking of heads, and when the clerk called the usher over, Judge Constant wrote something down in his red notebook.

'Perhaps you wouldn't mind leaving us for a moment, members of the jury?' Constant said. He then waited until the bemused twelve had sidled out of court.

Dan instinctively got to his feet as Len Constant addressed both counsel. 'There has been a request to . . . stay proceedings,' he said, clearly confused. 'An emergency request. From the Foreign Office.'

Julian Waugh moved threateningly along counsel's row towards Dan. 'What the *hell* have you done, Becket?' he said.

Thirty minutes later, a junior minister from the FCO insisted that his testimony should be heard *in camera*. The public gallery was cleared and half a dozen indistinguishable besuited men, who Dan assumed to be Special Branch, blocked the doors. They communicated to an unseen controller via black hand-sized radios.

The minister in the witness box was a fit man in his late forties with prominent eyebrows that met in the middle, a thick head of dark hair and the confident but guarded air of someone privy to the darkest secrets of the state. A lawyer from the Government Legal Service stood at the side of the court, but the minister insisted on addressing the court himself. It meant either that the politician wanted to make a name for himself, or that he wanted to expose one of his political rivals, or that he had something to hide and could trust no one else. Dan noticed that the DPP's rep, Andrew Short, had also come into court and was sitting two rows behind Dan.

'My Lord,' the minister said, 'I am answering a summons on behalf of the Foreign Secretary. The summons was served on the Foreign and Commonwealth Office this morning.'

Sophie had succeeded, Dan thought. She had done her part; now it was up to him.

'Who issued the summons?' the judge asked.

The minister began to look at the thin document in his hand, but Dan got to his feet. 'I issued it,' he told the judge.

'Well, *why*? What has the Foreign Office got to do with a war crime fifty years ago?'

'Everything,' Dan said casually. He realised that the Foreign and Commonwealth Office had responded with unparalleled speed. A minister had appeared in court an hour after service of a summons. There could only be one rational explanation: the Foreign Office had been monitoring the trial. It *knew* what was going on.

Waugh got to his feet in a fury. 'I'm afraid Mr Becket's flights of fancy have finally reached the stratosphere. What possible relevance can all this have to the alleged war crime?' He looked at the judge as if to goad him into action. 'When will this court call a halt to all these detours and dead-ends? This case is about—'

'MI6,' Dan said quickly. 'MI6 comes under the Foreign Office. Isn't that right, Minister?'

'Yes,' the man said. He stroked his bouffant hair with his right hand. Then the chalk-stripe sleeve of his three-piece suit fell back to his side. 'Perhaps I could explain—'

Dan cut him off. 'Since the court asked *me* to explain why I issued a summons, I will.' He could hear Short behind him puffing with annoyance. But he had to push on. 'A document has been brought to my attention. What is called a Contact Note, which the minister will be able to confirm is a classified communication between MI6 and the FCO. The note concerned arms to Iraq. Chemical arms and munitions to Iraq.'

Waugh again got to his feet. 'But what has this to do with the Neuwelt war crime in 1945?'

'Everything,' Dan said. 'If I can be allowed to ask the minister a few questions, I shall be able to—'

'This note is protected by the Official Secrets Act,' the minister said. 'I should *also* like to ask Mr Becket some questions.'

'So we'd like to question each other,' Dan said. 'It should be a very interesting conversation.'

The minister dropped the copy of the summons impetuously on to the rim of the witness box. Then he picked up another document. 'My Lord, I have here a Public Interest Immunity certificate signed by the Foreign Secretary himself. It states quite explicity that material about the *alleged* – and I stress that word – about the alleged sale of arms to Iraq falls into the category of evidence that potentially damages the public interest.'

'Your point being?' the judge asked.

'My point being that we wish this court to set aside the summons that Mr Becket has issued against the FCO. We refuse to divulge any further information concerning this topic. The investigation of these matters in a public forum would not be in the public interest.' The man smiled superciliously at Dan. His grin was so wide that his eyebrows crinkled slightly in the centre. 'What Mr Becket clearly fails to appreciate is that what is *of* interest to the public is not always *in* the public's interest to know.'

Dan was acutely aware of Waugh sniggering to himself at the comment. One of the Special Branch officers broke off from his hushed commentary into the radio and smiled too.

Dan knew that he had to strike back at once. 'There is of course another name for a P.I.I. certificate,' he said. 'A *gagging* order. Cases like Matrix Churchill make it crystal clear that it is the court that should be the final arbiter of what information should be disclosed. Now either the minister answers my questions or I shall invite the court to hold him in contempt and have him arrested.'

The man in the witness box glanced around at the judge, his cheeks crimson with outrage. Dan knew that this was the moment to attack.

'I'm a minister of the Crown,' the politician snorted.

'And I'm prosecuting on behalf of the Crown,' Dan replied. 'And this is a court of law, not a parliamentary talking-shop.'

'What *is* the relevance of this evidence?' the judge said.

'Montford has put himself forward as a man of good character. If the evidence proves that he had been a party to the illegal exportation to Iraq of weapons of mass destruction, in breach of United Nations embargoes, while one of Her Majesty's ministers, that might *just* show that *Mr* Montford is not quite the impeccable character he would have the jury believe.'

Dan handed the judge a photocopy of the Contact Note.

'This is absolutely preposterous,' Waugh said. 'There are rules preventing the calling of rebuttal evidence on questions of character. When will the court intervene to . . .' He broke off when it was clear that the judge was avidly reading the note.

'Is it true,' Dan asked the junior minister, 'that the Foreign Office knew of the sale of chemical technology to Iraq immediately before Simon Montford's resignation from the government?'

'I refuse to confirm or deny that,' the minister replied.

Judge Constant had finished reading the Contact Note and appeared to be furious. 'You *will* answer or I will personally—'

Dan wanted to press home the attack. 'British firms were breaching the embargo, weren't they?'

The man still said nothing.

'MI6 had recruited some of these British businessmen to spy on Saddam Hussein, isn't that right?'

The man looked down.

'The government knew? And encouraged? Arms were sold? Chemical components were sold?' Dan paused for breath and then began to fire questions at the witness. 'The gas Tarin A was sold? The gas developed by Klaus *Keller*? The gas developed at *Neuwelt*?'

Dan felt a violent tug on his gown. He spun around. It was Andrew Short. His usually languid face was contorted with rage. 'Shut up, Becket. Shut up right *now*.'

'Is that your advice?'

'That is my *order*.'

'On what authority?'

'On the authority of the DPP of England and Wales. On the authority that put you here and can sack you like that. So just *shut* up.'

'Is there a problem?' the judge asked.

Dan spun back to face the front, now feeling light-headed. 'I'm . . . just taking instructions.' He felt another tug from behind.

Short whispered, 'If you try to make any more of this information about chemical weapons public, you'll be sacked.'

'I'm going on.'

'Then you'll be off the case, Becket.'

'I'll go public with all this. I'll hold a press conference.'

'Then you'll hold it from Wandsworth Prison, because breathe a word of this and you'll be breaching the Official Secrets Act.'

'I might be prosecuted, Short, but what about all those thousands of Kurds gassed by Saddam? I might cease to be a barrister. But Montford won't cease to be a murderer. MI6 won't cease to be accomplices to chemical warfare. So you can take your threats, Short, and fuck yourself.'

'You'll live to regret this, Becket.'

'You know,' Dan winced, 'perhaps I won't.' He turned back to the court quickly, and was about to address the witness once more. But Short then uttered the only words that could have stopped him.

'You leave me no option. The DPP will take over the war crimes case and *drop* it. Montford will walk out of court and you'll walk straight into prison.'

It was not so much the personal threat which made Dan hesitate. It was Montford.

'Simon Montford will walk out a *free* man,' Short whispered. 'For ever. It's your choice, Becket. Your choice. You wanted to play the big bloody man. Well, here it is. The big decision. It's up to you. One more word and Montford walks out.'

Chapter 15

Sophie felt there was something too easy about what had happened at the Foreign Office. Once she entered the building and had presented herself, she was directed to a small room full of lawyers, standing around the walls in dark suits like disgruntled mourners at the wake of a decidedly unloved relative. They asked no questions about the summons. It was as if they had been waiting for precisely this.

Slightly bewildered, she was out on the Westminster streets again before she knew it. Then she wandered up Whitehall until she was able to hail a black cab by Downing Street. From there, it was no more than a ten-minute ride until she was dropped off at the Café in Soho. This hip establishment not only served great cappuccino, it also allowed visitors the opportunity to use the Internet. So before she had half finished her coffee, Sophie had discovered that the fax had already been sent by the hacker from California to the Old Bailey. She decided to join it.

The female guard on the security door of the Bailey recognised her immediately. So much for her disguise: her large hat and tightly wrapped scarf, her heavy make-up. However, the guard agreed to buzz Court 12 on the internal line to find out the state of proceedings in the Montford trial. Sophie did not understand the answer: the trial had just been adjourned.

She pushed past a group of three policemen, turned right and proceeded down the ramp, past the Royal Mail postbox – a unique feature of the Central Criminal Court – and took the lift to the robing rooms on the fourth floor. There she waited in the stairwell for signs of Dan.

He came winding his way up the stairs just over a minute later. She saw that his wig had slipped forward and was low over his eyes. There was a sprinkling of sweat on his cheeks, and he spoke silently to himself, lost in a world of his own.

She smiled at him widely, and began to unwrap her scarf. 'Bad day at the office, honey?' she said.

'Soph, what are you doing here?'

'Helping you win the case.'

'What if Waugh sees you?'

'Sod Julian Waugh, and all the rest of them. I'm sick of skulking around.'

'He said he'd *report* you.' His words resonated for a fraction of a second in the stairwell, and he looked down to the third floor to ensure that no one was behind him.

'Let him report me. I'll report him. We can report each other. We can have both hearings at the same time.' She also looked anxiously at the flight below. Suddenly the sound of people climbing the stairs could be heard.

'Soph, I don't want you to ruin your career because of—'

'Of what?'

'Because of me. This is my fight.'

'And you don't want me to be part of it?'

'I don't want you to get hurt.'

He looked directly at her. Protruding slightly on either side of his wig were the grey-tinged curls of hair she adored. His dark eyes burned with anxiety for her, and in front of them the long eyelashes batted slowly. She didn't care about the risk. She knew that this was the man she wanted to be with.

'If Waugh reports you to the Professional Conduct Committee—'

'Then what? What, Dan? I know,' she said, her words gathering pace. 'Why don't we call up the Lord High Chancellor and have a cosy little chat about legal ethics. Meanwhile Montford walks free, your daughter's safety is jeopardised and Julian Waugh fucks you over again.'

'What do you mean?'

'Come on, Dan. Like he did with the Kurd bombing case. Don't you see? The time for playing by the rules is over. There are no rules, or none that everybody agrees upon. This is no longer just a court case. It's a war. And the winners decide the truth. About what happened in 1945. About everything else.' She was breathing quickly and she felt sweat appearing on her neck. 'Now am I completely off my trolley?'

He paused as two barristers sidled past them on the stairwell. Neither was involved in the case.

Then he said, 'Not completely.'

'Thank you.'

'You're sort of hanging on by your fingertips, Soph.'

'Did you get the Querry fax?'

'Blew him out of the water.'

'What about the Foreign Office?'

'We need to talk. But not in here.'

'When is court reconvening?' she asked.

'After two. Len Constant has given me a couple of hours to decide how I want to proceed. The DPP's office has forbidden me from using any of the Iraqi gas stuff. There must be a way round it. But I just can't see it at the moment.'

'Right. Meet me outside. On the steps of St Paul's.'

'Give me five minutes.'

She brushed past him and couldn't resist the temptation to touch his face with the back of her hand.

'Dan?'

'What?'

'For God's sake, don't look so miserable. We're going to make Montford pay. We can still win this.'

'*Win?* The prosecution win no victories and suffer no defeats.'

'Bollocks,' she said.

As he left the Old Bailey shortly afterwards, Dan found himself once more in the centre of the lunchtime City chaos. All around him secretaries and office workers sped out of their offices and queued up at sandwich stalls or went into convenience stores. He wanted to shout out to these people, to this small cross-section of the British public: You must be told what your government is doing in your name. I know. And so must you.

Sophie was sitting calmly halfway up the steps of St Paul's, her legs crossed easily, chatting to the man who stood next to her. She waved to Dan as he drew nearer, but she continued to talk. She smiled easily at Dan, and then at the other person. A man in his fifties, with deep lines on his face. Yuri.

'Hi, Dan,' she said. 'This gentleman was watching the case this morning from the public gallery and asked—'

'*What?*' Dan snapped coldly.

'Chill out, Dan. He just asked if he could come inside the main building itself. He's a lawyer from—'

'Russia,' Dan said.

As soon as he uttered the word, Sophie stood up in confusion. 'But I thought you said you were from . . .' She stared at the man, bewildered.

'I lied,' he replied.

'Jesus, Soph,' Dan said, moving next to her. 'This is—'

'I *know*,' she said, shying away.

Yuri paced around them, inspecting the two English barristers, smiling to himself, but not maliciously. 'I'm sorry. It was just a bit of fun.'

'What do you want?' Dan asked, trying his best to show no fear.

'Follow me,' the Russian said, walking down the hill towards Ludgate Circus.

The three of them walked at a rapid pace, through the crowds oblivious to the tension between the parties; three people, three lawyers in a strange alliance. Dan was careful to place himself between Yuri and Sophie.

As they turned left at the main junction and headed towards the river, Yuri said to Dan simply, 'I can't get an expert to come today. But I have contacted one.'

'What expert? To say what?'

A woman with a blue pushchair suddenly emerged from the oncoming crowd and Dan had to leap to his left to avoid her. She tutted scornfully as she passed. Yuri again smiled at the high-farce element of the scene.

'What are you laughing at?' Dan said as they continued towards the river.

'Here I am telling you the answer to the case and you are being run over by a – what is the word? – perambulator.'

'Just tell me about the gas,' Dan said.

'Smile, Mr Becket. In Russia we learn to have a sense of humour.'

Sophie whispered, 'I bet Stalin was a *million* laughs.'

Dan was unclear whether Yuri had heard what she had said,

for Blackfriars Bridge loomed in front of them, and a barge on
the river below it sounded its horn repeatedly.

The Russian led them into one of the subways connecting the
pavement with the Tube station. Water dripped into yellow and
brown pools from the dirty concrete roof as workmen attacked the
stonework with pneumatic drills, drowning out all other sound.

Yuri stopped suddenly and faced Dan. Although their faces
were only inches apart, the Russian shouted at the top of his
voice, 'The post mortem reports show that Ira Gottlieb died of
asphyxiation.'

'With no sign of injury,' Dan added impatiently.

'He also had a hardening of the arteries.'

'So?'

Yuri looked suspiciously at one of the workmen who was
changing the bit on his drill. When the tumultuous noise of
cracking concrete once more bombarded their ears, Yuri spoke
again. A thin cloud of concrete dust floated up around them.

'The toxicologist says that slight hardening of the arteries is
a side effect of . . . Tarin A,' he continued. 'A few drops of the
liquefied gas put on the skin. You wouldn't notice it. It's an easy
way to kill someone.'

Dan looked at his watch; the minutes were racing by. 'I'll have
to head back to court soon. It explains why Neville Neale's heart
was cut out. If you've got time, make it look like a psycho *and*
hide the evidence of the Tarin A.'

Sophie took his hand gently, and then let go when Yuri looked
down at the meshing of fingers. 'Was the Foreign Office evidence
any good?' she asked, turning away from the other man.

'I can't get sight of any more dirt. The DPP will drop the
case.'

'He can't do that.'

'He can, Soph, and he will. We've got to go ahead with
what's left.'

Yuri crossed his arms impatiently. 'How much is left of
the case?'

'Montford's evidence.'

'You must destroy him.'

'I can try to dent him. But there still isn't a clear motive as to
why he killed . . .' Dan looked from Yuri to Sophie and then back
again. 'As to why he killed your father,' he said.

'You don't need to prove a motive.'

'In law, no. But if an English jury is going to convict an English war hero of killing a Russian, they will want a cast-iron motive.'

Yuri moved closer, his face virtually touching Dan's in the gloom of the subway. 'Well, *find* a motive.'

Dan was undaunted. 'In fifty years, have *you* found one?'

The man looked down.

'Well, *have* you? Because if you have, the time to tell me is now. In two hours I'll be cross-examining the man who killed your father and you still can't tell me why he did it.'

When Sophie looked at Dan, he saw surprise in her eyes, but the time for backing away from Yuri was over.

'Just do your best,' the Russian said.

'That's what I've been trying to do,' Dan said.

He put his arm around Sophie and began to walk to the steps that led out of the underpass. Yuri followed a pace behind them, lost in thought.

'Will there be any more evidence after Montford?' he asked Dan as they emerged blinking into the bright City light.

'They say they have a surprise witness.'

'Waugh's bluffing,' Sophie said.

'I hope he is,' Dan replied. He turned back to Yuri. 'If you want to do something to help, you could follow Montford tonight. See where he goes. Who he is meeting.'

They walked slowly back through the crowds, the couple walking side by side, lost in the mass of people. Along the way, Yuri fell further and further behind and soon they could not see him.

'How are you bearing up?' she asked.

'I think I'll cope with Montford. It's just—'

'Dan, I know Julian Waugh. There is no surprise witness. He's bluffing. He's trying to psych you out.'

'Doing a good job.'

'So are you, Becket.'

She stopped as they reached Ludgate Circus and stood in front of him.

'Dan, this thing is going to be over tomorrow. One way or another it's going to be over.'

'When I'm in the courtroom, I just can't see it ever coming to an end. I try to see you and me and Chris, but there is this trial always in the way.' He could feel her body moving forward until it leant gently against his. The curves of her body folded into the contours of his frame easily, naturally. 'You know, this morning, the strangest thing happened.'

'What?'

'Before he left, Jo ... well, Jo kissed me.' He paused as the curious moment played itself out again in his mind. 'For the first time in my life my' father kissed me and I can't understand why.'

'Because – despite everything – you're still his son, Dan. Because he loves you. Because,' she said, moving her lips millimetres from his, so that he could feel her warm, sweet breath on the lower part of his face, 'because you are very ... kissable.'

Their lips met for a fraction of a second. Each pair had been made hard by the cold December air.

Then she said, 'Now go back to court and kill Montford.' She reached into her jacket pocket and pulled out an envelope. 'I wasn't going to show you these photos – I mean, I still find them upsetting. But this is war, Dan. See if you can use them. Remember Helen's in that support group? They exchange stories, photos, experiences. She will *kill* me if she finds out.'

Chapter 16

Simon Montford gave his evidence in chief with a quiet assured-
ness, exuding the confidence of a man who was certain of his own
acquittal. His tone was understated as Waugh questioned him.
Yet Montford spoke with warmth and humour, and even with a
certain panache. It all had an effect. The jury was riveted by his
war stories, how he made little of his acts of undoubted bravery,
how he was mentioned in dispatches, how he was decorated.
Waugh then systematically led him through denial after denial
of Dan's case.

As he did so, Dan opened the brown envelope Sophie had
given him. Inside there were a dozen perfectly square Polaroid
photographs, the sort of snaps any proud parent would take of his
or her child. But Dan knew instantly what they were: photos of the
deformed children of the Gulf vets. As he flicked slowly through
the disturbing images, he was aware that Waugh's examination
was reaching a climax.

'Were you at Neuwelt in April 1945?' he asked Montford.

'Yes.'

'Did you *order* the execution of the Russian, Ivan Basarov?'

'Certainly not.'

'Was any British officer lost in action at Neuwelt?'

'Definitely not,' Montford replied emphatically.

'Did you commit any crime at all during the war?'

'I've never committed any crime during my entire life,' Montford
said. He commanded the court from the witness box as Dan had
seen no other witness do. The jury appeared to like him. They
appeared to believe him. But he still was not finished. 'My family
can be traced back to the Domesday Book, and apart from one
Montford who was sent to the Tower to cool off after making

rather too obvious an advance to Queen Elizabeth I, none of us has ever been in trouble.'

'Have you told the jury the truth?'

'I've told the jury, Mr Waugh, the whole truth and nothing but that. I am entirely innocent of these charges. I am an Englishman and I have fought for my country. Now here I am fighting for my good name. Well, so be it. I am not frightened of these accusations. They are lies.'

In his mind, Dan could almost hear the court breaking into patriotic cheers. Yet with every answer, he knew that his time was coming nearer.

Waugh looked at the jury to make sure they had soaked up the full force of Montford's finale. Then he said, 'I have no more questions. But Mr Becket *may* have some.'

Game on.

Each sentence, each word Montford had uttered had struck at the pit of Dan's stomach, making him queasy with the anticipation of this final confrontation. He knew that all he had was words to prove beyond doubt that this war hero was a murderer, the killer of an innocent man, a monster, a war criminal. Chaotic thoughts of the previous months washed through his mind, blurring his vision: images of Yuri, then Chrissy and Jo together, then the finding of Ira Gottlieb's body, Sophie smiling and kissing him an hour before, Jo again – his father kissing him and then leaving in the early hours.

'Neuwelt was an experimental camp?' he began. His own words sounded distant to him, like the words of a stranger, a different man from the one who had sat in a New York courtroom in January. So much had happened in the previous months, and it was always going to culminate in this moment. 'Was it experimental?'

'So I'm told.'

'Told? Didn't you see that with your own eyes?'

'I don't understand your question.'

'I think you do.' Dan waited until Montford had turned his body from its easy posture facing the jury. He was more tense as he confronted Dan directly. 'There were Russian Jews in Neuwelt?'

'Yes.'

'And what condition were they in?'

'Pretty awful.'

'One witness spoke of living skeletons. Do you think that is a fair description?'

'Yes,' Montford said clearly, not frightened of the answer.

'And there were laboratories at Neuwelt—'

'But you heard William Querry say that the gas chambers didn't . . . *couldn't*—'

'Oh, we'll come to the gas chambers, Mr Montford. Of that you can be sure.' Dan paused, trying to fight back a tic in his face that revealed his nerves. Where to go now? Keller? 'There *were* laboratories in Neuwelt? Will you answer my question?'

'Yes.'

'So who was in charge of those laboratories?' he asked casually.

'I don't know.'

'Yes you do. It was Klaus Keller, as you well know.'

'I know no such thing.'

'So did you make any effort to find out who was in charge of those laboratories?'

'I can't remember. I must have.'

'So who was in charge?'

'I . . . forget.'

Dan knew this was a mistake by Montford. Suddenly the forensic instincts he had honed over the course of years took over. 'You *forget*? You accept, don't you, that you found hundreds, thousands of Russian Jews more dead than alive?'

'Yes.'

'You found thousands more skeletons in a pit outside the camp?'

'Yes.'

'And if the labs and gas chambers did work, these were industrialised killing centres the like of which mankind had never before seen?'

'I suppose—'

'So tell the jury,' Dan shouted. 'Who *was* in charge?'

'I don't know.'

'If it wasn't Klaus Keller, then who was it?'

'I . . . don't . . . with the years, you see, I don't . . .'

These hesitations, Dan knew, were the best chance he was ever going to get to break Simon Montford.

'In 1945,' he said, staring hard at the witness box, 'you were

briefed to take into custody any Nazi scientists you came across
in the concentration camps?'

'Well—'

'Are you suggesting that you were briefed to *ignore* them?'

Montford paused to consider. 'You must understand that we all
believed a war with the Russians was about to start. The Germans
were keen to be taken prisoner by the Western Allies rather than
the Russians.'

'We have been told that the nerve gas, Tarin A, was developed
at Neuwelt. Do you have any reason to believe that is not true?'

'No.'

'It was said that a Nazi scientist by the name of Klaus Keller
developed Tarin A. Do you have any reason to believe that fact
is not true?'

'No.'

'When the British tanks entered Neuwelt in April 1945, you
took Klaus Keller into custody.'

'No, that's a lie.'

'But you did make your temporary headquarters the SS hut,
as the witnesses have said?'

'Yes.'

'And Klaus Keller put on a demonstration for you.'

'No.'

'He gassed Ivan Basarov.'

'*No*,' Montford shouted.

'Klaus Keller disappeared.'

'No . . . I mean, I don't know what you are talking about.'

'You said "No." How can you know one way or another? Or
do you really know more than you're prepared to say?'

'Nonsense.'

'Then, miraculously, the nerve gas Tarin A, the gas Keller
was developing, was researched in England after the war.' Dan
paused, waiting for a reply. Montford was silent. 'You have heard
that *did* happen.'

'Yes.'

'Tell the jury, where was Tarin A researched in England?'

Montford paused and Dan could almost see the man's mental
calculations as to the safest response to the question. 'Tarin A
was researched at Stamford Grange.'

'In your constituency?'

'Yes.'

'And in the 1980s you were in government?'

'Yes.'

'And this country covertly traded with Iraq?' Dan could sense Julian Waugh becoming restless to his left. He knew that there was only so much he could bring out without the plug being pulled on the whole case. Andrew Short coughed loudly one row behind him. 'The government knew of businessmen trading with Iraq?'

Waugh jumped to his feet. 'What relevance has this to 1945?'

This was Dan's chance. 'If this witness knows that MI6 was aware of Tarin A being sold to Iraq, it confirms that his links with Keller's gas didn't end in 1945.'

'That was a *speech*,' Waugh shouted, '*not* a reply to my objection.'

'Oh, I'm sorry. I thought Mr Waugh wanted to know why I was asking the question.'

The judge looked at the feuding lawyers in front of him. 'I think it is a relevant question. You may proceed, Mr Becket. *If* you are able.'

Behind him, Dan could hear Short whispering, 'Careful, Becket. Careful.'

Next to Short, Robert Lancing held his head in his left hand as he took a note with his right. Dan knew he had to find another way.

'Without giving away any government secrets, Mr Montford, it is already public knowledge that we sold *some* arms to Iraq?'

'Yes, as the Scott enquiry heard.'

'And we know that Saddam Hussein has gassed his Kurd population with chemical gases? The United Nations has confirmed that?'

'Yes.'

'And Tarin A was one of those gases?'

'Well . . .'

'Your expert William Querry didn't deny it.'

'No.'

'And have you heard of Gulf War Syndrome Two?'

'Of course.'

Dan looked at the jury and was met with a mixture of recognition and confusion. Two of the suited men nodded: they had probably read about it in their broadsheet newspapers. 'To assist those who are not as familiar with these matters as you are, Mr Montford, isn't it right that some British servicemen from the Gulf War are complaining – amongst other things – of anti-gas injections and being poisoned with chemical gases in Iraq?'

'There are such complaints to the MoD.'

'And their babies have been born with . . . *defects*?'

Waugh again shouted, 'I *object*, I strongly object. This is—'

'Nothing has been proved,' Montford said above Waugh's objections. 'I want to deal with this, Julian. You make these allegations but nothing has been proved.'

'Nothing has been *disproved*,' Dan replied, knowing that battle was joined. It was clear that Montford now took it personally. The defendant had emerged from the shadow of his counsel's protection; now it would be head to head. 'Children have been born deformed, with holes in their hearts, with eyes missing, with—'

Waugh tried to object again, but Dan held up the photos Sophie had given him. He shouted, 'Is this *proof* enough? These are facts. These are . . .' He looked at the contorted, small faces in the Polaroids. 'These are *children*.'

'Yes,' Montford said, 'but—'

'But don't you *see* what you've done?' Dan said, holding up another photograph.

Waugh got to his feet, but Montford insisted, 'No, I *want* to see them.'

Dan handed over the bundle via the usher and Montford flicked through the snaps impassively. As he did so, Dan continued questioning him.

'You recruited Klaus Keller at Neuwelt after he showed you how his gas Tarin A worked on the Russian, Ivan Basarov.'

'No.'

'Keller came to Stamford Grange, where he further developed Tarin A.'

'No.'

'And then we sold chemical components for this death gas to Saddam Hussein. When *you* were in government, Mr Montford.'

'No.'

'And now, because of the Gulf War, we've poisoned our own *children* with these Nazi gases.'

'You don't under—'

'Our children, Mr Montford.'

'No.'

'*Our* children.'

'No.'

'From father to son.'

'You don't *understand*.'

'*Make* me understand.'

'The Cold War was starting.'

'So?'

'The Russians had nerve gases.'

'So we wanted Nazi ones?'

'It was necessary.'

'It was politics?'

'It was *war*,' Montford said, his head dropping for the first time. He looked at the photos as the echoes of the exchange died away. The court suddenly became silent. Finally Montford put the photographs down carefully.

'It was war,' he repeated.

Dan sat down, exhausted. During the next few minutes, he was vaguely aware of Julian Waugh re-examining his witness, getting Montford to repeat the denials of the murder accusations. By that time, the usher had collected up the photographs from the witness box and had returned them to Dan. But he could not bear to look again at the faces. He turned the snaps over and it was then that he saw writing on the backs. Names. John, Annie, Julia. The photographs were of *different* babies. Yet they all looked the same: deformed, unfinished, cheated of a normal life by the effects of a gas a Nazi scientist had developed even before their parents were born.

Montford walked back to the dock slowly. He passed a matter of inches from Dan and the two men looked at each other silently.

'Is that your case, Mr Waugh,' Len Constant asked, 'or do you have any more witnesses?'

Julian Waugh looked at Dan and smiled. 'We have no more witnesses,' he said.

So Sophie was right. Waugh had been bluffing about the surprise witness all along.

'Well,' the judge said, 'we will hear closing speeches tomorrow and then I will—'

'I'm sorry,' Waugh said. 'Your Lordship has misunderstood me. We have no more witnesses – except *one*.'

Dan's eyes darted at Waugh, and he saw the defence counsel turning towards the door behind him.

Over Dan's head Waugh shouted, 'Call . . . Josef *Rosen*.'

Chapter 17

Jo walked into court slowly, his steps more deliberate, more pained than Dan had ever seen. The usher helped him climb the two or three steps that led into the witness box, and it was only when Jo was settled there that he turned towards his son. Their eyes met. He did not blink as he looked at Dan, but his face was grim and determined. The muscles in Dan's stomach knotted with worry. He feared what his father would tell the court, what he was about to hear, the damage it could cause, to the case and, more importantly, to their relationship. He worried about Jo, laying himself open in the most public of places, in the most scrutinised of trials. But it was too late.

'What is your religion?' the usher asked.

'Jewish.'

The usher straightened her black gown and then handed the Old Testament to him. He read the oath aloud in his composite accent, with the hints of Yiddish and Russian and English and American. He wore his familiar grey coat, and Dan could see that the New York Yankees baseball cap was shoved in the left pocket. He had shaved more carefully than Dan had ever seen before, but nonetheless there were some stray grey hairs where the underside of his face met his neck.

He cleared his throat. 'I swear by Almighty God that the evidence I shall give shall be the truth, the whole truth and nothing but the truth.' He put the card down. 'So help me, God.'

'Thank you,' Julian Waugh said, 'but in this country, Mr Rosen, we don't use the last few words – unlike our American cousins.'

No one in the jury box stirred. There was no writing of notes or doodling. Everyone watched the slightly bent Jewish man. It was as if Dan had disappeared from the court, though he stood not ten feet away from his father.

'What is your full name?' Waugh asked.

'Josef Rosen.'

'And where do you live, Mr Rosen?'

'New York. Brighton Beach, New York.'

'And your occupation?'

'I run a deli.'

Waugh took a sip of water. 'I want to ask you about 1945. Is that all right?'

'That's why I'm here.'

Again Dan felt Jo's gaze, no more than a glance of his lateral vision as his father's head moved three or four millimetres to the left. He knew that this was the time to admit the fact of his blood relationship with Jo. Professional etiquette demanded that he withdraw from the case. The jury would have to be discharged. The case would be over for ever as far as Dan was concerned. For a moment he remembered Yuri's threats, that if he withdrew from the case because of Jo then Chris would not be safe. But he was no longer afraid of the son of Ivan Basarov. He began to see that, like Yuri, he was himself another victim of Neuwelt. Thus his professional concerns were overridden by a far more powerful force: curiosity. He wanted to hear what Jo really knew of Neuwelt. He wanted to know the whole truth. He really wanted to hate him.

'What happened to you during the war?' Julian Waugh asked.

Jo looked at the jury and said in a steady voice, 'I was captured by the Germans when they invaded Russia. Then I was sent to various camps as a prisoner.'

'Where did you end up?'

'Neuwelt.'

'For how long?'

'Until . . . liberation by the British tanks.'

'We know that was April 1945,' Waugh said.

'I don't know. Time meant nothing to us. It had stopped. We were already dead.'

'What did you do in the camp?'

Jo hesitated, glanced again at Dan and then said, 'I survived.'

It was the familiar answer.

Dan watched as Waugh glanced down at Jo's statement. He

paused, clearly deciding how best to form his next question. He took another sip of water. Dan wished he could see what had been written down, but it was a long-standing rule of law that the defence did not have to disclose the statements of its lay witnesses to the prosecution.

'Mr Rosen, did you get to know any of the other Russian prisoners in Neuwelt?'

'I think we all knew each other. So much as we were able. We all tried to know each other, it was all there was.'

'How did the Russian prisoners respond when the British tanks arrived?'

Jo looked slowly from the front row of the jury to the back. 'Let me tell you, we had *dreamt* of the moment all the time we were in that camp. We imagined that we would fall on our knees and pray or something. But when they came, we were just tired, and the joy was too much. Mostly, we sat and watched. I didn't even cry.'

'What did you think of the British?'

'They were our saviours.'

'Was that view shared?'

'When we first saw the tanks, we thought we must have died and this was heaven. Or we was dreaming and this was the cruellest dream. When we knew it was for real? We thought these guys were our saviours.'

Waugh turned the pages of Jo's statement noisily. He was reaching the crux of his evidence. 'Now, you know that Simon Montford is charged with ordering the execution of a Russian soldier who killed a British officer.'

'So I'm told.'

'The case against my client is that the execution by gassing took place because the Russian, Ivan Basarov, had killed a British officer.' Waugh raised his voice and looked around the court slowly. 'Now, please tell the jury as clearly as you can, was any British officer killed by a Russian prisoner who had just been liberated?'

Jo paused. His eyes met Dan's. The rest of the court was in total silence.

'Mr Rosen,' Waugh repeated, 'this is of the utmost importance. Did any Russian kill a British officer?'

Jo took a deep breath. 'No,' he said.

'Are you sure?'

'I'm sure.'

'How do you feel about the allegation?'

'It is ridiculous.'

'The case against Simon Montford is that he ordered the execution of Ivan Basarov because Basarov had killed a British soldier. Did such a thing happen?'

'No. How many *more* times? I put it in my statement. No. No. *No.*'

Suddenly, Julian Waugh sat down. But Dan stayed in his seat, crushed, for he knew that his father had finally saved Simon Montford.

The court reverberated with excitement. The jury chattered in pairs. Above and behind Dan, there was movement and debate in the public gallery. But Dan remained seated, gazing at Jo, at his profile. The features were those that he recognised as his own: the long eyelashes, the dark eyes, the swarthiness that had come to dominate Dan's appearance. He now saw them as dishonest features, treacherous, soiled. He felt sick.

'In view of the time,' the judge said, 'I'll allow you to cross-examine this witness tomorrow, Mr Becket. No doubt you and your team will have some enquiries to make before you do.'

The judge stood and so did the whole court. Dan noticed that his hand did not shake, his breath was still and his knees did not tremble when he got to his feet. It was over. Ten feet away, Jo shut his eyes as the court was officially closed.

Chapter 18

Dan sat with Sophie in the lounge, beside a dying fire. Outside were the first signs of an evening wind getting up, not yet violently, but with sufficient force to cause the flames to flicker unpredictably in the fireplace. Chris had gone to bed five minutes earlier and the two of them had their first opportunity to talk.

They both had a glass of whisky on the coffee table next to the sofa. When he looked, Dan could still see the faint scuff marks of Jo's shoes on the tabletop. Jo, of course, had not come home. They sipped the strong single malt from heavily cut crystal glasses without speaking, until the silence became unbearable. Dan held his glass up between his eyes and the flames and turned it slowly, creating a kaleidoscope of colour finished off by the rusty tones of the swirling whisky. All the lights in the room were off except a lone table lamp covered in a parasol-like tortoiseshell shade.

He finally said, 'I just let things drift before. While Chris was growing up, I was too obsessed with my work, with my career at the Bar . . . with success. I don't want that to happen again.' He put his glass down and took her hand. He was always amazed by how small it felt in his, but despite her slight physical presence, Sophie seemed able to cope with so much. 'I want you to know, I want to be honest with you, I will always love Viv, or some part of me always will. I don't think that will – *can* – change, Soph. But that doesn't mean that I can't love you.'

'So you do love me?'

'What do you think?'

'You've never said it.'

'I've loved you for longer than I dare think, Soph. In the months after Vivienne died, when things looked bleak, it was your face that I saw. I guess I didn't always understand it. I thought it was some kind of desire to get back to work. You know, to get back among barristers. But it was *you*, Sophie.'

'Why didn't you say anything?'

'Because I was a fool. Because I'm a man and men don't say things like that. Or if they do, most people just want to throw up. But I see you with Chris and I can see her happy, healing even – and I just can't believe it.'

'She's a great kid.'

'She had a great mother. Viv will always be her mother, no matter what happens to us. Can you deal with that?'

'I think so. But where do we go from here?'

'Ask me the same question in twenty-four hours.'

'Do you have any idea what you're going to do tomorrow?'

'If I say who Jo is, the jury will be discharged.'

'So? At least there will be a retrial.'

'There's no guarantee after this fiasco that the prosecution will be brought again. Especially after all the Gulf gas stuff we've uncovered. It's too embarrassing to far too many people.'

'So what's left?'

'If I leave things as they stand, then Montford is bound to be acquitted.' He paused and tried to summon up a hopeful look. 'Unless Helen has come up with anything about that British officer,' he said. 'The one Basarov is supposed to have killed.'

'She's trying, Dan. But so far—'

'Just a thought,' he said.

Sophie suddenly stood up. The expression on her face changed almost into a smile as the realisation washed over her. 'I think you *know* what you're going to do.'

'I think so.'

'Dan, consider what it might mean. For Chris, for you. For all of us.'

'That's all I've been thinking about.'

'So there's no alternative?'

Moments later, Dan heard a light rap on the window by someone who was obscured by the drawn curtains. He knew who it must be.

'You don't have to see him,' Sophie said.

He went to the door.

Jo stood at the bottom of the steps as he had months before on his first arrival in London. His head was cocked slightly to the right, and he wrapped his arms around his body against the cold. His face was partially illuminated by the streetlamp, but the peak of his baseball cap cast a shadow over his eyes.

'I had to come,' he said.

Dan did not reply.

'I just want to *try* to explain ... it's something I had to ... look, you don't understand, Dan ... son.'

The word, for it was the first time Jo had called him 'son', filled him with a confused joy, but also with regret.

'It's taken all this to call me ... that?' he asked.

Jo did not reply immediately. He took his baseball cap off and looked down. 'You got to trust me.'

'What do you think I've been doing? Since January?'

'One more day.'

Dan shook his head. 'More,' he said. 'It will have to be more. Because if we say nothing about ... us ... then we're going to live with it for ever.'

'I already put in fifty years.'

'And you've achieved what? Saved Montford?'

'One more day,' Jo said.

'Why didn't you tell me about all this?'

'I couldn't.'

'Why not?'

'You wouldn't understand.'

'No,' Dan said. 'I don't think you wanted me to understand.' He paused and took a breath. 'Look, I wasn't going to criticise ... condemn you for what you did at Neuwelt. You're still my father.' He took Jo's arm. 'Whatever you did, you're still my father.'

'So you think I was wrong? Working the labs.'

Dan was silent.

'Since you won't criticise me, tell me I was right to work in the labs.'

Dan stared back but could not reply.

'Tell me,' Jo continued, 'you would have done the same thing. *Tell* me.'

'I ... I can't.'

The old man nodded his head as if he had finally heard what he had already known. 'I ... I just wish one time ... that you was proud of me.'

'You survived. You did what it took. I'm proud of that.'

'Then do what it takes tomorrow.' Jo hesitated for a few moments. 'Say nothing . . .' He waved his cap from his body to Dan and back.

'I don't know.'

'Give me one more day,' Jo said.

'To do what?'

'To save myself.'

Behind Jo the streetlamp illuminated a shroud of freezing fog, and Dan suddenly felt the chill biting into his body. Icy crystals were forming in Jo's grey hair, and they shone brilliantly in the light that spilled out of the hallway and into the darkness outside.

'Come in,' he said.

'I got to be alone. Just tonight.' Jo turned around and began to walk away from the house.

Dan stepped out into the cold air, catching him up at the small gate.

'I don't know what you're doing,' he told him.

'That makes two of us,' the old man replied in a sing-song voice.

'No, don't do that.'

'What?'

'Joke. I do it, too. All we ever do is joke or banter or argue. When do we ever just talk?'

Jo nodded, smiling mainly with his eyes as small wrinkles traced paths down each side of his face.

'I don't know what the hell you're doing,' Dan repeated. 'But I do know that you're my father and—' Jo tried to interrupt but Dan talked over him. 'No, let me finish. Look, you may not need me – or want me. But I need you in my life, Jo. So does Chrissy. We both want you in our lives.'

The smile had vanished from the old man's eyes. But it was replaced by a distant, deeper look, one Dan had not seen before.

He said softly, 'I regret not seeing you grow up. Missed the lot. But sometimes . . . I used to talk to you. Quietly. In New York. Tell you all sorts of things I couldn't even tell Ira.' He shook his head slightly. 'All sorts. Sometimes I thought you heard me.' He paused and looked intensely at Dan. 'Did you hear me?'

Dan tried to smile back but could not answer.

'Thought not,' Jo said.

'But I saw you,' Dan protested. 'When I was lonely. I thought – hoped – somewhere you were thinking of Mum and me. Hoped one day we'd be together.'

'Did she ever talk about me?' Jo asked, his eyes full of optimism.

Dan hesitated and wondered what he should say; after all, how much could one small white lie cost when the truth would hurt so much? But as he gazed at his father, he knew he had to tell the truth. So he shook his head in reply.

Jo's eyes dropped.

'Chris really loves you,' Dan said.

'She loves everyone. That's her gift. She's a blessing upon you because you're a good man.' He half chuckled to himself at what he was about to say. 'Hey, someplace down the line I couldn't have screwed up. 'Cause at least I have that. A good son.'

There were a few seconds of silence between them until Dan said, 'Come in?'

Jo shook his head. 'What will you do tomorrow?'

Dan shrugged. 'You?'

Jo raised his eyebrows. 'I just want you to know. This morning? When I kissed you? I meant it, son.'

Dan was too choked to reply.

'One more day,' Jo said.

'Yes, one more,' Dan whispered.

Jo reached for the latch on the gate but with the cold in his fingers couldn't open it. Dan took charge and let his father out. He watched in silence as Jo walked up the street, intermittently moving between pools of frosted yellow light and semi-darkness, until the old man completely disappeared.

He returned to the house and shut the front door. For an instant, he caught sight of his face in the painted mirror behind the door. There, among the yellow and blue flowers, were the features of a son in pain. Dan's face, Yuri's face. They were the same, he realised. These two sons. Ultimately the same. In pain.

A little later Dan silently opened the door of Chrissy's room. The streetlight under which Jo had stood sent diffracted yellow rays through the tops of the curtains. There was a delicious warmth, a clean fragrance in his daughter's room, a mixture of her small collection of perfumes, potpourri and scented candles.

'I'm not asleep, Dad.'

He moved quickly to the bed and sat on the window side, as if he somehow wished to shield her from Jo.

'Who were you talking to?' she asked.

He stroked her hair as it fanned out on the pillow, and he saw the approach of sleep in her eyes. The last thing he wanted to do was lie. 'It was your grandfather.'

'Why didn't he come home?'

'He just can't.'

'Dad, you've *got* to sort it out. Look what happened when you argued with Mum.'

He held her tight and felt her comforting breathing on his arm as she turned her head to one side. 'Chris, I just don't know how much I can tell you.'

'How about . . . everything?'

'Don't be so precocious,' he smiled.

'All right. *Almost* everything, then.'

'It's to do with the case. Jo is a witness on the other side and because of him we are going to lose.'

'He's still Jo. Isn't he still my grandfather?'

'Yes, but—'

'Dad, I still love him. I don't care about your stupid case.' She sat up, the tears suddenly exploding from her eyes. 'You always cared about your stupid cases more than you cared about us. That's why you argued with Mum that night – wasn't it?'

He suddenly saw himself in the lounge below where, instead of Sophie, Viv was pacing the room. It was early the previous summer and he had just resigned from the Kurd bombing case. He could hear again the shouts, the screaming row, the hurtful words that he had never been allowed to retract. He saw the drinking, the gin, and Viv grabbing the car keys, storming out, never to come home.

'Chris . . .' he said. How could he broach it? This was the time, but where were the words? Words always came to him in court when he was talking about other people's problems. Surely they should come to him now? He carefully examined his daughter's face. Her eyes were wide with grief. 'I'm going to tell you the truth, but I don't want you to say anything until I finish. Do you agree?'

She nodded silently.

He felt her body slide back into the mattress and she pulled the duvet up to her neck. She held it there, though her hands were obscured, with a small piece of cover against each of her cheeks.

'I did something wrong, Chris. Look, I know, I was always doing things wrong, but this was special ... I mean, especially wrong. Mum fought tooth and nail to help me become a barrister. She did all sorts of horrible jobs, but she was always there for you. She made time. I didn't. I see that now. But I always loved you, Chrissy. Sometimes we don't understand why our parents do things, we forget that they are people too, that they can be wrong. I know that now. But I always loved you.'

He stroked her hair, smoothing it again over the pillow, and looked at the drawn curtains. The light still filtered through the fringes.

'Last year, I had a big case. It involved some men who I think were innocent, but because of ... politics, because sometimes our government does things it shouldn't, these men were sent to prison. I was told they were innocent but I wasn't allowed to say – it was a secret. So all I could do was resign. It was what your mum and I had worked for, for me to be a top prosecutor, and I threw it away without even asking her. That was wrong. I should have discussed it all with Mum first. Perhaps there was another way out, I don't know. I've tried *so* hard to work out what I could have done but I just don't know ...'

He stopped when he felt the fingers of her left hand coming out from under the duvet and holding his arm, tightly. She used her other arm to lever herself up and hugged him. For a while neither of them spoke.

'Dad, if I do things wrong, you go bonkers for a bit ... but then you forgive me.'

'Yes.'

'So why can't you forgive Jo? He would never hurt us, Dad. Just like I know you'd never hurt those men.'

'But I did, Chris.'

'So where are they now?' she asked.

'Still in prison.'

'Is it too late to help them?'

Dan considered this while they continued to hold each other.

His chin rested on her shoulder for what seemed like ages. 'It's not too late.'

'And can *you* help them?'

He nodded.

Chapter 19

The fourth day of the trial was plagued with low clouds. Rolling mountains of cumulonimbus were driven from the west by a blustering gale, and in the process they were broken up, occasionally revealing a small patch of sky before the gathering storm once more swallowed up the fleeting island of blue. The wind gusted at speeds of seventy and eighty miles an hour as it hurtled through the London streets. Glass shopfronts rattled, telephone wires and cables high above the street started to vibrate and then, when a critical frequency was reached, they let out high-pitched, eerie whining.

When Dan arrived at the Old Bailey that morning, there were already police riot control barriers outside the court. Back-up vans full of heavily armed officers patrolled the narrow street, backwards and forwards, ignoring the fact that it was one-way. There were thick metal grilles lowered over the windscreens of the vehicles. Clearly the police expected trouble: for it had been announced that the jury would soon go out in the war crimes trial.

There was a crowd that was separated into two parts, each shouting at the other, while their threats and insults were intermittently drowned out by the wind. Some people had banners that were being stripped by the force of the gusts. There were Orthodox Jews and Zionists. On the other side there were extreme right-wing activists holding banners denying the Holocaust. And in front of all this, the media of the world: Japanese reporters doing pieces to camera, American photojournalists taking shot after shot of the seething crowd, a French radio team trying to find a quiet corner.

Dan entered the Bailey alone. There was in fact a back entrance to the building that was used by Treasury Counsel and judges. It allowed select barristers to avoid the mêlée outside court on days such as this. Dan no longer had this perk and no longer cared. He wanted to go in by the front. Chrissy's words echoed in his head as he reached Court 12. It was not too late to help the imprisoned Kurds. The only question was how.

When he arrived in court, he looked at the dock, the jury box, counsel's row and the witness box where Jo had stood the previous day. He was barely aware of the warring parties assembling, the court staff convening, the judge coming in, owing to the tumult of emotions he was forced to confront because of Jo's actions. He was steeling himself, trying to swallow the pain. He told himself to focus his anger. Use it. Moments later, when the judge invited him to cross-examine the witness, Josef Rosen, he knew what he had to do.

He rose to his feet slowly. Jo, he noted, was in the same suit and coat he had worn the previous night. He looked tired; his eyes were no longer alert, as though he had not slept at all. Well, good, Dan thought. You deserve it. I offered you my home, my trust, my love, and what did you do? He wanted to translate these sentiments into questions in court. But where could he begin? What could he say? What would anyone say if they had the chance to cross-examine their father on oath?

'Your name is Josef Rosen?' he asked simply.

Jo nodded, without looking at him. He had not shaved since the previous day and greying stubble like a film of old sawdust covered his cheeks and chin.

'And you are Jewish?'

'I am a Jew.'

'Are you proud of being a Jew?'

'I am proud of being a Jew.'

'And you were born a Russian?'

'Yes.'

'Are you proud of being born a Russian?'

'Yes.'

'And what did you do in Neuwelt?'

'I . . . survived.'

Dan raised his voice. 'You said that *yesterday*. What else did you do?'

'I survived. Isn't that enough?'

'Not for me. Now you tell the jury. Did you work?'

'Yes.'

'Where?'

'In the camp.'

'*Where* in the camp?'

Jo looked frantically around the court, towards Julian Waugh, then to Montford in the dock, then to the judge. 'Hey, am I on trial here? I was a prisoner for Chrissake.'

'There are different degrees of captivity,' Dan said. 'Now what did you do?'

Jo remained silent.

Len Constant, burdened down by the case, leant forward wearily and said, 'You must answer.'

Dan's eyes bore in on Jo. Yet his father stared back at him resolutely, as if he were somehow proud of what he was doing.

'I worked in the . . . labs,' he said.

There was an outburst of astonishment around the court. People were suddenly hissing at each other and arguing high above Dan in the public gallery. The rank of solicitors behind Waugh desperately searched through the notes of their interviews with Jo to see how they could have missed such a crucial detail. Julian Waugh spun around and stared at Montford. But father and son held each other's gaze.

'You worked in the laboratories at Neuwelt?'

Jo paused, his head rolling forward fractionally, his shoulders hunched. 'I am not proud of that.'

'So why did you do it?'

'To survive.'

'And what did you have to do to survive there while thousands of others were murdered?'

Waugh was on his feet objecting. 'This is *not* admissible evidence. I *object*—'

'Why isn't it admissible?' Dan shouted back. 'This . . . man is your witness.'

'I still object.'

'Why don't you just let the truth come out?'

'That is an outrageous remark.'

'And hiding the truth is an outrageous thing. Now,' Dan said, turning back to his father, 'what did you do?'

'So I helped in the lab. It was only menial work. Cleaning things, sorting chemicals mainly.'

'Mainly? So you did other things?'

'I sometimes had to help with the experiments. Chemical control tests. But never experiments with people.'

'Who was in charge of the labs?'

Jo affected not to want to say, but Dan was beginning to sense that the old man might be putting on an act.

'I was told I don't have to talk about that,' Jo told the judge.

'Who was in *charge*?' Dan repeated, louder.

Jo hesitated, the pause silencing the crowd. 'It was ... that man.'

'Who?'

'Klaus Keller.'

Again the court erupted, and a scuffle broke out in the public gallery. Those involved were quickly dragged out by a bailiff.

'You said,' Dan continued, 'that no Russian killed a British officer. Is that true?'

Jo did not answer.

'Is that true?'

Jo looked at Julian Waugh. 'Yes.'

Waugh exhaled in relief.

'But,' Jo continued, 'a British officer was killed. By Simon Montford.'

Another explosion of noise. The judge shouted repeatedly at the gallery and again the bailiffs moved among the occupants, but Jo carried on speaking through the chaos.

'I was in the lab, no one saw me, and Montford came in with this young officer. I often hid under the worktables when I had something to eat – otherwise you get robbed. The other guy was from some different part of the British Army. He talked all the time about his duty to arrest war criminals. Montford said that Military Intelligence wanted to recruit Klaus Keller but the other man would not even give him the time of day. He wanted to arrest Keller. They argued, and Montford said Keller had a bundle of money from the Jews and he could cut the other soldier in. The argument got worse. The man shouted he was going to report Montford and ...'

'And what?' Dan asked.

'And Montford shot him.'

The court was now stunned into silence. Montford sat in the dock with his head in his hands and Waugh leant back in the front row, crossing his arms, refusing to take notes.

'A Russian prisoner was accused of killing the British officer,' Jo continued. 'The Russian was called Ivan Basarov. I reckon he was chosen because he was in a worse state than the others. He would probably have died soon anyways. He gave his food – well, the little he had – to others, to younger guys, fitter guys, guys who had a better chance of living. That's why they chose to execute him. They took him in the night. He didn't struggle. And they gassed him.'

'Was Simon Montford there?'

'He didn't miss a moment.'

'But other British soldiers have spoken about the gas chamber not functioning properly. About Basarov dying in excruciating agony. Do you know why?'

Dan saw his father's face redden, and there were tears in the old man's eyes.

Jo said, 'I don't know. They killed him. That's all I know. And . . . Ivan Basarov . . . he was a good man. You know, gentle. He'd save seeds from the bits of food we was given. He dug holes along the walls of the hut. Then he planted them.' Jo smiled distantly. 'Usually nothing happened. Not a goddamn thing. But twice we saw shoots. Little green shoots coming up out of the earth – in *that* place. Something growing. When I was released, after Ivan was killed, I dug up them plants. Wrapped them, roots and soil, in a wet old cloth. I brought them here. To England. In my pocket. But they died.'

When Jo finished speaking, there was again utter silence in the court.

After a short break, Julian Waugh was given leave to cross-examine Jo as a hostile witness.

Andrew Short came up to Dan's shoulder and hissed, 'I don't know who Uncle fucking Vanya is, but no British soldiers died at Neuwelt. Grail checked the records.'

Jo was attacked as Dan had never seen before. But by now, Dan was so raw emotionally, so numb, he didn't know whether to curse the old man or to praise him. His father had been extremely sharp with Montford's solicitors, and had restricted his statement

to the fact that no British officer had been killed by a Russian.
He had told half-truths, saying that he couldn't be sure who had
run the Neuwelt labs, and there were small contradictions in his
story which Waugh tried to make much of in order to decimate
his character. But the essential truth of it, the kernel of history
that Jo related to the jury, remained intact – until Waugh reached
the climax of his cross-examination.

The barrister's body was tense, and he leant on the knuckles
of each hand, inclining towards Jo. His voice exuded controlled
venom, and he spat out the words with obvious disgust.

'Let me understand what you *now* tell the jury, Mr Rosen.'
He paused. 'Josef is your real name – you haven't lied about
that, too?'

'I haven't lied about *anything*,' Jo said indignantly.

'But you betrayed Mr Montford?'

'I was never on his side.'

'But you pretend to help him?'

'I . . .'

'So you *deceived* him. Like you're trying to deceive the jury.'

'*No*,' Jo shouted.

'I understand that you now swear on oath that Mr Montford
murdered a British officer.'

'Yeah, that's what he did.'

Waugh stood up perfectly straight. 'Oh, but the prosecution
will not dispute that there is no record of *any* British soldier lost
during the taking of Neuwelt. What do you say about that?'

Waugh looked defiantly at Dan, but Dan had no material with
which to contradict him.

Jo replied, 'I don't know what to say.'

'Let's see what else you don't know about. What was the name
of the officer?'

'I don't know.'

'Oh, the unknown soldier?'

'No, I just don't—'

'Ever try to find out his name?'

Jo paused and his face flushed red. 'No.' Then he tried to add,
'I didn't think it was my place to—'

Waugh ignored him. 'What colour hair did he have?'

'I don't know.'

'Eye colour?'

'I don't know.'

'A big nose? Small nose? Full mouth? Thin lips?'

'I don't know.'

'Can you describe his face at all? Well, *can* you?'

'No,' Jo said quietly.

'Why not?' Waugh sneered. When there was no reply, he continued, 'Why not, Mr Rosen? Why *ever* not?'

Jo exploded. 'Because he had no face. He had no face, all right? What the hell do you want me to say?'

'How about the truth?'

'I'm telling the truth. Truth is the guy had no face. Like all his features had melted—'

'Into air? Into thin air?' Waugh interrupted. Then he continued the quote from *The Tempest*. '"And, like this insubstantial pageant faded, leave not a rack behind"?'

'I dunno what the hell you're talking about now,' Jo said.

'It's Shakespeare, Mr Rosen. A quite well-known *English* dramatist. Does it not describe your ludicrous evidence perfectly? "Such stuff as dreams are made on."'

Jo gripped the edge of the witness box and Dan could see his forearms shake with the force of his grip. His face twisted as if he were fighting back a clutch of inner demons. Suddenly he held up his left arm and rolled back his sleeve.

'*Dreams?*' he cried, showing the jury his concentration camp number. 'You think that's a *dream*? Let me tell you, it's a nightmare. A nightmare I've lived every goddamn day for fifty years. So, no – I can't answer your questions. But the guy didn't have a face, all right?'

'Mr Rosen,' Waugh said, exhaling, as if he had heard it all a million times before, 'you can carry on in this fashion for as long as you like, but I've finished with you now.'

'Well, I ain't finished with you,' Jo snapped back. His face was now becoming purple. His eyes were bloodshot.

Dan knew his father was losing it. Very soon he would go crazy – he'd seen witnesses this way before when the truth was so fantastic no one could believe it. Then he might even mention his son. But before it went that far, Dan glimpsed Sophie at the door of the court. Beside her was her sister, Helen.

Chapter 20

From where Sophie had stood in the vestibule between the outer and the inner courtroom door, she could see Dan sitting in the front row, watching intently as his father was being annihilated by Julian Waugh. Dan was in profile. His black gown slowly slipped off his shoulder, though he did not seem to notice this as he stared, without blinking, at the old man standing in the witness box a matter of feet away. It was odd to her how, despite the importance of her mission, she still noticed the small details: how Dan's forehead and chin were precisely the same as Jo's, more pronounced and craggier than was common; how their noses were different, with Dan's being slightly more angular, but how the eyes and eyelashes – the long black lashes, the large sad eyes – were identical and told the tale of their common blood. Why had no one else noticed?

Just before she pushed open the inner door, Helen had taken her right hand and squeezed it once. The two looked at each other momentarily. Sophie was always slightly taken aback by how imposing Helen looked in her army uniform. The blond hair was tightly pinned behind her head. She wore the peaked cap low over her eyes. But although the military uniform made her look grown up and important, Sophie knew that Helen was just as frightened as she was.

'Think it will work?' Helen asked.

'We've got to try, sis,' she whispered back. 'You know you're going to get into trouble.'

'For telling the truth?'

'Yes.'

'Bugger that.' Helen smiled. 'Forward, Private.'

Sophie smiled back. 'Only private? Thanks.'

But Helen did not have the opportunity to reply. For when the door was opened, they were both struck by the crushing solemnity of the courtroom and the sudden loudness of Julian Waugh's voice as he shouted at Jo.

Sophie gestured with her left hand to Helen to take a seat at the side of the court and approached Dan. Before she did so, she took the vital documents from her sister. Julian Waugh tilted his head to the right and focused exclusively on Sophie. His stare was cold and narrow-eyed, his hatred obvious to everyone. But she matched Waugh's stare. She refused to look away.

When she arrived at Dan's shoulder, he breathed, 'Soph, tell me some good news.'

Sophie glanced over her shoulder. Above them, the packed public gallery watched in unison. The array of disparate faces – white, black, young, old, female and male – was frozen in anticipation as they stared down like a Goya etching.

'Soph, I said—'

'You look tired.'

'Soph, the court is waiting—'

'Are you prepared to win this case?'

'Of course.'

'By any means necessary?'

'Yes, but—'

'Even the truth?'

Dan glanced around the court. He paused briefly when his gaze fell upon the stricken figure of his father standing alone in the witness box. 'Even the truth,' he said.

The judge leant forward in his high-backed chair. His voice boomed from the front of the court. 'Mr Becket, do you or do you *not* have any further examination of this witness?'

Sophie was by now seated in the row directly behind Dan. 'Yes,' she whispered.

He glanced round. His expression was confused, his eyes wide, slightly lost.

'Yes,' she said again.

Dan stood and pulled his black gown tightly around his shoulders. 'Yes, I do have further examination.'

She heard a rustle to her left as Waugh jumped to his feet. 'Well, what is it? The prosecution has already had *one* opportunity to examine this . . . man.'

'Mr Becket?' Constant asked.

'There's new evidence,' Sophie whispered.

'There's new evidence,' Dan repeated. When he realised what he had said, he suddenly turned on her. 'What new evidence?'

Waugh shouted, 'This is an *outrage*. The prosecution has closed its case. It's too late to adduce new evidence.'

'No, it's not,' Sophie hissed.

'No, it's not,' Dan repeated. Again he turned back to her, whispering, 'It's *not*?'

She gave him the photograph and the file that Helen had given her. 'You said Montford testified on oath that no officer was lost at Neuwelt? This is a rebuttal of that.'

When Dan looked down at the sepia photograph, with its curled-up corners and official stamps, he smiled. Small lines appeared at the corners of his eyes and, as the smile grew, a wrinkle appeared. So men get wrinkles, she thought. There *is* a just God.

He glanced at the medical record too, and then said, 'Leave it to me, Soph.'

'My Lord,' Waugh shouted, 'I *still* object.'

'Perhaps,' Dan said, 'my learned friend should wait until he knows what the evidence is before he objects – *unless* he already knows precisely what the evidence consists of.'

'That is *scandalous*,' Waugh cried. 'What is he suggesting?'

'I'm suggesting that a British officer *was* lost at Neuwelt in April 1945.'

'Who?'

Sophie saw Dan look down at the medical record, the yellowing paper, the official heading. As he spoke, she mouthed the name silently to herself.

'His name was Lieutenant-Colonel Charles Hammett.'

Waugh raised his voice still further. 'But My *Lord*, the defence should be *served* with this evidence in advance.'

'Not if it's just been discovered,' Dan replied. 'Not if there has been a concerted attempt to conceal it.'

'I am appalled—'

'We should *all* be appalled by what has happened in this case,' Dan interrupted. He held the photograph up towards Jo and asked, 'Who is this man?'

Sophie knew that the photo depicted an army officer whose

face had been blistered and burnt unrecognisably.

Jo peered towards his son.

'Have you ever seen this man?' Dan repeated.

'Can't say,' Jo replied.

Sophie could see along the length of Dan's arm – the black cotton of the gown ending at the elbow, then the midnight-blue suit, then the brilliant-white double cuff. The photograph shook in Dan's hand between his long fingers.

'Is it that,' he said, 'you cannot say because you can't see?'

'My eyes,' Jo said. 'They ain't so good.'

Dan quickly handed the photo to the usher who conveyed it across the well of the court to the witness box. Sophie noticed that the sleeve of Jo's left arm was for some reason rolled up and, as the old man held the photograph up to his face, the tendons and root-like veins flexed and bulged. He examined the picture for what seemed an age.

Finally he nodded towards Julian Waugh. 'Like I said, the officer had no face.'

The court exploded with noise. Montford's solicitor, Douglas Wallace, in the row behind Sophie, gasped with despair, and a younger assistant said 'Fuck' under his breath. The judge tried to call for silence.

Dan turned and grinned at Sophie. 'Thanks,' he mouthed.

Waugh shouted above the din. 'My Lord, these documents are inadmissible because they have not been properly proved.'

Dan shouted back. 'That lady – that soldier – is Captain Helen Chase of the Royal Army Medical Corps. She produces these medical records to testify that Lieutenant-Colonel Charles Hammett was gassed at Ypres in 1918 with phosgene. His face was blistered and burnt beyond recognition. His medical record ends with the fact that he went 'Missing in Action' in April 1945 at Neuwelt. All other army records have vanished. Mr Waugh can have as long as he likes to check these documents. But those are the facts.'

Sophie looked at Dan and then to her right, at her only sister Helen, who stood to attention in full uniform at the door of the court. Whatever Waugh might do to her, Sophie knew she would treasure these moments for the rest of her life.

Chapter 21

In contrast to the United States, the convention in England was that the prosecution should make the first closing speech. Although it was normally an advantage to speak second, Dan was grateful to go first. He wanted to say what needed to be said, what could be said, and when he sat down he wished to begin the process of putting the war crimes trial behind him.

Over the weeks and months since January, he had many times imagined this moment; standing up at the end of the case and facing twelve strangers, the jury, and asking them to convict Montford of a crime perpetrated fifty years ago. He had considered many opening comments, some tried and tested in other cases through the years (speaking about the burden of proof, or the elements of the crime charged), some more unconventional, grabbing the jury's attention by quoting something relevant from the Bible or Shakespeare. He had made brief notes on them all.

But as he stood in the front row of Court 12 at the Bailey, he was in no mood to read his speech. For the first time in his professional career – and possibly for the last time – he wanted to speak as directly as he could from the knot of angst and emotion inside him, from the heart. He wanted to tell the jury how he really felt about the case. The twelve jurors were perhaps thirty or forty feet away from him. He wished he could walk right up to them and speak face to face, like the attorneys in that Manhattan courtroom had been able to do. But there were still the professional courtesies of the English court to be observed: Waugh was his learned friend, Montford was presumed innocent. Dan turned to his left. His line of vision took in Montford sitting in the dock between two jailers at the back of the court, and Len Constant making notes on his speech at the front.

'Members of the jury, the Hebrew word for Holocaust is *Shoah*. Some of you might know that means a great and terrible wind. And it was a terrible wind that took up and scattered the best part of the Jewish nation. That wind still blows through the lives of thousands of ordinary people: survivors, the families of survivors, their sons and their daughters.

'I hope that during this case, no matter what your religion or background or age, you will have been touched just a little by this tragic fact of history.

'When you look at the dock, what do you see? There sits an Englishman through and through. Someone who has fought for our country, who has been elected by his peers and who has served in government. And what must you think? What *must* each of you think when I stand before you and say that this man is a war criminal, that he is a murderer, that he has committed a monstrous crime against humanity? He is not a Rudolf Hess, Mr Waugh will tell you. Nor is he a Klaus Barbie. Simon Montford fought *against* the Nazis. Do not be misled. That is not a defence to this charge.

'The issue is simple: have the prosecution – have I – proved to you beyond reasonable doubt that this man ordered the gassing of a Russian called Ivan Basarov? If you believe the evidence of the two soldiers, if you can accept the evidence of the ...' Dan paused to think how he should best describe Jo. '... of the defence witness, Josef Rosen, can there be any doubt that this man is guilty?'

After giving his evidence, Jo had been ushered from the courtroom, leaving by the doors behind Dan, and at that moment Dan had wondered when – *if* – he would see him again.

'But I want to confront head on the most difficult obstacle standing in the way of conviction. It is this. Simon Montford is one of *us*. He speaks our language, he lives in our country. So why should we convict him of a crime committed fifty years ago, in a country beyond the seas, when the victim is a man none of us knows. A Russian. Who cares? *Who* cares?

'But, even if some of you, all of you, have no feelings for Ivan Basarov ... or even his family,' Dan said, seeing the scarred face of Yuri in his mind, 'how important to you is our system of justice?

Keep it in proportion. This is only one case. But by your verdict you can send out a message. You can send out a message that says that this country condemns war crimes. Because they did not end fifty years ago with the Holocaust. You will find them all over the world today. Whether they are called ethnic cleansing in Bosnia or tribal unrest in Rwanda or sectarian conflicts in a dozen different places elsewhere in the world. We *need* to be able to say that if British residents get involved, one day, even if it takes years, even if it takes fifty years, they will be caught and prosecuted and tried by their peers and convicted.'

No one in the jury box was taking notes. Dan did not know whether that was a good or a bad sign. There was no sound except his voice and the fleeting echoes his words made in the vast space of the courtroom before they faded and vanished.

'The Hebrew for Holocaust is *Shoah*. That great and terrible wind blew through Neuwelt concentration camp in April 1945. Then the British came. Our army came to liberate that camp, to put an end to the suffering. But Simon Montford did nothing to shield one of its victims, Ivan Basarov. Why did he do it? I cannot tell exactly. Greed? Politics? Curiosity? Cruelty? Perhaps a strange combination of these things. But he chose to do the wrong thing and two innocent men died. After all these years we need to do the right thing. Simon Montford is guilty of murder, he is guilty of war crimes, he is guilty as charged.'

Julian Waugh's speech was a clinical demolition of the evidence Dan had called. As he spoke, Dan took no notes; he barely listened to the cunning oratory of the QC. Waugh said that Josef Rosen's evidence was the best possible reason to acquit Montford. It demonstrated the depths to which people would plunge to convict this pillar of the British community. Judge Constant summed up the case in less than an hour and before lunch the jury bailiffs were sworn.

Two ushers held up the Bible in their right hands and said, 'I promise to keep this jury in a convenient and private place. I will not suffer others to speak to them, nor will I speak to them myself unless it be to ask whether they have agreed upon a verdict.'

Dan couldn't bear to wait in the building over the luncheon

adjournment, and as the judge had agreed not to take any verdicts until after two o'clock, he left Robert Lancing in court to deal with emergencies.

The wind was still blustery as he left the security doors, and he was cheered and booed in about equal proportion by the demonstrators outside the Bailey. At Blackfriars Bridge, the water was choppy and rushed under the arches with a dizzy speed, carrying with it bits of wood, bags, a tyre, large cans. While he was standing on the north side of the bridge he saw Yuri emerge from the subway that led to the Tube.

'Tide going out?' he asked Dan as he joined him.

'Or in. I can never be sure.'

'It was a good speech.'

'Waugh's was better.'

'No, it was a good speech. Even if the jury acquits Montford, it was a *good* speech. Thank you. My father would have ... I don't know.'

Dan looked at the Russian. There was a calmness in Yuri's face that he had never seen before. To be thanked by this man who had threatened him for so long made him feel uneasy. A huge gust of air blew straight across the surface of the water. The banks and buildings on each side acted almost as a chute, concentrating the force.

'I did what you said,' Yuri shouted over the noise.

'What?'

'I tracked Montford last night.'

Dan had forgotten what he had asked him to do. Yuri took out some long-distance photographs, obviously taken with a sophisticated camera. There was a mass of digital information printed in small yellow letters along the bottom of the prints.

'Who is that with Montford?' Dan asked.

'Here, look at another, there's a close-up.'

Dan took the photo and held it up into the dull winter light, almost losing it in the wind. He found himself looking into the face of Grail.

'Grail's been working with Montford all along,' Yuri said.

'But why?'

'Montford was always going to be prosecuted. There had to be a trial. So he did the best thing. He destroyed it from within. Grail was a—'

'Trojan horse,' Dan said. 'So where is this place they're meeting?'

'The Global Chemical Corporation warehouse, Tilbury.'

'I don't understand.'

Yuri flicked to another photograph. 'Montford is a non-executive director of GCC.'

'So?'

'GCC has been shipping Tarin A to Iraq.'

He examined Yuri closely. 'Did you know about my father? Did he infiltrate the defence with you?'

Yuri laughed.

'Did he? I need to know, Yuri.'

'Never discount a Russian. No, *J*osef *R*osen,' he said, pronouncing the name with a strong accent, 'did it all by himself.'

Above the wind Dan heard a faint bleeping. Yuri took a small black pager out of his pocket.

'What is it?' Dan asked.

'A verdict.'

'But the judge said he wouldn't take a verdict until after two.'

'Still, the jury have reached one.'

'How do you know?'

'We've made some friends among the court staff. They get paid very badly.'

'Is it guilty or—'

'They're not *such* good friends. You better go back to court, Mr Becket.'

Chapter 22

Jo stood by the stairs on the third floor, at the beginning of the corridor that led to Court 12. He had his hands in the pockets of his long coat and his collar was turned up, even though the central heating in the building was suffocatingly hot. He wore his faded blue baseball cap with the peak low over his eyes. As Dan went up to him, he could still picture a box around him, as though the old man were still about to give evidence. He was no longer just his father. He was a witness.

'Bet you don't want to speak to me right now,' Jo said.

'There's a verdict.'

'You hate me?'

'Yuri says you did it on your own. Is that true?'

Jo looked at the ceiling distractedly as a Tannoy summoned all parties back to court. 'We can't talk here, Dan. People will see.'

'I don't care.'

'Don't blow it now.'

'And what would we achieve, Jo?'

'We convict the bastard.'

'And we get . . . what?'

'Justice.' Jo moved forward and looked at the horsehair wig on Dan's head. 'You should know about justice, Mr Barrister.'

'You deceived the defence. I've deceived the court.'

'What about Ivan Basarov?'

'I can see how important he is to you. How you have to nail Montford. But what about us, Jo? What is it doing to us?'

'*Don't* blow it now. We're almost home.'

'Home? I invited you into mine last night, but you refused.'

'So I got no home. But at least I got some . . . some guts.'

'Guts?' Dan asked. 'It takes guts to commit crimes? Because that's what we're doing, we're committing a crime.'

'For the greater good.'

Dan shook his head. 'I know you're trying to do the right thing. But don't you think I am, too? Those books I read. Know what they said? One of the first things the Nazis did, they hijacked the courts. That's what they all do, Jo. Every single one of them who thinks they know the truth. They break the rule of law. They impose their view of right and wrong. And the thing is . . .' He paused and moved closer to his father, holding the left hand that now held the baseball cap. 'People can be wrong. I . . . I was wrong. About you. You are a brave, stubborn . . . exceptional man. But if there are rules, we should stick to them. If we don't like them? Change them.'

'It's as simple as that?' Jo snapped.

'No. But we can't play God with the system – with the rule of law.'

'Why the hell not?'

'Because if we play God enough, finally someone comes along and plays the Devil.'

'So you don't believe me? About Montford?'

'Of course I believe you. But it's not good convicting him now only to see him walk on appeal. Let's get him. Properly. If it takes more time, I'll find more time.'

'I got to do this for Ivan. You don't understand . . . Look, I wanted to . . . I might not get another chance, but the reason I left England—'

'Jo, it's the wrong time.'

'No, I want to tell you.' He grabbed Dan's gown tightly, pulling it away from his shoulder. 'Goddamit, I *had* to leave. I *killed* a man. At Stamford Grange. In 1955.'

Dan stared back, staggered.

The woman usher came out of court with small rapid steps. 'Mr Becket? Mr Becket, the judge wants to convene the court. There's a verdict.'

Dan looked from the woman to his father. 'But . . . I need time to—'

'The judge says *now*,' she insisted.

At that moment, Lancing rushed up behind her. 'Come on, Becket,' he snapped.

* * *

Five minutes later, the foreman of the jury was on his feet. It was one of the young Asian men. He had a folded piece of paper in his hand, and Dan knew that Montford's fate was written on the sheet. Through his head the scene with Chrissy the previous night kept playing. It was not too late to help the Kurds, if only he knew how.

The clerk standing just below the judge asked, 'Members of the jury, have you reached a verdict upon which you are all agreed?' The clerk held up the indictment, a sheet of white paper with the charge upon it.

'Yes.'

'On the first count, on the charge of committing an offence contrary to the War Crimes Act of 1991, do you find the defendant, Simon Sinclair Montford, guilty or not guilty?'

Dan spun around in his seat and saw Montford standing in the dock at the back of the court. Their eyes met. There was to be a verdict on each of them.

'We wish to make a statement,' the foreman said. He wore a white cricket jumper and he nervously pulled the cuff of his left sleeve over his fingers.

There was a murmur in the public gallery.

'Silence,' cried Judge Constant. Then he turned slowly to the jury. 'By law you are obliged to answer simply guilty or not guilty. Mr Clerk, please repeat the question.'

The clerk coughed and held the indictment higher. 'On Count 1, do you find the defendant, Simon Sinclair Montford, guilty or—'

He did not finish. For suddenly there was chaos in court. People shaking their heads, speaking, although Dan heard no sound.

He had got to his feet.

There had to be *some* end to the corruption.

What if Montford was convicted on Jo's evidence? Would that be justice? Or simply vengeance? Dan and Jo would be condemned to spend their lives hoping that no one found out about their blood relationship. Was that a price worth paying? Sophie knew about Jo, so Dan's silence would force her to become his accomplice. And anyway, the moment Dan's link to Jo was discovered, Montford's conviction would be quashed. He thought briefly of Chris and how much he loved her. He wanted her to be proud of him and she would not be able to be proud in safety if he continued the deceit. He had to say something. The images of the Kurdish defendants the previous year swept into his mind, men wrongly convicted because he had stayed silent. He quickly glimpsed Viv storming out of the door that fateful night; he had not communicated his feelings to her, he had not trusted her love for him. But now he had to trust himself.

'My Lord,' he said. 'There is something I have to tell the court before there is any verdict in this case.' He looked to his right. Jo was standing by the door of the court with his cap in his left hand, the hand above which was carved the concentration camp number. 'Josef Rosen—'

'The witness?' Constant asked, astonished.

'Josef Rosen is . . . my father.'

Instead of another outburst, there was utter silence in court. Dan heard the blood rushing in his ears and his heart pounding. All around him, he felt people reassessing the position, gauging where the advantage lay. He felt so alone, standing in the silent courtroom. Jo could only have been fifteen feet away, but it seemed like a vast, unbroachable distance. The front rank of counsel's row now seemed to Dan to be an island, a stage, a confessional, a prison. Here he would have to stand and await his punishment.

Julian Waugh was the first to speak. He got to his feet and demanded, 'This jury *must* be discharged.'

'I agree,' the judge said.

The first hints of outrage from the jury box. 'But we've reached a *verdict*,' the foreman said.

'I cannot accept it,' Constant replied.

'But we've found him—'

'I *cannot* accept it.'

'We found him *guilty*.'

'One more word and I shall have you arrested for contempt. This jury is discharged. Usher, please take them away. Mr Montford remains unconvicted. There will have to be a retrial.'

One juror threw down his notes petulantly. Another, in an expensive suit, made a sharp comment Dan could not make out. But they were all removed from the court.

The judge then turned his attention to Dan. He pulled his judicial gowns around him and tightly crossed his arms. 'Mr Becket, you realise of course that this is a matter of the utmost gravity which could lead to serious professional consequences for you.'

'Yes.'

'Mr Waugh, do you have any comments?'

Julian Waugh glanced sideways at Dan and sneered, 'It's no more than I have come to expect.'

When Dan glanced at his junior, Lancing said nothing but tried to conceal a smirk of satisfaction, as if he had been working for precisely this moment, Dan's downfall.

But Dan knew that he had to confront the past fully. If ever there was a time it was now. 'I have to tell the court,' he said, 'that there are innocent men languishing in prison.'

'What do you mean?' the judge asked.

Waugh shouted, 'This is *irrelevant*.' He struck the bench in front of him hard with his fist.

'No, it's very relevant. As Mr Waugh well knows. There are innocent Kurdish men in jail and the government knows about it. Mr Waugh knows about it. And I have known about it since last year. But I did nothing about it. And now I shall.'

With this the courtroom finally disintegrated into anarchy. The bailiffs and security police cleared the public gallery and the judge stormed from the bench.

A cluster of reporters surrounded Dan at the front of the court and fired question after question at him. He talked without thinking. Repeating the words he had wanted to say for over a year, since the night Viv had died. As he talked, he looked into the back of the court, where he saw the devastated figure of his father.

Chapter 23

When Dan finally got home, it was dark. Some of the houses already had their Christmas lights up and they flashed on and off, heralding a festive season he had totally forgotten about. Two tall trees had been blown over on the edge of Shepherd's Bush Green, and this caused a tailback stretching to the Uxbridge Road, all the way to the police station.

As he reached the steps outside his front door, he saw the curtain pulled back slightly and then heard rapid padding from inside. Suddenly the door flew open and Chrissy ran up to him in tears. Her hair was down around her face, long strands on each side curled around her cheeks, and she could not have looked more like Vivienne if she had tried.

'There was a news flash,' she said. 'The phone hasn't stopped ringing. Sophie was going to take it off the hook but we thought you might call. Oh, Dad. You did it. You *did* it.'

He hugged her for what seemed like ages. She clung to him and would not let him go, so he had to lift her off her feet and carry her into the hallway. Sophie stood at the door to the lounge, leaning against the frame with her legs crossed. She tried to smile.

'Jo?' he mouthed to her.

She shook her head.

They spent the next two hours in front of the television with the radio blaring away simultaneously. The case made all the news stations. High-powered political editors, more accustomed to Downing Street, stood uneasily with their microphones in front of the warring crowds outside the Old Bailey. There was no sign of the factions dispersing. Several scuffles between Jews and extremists had resulted in arrests and the riot police were on stand-by. No one quite knew what to make of it.

Chrissy surfed the channels as the sensational headlines filled the room:

'Today the Old Bailey was stunned by revelations of senior government corruption . . . Simon Montford remains an innocent man *despite* being convicted by a jury . . . The integrity of our prosecuting authorities lies in ruins today after barrister Daniel Becket revealed that secret deals had been done with Iraq, condemning two innocent Kurds to jail and sending others to their death . . . Have we armed Saddam with chemical weapons of mass destruction? We'll examine the evidence after the latest sports news. Another bad day for Chelsea . . .'

Eventually, Dan got up and switched both the radio and the television off after the BBC had reported: 'Senior legal sources tonight announced that they *would* retry Simon Montford for the Neuwelt war crime.'

As the echoes of the reports died away, he stood in front of Sophie and his daughter. His two favourite women sat side by side on the sofa and stared up at him expectantly, but he just wanted to look calmly at the faces he loved.

Sophie spoke first. 'Did you have to turn it off?' she asked. 'I was just beginning to enjoy that.'

'I've always wanted a famous father,' Chris added.

They continued mocking him gently and he smiled but did not reply.

After another minute, Sophie said, 'So what do we do now?'

'Nothing,' he replied.

'Nothing?'

'It's over. Well, for us. Let's just get on with our lives. There are going to be some changes around here. Firstly, I'm leaving the Bar.' He held up his hand when Sophie began to protest. 'I suppose they'd kick me out anyway so it's no great decision. But more importantly, I want to spend more time with you, Chris – if you can bear it. And Soph, I want you to know that whenever you think it's right, you can live here with us . . . with me. Helen, too.' He gazed at each of them in turn. Sophie's hands were in her lap; Chris cupped her fingers behind her head. 'Right, that's about it. Except *don't* put your feet on my coffee table.'

They got up, Sophie moving around the coffee table, Chris

clambering over it, and took hold of him from the left and the right. They didn't speak; there seemed to be no need. But then a noise intruded on his thoughts: the distant ringing of the phone. After a couple of rings it abruptly cut off.

'The fax,' Dan said.

Chris ran into the hall. 'Maybe it's a film offer.' Then she called back, 'It's for . . . Sophie.'

Dan looked at Sophie and she shrugged.

'I gave this number to my Kurd's solicitor. Hope you don't—'

'Don't worry. But I thought he couldn't afford one.'

'After he was in the news, we had to fight them off.'

From outside, Chris shouted, 'It's some kind of . . . letter.'

The two adults moved into the hall. The Home Office logo was just appearing at the top of the fax.

'Oh, God,' Sophie breathed. 'They've decided to deport him.'

The name of her client and his case number appeared, then a series of convoluted sentences full of legalese. Sophie read it out.

'With regard to the case of Abbas Bicak . . . blah blah blah . . . the Secretary of State – the bastard – has decided . . . to . . .' Suddenly she stopped reading and looked at Dan. 'Oh – my – God,' she said. 'They're only allowing him to stay. They're only sodding allowing him to stay.'

She grabbed Dan and he hugged her, the two spinning around until they bumped into the wall.

'I'll make some tea,' Chris said.

Sophie and Dan continued to embrace, her head now on his shoulder. She was in tears.

'You did a good thing,' he said.

'Oh, thank God,' she whispered. 'Thank God. I'd better ring the solicitor.'

'Sure.'

They let go of each other. Sophie was about to dial when the phone rang again.

'Shall I get it?' she asked. 'Could be another damn reporter from the Press Association. Go on, give me permission to be rude and obnoxious.'

As he moved to pick up the phone, he steeled himself once more. He had decided that the whole truth had to come out and he had resolved to answer any question truthfully. Now he had made the whole affair a matter of public debate, he knew that he had that obligation – at least until the full story of the Kurds and the Iraqi gas scandal was known.

He breathed deeply and slowly picked up the receiver. 'Hello, this is Dan Becket.'

'You . . . got to come,' a faint voice said, trailing off as a mobile phone line broke up. 'You got to . . .'

'Hello?'

'Dan, it's Jo.'

'Where are you?'

'I told Yuri.'

'What?'

'What I did at Neuwelt.'

'Jo, I don't—'

'Dan!' There was a sudden change in his father's tone. '*Don't* come. He wants you to come. But I'm *begging* you not to.'

There was a rumbling as the phone was snatched. 'This is Yuri Basarov. I know you want the same thing as me, Dan. I know you want the full story. Well, I'm going to get it. Now. Here. I've got Grail. With or without you I'm going to get the whole truth.'

Dan held the receiver away from his ear for a moment and tried to think. 'Where are you?'

'I'm going to tell you, Dan. I know it sounds madness, but I think I can trust you. This is now part of you as well.' He paused as the line crackled loudly again. In the background, Jo shouted: 'Don't come.' Yuri added, 'But if you do call the police—'

'Grail is part of the police, I know that.'

'—and they come here, then I don't know *what* I will do.'

'For God's *sake*, Yuri, where are you?'

'The GCC warehouse. Tilbury Docks.'

Then the line went dead.

Dan looked around, catching his face in the mirror. He noted that the colour had drained from it and his features were translucent and unreal.

'What's happened?' Sophie asked. She moved closer and took his arm softly. 'Dan, speak to me. What the hell has happened?'

But he did not reply.

Chapter 24

Dan took Sophie's mobile and, as he drove across London, he obtained the location of the warehouse from directory enquiries. At first the operator had refused to disclose the address. She said it was policy not to. But when Dan shouted down the phone that it was a genuine emergency, she relented. She asked whether she should call the police, and when she did, he cut her off. Grail was the police. Grail could not be trusted. The police could not be trusted.

He made the mistake of putting the radio on as he drove along the Embankment. Further reports and updates on the war crimes trial blared out. But by now he was sick of the same old stories, so he switched it off and accelerated well past the speed limit as he sped along the river.

The wind had veered around to the east and the Volvo laboured into it, buffeted by the ferocious gusts. The tyres slid dangerously on the road, one way and then the other, barely under control. The car just missed a coach near London Bridge, hitting the kerb and jolting back towards the centre of the road. But all Dan could think of was Yuri and Grail and Jo alone in what he imagined to be the cavernous GCC warehouse.

The industrial estate at Tilbury was a sprawling series of prefabricated hangars and storage facilities. Arc lights hung high from posts around the perimeter, and they washed the scene in a chemical brightness, creating an artificial daylight.

Dan parked his car two hundred yards from the outer fence. As he got out, the wind blew the stench from a cluster of tall chimneys into his face. It smelt of burning rubber and made his stomach churn. The wind rattled the chain fences, and he could

see that part of the perimeter fence towards the water had been
blown away. He headed for the gap. The icy gale cut straight
through his clothing, burning his skin with the cold. Papers blew
in front of him; an aluminium can was lifted and flew straight for
his face, forcing him to duck. He skidded and fell over, dirtying
his hands in an oily puddle.

The Global Chemical symbol stood out in letters twenty foot
tall on an aircraft hangar-like warehouse by the river's edge. A
sliding door made out of corrugated metal was slightly ajar at the
rear, and glancing out of the opening was Yuri. With a gun.

Most of the hangar was in darkness. Huge metallic drums were
silhouetted by a single strip light near the entrance; there were
twelve of them, evenly spaced, each over six feet high. Yuri
ushered Dan in using the gun, but not pointing it directly at
him. He pulled the door to after Dan had entered. It created
an awful grinding sound as the lock crunched uneasily into its
housing.

Grail was directly in front of him. He was in a yellow folding
metal chair. Bound and gagged. He shook his head from side to
side as the whites of his eyes caught the strip light, all the time
struggling against his restraints to no effect. Jo stood near him
and glared at Dan. There was another metal chair to Grail's
right. This one was empty. The chairs were each propped against
a drum.

'Told you not to come,' Jo said quietly.

'This thing has to be sorted out, Jo.'

'Begged you.'

'Shut *up*,' Yuri hissed from the door.

Grail moaned as loud as he could through the gag, but Yuri
pointed the gun at him and then he was instantly silent, his eyes
bulging with fear. That was the last thing Dan saw. Yuri suddenly
switched off the light.

In the darkness, Dan heard a generator somewhere on the far
side of the hangar ticking over, and then there were whispered
calls from outside the building. At first they were indecipherable,
but then it became clear that someone was calling repeatedly:
'Grail, Grail, *Grail.*'

The door creaked open and Dan saw Simon Montford framed
by the opening, momentarily backlit by the arc lights from the
perimeter fence.

As he moved forward, Yuri hit him violently across the skull with the gun.

Yuri forced Jo to tie Montford into the second chair. Then he pointed his gun in the direction of the two seated men while Dan stood to one side, trying to assess what to do. He noticed that a trickle of blood ran behind Montford's ear and then disappeared below the collar of his coat.

Above the chairs ran a metal rail which traversed the length of the hangar. Various sharp metal hooks were suspended at intervals along the rail. It appeared that they could be used to move heavy objects from one end of the warehouse to the other. They reminded Dan of a B-movie he had seen about the Russian Mafia in New York. Bodies of victims had been hung upside down from just such hooks.

'What are you going to do?' he asked.

Yuri did not reply. Instead he picked up a metal pail, full of dirty water, and, advancing quickly, threw it over Montford. The splashes almost reached Dan, though he stood ten feet to the left. Montford groaned and his head rolled from one side to the other. He coughed twice, spitting out the fetid water as it dripped down his face. His eyes were still bleary from the blow. He looked about him, desperately trying to focus, until eventually he saw Dan.

'Becket?' he gasped. He shook his head to try to clear his vision further. Then his head lolled on to his chest.

Dan turned to Yuri and asked, 'How did you get them here?'

The Russian smiled. 'I persuaded Grail, or rather my gun persuaded him, to bring me to the warehouse. Grail called Montford saying he had captured Josef Rosen. There is going to be another war crimes trial. But these cases take so long before they come back to court and there are so many ways in which an old man can die. Who knows? In all the excitement of the trial, Comrade Rosen might have got a curious ... *hardening* of the arteries. And then Montford would win the retrial.'

'Who are you?' Montford asked, his voice rasping.

'Yuri Basarov.'

'Basarov?' Then realisation flooded through him. 'Oh, my God.'

Yuri pointed the gun at Jo. 'I would get you a seat, Mr Rosen, but there are none left.'

Dan took a step nearer the Russian, but the gun rotated towards him. 'Look, Yuri, what are you going to do?'

'Punish the guilty and . . . I haven't thought about the innocent. There don't seem to be too many innocent men tonight. Take the gag off Grail.'

Jo complied. Grail spluttered and spat the taste of the gag out of his mouth.

'Who killed Ira Gottlieb?' Yuri asked.

'I don't know,' Grail said.

The Russian walked slowly forward, rubbed the tip of the gun in the blood on Montford's head then put it carefully to his temple. Montford moved his head away from the barrel but couldn't move far enough. 'Does that assist your recollection?' Yuri asked.

Grail shook his head.

'For God's *sake*, Grail,' Montford screamed, '*tell* him.'

Yuri pulled back the hammer.

Montford closed his eyes. 'Tell him. *Tell* him.'

Grail rocked backwards and forwards as he said, 'All right, all right. I killed him.'

'Why?'

'Ira could link Keller to Montford.'

'And Neville Neale?' Dan asked.

Grail looked murderously back and bit his lip, but Yuri moved the gun from Montford's head to that of the detective.

'All right,' Grail said. 'I killed Neale, too. He had got the MI6 Contact Note from that anonymous source.'

'And you frightened off the informer?' Dan asked. 'Ensured he'd never testify against Montford?'

Grail nodded slowly and then tried to spit some fibres from the gag out of his mouth.

Yuri smiled.

'So I told that stupid boy about Neuwelt.' Montford smiled back crazily. 'Fuck you. You're going to kill me anyway. I'm not playing this game any more, Basarov.'

'But why did you tell the informer all this?' Dan insisted.

'Because I couldn't keep it to myself any more,' Montford said. 'He was supposed to be the great young hope of the party. A brilliant student. A friend's son. Look at him now.'

Yuri looked at Montford with disgust. 'Your death is certain. But I'm offering you something else. A quick death. A death without unnecessary pain. The type of death *my* father never had. I'm not going to waste time. Montford recruited Keller and killed the British officer. But why did my father suffer so much?'

Dan saw Montford's eyes drop for the first time. A wave of fear washed over the former major's face, diminishing the features, setting the chin rigidly against his chest. He closed his eyes.

'*Why?*' Yuri repeated more manically.

Now Jo looked towards Montford.

'I don't know,' Montford whispered. 'Really—'

But his sentence was interrupted by Yuri charging with desperate strides across the room and tearing at Montford's silver hair, yanking it upwards, forcing the older man to look up into the barrel of a gun.

'*Why?*' he shouted again.

Montford shook his head.

'Why did he suffer so long?'

'I don't *know*.'

Yuri took the metal tip of the gun and pushed it into the corner of Montford's right eye. The blood on the tip smudged on his eyelid before the metal distorted the eye socket, making him wince with the terror.

'Tell me or I shoot,' Yuri cried.

'I don't *know*.'

Dan rushed forward. 'Yuri, for Christ's sake.'

The Russian raised his other hand, stopping Dan in his tracks, and then the hammer of the revolver was pulled back.

'I'll blow out your eye—'

'Yuri, *stop*,' Dan shouted.

'The bullet will smash through your brain.'

'I don't *know*.'

'You're going to die now.'

'I told you, I don't—'

Jo shouted, '*Stop*. Stop, stop, *stop*.'

Dan saw Yuri's finger move. The blood had been squeezed from the trigger finger. He saw the chamber begin to revolve.

Montford screamed.

The hammer crashed back.

Again Montford screamed horribly, making a sound the like of which Dan had never heard.

Then there was silence.

But when Dan looked, Montford was still alive, crying, sobbing to himself, but still alive. There was no bullet in the chamber.

Jo moved forward. 'It was my fault,' he cried.

Yuri raised the gun and pointed it directly at Jo.

Chapter 25

'What are you saying, Jo?' Dan asked his father, all the time trying to look into Yuri's eyes and not at the barrel of the gun.

Behind him, he heard Jo say, 'I tampered with the gas mechanism at Neuwelt.'

'*Why?*' Yuri demanded.

'I tried to . . . wreck it. I tried to stop the gassings. But I just made it worse.'

Dan felt his father put his bony hands on his shoulders.

'Yuri,' Jo continued, shielded by his son, 'I'm sorry. I know it won't make a whole lot of difference, but I am. Sorry. You know, all my time at Neuwelt, I didn't do the right thing. Working in the labs while people died, and I said, well, live but live with a purpose, *do* something with it. Something good. Then the first time I try to do something, to do the right thing, I make it worse. Yuri, those bastards – Montford and Keller – they was intent on killing your father. I tried to stop them that night. I figured, if I could save Ivan until the next day, just one day, then maybe other soldiers would come, perhaps Americans or Russians. We didn't know where the armies was going to meet. I'm so sorry, but believe me, I've lived with your father's screams down all these years – they never left me.'

The Russian relaxed his arm, as if some vital force were draining out of him. He appeared confused by this twist of fate that had resulted in Dan's father killing his own.

Jo moved in front of Montford and Grail. 'Your father was a good man, Yuri. You should know that. I'm not just saying that because . . .' He nodded at the gun. 'He saved other people. There are people alive – *somewhere*, Christ knows where, but somewhere on this planet there are people or their descendants who owe their lives to your father. And he would have been proud of you, just as I'm proud of my son.'

The Russian played with the rotating cylinder of the revolver, rolling it with his left hand as he held the handle in his right. Dan heard the unnerving *click*, *click* sound as the grooves moved around the barrel.

'What about Keller?' Yuri asked Montford. 'Where is Keller?' But the Englishman was too drained, too distraught to reply immediately. 'Where – is – Keller?'

'Klaus Keller is dead,' Jo said.

'Dead?'

'I killed him.' Jo looked at Dan. 'That's what I tried to tell you,' he said. 'Keller worked at Stamford Grange in the fifties. So did I. They had changed his appearance, but I still recognised him. You can't change someone's eyes, not completely. You know that stuff they say about the eyes being the windows to the . . . I reckon it ain't wrong. I knew it was Keller. He could call himself by another name, he could say he was Swiss, but I knew.'

'How did you kill him?' Yuri asked.

'Gassed him,' Jo said. His voice eased as he said it, not so much with pride as with relief, that after all these years the secrets he had struggled to bury within himself had come out. 'I gassed him in one of his own fucking little gas chambers – with Tarin A.'

Montford looked up at him. '*You* did that? It was an accident.'

'The only accident was he didn't recognise – *you* didn't recognise – a shrivelled little Russian Jew who after ten years was not quite so shrivelled. But, hey, whose gonna recognise a skeleton?'

'Where is Keller's body?' Yuri asked.

Jo looked at Montford as he said, 'There is an unmarked grave in the chapel graveyard outside Stamford Grange. It says simply 1955.'

Yuri nodded at Montford. 'So all there is left is you and Grail?' He slowly pulled back the hammer of the gun, taking two paces backwards. He took aim firstly at Montford, at his heart. Dan saw sweat on his forehead, tracing the contours of the scars on his face as it trickled down. The Russian's hand started to tremble. He narrowed his eyes as he aimed, while the tip of the gun shook.

'Go on,' Montford said defiantly. 'If you're going to do it, do it now.'

Dan looked from the Russian to the Englishman, and saw a look of arrogance on Montford's face as his mouth twisted grotesquely into a sneer.

'Go on,' Montford repeated.

'Shut up!' Dan shouted.

But Montford continued to goad the Russian as the man's arm began to move. The end of the barrel defined a small, crazy circle in the air as Yuri struggled to compose himself.

'Go on, Basarov.'

'For Christ's sake, Montford, he'll kill you.'

'Go *on*, Basarov.' Montford trained his eyes on the barrel of the gun.

Yuri breathed heavily, screwing up his face. More sweat appeared, but the gun shook more violently the more he tried to control it.

'Kill me, then,' Montford shouted. 'Kill me, kill me, *kill* me.'

Yuri shouted, his teeth flashed.

Dan couldn't stand it. He stood in front of the gun. He held his hand out towards the man who had threatened the life of his daughter, who had made his family live in fear for most of the year, but he wasn't frightened. For the first time, Dan felt he was stronger than the Russian. 'Yuri, it's *over*,' he shouted.

The gun barrel still shook inches away from Dan's body. It moved from his eyes to his neck to his chest, then back to his eyes. 'You can't execute them, Yuri,' Dan said.

'Why not?'

'That's what Montford and Keller did to your father. You can show you're stronger than they are. Spare them.'

'No.'

The gun was only eighteen inches from Dan's face, and he could see the oil smears along the barrel, the blood on the tip. He looked directly into Yuri's eyes. They were filled with hate and fear.

'Get out of the way,' he hissed.

Dan shook his head.

'Get out of the *way*,' he shouted, gesturing with the gun. 'I don't want to kill you, but I will.'

He pulled back the hammer.

Jo shouted, 'Dan, for *Chrissake*.'

Yuri turned his head momentarily towards Jo and that was Dan's chance. He lunged at the gun.

Yuri screamed, his hot breath on Dan's face as the two of them struggled for possession of the gun. That was when the first shot rang out.

The first pain Dan felt was in his ears – his eardrum exploded with the report. The air around him was suddenly acrid. Out of the corner of his eye he saw Jo screaming something but he could not make out what.

Behind him there was a terrible hissing. And flames. Terror in Yuri's eyes. The gun dropped to the floor.

Montford and Grail cried out as the metal drums behind them spewed out chemicals. Jo ran towards Dan, but he didn't make it. He slipped and convulsed on the floor, as if he were having a stroke.

'It's chemicals for *Tarin*,' Montford screamed. 'It's *Tarin*. For God's sake get us out.' But the spray continued to rain down.

Dan spun around. He saw Jo on the ground, his face now purple. His left arm shook, and still the chemicals behind them spewed out. A deathly flame had been ignited on the second drum. Dan knew he shouldn't move Jo, but the drums were going to blow. He knelt and took Jo's legs, grabbed his ankles, and dragged the old man as Jo continued to convulse.

Montford screamed, 'It's Tarin. For God's sake help us.'

Where was the door? Dan dragged Jo backwards, and as he did so he faced the two chairs and the cries of the two men tied to them. The chemicals sprayed out like a toxic shower and a multi-coloured flame burnt madly, illuminating Simon Montford with an awful unnatural light.

Where was Yuri?

Dan kept pulling his father and crashed back against the corrugated iron door. There was the Russian, trying to open it. But the lock was jammed, and the chemical flames were getting larger, like some sort of fuse that was reaching its end.

Still the door would not open.

Yuri ran back towards Montford as the two men screamed. He retrieved the gun he had dropped in the struggle and raced back to the door. He fired twice. The bullets blasted sharp fragments into Dan's face. Blood immediately trickled from his cheeks. But Yuri still could not open the door. Dan dropped Jo's feet and pulled with all his strength. There was a grinding noise as the door crept open a fraction.

Together they pulled Jo through and out into the night where the wind howled. A gust of air shot through the narrow gap and fanned the flame from the drum. The tongue of fire virtually reached Montford's head and he screamed again, but his words were lost in the cry of the gale outside.

'We've got to get them,' Dan said.

'It's going to explode.'

'You *can't* just leave them there to die.'

Yuri stared deep into Dan's eyes and grabbed his shoulders. 'I'll go,' the Russian said. 'You take your father, get him safe.'

'It'll only take us a second together.'

'No. Save your father, Dan.'

'But—'

'I'm sorry for what I did.'

'You loved your father.'

There was a blast from inside as more chemicals spat out, expanding with the growing heat. Dan pulled Jo again. He heard the bones in the older man's ankles cracking as he dragged him. Yuri looked back at Dan for a second. Their eyes met, then the Russian went back into the warehouse.

Dan soon reached smoother ground where Jo's body slid more readily. The wind cried out terribly, roared in Dan's ears, blocking out all sound until he reached the next warehouse. He turned the corner and pulled Jo's arms after him. He had to rest – his lungs heaved desperately for air, his back was locked with pain. Jo had stopped shaking. He opened his eyes and looked up at his son.

Then there was a monstrous explosion. Flames shot hundreds of feet into the night sky, rocking the walls of the other warehouses, and Dan knew that the people inside the GCC building had been obliterated.

A multi-coloured chemical fireball climbed into the London air, a monstrous burning toxic flame, the chemical components of Klaus Keller's lethal nerve gas, Tarin A, blown by the rising wind over the country that had sheltered him after the Holocaust.

In the distance Dan heard the screaming of police cars and fire engines. When he looked at his father, Jo had closed his eyes.

Dan began to panic, unsure what to do. He put his ear to his father's mouth to check that he was still breathing. Although there was still breath, it sounded as if the lining of his throat had been ripped.

'The . . . o-others?' Jo whispered.

'Dead.'

'Yuri?'

'Don't try to speak.'

Jo opened his mouth but nothing came out except pained breath. He tried again to say something but it was too faint to be audible.

Dan moved his head closer to his father's face.

'Tab-lets,' Jo whispered.

Dan searched frantically through the old man's coat, finding nothing in his outer pockets. He opened up the buttons, searching the jacket, finally finding a small plastic bottle inside. He took a yellow capsule out and put it in his father's mouth, saying, 'Jo, we've got to move on. The gas has escaped—'

Jo shook his head. Dan saw that the tablet had not been swallowed but was melting on Jo's tongue as he talked.

'Jo, I'm going to move you. You survived Neuwelt, for Christ's sake, you're not going to be poisoned by Tarin here.'

The old man smiled.

'*What?* Jo, I'm not going to let you die like this.'

There was another explosion, and the surreal toxic flames climbed higher into the night air. It was a brilliant, blinding illumination.

'I ain't moving,' Jo rasped.

'If we stay here—'

'Ain't . . . mixed,' he whispered, the effort forcing him to gasp for breath and then cough horribly.

'The gas?'

Jo shook his head faintly.

Dan laughed and glanced around the corner of the warehouse. He saw a mass of emergency vehicles surrounding the GCC hangar. Lights of all descriptions whirled on top of the police vans and fire engines. An emergency team dived out of one of the trucks, decked out in gas masks and protective suits. They looked like soldiers from a futuristic war as they sprayed the poisonous flames with thick foam.

'There's an ambulance back there,' Dan said.

Jo shook his head.

'Jo, you need medical—'

Again he shook his head.

'So what are the tablets?'

'Stroke. Last year.'

'Why the fuck didn't you say?'

The purple flush on Jo's face was fast disappearing, leaving his skin dead and ashen. Dan felt his arms begin to stiffen, and he saw his father's eyes fill with tears.

'Oh, shit. Oh *shit*, Jo.'

With great effort the old man gritted his teeth and said, 'I love you, son.'

Dan raised his fists, but he didn't know what to do. Should he bang on his father's chest? 'Jo, don't die. Chrissy will never forgive me.'

Jo shut his eyes.

'Jo, *Dad*, don't go, not *now*.' Tears fell from his eyes uncontrollably. He felt his father's left arm beginning to go cold. He put his ear to Jo's mouth but could barely detect any sign of breathing. 'Oh, shit,' he said, banging on his father's chest. 'Jo, I'm not going to *let* you die.'

He banged again, violently, then again, first the left and then the right fist, again and again and again until his knuckles were raw. He glanced around the corner, saw the ambulance, screamed for help, but his words were drowned out by the terrible wind as it raced from the east, like the cries of a thousand victims in the chambers of Neuwelt.

He got up and started to run towards the ambulance, but stopped. He could not reach the paramedics. His path was blocked by armed police.

Chapter 26

They waited all night in the dedicated burns unit of the City of London Hospital, the most specialised facility in the South-East. Dan sat by his father's side, lightly touching his fingers. As he waited in the clean, safe, if unnerving room, he tried not to listen to the buzzing of the mass of machines that surrounded the old man.

Sophie sat in a waiting room with Chris. When Dan peeked into the room at 5 a.m., the two were finally sleeping, their heads propped against each other. He didn't have the heart to rouse them. He went back into Jo's room. He had told the police everything he knew, and although they wanted to question him again, they did not seem disposed to challenge his story.

He sat in the uncomfortable plastic chair a nurse had placed at the side of the high bed. Jo's fingers were still cold and grey, but the machine that tracked his heartbeat peaked sufficiently to give them all hope. Dan was more tired than he could ever remember being in his life. He watched Jo's face, calm, almost tranquil, displaying the serenity of someone who is reconciled to the inevitable. His eyelids began to shut and he thought that it wouldn't hurt, just for a few moments, to give in. Suddenly his head's weight seemed enormous and he rested it on the clean white sheets of the bed.

His breathing became slower and heavier as he drifted off. He thought again of Yuri and the half-smile that the Russian had given before going back into the warehouse to save his father's killer. He thought of Montford, burning to death in a shower of chemicals he had recruited Klaus Keller to develop. But most of all he thought of Jo, and how he had found his father after forty years, how they had both struggled to get on, how the secrets

from the past, the legacies of Neuwelt, had almost made father
and son fall out for good. He wondered whether Yuri knew he
was going to his death, and whether, having avenged his father,
he had no further purpose left in life. Perhaps he wanted to join
the Russian soldier and war hero, Ivan Basarov.

He didn't know how long he had been asleep when he felt
something moving in his hair. He tried to brush it off without
opening his eyes, but there it was again, annoying him like a
fly. It would not leave him alone. So he raised his head, slowly
opening his heavy eyelids, and saw his father, now conscious.

'Jo,' he cried.

The old man moved his head fractionally, and creases appeared
at the corners of his eyes.

'Jo, don't try to talk, do you understand?'

His father nodded once.

'The doctors say you're probably going to be all right. You'll
need to rest and take it easy – no more shoot-outs in warehouses,
that sort of thing. But essentially, you're as tough as old boots and
– with a bit of tender loving care – you're going to be all right.'

Again Jo nodded, and a single tear appeared in the corner of
his right eye.

Dan took his father's fingers carefully. They appeared shrivelled and small, like those of a baby. He looked past the old
man's long eyelashes and into his still-youthful eyes. 'I love you,
Jo. We've both been through the wars, but now it's finished, and
I want you to know . . . that I love you.'

Jo's head moved again, just an inch, beckoning Dan to his
mouth. 'I want . . . to go home,' he said.

His fingers gripped Dan's once, but this time more firmly. The
hospital had put a clear plastic identification tag on the old man's
wrist on which a nurse had scribbled 'Rosen, Josef'. But on the
skin below there was another mark that spoke just as graphically
about who Dan's father really was: his concentration camp
number, his certificate of pig-headed, miraculous, extraordinary
survival.

Dan went to the window and drew back the curtains.

The hospital room was high up and gave a spectacular view.
To the south Dan could see the river dividing the city in two,
flowing slowly out of London, past Tilbury, and into the stretch

of water that separated England from continental Europe. The wind had blown itself out and the first traces of dawn stained the horizon far to the east. It was a staggering sight.

As the room filled with brilliant morning light, he wondered if there was a similar dawn over Germany on that day in April 1945 when the British tanks rolled into Neuwelt, the camp where a Russian Jew called Josef Rosen witnessed a war crime; and by his stubbornness and courage fifty years later, revealed to the world its final solution.

Acknowledgements

This is my opportunity to thank the many people who have assisted me in the publication of this book. Firstly, I would like to thank my sickeningly brilliant agent Mark Lucas, who persuaded me to be more ambitious and to reach for what lay at the core of this novel. Even if it sometimes felt like death by a thousand revisions, it is in no small measure due to Mark's patience, persistence and editorial genius that the book began to edge towards the potential of which it was capable. Thanks also to my other agents: David Black in New York and Nicki Kennedy at the Intercontinental Literary Agency. I would also like to acknowledge John Pearce at Doubleday, who found the time while publishing a certain Mr Grisham in Canada to show an interest in this book and my next. As ever, I am grateful to the whole team at Hodder & Stoughton, but in particular to my editor and fellow Chiswickite, Carolyn Caughey. Outside the rarefied atmosphere of publishing, my outrageously successful brother Mike has always supported my work and helped me to dream of still wider canvases. Antoinette Jones deserves praise, too, for being such an avid and reliable reader – as does Jessie Ripley. Eileen was good enough to assist in the typing of the second manuscript. Lucy and Bella kindly provided much expertise on the mysterious world of teenage girls and their shoes. Madeleine has brightened the lives of all who have met her and does great credit to her wonderful parents, Helen and David. Phyllis sat with me throughout the breathless summer of '95 and ensured in her inimitable way that I was never lonely while writing – I shall miss her terribly. Colin Cook, the clerk to my chambers, has been over the years the best senior clerk in the Temple and – as importantly – a cherished friend. Finally,

I would like to thank my mother, a woman of rare talent, whose encouragement and constancy through the years have made everything else possible – I couldn't have done any of it without you.